Broken Voices

MUSIC AND PERFORMING ARTS OF ASIA AND THE PACIFIC

Series Editor: Frederick Lau

Broken Voices

POSTCOLONIAL ENTANGLEMENTS AND THE PRESERVATION OF KOREA'S CENTRAL FOLKSONG TRADITIONS

ROALD MALIANGKAY

University of Hawai'i Press
Honolulu

KOREA FOUNDATION

The Korea Foundation has provided financial assistance for the undertaking of this publication project.

Paperback edition 2020

Printed in the United States of America

25 24 23 22 21 20 6 5 4 3 2 1

Library of Congress Cataloging-in-Publication Data

Names: Maliangkay, Roald, author.
Title: Broken voices : postcolonial entanglements and the preservation of Korea's central folksong traditions / Roald Maliangkay.
Description: Honolulu : University of Hawai'i Press, [2017] | Includes bibliographical references and index.
Identifiers: LCCN 2016059836 | ISBN 9780824866655 (cloth ; alk. paper)
Subjects: LCSH: Folk songs, Korean—20th century—History and criticism.
Classification: LCC ML3752.5 .M35 2017 | DDC 782.42/162957—dc23 LC record available at https://lccn.loc.gov/2016059836

ISBN 978-0-8248-8833-6 (pbk.)

University of Hawai'i Press books are printed on acid-free paper and meet the guidelines for permanence and durability of the Council on Library Resources.

For Shuge and Lucas

CONTENTS

ACKNOWLEDGMENTS

THE completion of this book is owed to the kindness of a great many people. Among those who have played a crucial role in my academic life over the years, I wish to first thank Boudewijn Walraven for introducing me to folklore studies and to many a soju-guzzling, chain-smoking, spirit-whispering shaman at the foot of Seoul's Namsan in the early hours of the weekend. Koen De Ceuster and Remco Breuker crucially guided me further into the world of Korean studies and to many visual, audial, and palatable delights. Nathan Hesselink encouraged me tremendously when I set first foot on the shaky ground of academia, and like the others and Keith Howard, he continues to be an inspiration. Keith, my doctoral adviser, never ceases to support and motivate me, for which I am extremely grateful. Jacqueline Vel, Mario Rutten, Willem van Schendel, and Leo Douw provided me with my first institutional home in Amsterdam, a place full of wonderful synergies; one I have become increasingly nostalgic about since leaving for Australia, perhaps because it no longer exists. As soon as I took up a position at the Australian National University, however, I began to make many new friends. Those who have since provided very helpful feedback on my work in general include, in no specific order, Ruth Barraclough, Hyaeweol Choi, Marcus Mietzner, Benjamin Penny, Katarzyna Cwiertka, Theodore Jun Yoo, Stephen Epstein, Jo Elfving-Hwang, Ross Tapsell, Michiel Baas, Geng Song, and Tessa Morris-Suzuki. In developing this manuscript in particular, I am hugely indebted to Clark Sorensen, who graciously dedicated much of his time giving invaluable, detailed advice on many aspects of the first draft. His comments have significantly improved my approach toward various aspects of my work and I hope the changes I made after his review do his efforts justice at least to some degree. My good friend Benjamin also provided sharp and insightful thoughts on one of the chapters. At University of Hawaiʻi Press, I was very fortunate to gain the magnificent support of Masako Ikeda, who provided important feedback on my manuscript and graciously guided me through the various procedures. Kristen Bettcher, finally, did an amazing job seeing this book through the production process.

The people and institutes who have helped me in Korea are too numerous to mention by name. I wish to sincerely thank, first and foremost, the Korea Foundation for its enormous support over the years. I was fortunate enough to receive one of the PhD scholarships it funded through the School of Oriental and African Studies (SOAS), and was able to rely on its support for a number of essential fieldwork trips. I am again grateful to the Foundation for the subsidy it provided for this publication. Another institute I wish to thank is the National Gugak Center. It has provided many occasions for me to meet people, and even after she took up the role of Director of the Busan National Gugak Center, So Inhwa and her network of peers have continued to go out of their way to respond to my queries and requests. Others who always offered generous assistance and hospitality to me on various occasions include performers Yi Ŭn'gwan, Yi Ŭnju, Muk Kyewŏl, Hwang Yongju, Yi Juna, Pak Chunyŏng, Yu Sangho, and Yu Chisuk, as well as professors Shim Usŏng, Im Tonggwŏn, and Kwŏn Oh Sung. Professor Yi Pohyŏng, in particular, never seemed to tire of my questions and requests and always welcomed me to his study, where he would dazzle me with fascinating anecdotes and collectibles. Jocelyn Clark gave important advice on my hypotheses, helped me on a few complicated quests, and along with Cecilia Heejeong Kim offered generous scoops of makkŏlli when my battery needed recharging. Together with her late husband and her daughters Ji Eun and Chihye, Chŏn Misuk provided a loving home in Seoul, heaps of yummy food, and many hilarious descriptions of Korean culture. Mr. Yi Sŏnggon at the National Folk Museum of Korea made it possible for me to reproduce the beautiful image on this book's cover, while Mr. Tony Jung was extremely generous with his time helping me with several other illustrations. None of these delightful people are responsible for any of the incorrect or uninspiring parts of this book for which I take full responsibility (though, if urged to do so, I might pass the buck to the Boogie, rather than Australia's sunshine).

I owe much gratitude to my family for always inspiring and supporting me. They are often missed, in part for their creativity and many passions and for making my work peeves seem so delightfully insignificant. I mention Shuge Wei only at this point, but she comes first in thought. With much love, wit, and care, she has turned my life into an adventure, and I find myself hoping time will slow down. These acknowledgments would not be complete, however, without an ode to Poktori, who for almost seventeen years accompanied me during my work while reminding me of shared meal times, until he sadly passed away during the final months of writing. Fortunately, Shuge and I were able to welcome another amazing boy into our lives not long after. I dedicate this book to her and our dearest Lucas, in loving memory of the greatest food thief who ever lived.

ROMANIZATION AND OTHER CONVENTIONS

BECAUSE the official Korean romanization system promulgated at the start of the new millennium can render unfortunate (and in some cases hilarious) connotations, I use the McCune-Reischauer system instead, albeit in the revised form created by the Korean Ministry of Education in 1988. This allows me to use "shi" for sounds previously transcribed as "si," which does not represent the actual sound and therefore defeats the main purpose of transcription. I make exceptions in the case of commonly accepted alternative spellings, such as Seoul and Pyongyang, and where Koreans used an alternative spelling of their name in an English language publication. In the bibliography references to the latter are listed under that name, followed by a systematic transcription between brackets. In the narrative I retain the order of people's given and surname as common in what I take to be their country of residence. When referring to place names, I occasionally leave suffixes like—*san* and *-dong* untranslated when they are commonly treated as part of the township's name in English. When the vernacular clearly deviates from the McCune-Reischauer system, such as with words like *pohopŏp* and Sejon-kut, which the system would have me romanize as *pohobŏp* and Sejon-gut, I disregard the rules and transcribe the word as I hear it pronounced. Although I add hyphens to separate suffixes from nouns and numbers, the transcription reflects how the sound of the noun's final consonant is inflected when it is followed by the initial vowel of a suffix. Therefore, rather than *pohopŏp-ŭi* I use *pohopŏb-ŭi*. In order to avoid confusion I also add a hyphen when a single compound word is separated upon romanization, as in "30-nyŏndae" (1930s) and "1970-nyŏndae" (1970s). I have transcribed Chinese terms according to the pinyin system and Japanese according to the Hepburn system.

All translations are mine unless otherwise specified. In my transcriptions and translations of printed text and recorded interviews I have tried to stay as close to the original as possible, but I have slightly corrected the grammar and terminology where, for example, it was absolutely necessary in order to maintain the flow of the text or where an informant used more profanity than even I thought was cool. Song titles are given in romanized Korean, followed by, where possible, a translation or the official English title. Although I was not always able to find them, I provide birth and death dates for those I believe played a crucial role in the events and traditions deliberated. I omit such dates for scholars unless seniority may have awarded them particular leverage in decision-making processes.

Broken Voices

Introduction

PROMOTING TRADITION IN KOREA

On my first visit to Seoul, in early August 1988, I visited the National Museum of Korea when it was still located on the grounds of Kyŏngbok Palace inside the monumental building formerly used by the Japanese colonial government. Relishing the respite from the humid summer heat, I slowly shuffled through the large open halls, occasionally followed by the stares and whispers of groups of school children, who were unaccustomed to seeing foreigners, let alone teenage civilian ones. The high ceilings and thick walls made the interior seem very impressive, and yet I could not shake the feeling that there was something sad about the exhibition as a whole. If anything, it looked empty. To postpone re-entering the stickiness outside, I visited the museum's bookshop. But looking through the exhibition catalogues and books, I realized that many of the images offered in print were identical to those I had just seen behind glass. I learned not long after that several of the items on display at the museum were, in fact, copies of the originals.[1] Not only had many artifacts been destroyed during the Korean War, but tens of thousands of items had also been taken abroad by foreigners over the course of the twentieth century, and the government was attempting to retrieve them. Despite my first impressions, though, the replicas on display served an important purpose. Many of them featured in publications and commercial products both as decoration and tokens of national pride. Koreans often told me about their cultural heritage with pride, could recite a list of important "national treasures," and were quick to point their finger at the Japanese for having tried to destroy or erase them. Museum collections, it became apparent, comprised mementos rather than specimens of Korea's national heritage. In the South Korean government's attempt to nurture national pride, propaganda proved more important than either the size or authenticity of the country's heritage.

Since the late 1980s, major sports events, global brands, and the Korean Wave—the worldwide success of South Korean (hereafter Korean) popular entertainment since the late 1990s—have tied Korea's national heritage to images of prosperity and celebrity. Korea's cultural icons had to play catch-up with those of its neighbors, at least in the eyes of policy makers, but they have proved quite successful, and features of traditional culture now appear prominently in popular entertainment, tourism, and general retail. A modified copy of the traditional costume (*hanbok*) is a popular formal type of dress, worn by people on a wide range of occasions; and traditional crafts are used everywhere for decoration, from modern hotel lounges to car interiors and restaurants. Even the popularity of traditional folk ceremonies and religious rituals has grown, if perhaps more for sightseeing than participation. The success of such iconic traditions has derived as much from economic growth as from the effectiveness of Korea's cultural policy. Of particular importance in this regard is the ongoing impact of the Korean Wave on foreign shores. Although it is significantly amplified by the global success of Korean business conglomerates, it is inconceivable that Korean popular entertainment could have become such a phenomenon without the features of traditional culture it incorporates. Korea's heritage gained significant commercial importance only after the Wave began; until then the country's cultural traditions were principally used to express a range of sociopolitical concerns, and evoke feelings of patriotism and nostalgia. Today, many consumers across East and Southeast Asia avidly keep up with the latest Korean traditional costume dramas, populated by casting agents from among a broad arsenal of idol K-pop stars.

The commercial success of Korea's cultural policy is owed partly to the image of Japan overseas, in particular in China and Taiwan, Southeast Asia, and the West. This may be because of familiarity with or fond memories of Japanese popular culture, or resentment of the Japanese government's unwillingness to discuss its war crimes or its position on whaling. Japan's image has affected the world's view of Korean contemporary culture as well as Korea's national heritage. In this book I investigate Korean government policies created to preserve and promote its intangible heritage, and focus especially on the professional folksong traditions from the central provinces. I discuss the major factors that have made an impact on the alleged authenticity of the Korean traditions and show that the experience of Japanese imperialism has been a major factor in both their configuration and conception.

Studies that scrutinize Korea's heritage management are generally concerned with either tangible or intangible cultural properties. In her extensive, seminal work on the presentation and preservation of Korean archaeology and tangible properties, Hyung Il Pai deliberates the crucial impact of nationalism, modernity, and colonialism on the valorization of Korean objects and the development of Korean preservation strategies.[2] Others, such as Yang Jongsung, focus on strategies toward the preservation of specific elements of Korea's intangible heritage. Among his major contributions is his analysis of the impact of Korea's heritage management on the reinvention of *Kangnyŏng talchum*, a mask dance-drama from the town of Kangnyŏng (National Intangible Cultural Property no. 34). As a former performer in the group that preserves the tradition, and an occasional adviser to the government on heritage-related issues, he is able to share many insights related to the decision-making processes.[3] Keith Howard is concerned with the use of traditional arts and crafts in the construction of identities on either side of the Korean Demilitarized Zone. Although he critically investigates the challenges posed by the requirements of authenticity and transmission, he is particularly interested in the motivations of those involved. He includes folksongs in his analyses, but focuses on the less prominent genres from the southern part of the peninsula.[4] While I carefully consider the roles identity formation and globalization play in approaches toward heritage and its management, in this book I deviate from the work of these scholars by presenting the primary argument that strategies and notions developed by the Japanese during the colonial period have impacted Korea's folksong traditions.

Apart from Japanese strategies and notions, major factors in how the management of Korea's national heritage was conceived include a range of sociopolitical concerns and economic pressures. In the early days of South Korea's existence, funding constraints significantly affected the scope of national heritage management. The enormous devastation of the Korean War left little room for a policy that concerned itself with heritage preservation or the nurturing of cultural activities. Rather than promoting the development of culture or investing in sizeable restoration endeavors, therefore, from the mid to late 1950s new legislation regarding culture was mostly administrative and regulatory. Since establishing a comprehensive system of heritage management in 1962, however, Korea has undergone dramatic sociopolitical and economic transformations. Bolstered by feelings of loss and nostalgia, efforts to preserve and revive Korean heritage have tried to keep up with the ensuing changes, but they frequently required adjusting. As properties, both tangible and intangible, became damaged, moved abroad, or risked becoming lost, constant maintenance and policy revisions became necessary.

In the early 1960s, at the first signs of economic recovery, the administration of Park Chung Hee (Pak Chŏnghŭi, 1963–1979) began to heavily involve itself in activities to preserve what it defined as national heritage: "Culture must be a part of the daily lives of the people to hasten the renaissance of our national culture."[5] Believing that its sociopolitical and economic goals could only be achieved through concerted sacrifice by the Korean people as a whole, the administration laid out a cultural policy that promoted national pride using a single historical narrative that emphasized the uniqueness of the Koreans and their culture, which past invaders had tried hard to eradicate.[6] In doing so, it executed a cultural policy that was colonial at its core (although it would strongly deny this).[7] Several of Park's developmental policies and strategies were noticeably inspired by Japanese ones, including those dealing with Korean heritage. Indeed, in devising his policies and strategies Park would have drawn substantially on his years serving in the Japanese imperial army in Manchukuo.[8] It is likely that in exchange for considerable economic aid and investment, US representatives also urged Park to adopt schemes similar to those that had proven successful in Japan in earlier years. For the purpose of reviving the Korean economy and advocating unity in the face of North Korea's belligerence, Park openly embarked on a policy of reconciliation with Japan.[9] His efforts were explained as necessary to secure loans and develop an economy strong enough to hold its own. Since they were intent on making South Korea "impervious to further outside influence," the government sold them to the public as patriotic.[10]

In spite of the emphasis they placed on traditional Korean values, Park's policies were fully supportive of capitalism. Yet they sought to define the modern Korean nation as decidedly non-Western. Chatterjee has shown that in India, in response to British colonialism, a non-Western nationalism led to an exploration of the spiritual and cultural essence of the East, whereby traditional values retained their relevance at home and global values held sway outside. According to the protagonists, Chatterjee asserts, Britain had failed to destroy the inner, essential identity of the East, which lay in its distinctive and superior spiritual culture. The nationalists were nevertheless intent on people studying "the modern sciences and arts of the material world from the West in order to match their strengths and ultimately overthrow the colonizer."[11] In Korea, where Japan was virtually synonymous with the dominant West, Park chose to follow a similar approach. To rally the people behind him in his bold pursuit of idealized Western living standards, he used a similarly self-orientalizing rhetoric: "Orientals possess a mysterious, unified, and harmonized spiritual culture that can scarcely be understood by Westerners, who have different ways of thinking and different systems of logic. Although it is risky to generalize, it is clear that Oriental cultures have a certain gentle, mild rhythm and harmony."[12] To promote this view, government propaganda began to use the slogan "spiritual mobilization," originally a Japanese wartime term whose adoption under Park was again no coincidence.[13] And to foster the study of this unique, spiritual culture of Koreans, in 1978 Park established the Korean Spiritual Culture Research Institute (Han'guk chŏngshin munhwa yŏn'guwŏn; renamed Han'gukhak chung-ang yŏn'guwŏn, or Central Research Institute for Korean Studies, in 2005), known in English as the Academy of Korean Studies. On its current home page, the institute explains that its mission is to overcome "the ethical confusion that has emerged alongside rapid industrialization."

Apart from making efforts to implement policies from Korea's former colonial power while publicly denouncing them, Park emphasized the danger of renewed North Korean aggression, communism, and foreign cultural imperialism. In his inaugural address on December 17, 1963, for example, he said, "The difficult times that followed the turn of this century included [our] blind acceptance of unsuitable foreign customs and manners at the end of World War II. This half century of shame and disgrace degraded our traditions and customs, and lowered public and private morality."[14] While primarily aimed at encouraging Koreans to work toward a common goal—the pursuit of Western materialism—and refrain from dissident activities, the denial of the plurality (and indigenous agency) of colonial modernity,[15] and the focus on Korea's unique culture also served to prevent negative reactions to the effects of economic growth (e.g., increased economic inequality and new values in conflict with official policy). At the same time, Park may have hoped that the emphasis placed on protecting Korean traditions would help prevent accusations of being unpatriotic in light of his efforts to reconcile with Japan.

The inability to abandon the standards and hierarchies of the colonial past has long represented one of the major predicaments of postcolonial nationalism. Indeed, Park's penchant for comparing Korea with Japan would have resonated with many of his contemporaries, including US representatives. Sorensen notes that after liberation, many among the business and intellectual elite, who had maintained "uncomfortably close ties with the Japanese authorities" during the colonial period, believed that Koreans had a lot to learn from the Japanese.[16] Possibly compounded by the geographical proximity of its former colonizer, which achieved fast economic recovery after the Pacific War and benefited from the United States having a relatively higher opinion toward its recent adversary, a cultural cringe manifested in the first few decades of Korea's post-Liberation era.[17] Many norms introduced by the Japanese during the colonial era prevailed, as the former colonizer remained, alongside the United States, one of Korea's primary yardsticks in terms of cultural prowess and economic development. The cringe dissipated only in the final years of the previous millennium, when the Korean Wave began to divert considerable soft power away from Japan, and Japanese pop culture, which had been banned for decades, became widely available in Korea for comparison.

Park's cultural and education policies would have a profound effect on the national "popular" image of Japan. Along with a cultural cringe, they fostered anti-Japanese sentiment, which remained strong at least until the mid 1990s. Although the administration could not openly promote negative opinions of Japan, it ensured that their adherents occupied key positions in public information and education while prohibiting the import and public display of cultural products from Japan, including the employment of Japanese entertainers. It also made efforts to educate foreigners about Korea's suffering at the hands of foreign invaders. An English-language publication by Samsung from 1991 is testament to the lasting impact of Park's public information and education policies. Entitled "Misconceptions about Korean History," it sets out to correct factual errors in the descriptions of Korean historical events in foreign textbooks and in the process conveniently lists endless examples of Japanese aggression.[18] Two years later, Jeon Yeo-ok (Chŏn Yŏok) published a collection of essays that attacked Japanese culture under the title *There Is No Japan* (*Ilbon-ŭn ŏpta;* 1993), which became a bestseller within months.[19] Although the government did not directly subsidize either publication, the latter's initial popularity, amid some criticism, suggests that it did not reflect the opinion of the author only. A critical view of Japan had become widespread.

In 1962, the government promulgated the Cultural Properties Protection Law (*Munhwajae pohopŏp*), which set up a system to protect, transmit, and promote Korea's cultural heritage, both tangible and intangible. It initially won the approval of many students and intellectuals who wanted to uphold Korea's folk heritage, which they claimed the Japanese colonial government had tried hard to erase.[20] Despite their support for the government policy, they would later join the antihegemonic *Minjung* movement, which, among other things, spurred criticism of the way the government went about protecting and reviving Korea's folklore. Although several other laws related to culture were passed around the same time, the administration's economic strategy prevented the system from receiving adequate funding until the end of the decade.[21] Active sponsorship and promotion of cultural activities began with the enactment of the Culture and Arts Promotion Law (*Munhwa yesul chinhŭngpŏp*) in 1972. This law, last amended in 2016, forms the basis of Korea's present cultural policy. The most comprehensive measures for the promotion of culture taken since then include two five-year plans (1974–1978 and 1979–1983), a ten-year plan initiated in 1990 by the newly established Ministry of Culture,[22] and the 1999 Basic Law for the Promotion of Cultural Industries (*Munhwa sanŏp chinhŭng kibonpŏp*), which provided major incentives for the production and promotion of Korean popular entertainment.[23]

In the late 1960s, when it was still making regular adjustments to its overall approach toward preserving and promoting national heritage, the Korean government split with the US government over issues of defense and security. Tension built up between President Park and Korean Christian leaders, who had long kept close ties with their American counterparts.[24] Partly in order to secure the allegiance of his political base in the Yŏngnam region of Kyŏngsang province, a Confucian stronghold, Park began to actively promote Confucian activities, including the concepts of *ch'ung* and *hyo* (loyalty to one's superiors and filial piety). This was intended to encourage compliance with official regulations and the endorsement of national economic plans. The Cultural Properties Protection Law from 1962 fit well into this policy, as it could be used to promote specific customs and traditions, including traditional values (though by the late 1980s the new rituals and principles included a few with strong shamanistic associations, which Park had tried hard to eradicate).[25]

Initiated in 1971, the New Village Movement (*Saemaŭl undong*) was another major program intended to develop the Korean economy and the people's communal spirit. It followed Park's plans to reduce the economic and ideological differences between urban and rural areas and to boost agricultural production. Rapid urbanization was leading to a fast-growing age gap between rural and urban populations, causing rural communities to become ill disposed toward new policies and farming methods. Crucial to the success of the movement, therefore, was an upgrade of farming methods and technologies, and for this the government had to interfere extensively in village matters.[26] In order to achieve significant technological innovation, the government tried to break down the traditional Confucian hierarchy of the village and to install younger, more modern men in leadership positions. It also advocated for a New Mind Movement (*Saemaŭm undong*) and New Village Spirit (*Saemaŭl chŏngshin*), which underscored the importance of harboring ideals equivalent to those of *ch'ung* and *hyo* while promoting self-reliance and a cooperative spirit.[27] The movement's emphasis on frugality and the value of moral and physical education once more revealed the influence of earlier Japanese programs, specifically the colonial Rural Promotion Movement (*Nongch'on chinhŭng undong*) and the New Life Movement (*Shin seikatsu undō*), which was introduced in Japan in the late 1940s and reached its height in the 1950s. The wide distribution of entertainment and sports programs served the additional purpose of swaying the populace by giving them a taste of what the movement's primary slogan—"let's try living well" (*chal saraboja*)—implied.[28] Yet, as it was believed that the success of the New Village Movement lay in modernizing the villages to the level of the cities,[29] those rituals and traditions thought to stand in the way were oppressed or forbidden.

Many Koreans opposed the focus on secular rationalism and Westernization as well as the unfair treatment of workers and police violence that persisted during the regime of Park's successor Chun Doo-hwan (Chŏn Tuhwan, 1979–1988). In the 1970s a populist *Minjung* movement began to emerge that engaged industrial workers, artists, students, and young intellectuals. Although relatively obscure at first, it gained momentum following the ruthless government crackdown on a popular uprising in Kwangju City in May 1980, which later also became known as the Kwangju massacre. The violent episode firmly established *Minjung* as the dominant ideology of the working class.[30] Several years ahead of the 1988 Olympics in Seoul, when the world media feasted on footage of students hurling rocks at military police across torn-up streets clouded by tear gas, the *Minjung* political protests concentrated on cultural symbolism. Protagonists expressed their discontent in a way that stood in sharp contrast to the cultural features of the regime.[31] They advocated traditional Korean culture, which they defined as rural and largely agricultural, in opposition to Western culture, and accused the government and the elite of too eagerly embracing North American culture and its associated norms. In its stead, they sought "a national community where humans are liberated" from "individualistic materialistic culture and administrative force."[32] Seeing as it advocated a return to the traditional, preindustrialized village values, the *Minjung* movement promoted principles that conflicted a little with those underlying the New Village Movement. But *Minjung* proponents' active opposition to cultural imperialism and their anger over Japanese aggression in some ways mirrored the government's own cultural policy and may have been a partial outcome of it.[33]

In protest against the government's advocacy of Western values and the oppression of Korean traditions, many *Minjung* practitioners turned toward the study of traditional arts and religion, masked dance drama, farmer's music and shamanism in particular—aspects of Korean culture that were not institutionalized and had long been suppressed. Masked dance drama appears to have preceded shamanism as a metaphor of political resistance. Having traditionally provided political satire for the working classes, its very image represented resistance to the military dictatorship, regardless of its script.[34] Some students started playing the music of farmers' percussion bands (*p'ungmul*) in small ensembles, dressed in the costumes of folk musicians. Their number grew considerably in the mid-1980s, when their activities became a common sight on university campuses. For a while, shamanism became a popular form of entertainment and field of study. Kim Kwang-ok points out that the use of shamanistic ritual items as an integral part of the student rallies symbolized protest against the government's official cultural policy in two ways: it was a reaction against Western cultural imperialism and a demonstration in favor of an authentically Korean belief system that governments had long attempted to eradicate because it was thought to be superstitious and retrogressive.[35] Tangherlini argues that, in addition, because shamans were predominantly female, their publicly taking center stage symbolized a rejection of the traditional Confucian social order.[36]

The Park and Chun administrations strongly endorsed sports activities not only to nurture patriotism, but, along with cheap, erotic entertainment, also to divert the public's attention away from politics.[37] At the same time, they maintained a system of strict censorship to silence critical voices and drown out dissonance. For decades, government propaganda and the apparatus of censorship worked overtime to mold the Korean people into conscientious workers and to quiet subversive thoughts that spurred *Minjung* or any other form of activism.

Widespread propaganda emphasized proper morals and a strong work ethic and reminded people of the hazards of foreign imperialism and aggression. The government even scrutinized the public performances of folksongs it had officially designated as cultural properties,[38] making sure their performers did not abandon the script for the sake of entertainment. The rules for censorship were left intentionally vague, but expressions of support for North Korean or Japanese society and culture could result in incarceration and even torture.[39] In 1999, the second democratically elected government acknowledged that there was no longer a purpose for such policies and abolished many of the propaganda and censorship committees that had scrutinized the entertainment media and public performances.[40] Government-disseminated information nevertheless continues to be an important political tool and efforts to protect Korean moral standards persist, albeit in reduced form. As many forms of commerce and political activism have moved online, the Korean government has established new agencies to survey online activities. While some of these may be politically motivated in their investigation of potentially subversive or otherwise illegal activities, others, such as those protecting Korean copyright, may be driven mostly by the possible loss of revenue.

Korea's cultural policy thus continues to adapt to the changing sociopolitical and economic climate. This applies equally to the way in which the government manages national heritage, but the changes in approach have been subtle, as compromises have been made. Those compromises are arguably most noticeable among intangible cultural properties, a category that comprises a range of practices and skills that have been passed on from generation to generation and include the performing arts and a number of crafts. But preservation efforts must be sustainable. Since the heritage preservation system relies on transmission, it must generate an interest in its traditions among future generations, while recognizing that the changing makeup of Korean society will dictate what captures the imagination of future practitioners and domestic audiences alike. In the future, people may highlight and further develop specific aspects of some traditions that are not necessarily of particular note today. The use and performance of these and other traditions may become associated with different social groups, which, in turn, will affect how the traditions become interpreted. The preservation system does not officially incorporate the possibility of adaptation as such, but many of the traditions under the system's tutelage have either been adapted or promoted differently to maintain their contemporary significance—with the fast-growing number of mixed marriages and Koreans born overseas likely creating the need for further adjustments in the future.[41] Despite being left undefined, since the notion of authenticity remains essential to the system, conspicuous forms of adaptation challenge the effectiveness of its approach.

Managing the Intangible

Government policies that focus on national intangible heritage can be found all over the world.[42] Their stated objectives are likely to highlight the cultural and social capital of the art forms concerned, but as they support the general objectives of their respective administrations, they may not be all-inclusive or aimed at the preservation of the art forms for future generations. In North Korea, for example, legislation does not incorporate intangible cultural properties.[43] Following the inauguration of the Galloping Horse Movement (*Ch'ŏllima undong*) in 1957 and the subsequent Juche ideology, concepts such as "collective art" (*chipch'e yesul*) and "collective creation" (*chipch'e ch'angjak*) were introduced that did away with individualism and the evils of the feudal past and paid homage to Soviet influence.[44] Traditions were subsequently revised introducing, among other things, new instruments and harmonic arrangements.[45] In the south, rather than relying on the masses to recreate and innovate, policies for intangible heritage aimed, instead, at emphasizing the historical uniqueness of the Korean people and their culture. Although it may seem ironic that the pivotal 1962 Cultural Properties Protection Law (CPPL) closely followed a Japanese model (see chapter 1), including a category of intangible (*muhyŏng*) cultural properties that comprised performing arts, crafts, and martial arts, it differed from its Japanese counterpart in that it prioritized folk arts and crafts rather than the arts of the nobility. Howard argues that this shift of emphasis was intended in part to avoid foregrounding art forms that had been limited only to a privileged few and were marked by Chinese influence, and in part to allow the inclusion of folk traditions that had been oppressed by the Japanese.[46]

In order to regulate the decision-making process for listing cultural properties, the CPPL established a committee made up of specialists from different fields of study, the Cultural Properties Committee (*Munhwajae wiwŏnhoe;* CPC). CPC members travel throughout the country to survey and write reports on cultural items, and on the basis of these reports, which often define an item's "original form" (*wŏnhyŏng*), the CPC may recommend their recognition as cultural properties. The CPPL ensures the protection, promotion, and, if appropriate, the restoration of such properties. It "maintain[s] the right to authorize or otherwise control the performance of designated items or the activities of the performers."[47] To safeguard the transmission of these so-called Important Intangible Cultural Properties (*Chungyo muhyŏng munhwajae;* IICPs), "holders" (*poyuja*) were appointed. These holders are required to perform and teach their art, and since 1968 they have received a monthly stipend to help them do so. To encourage and support the study of intangible cultural properties, the government also financially supports promising students.

Opinions about what constitutes a successful preservation scheme differ considerably. Studies and reports document the conflicting concerns and approaches of various stakeholders involved in intangible heritage management across the world, such as private entrepreneurs, academics, the general public, and governments, and the values that each group ties to specific cultural expressions.[48] A study of these reveals a consensus that today, one of the greatest challenges to the sustainable preservation of cultural items and activities is the tourism industry.[49] Even so, efforts to protect cultures from the negative effects of tourism cannot guarantee their survival. Although an interest group may be successful in its preservation efforts, it is likely that its objectives will change over time and that the cultural elements preserved will acquire a different symbolic value as a result. Specific items can maintain their significance and even outlast the communities and customs that initially sustained them,[50] but this may require the readjustment of strategies and even the invention of a new historic continuity.[51]

It might seem that loss of authenticity would render heritage management impossible, but equally, any system that seeks to freeze aspects of culture will eventually have to justify their importance time and again as society changes. Even traditions recognized for their historical cultural value may ultimately yield to the forces of change, such as technological innovation, new notions of beauty, and demographic shifts. In Korea, the legislation does not include provision for the adaptation of traditions, although those involved in the designation of intangible cultural properties acknowledge the inevitability of change. As long as people are involved, some change will occur, but many studies nevertheless challenge the authenticity of traditions based on their alleged unnatural development. Such studies presumably assume that "authentic" traditions are relatively stable. And yet traditions rarely develop along a steady chronological line and sometimes incorporate modern elements from a very different origin.[52] Andrew Killick notes that when *ch'anggŭk*, a traditional Korean opera, borrows from other genres, the elements brought in are rarely "pure and unified" themselves.[53] In the case of Korean traditional performing arts, at least, the issue of authenticity does not, therefore, apply so much to the inclusion of new ingredients per se, but rather, to forms of art that have adopted this practice more recently.

In Korea, debates regarding heritage management have often revolved around the issue of authenticity. As they were concerned with the re-evaluation and preservation of Korean culture, the magazines *Space* (*Konggan;* since 1966) and *The Deep-rooted Tree* (*Ppuri kip'ŭn namu;* since 1976) both featured regular discussions of the government's cultural policies. While *Konggan* viewed traditions as constantly evolving elements of culture, *The Deep-rooted Tree* expressed a fervent concern for the erosion of the authenticity of traditions under the state's guardianship.[54] The Chun administration finally banned *The Deep-rooted*

Tree in 1980 under the National Security Act,[55] an action the magazine's founder, aesthete Han Ch'anggi (1936–1997), explained as having been driven by the notion that "intellectuals read it."[56] Although Han was not critical of the concept of heritage preservation as such, he was scathing when he discussed the widespread corruption in the system and the fact that it was encouraging artists to change their traditions in order to be noticed:

> With regard to the current preservation system I think they fail to project it into the future. They do a lousy job too. Usually they designate [as holders] the people who are friends with the researchers. These people are very diplomatic, certainly not the best artists. Real artists are temperamental. . . . so they designate the wrong people, the kind of people that do a great job of explaining their art. . . . You see, they also designate useless things like embroidery. This craft—*hwarot*—was prosperous until the Chinese moved in. The coats are very expensive. Without appointments there would be competition and lower prices. Now they sign their product. The same with shoes. There was this man who was very skilled at making shoes so they appointed him, but he started making his own designs and then he even started to make tables. Very ugly tables, outside his field. Now look at this ink stone. Our ink stones used to be very simple, but if you go to Insa-dong now all stones are decorated too much, like baroque. At the National Handicrafts Contest one has to make big things in order to win. The country lets them compete. . . . There was this guy who could make really nice knives, the kind Koreans wore on their belts, but he got no attention. Someone told him, "you should make a big sword."[57]

Since the fall of the military dictatorship that banned the magazine, the majority of Koreans have come to embrace the system as a whole, though the issues Han raised continue to complicate its effective implementation.

The official designation of intangible cultural properties implies a change in the social and cultural capital of the art forms. This inevitably leads to a reduction of diversity. When the Korean government began to designate traditions as cultural properties, it chose one or two versions of a tradition as they existed at a specific point in time. It disregarded alternatives and the possibility that a few elements had been changed in recent years.[58] Although the authenticity of many Korean art forms had been the subject of debate well before the heritage management scheme was put in place,[59] the official designations have led to much criticism among scholars and practitioners. While some condemn the exclusion of alternative forms, others argue that a number of the traditions the government claims to protect are not being preserved in their "original form" (*wŏnhyŏng*).[60] Scholars have also pointed out a lack of depth in several reports that document why an art form was designated, and they have questioned why candidates put forward for appointment already held authoritative positions in their fields.[61]

While many of the changes to the three folksong genres discussed in this book are relatively recent inventions, they do not necessarily jeopardize the value of the genres as cultural heritage as long as the particular values they have been chosen to represent remain unaffected.[62] What is more, artifacts and traditions have more than cultural or nostalgic value; they may provide an income and perform a social function, factors that require a degree of flexibility on the part of both the performers and their audiences. When inventions do occur, the inventors themselves may be unaware of them, and even when they are, they may not always consider them "changes"; they may believe in their own creations as long as they benefit from them.[63] Eyerman and Jamison argue that in today's world, traditions have come to remedy the breakdown of communities. More individualized than in the past, people select them to define themselves.[64] Traditions increasingly represent different things to different people. Even within a fairly homogenous society such as South Korea, the general public, intellectuals, and others may variously criticize the legitimacy of traditions.[65] Their opinions are shaped by sociopolitical and economic change, to which, along with technological innovation, cultural development occurs in response.

To link the uniqueness of a culture to history by stressing "authentic" traditions can therefore be misleading. A number of Korean scholars have nevertheless emphasized the historical legitimacy of Korean culture in order to justify the nation's existence, as if the absence of true change somehow explains its many accomplishments. Kim Young-soo, for example, claims that without a firm notion of "national culture," "race would lose its spirit and finally fall into a colonial country in the political dimension. If this abnormal state extended over a long period of time, the race would stand on the brink of perishment. Only by elucidating the right tradition of national history upon the tradition of national identity and at the same time accept and assimilate foreign culture in our own way, can we create a new and high culture and history."[66] In other words, a Korean identity based on a clearly defined single history is the basis of national legitimacy and it is tied to the concept of national culture, regardless of whether the latter is based on mere assumption as opposed to fact. Kim's words certainly apply beyond Korea. Benedict Anderson argues that in general, among the various imagined communities that have emerged around the world since roughly the eighteenth century, "the objective modernity of nations in the historian's eye exists alongside their subjective antiquity in the eyes of nationalists." He notes that this position is not a universal one, since Swiss nationalism, for example, appears to be characterized by modernity rather than antiquity.[67] Richard Handler finds that the justification of nationhood through heritage is common. Quoting a Quebec high school student who claims that Quebec constitutes a nation because it has a culture, he contends that it reflects the Western materialist idea that a people's identity is manifested through its possessions.[68] He cites a principle formulated by a UNESCO panel in 1976 that recognizes the importance of repatriating cultural properties to their countries of origin on the basis that they constitute "a basic element of a people's identity."[69]

Despite the importance of claims to historicity, heritage management always disrupts the continuity of traditions. It cannot maintain the historical social contexts in which traditions grew, and it will affect the purpose of the art forms and that of the people involved in them. Shalom Staub is right, therefore, to question whether the authenticity of traditions lies in the objects themselves (even if the original function is lost) or in their function.[70] The Korean government pursues the protection of cultural properties through preservation and transmission,[71] but it is inconceivable that one might successfully pass on a folk tradition endlessly without sacrificing its authenticity. Since societies change, so do traditions. The alternative to freezing a tradition in time lies in allowing it to reflect changing societal contexts. Especially in music, which not only carries meaning and a link to the past but also functions as entertainment, preferences change considerably over time. To freeze all elements of a traditional music would deny its practitioners the ability to modify their art to relate to contemporary entertainment and expectations, including their own. Bruno Nettl posits that preventing music from changing will eventually turn it into "an artificially preserved museum."[72] Even so, attempts to freeze traditions can certainly serve a purpose. Museums provide a reference for questions of identity and definitions of a culture. They may play a role in the revival of traditions and use them to demonstrate a culture's continuity. And even when they merely document that which identifies a cultural group, museums serve to embellish the identity of that group and summon feelings of nostalgia.

The difficulty of dealing with change in the performing arts is partly due to oral transmission and interpretation. Since interpretation—and improvisation—is an inherent aspect of the folk performing arts, it needs to be incorporated in the preserved art form, to some degree at least. Folk performing arts are generally transmitted orally, through rote learning, and performers rely on what they recall having been taught, though the more senior they are the more room for interpretation they are likely allowed. They may add and omit elements intentionally or unintentionally, based on the conditions of performance, all within the tradition. Nettl argues in favor of allowing change because it constitutes a basic element of folksong performance: "A folksong may be sung differently by a singer on various occasions, each performance representing a change from the past, but the artifact remains an unchanged unit of musical thought."[73] The degree to which some traditions allow improvisation, however, varies. Nettl notes that while the Samaritans of Israel and the Navajo were anxious to preserve their liturgical tradition, in other cultures people may be much less concerned about preserving the lyrics or music of their folk art because its essence does not lie in those elements.[74] In folk music, improvisation will in many cases result from participants either not knowing or failing to remember parts of a piece of music. Roger Janelli and Dawnhee Yim Janelli found that ignorance is a standard characteristic in the performance of Korean folklore: "Ignorance, or 'not knowing,' need not be regarded as a lapse of memory, a faltering of tradition, or any other deficiency in either the folklore performance or transmission progress. Ignorance may be characteristic of highly effective performances, enhance their very effectiveness, and help maintain a vigorous and healthy tradition in its present form."[75] Joshua Pilzer points out that for elderly Korean women, particularly those living in the southwestern *namdo* area, self-expression is prioritized over the accurate rendition of versions of songs passed on to them.[76]

Korean society has changed considerably since the enactment of the Cultural Properties Protection Law, and social values and norms have adapted accordingly. The Korean government's cultural preservation system may allow a small degree of adaptation, but it cannot allow it to lead to further development. The designated cultural property sets an ideal that the heritage system hopes will be followed, irrespective of its authenticity. This book focuses on those who are expected to preserve the traditions they represent and personify, regardless of whether that allows them to convey personal emotions. Although I describe aspects that have changed from the audience's point of view on a number of occasions, I am not concerned with change itself and concur with Bruno Nettl in regarding studies concerned with "continuity and change" as clichéd.[77] Rather, I attempt to show how Korean folksong traditions have evolved and what factors have caused them to change. Why, in other words, they have either gained, maintained, or lost their relevance in changing conditions.

Establishing Motives

Upon examination, it is clear that a number of intangible cultural properties have been altered since their designation. The changes are diverse: some folk traditions have been modified to gain an advantage over similar traditions, for example, by adding a colorful uniform or unusual stage props; others have changed the gender composition of the performers due to a lack of male or female interest; and others still have reverted to an earlier form as a conscious decision of its performers. These changes reflect personal and artistic priorities as well as sociopolitical and economic pressures. Because a tradition can stress the uniqueness of a people as a whole and serve as a cultural icon, it can extend cultural and social capital to those involved. It is difficult, therefore, to isolate a single agent of change, not least because various interest groups are intertwined: both scholars and performers are among those who have been involved in executing government efforts to preserve traditions. Although it is easier to determine the effect of changes in folk traditions than to identify their cause, it is sometimes possible to establish a particular motive, even among the vast body of Korean folksongs. Folksongs rarely require special skill and are easily performed and transmitted by large groups of people. The common anonymity of the songs may cloud the rationale for particular changes, but among preserved genres such as those examined in this book, which require considerable special training and are passed on by a relatively small number of people, the cause for change can occasionally be determined.

At present, a total of eight folksong traditions are listed as National Intangible Cultural Properties (for a detailed list, see chapter 1), but this study is concerned primarily with *Sŏnsori sant'aryŏng* (Standing Mountain Songs), *Kyŏnggi minyo* (Folksongs from Kyŏnggi Province), and *Sŏdo sori* (Folksongs from the Western Provinces). These three genres have the largest number of folksong practitioners. Unlike many other folksong genres, they have been transmitted in and around Seoul, where they have been subject to considerable change and their performers, music, and repertoires have become interconnected. They therefore present major challenges when discussing authenticity. In the case of *Kyŏnggi minyo* and *Sŏnsori sant'aryŏng,* for example, the issues are tied very much to gender. Although once sung by either men or women, both genres are now sung predominantly by women, which affects the sound, movement, and semiotics of performance. Because the CPPL lends authority to the form of these folksongs, their sound and presentation will become set in the minds of audiences for the foreseeable future. The preservation of *Sŏdo sori,* on the other hand, ties the issue of authenticity to the question of roots: How can performers successfully pass on a tradition when they have never visited the native land from which it derives—and, in all likelihood, never will—and to which its music and lyrics refer?

In this book I investigate how the three major genres have developed over time and what impact the official preservation system has had on their alleged authenticity. I analyze the historical development of these three traditions from the viewpoint of repertoire, pedigree, music, and representation (or performance) and pay attention to what factors have influenced decision making. One major factor in their transition to intangible cultural properties is postcolonialism. Resentment towards the Japanese, for example, continues to smolder. Until recently, many Koreans resented the Japanese colonial government's alleged suppression of many forms of Korean folk performing arts. In response, some of the custodians of these genres have emphasized their anti-Japanese credentials, while others have created them. In these cases, the indignation over the colonial experience may have been fuelled by the desire to stand out among competing folk traditions. In 1998, for example, "Tondollari," a dance with song from south Hamgyŏng province was listed under a special category of cultural properties (see chapter 1), even though those involved had made obvious adjustments to it in order to compete with similar traditions and become noteworthy as a unique remnant of anti-Japanese resistance.[78] Its developers probably drew inspiration from "Kanggangsullae," a women's circle dance song, which in 1966 became the first folksong genre to be appointed an IICP and was included in UNESCO's Representative List of the Intangible Cultural Heritage of Humanity in 2009. There are many theories regarding the latter's origin. One of the most popular holds that the tradition dates from the time of the Hideyoshi invasions (1592–1598), when the women's movements were intended to lead the Japanese Navy to think that Korean troop movements were a preparation for battle on the shore.[79] According to a 1954 English language publication of Korean folksong scores by the "National Music Research Society of Korea," on the other hand, a "rather reliable" theory holds that the song was composed by Admiral Yi Sunshin, who was responsible for defeating the Japanese Navy on numerous occasions. Intended as a warning that the Japanese Navy was approaching, the song title therefore ought to be interpreted as meaning "the ferocious enemy is coming across the sea."[80]

Korea's most widely known song, "Arirang," meanwhile, was included on UNESCO's list in December 2012, first as a South Korean song and then again on November 24, 2014, as a group of songs that came from different provinces in North Korea.[81] Although it already existed in many forms in the nineteenth century, the version preserved gained much popular appeal when in 1926 its lyrics appeared on screen at the end of Na Un'gyu's controversial silent film of the same name. Both the narrative of the movie, which highlighted the Japanese colonial government's violent oppression of the Korean people, and the film narrators (*pyŏnsa*) who performed it lent the song an undertone of political resistance not actually reflected in its lyrics.[82] Despite the active promotion of a mere romantic reading of the lyrics by the Japanese,[83] the popularity of the song with the Japanese in the ensuing years nevertheless authenticated its power, as both a form of entertainment that could compete with that of Japan, and as a symbol of colonial-era retribution. Many Korean government-produced materials, including the previously mentioned English language volume, have highlighted the standardized song as an expression of the Koreans' colonial experience: "Under Japanese pressure, we shed tears of national indignation singing Arira[n]g and now swear to realize our wishes singing this warm-hearted song. . . . The melancholy melody of this song . . . seems to symbolize the sorrowful and painful fortune of our nation. We cannot overlook that this melody holds firmness of purpose desiring final victory against the enemy through national trials and tribulations."[84]

Popular folksongs play a significant role in the experience and representation of postcolonialism. For many years government-sponsored performing troupes traveling overseas have incorporated "Arirang" alongside elements of dubious heritage or authenticity in their performance. While the latter were aimed primarily at boosting the shows' visual appeal—they sometimes featured a few scantily clad male drummers beating oversized barrel drums, an image strongly reminiscent of a Japanese *wadaiko* performance—the inclusion of "Arirang" was intended to promote the song's recognizability as a symbol of Korea. Both characteristics were, however, also aimed at stirring feelings of nostalgia and national pride among Koreans in the audience. Perhaps because "Kanggangsullae" would require a considerable number of young female performers, the song rarely forms part of the programs. It appears that "Tondollari," which is not as strongly associated with a particular age group or gender, has taken its place. In October 2014, for example, the Korean Ministry of Foreign Affairs welcomed a large number of guests to an extravagant *kugak* (Korean traditional music) show touring Australia to commemorate the opening of the G20 Leaders Summit in Australia. Although it comprised folk, fusion, and B-boy dance music, the program included no less than five folksong renditions: four of "Arirang," and one of "Tondollari." The Korean national flag appeared both on stage and in a slick tourism video, which was projected halfway through the concert and highlighted some of Korea's major achievements in culture, science, and business.

Considering that all Japanese cultural products, including traditional performing arts, were banned in Korea from the time it was liberated, it seems unlikely that they would have had any significant impact on Korean art. And yet their image has long affected the interpretation of Korean traditions, including folksongs. Unable to shake the cultural cringe, performers, scholars, and policy makers have sought to establish Korean icons that could compete with those of Japan.[85] Much like folksongs with anti-Japanese lyrics, the three folksong properties seek to heal the wounds of Korea's colonial past, and they remind us of its suffering through the broken voices of the singers. Changes that epitomize this purpose have occurred in the traditions of *Sŏnsori sant'aryŏng* and *Kyŏnggi minyo* since the colonial period. In dance, vocal style, costume, and the gender of its primary performers, the two genres have been developed as Korean alternatives to the iconic sound and image of *koto*-playing geisha. Chapter 3 describes how these traditions came to be reconfigured, in part, to outdo their imagined Japanese counterpart.

There are, however, other factors that have led to the reconfiguration of Korean folksong traditions. One is that Korea now has a significant Christian population, which, though still a minority, exhibits significant intolerance toward shamanistic, Buddhist, and Confucian features, particularly where its own activities are concerned.[86] Another factor is the diminished career prospects offered by the folk arts. Although the Korean Wave has boosted the visibility and marketability of Korean traditions both domestically and overseas, the possibility of performers earning a decent living through folk arts remains small, leading to a steady demise in the number of male professionals. A third factor involves the nostalgic value of folk arts from what is now North Korea. While the likelihood of reunification was great enough to inspire the many students who took part in the *Minjung* movement, the failure of President Kim Dae Jung's Sunshine Policy (1998–2007), and continued North Korean aggression since then, have diminished nostalgia for the north and its customs. It is therefore possible that the tradition of *Sŏdo sori,* which comprises songs that originate from and relate to the now North Korean Hwanghae and P'yŏngan provinces, may summon stronger feelings of nostalgia if the idea of reunification is abandoned. Equally though, the genre may lose these feelings for good because neither its current practitioners nor the majority of their audiences were born or trained in the tradition's native land.

Contemporary folk artists must meet other demands that are not directly related to their art per se, such as networking, liaising with private benefactors, and sometimes even converting to Christianity or undergoing cosmetic surgery.[87] Such demands are a consequence of changes in society and may be inspired by developments in popular culture. Oskar Elschek argues that cultural policies can only "speed up or slow down processes of change that are already taking place,"[88] and yet it is commonly expected that the holders and students of intangible cultural properties adhere as close as possible to the "authentic form" designated by the CPC, even though this is not specified in the CPPL. This book does not seek to account for all the social factors implicated in the changes that have occurred within the folksong traditions, but acknowledges the significance of major sociopolitical and economic shifts. I contend that the Korean preservation system has both effected and consolidated changes in folksong traditions in the process of selection, and that it has chosen not to rectify modifications that have since taken place.

Some of the material presented in this book is based on fieldwork from the mid-1990s. Drawing on standard methodologies of anthropology, I have applied in particular ethnomusicology's "critical method," which highlights the contextualization of music and performance. It urges caution when interpreting fieldwork data, paying due account to the potential impact of the recording process on the actions of informants and their audiences.[89] The importance of contextualization also pertains to the use of particular sound or image media. Considering, for example, the cost and practical operation of gramophone recordings in the past should allow more accurate conjecture regarding the media's application and audience. This can be of use in trying to avoid making false claims on the basis of materials that do not represent the conditions described,[90] and allows readers to infer caveats on claims made by informants.[91] Although the many methods used to notate music and lyrics in the past ought to be included in such considerations, I have chosen to discuss only those I consider to have had significant impact on the performance or transmission of specific forms of music.

The prominence of musicians' personal stories in this text acknowledges the individual conditions in which the musicians studied and performed their art over time, which intimates to some degree the basis of their position within their music scene and outside. In addition, it sheds light on the possible rationale for a number of the changes traditions incurred under their helm. The information I was able to gather on the singers' past is limited by lack of access to their backgrounds. As a result, the conclusions I arrived at in regard to the effect of postcolonialism on their traditions are more likely to appear assumptive. While the focus and detail of individual accounts as well as the time of their composition will bear on the value of any musical ethnography, Timothy Rice presents a strong argument that by considering the experience of music, an overemphasis on the role of particular individuals (including the ethnographer) can be remedied. What, indeed, led them to take up studying music in the first place? And how did they respond to modernity and the changing significance of their practice?[92] Since an emphasis on adversity is nevertheless likely to highlight and possibly romanticize individual accomplishment, I have included the personal stories of a range of performers across different genres. This should underscore the importance of recognizing the individually dissimilar experiences of certain sociopolitical or economic changes.[93]

The conditions under which I collected fieldwork data differed over time. Sometimes, a professor or musician would provide the necessary introduction to an informant, but in most cases I was able to approach people of my own accord. The value of the eventual interview would rely on a fortunate culmination of factors, such as the informant being in the right mood, and perhaps intrigued by a young foreigner who professed an interest in Korean heritage, as well as him or her having faith in my ability to understand and represent the information requested. Interviews ultimately became easier as my language skills improved, and as I became older and was affiliated with a Western educational institution, all of which lent me more legitimacy. It is unavoidable that my being a foreigner affected the informants' rendition of events to some degree. It certainly led several elderly informants to simplify their accounts and spend time recounting what was fairly common knowledge, even after I provided evidence of having previously studied the topic. Meanwhile, the practicalities of conducting interviews also changed. In my early days as a researcher, I would turn up with a paper notebook and a cassette recorder and place the latter within sight of the interviewee. These days I continue to take notes by hand during interviews, but I use a smartphone app to record the sound, which due to the standard practice of placing phones on tables has become fairly unobtrusive. Most of the interviews took place at someone's office or school, though on occasion, research-related matters were discussed over dinner or while at a "3-ch'a" (third—and thankfully last—consecutive drinking venue). In those cases, I would remind my informants of both the question and the fact that I was recording their words, lest intoxication would cause them to forget.

I often contacted singers multiple times. While my own aging afforded me easier access to some of the very old singers, their age made it increasingly difficult for them to spend much time talking or even meeting people. When I started fieldwork in 1995, most of the key singers were already in their seventies. An Pich'wi (d. 1997) told me she was too ill to meet me, and when I first met Muk Kyewŏl and Yi Ŭn'gwan, they both had to rest after they had climbed the many stairs to their institutes where they had agreed to meet me. In addition to their physical frailty, they sometimes had difficulty recalling events in detail. On my last visit to Yi Ŭnju in July 2013, for example, she began to recount the days of old in response to questions regarding the activities of her peers in recent decades. Had I not had the assistance of her senior student Yu Oksŏn, I would not have pursued my questions further. Although I also intended to conduct an interview with Muk Kyewŏl that month, a few singers told me that due to her weakliness it would not be worth the trouble I might cause her. She died less than a year later, on May 2, 2014. While Yi Ŭnju and Hwang Yongju were ultimately still able to provide fairly detailed descriptions of past events, Yi Ŭn'gwan became quite fuzzy. On more than one occasion, he would respond to my questions about a certain event or singer dismissively or give me information that conflicted with what he had told me before. Keen though he generally was on providing me with the right details, he regularly contradicted his earlier statements. When I had conflicting accounts, I either pointed them out in the notes or chose to rely on different sources.

Rather than freezing the folksong traditions of *Sŏnsori sant'aryŏng, Kyŏnggi minyo,* and *Sŏdo sori* and jeopardize their survival, the preservation system has allowed them to adapt to the changing sociopolitical and economic climate and to incorporate a degree of technological innovation. Whereas the decisions made by the parties involved in official recognition are mostly left unjustified, they have defined genres in ways that differ from the often more diverse forms they had prior to being designated. It is possible that performers and those involved in the traditions' designation were influenced by, among other things, loyalty to peers, a desire to compete with Japanese cultural icons, commercialism, and individual pride. While considering these factors, I concern myself primarily with the development of the folksong traditions and the ways in which they have been affected by the preservation system, positively or negatively. I discuss the changing conditions of performance over the years, and the various forces behind those changes, while paying attention to the key individuals involved in the preservation of the three folksong genres.

In chapter 1, I chart the history of legislation related to the protection of cultural properties and the influence of Japanese colonial rule. Because the notion of a particular item having cultural significance to the Korean people may have affected the decision making of performers even before the promulgation of the Cultural Properties Protection Law, I discuss how the development of Korea's heritage management policies reflects a growing recognition of cultural property as representing historical, cultural value beyond mere private possession. In the second part of the chapter, I examine current legislation and the various measures and procedures established concerning intangible cultural properties. I investigate, among other things, the rationale for focusing on folk traditions and demonstrate that the requirements for holders are not explicitly supported by law. Chapter 2 discusses the characteristics and terminologies of Korean folksongs, such as their melodic style, structure, and the pressures imposed by Confucian morals. Here I lay out the primary regional characteristics and the main factors currently affecting the performance of Korean folksong traditions, such as the increasing number of Christian practitioners and the ongoing decline in the number of male professionals.

Chapters 3 and 4 explore the history of the folksong genres *Sŏnsori sant'aryŏng*, *Kyŏnggi minyo*, and *Sŏdo sori*, including the tradition of *Paebaengi kut*, a partly sung, partly narrated performing art that was categorized under the latter category. I examine the development of repertoire and discuss the ways in which the government's efforts to preserve folksongs have either prevented or encouraged change in the three genres. As I discuss the transmission of the traditions in recent years, I also observe the impact of iconic Japanese traditions on their presentation and performance. The life stories of the first holders of the three genres testify to the significant impact of changes in the sociopolitical and economic conditions on their work. They detail the impact of the Japanese colonial period on opportunities for employment and conditions of performance, and they highlight the importance of personal networks and the media for the performers' careers and the preservation of their art.

The book concludes with a recount of the changes and compromises made to the three folksong traditions. I discuss how the folksong traditions have come to be promoted as the valuable property of the Korean people as a whole, including the growing number of Koreans born overseas. While the direct recollection of the colonial experience is waning, the changes it has effected in the three genres—the substitution of "authenticity" with popular, iconic appeal—may be permanent. Rather than being threatened by a loss of authenticity, however, I contend that folksongs have retained their appeal, albeit for less practical and more political reasons, such as tourism, nostalgia, and community pride.

CHAPTER 1

Colonial Foundations of Korean Cultural Policy

UNTIL 1910, when the Japanese annexed Korea, official measures for the preservation of public or private property did not consider the notion that either could have what Bourdieu would regard as "symbolic capital." While retaining economic and functional values, which require no audience to be valorized, such capital would serve to positively distinguish the owner (or owning body) in society.[1] Because the Chosŏn dynasty (1392–1910) was fairly stable, it is unlikely to have spawned many creative applications of tradition.[2] But whereas the aristocracy (or royal house) would be impervious to the mundane, banal social pressures that drive the general public to pursue particular properties, they would have been well aware that particular forms of capital, such as that represented by ancestral shrines,[3] could be used to symbolize their own lasting, unique legacies of which their subordinates formed an integral part. These days, when cultural policies preserve and promote objects' public ownership, they prioritize symbolic over other forms of capital because the suggestion of historic continuity serves to underpin nationalism and loyalty to the state. Gellner argues that preindustrial societies were too segmented to execute "cultural imperialisms, the efforts of one culture or another to dominate and expand to fill out a political unit," but their culture (and ancestry)—as represented by property—would have helped determine the legacy of the privileged for centuries.[4] While legislation in regard to property management therefore did not show concern for its potential use to define either the aristocracy or the royal house and their respective communities of subordinates, either group is likely to have recognized the notion of "symbolic capital."[5]

The history of the protection of national heritage through legislation technically could be said to have begun almost five centuries earlier, in 1471, when a criminal justice system known as the Great Code of Administration (*Kyŏngguk taejŏn*) was put into effect. It constituted a revision of the Literal

Explanation of the Ming Code (*Tae myŏngnyul chikhae*), which had been translated from Chinese in 1395. The code was in effect roughly until the end of the Chosŏn dynasty (1392–1910).[6] It was ordered according to six sets of regulations, each of which corresponded to one of six government ministries. Under the sixth set, which comprised laws regarding public works, a regulation called "management of repairs" (*yŏngsŏn*) dealt with the restoration of palace buildings:

> The palace [is managed by] the *Chŏnyŏnsa*, and the buildings of the [surrounding] *kwana*[7] are divided up and guarded by each of these buildings' own officials, and when there is a place where the rain leaks through or where it is crumbling, they report it to the main office and it is repaired. Every year, in spring and autumn, [people from] the main office conduct an inspection tour and [then] report to the king. The repairs on the buildings of local government offices are undertaken after a report has been made to the king. As for the harbor platforms where Chinese envoys come and go, the responsibility is partially taken by the nearby counties and they make sure repairs are undertaken. As for the harbor platforms where the Japanese and the Manchus come and go, they are repaired by the local counties.[8]

Incorporated in the code were the *shibak* (*ship* = ten, *ak* = crimes), the ten worst crimes one could commit. Listed among them was an offense called "conspiracy" (*modaeyŏk*), which constituted the destruction of the ancestral temples that held memorial tablets to generations of kings, the kings' tumuli, and the royal palaces. The family of anyone found guilty of one of the *shibak* would have had little reason to celebrate their relative's rebelliousness. In the most extreme case, the principal offender would be left unburied with his head, arms, and legs cut off, while his father and those sons older than sixteen years would be hanged. The remaining family members would all be made slaves to a meritorious official, with the exception of very ill men over eighty or incurably ill women over sixty.[9] It is obvious why the code did not consider recidivism.

The regulations show no sign of having been set up in order to protect the cultural, historical value of the properties. They were primarily preventative, concerned with the protection of property on the basis of it belonging to the royal house (no doubt intended for public admiration) and a matter of religious concern. Even the sizeable restorations performed on the royal palace from 1865 to 1867, which were aimed at restoring the prestige of the dynasty, failed to appeal to a sense of pride over the site's cultural, historic importance.[10] In December 1894, following the initiation of a series of changes to government policy under the name Kabo Reform (*Kabo kyŏngjang*, 1894–1896) in July that year, the Korean government was reorganized and a Japanese-style cabinet formed with seven ministries. One of these, the Ministry of the Royal Household (Kungnaebu), oversaw the Ceremonial Court (Changniwŏn), which was responsible for the management of mausoleums, cemeteries, and tombs.[11] By separating the Council of State Affairs (Ŭijŏngbu) from the Ministry, the latter was stripped of its governing powers and turned into a ceremonial institute.[12] The new administrative structure thus effectively eroded the power of King Kojong, who had tried to resist the measures for years.

When they set out to colonize Korea, the Japanese anticipated that in light of their loss of autonomy and the significant social change that modernity was ushering in, the effects of which they had only recently experienced firsthand,[13] Koreans would come to long for markers of their heritage. Recognizing in addition that as they transitioned into the full annexation of Korea they could make use of the royal institution as a channel for the proclamation of sociopolitical measures at least for some years,[14] the Japanese government refrained from removing all symbols of the Korean traditional hierarchy and prepared their maintenance as hollow, ceremonial institutes and monuments. Their eventual exhibition on museum grounds was to serve as a reminder of a foregone past. Rather than portraying them as "living" treasures, they deprived them of their religious significance and turned them into objects of nostalgia and wonder. To rid royal palaces of their mystic status and meet the growing demand for Japanese tourist attractions, the Japanese not only rearranged them but also opened them to the public—they had long been hidden from view, like similar palaces elsewhere in East Asia. The first of a series of museums was the Prince Yi Museum (*Riōke hakubutsukan*). Construction for this museum, which focused on the possessions of the former royal household, began on the premises of Ch'anggyŏng-wŏn royal garden in November 1908. It was part of a large public entertainment park modeled after Tokyo's Ueno Park and carried a name that revealed the colonial government's intention to market Korea's royal house as a curiosity, the ornate shell of a former kingdom.[15] Another major museum in the center of Seoul was established on December 1, 1915, on the grounds of Kyŏngbok Palace. Named after the Japanese colonial headquarters, the Museum of the Government-General of Korea (*Chōsen sōtokufu hakubutsukan*) was a colossal building constructed right behind the main gate to the palace grounds between 1916 and 1926. This museum was the first to focus on archaeological finds.[16]

On November 27, 1907, the Royal Household Minister declared that an office would be established for the purpose of managing and maintaining "movable [*tongsan*] and unmovable [*pudongsan*] property in the possession of the [Korean] royal family."[17] This so-called Office for the Management of the Royal Family's Property (Cheshil chaesan chŏngniguk) would be small in size, with six positions to be filled by nine people in total. Although the edict suggests recognition of the royal household's cultural as opposed to mere exchange value, a

Japanese reprint of this edict shows that the measure was little more than a justification for drawing a full inventory of the royal family's property, with the intention to eventually transfer its management to the colonial government.[18] In 1911, the office was renamed Yi [Chosŏn] Royal Household Office (Yiwangjik) and considerably expanded. From February 1 onward, it would be staffed by no less than ninety-seven people, with the number of Korean aristocracy eligible for employment limited to eleven.[19] One important reason for the expansion was that the office was made responsible for managing the Prince Yi Museum.

The cultural policy of the Japanese colonial government—Chōsen sōtokufu (Government-General of Korea, r. 1910–1945)—focused, primarily, on cultivating loyalty to the Japanese empire through public information and education. From the turn of the century it had steadily increased its control on the media by taking over newspapers and implementing censorship of Korean publications. By 1910, after various takeovers and bans, all newspapers intended for Korean readers had been converted to propaganda organs of the Japanese government. To prevent the pervasion of dissident voices, the government-general's comprehensive censorship apparatus scrutinized many aspects of public life.[20] The instruction of Japanese, both as a condition for assimilation and a propaganda medium, became a priority. It is sometimes said that upon annexation, the Japanese discovered that the vast majority of Koreans were illiterate,[21] but already in 1898, Isabella Bird Bishop had found that most uneducated men were able to read texts in the vernacular *han'gŭl,* so it appears that establishing proficiency in Japanese was more important than literacy itself.[22] The Japanese provided Korean children with four years of elementary schooling, as well as an additional three and four years for girls and boys respectively. There was also the possibility of attending a technical or professional school, or even, if their parents could afford it, college in Japan. But prejudice significantly limited their access to higher education.[23] All preexisting public and private schools came under strict control of the government-general, their curriculum dominated by language training, with science only introduced in the third year. Music education, meanwhile, was strongly based on Japanese standards.[24] All courses were aimed at developing the students' fluency in Japanese and introducing them to new morals, including a revised reading of Korean history and culture. Rather than educating Korean students per se, the curriculums were ultimately intended to ease their assimilation into the Japanese empire.[25] Unless they could extend their education in Japan, the basic education allowed Koreans little opportunity for success; the Japanese authorities believed that overeducating Koreans would make them critical of their situation and too well equipped to voice their discontent. To frustrate patriotic appeals, it discouraged and oppressed the expression of Korean culture in words and behavior and pushed the adoption of Japanese customs and norms—such as those on hygiene and ethics—

instead.[26] In spite of the ambitious education policy, however, many Koreans still missed out on basic education. By 1945 less than 20 percent of the population had received any form of schooling.[27]

The government-general portrayed Korean culture as inferior to that of Japan. Targeting its spiritual life in particular, it banned a large number of religious and folk rituals.[28] Using terms such as *dozoku* (indigenous) and *minzoku* (folk) to refer to Korean customs and belief systems, the Japanese authorities described Korean culture as uncivilized and barbarian, and in dire need of replacement by Japanese modernity. Although the terms were targeted at shamanism and Confucianism, they were equally applicable to Christianity and other forms of folk religion. The Japanese initiative to develop a public cemetery was another demonstration of their considerable disregard for Korean rites and customs. Since it was intended to facilitate the cultivation of particular land for farming or construction projects, the public gravesites did not follow the directions of a geomancer and disallowed Koreans to be buried near their ancestors.[29] Another example entailed the conversion of many village shrines across the country into shrines for Japan's native Shinto. In 1912, the government-general issued an order that authorized the investigation and subsequent purging of all superstitions and "fake religions"—such as small cults and Ch'ŏndogyo (Religion of the Heavenly Way)—by the Bureau of Sanitation.[30] Atkins argues that the Japanese government treated shamanism with "resigned tolerance,"[31] but according to Kim Kwang-ok, the police carefully monitored the activities of shamans and sometimes arrested or tortured them. He contends that because they regarded shamanism as a common enemy to their views on enlightenment and modernity, even the Korean adherents of Christianity, Buddhism, and Confucianism in some cases "reluctantly" cooperated with the Japanese in their efforts to eradicate the practice of shamanism.[32]

While the Japanese colonial government made considerable efforts to export its native religion, Shinto, for example, by ordering its colonial subjects to pay a large number of visits to one of its shrines,[33] it also manipulated Korea's own major belief systems. Having reorganized the Korean monarchy as the colony's main pillar of Confucianism, it shifted its attention to Christianity and Buddhism. Christian missionaries were considered a potential source of patriotism, and, presumably in an attempt to threaten them into submission, in 1911 and 1912 the Japanese arrested and tortured hundreds of men—many of whom were Christian—over allegations of conspiring to assassinate the Governor-General Terauchi Masatake.[34] The government-general would apply further pressure on Christians from 1919, when a large number of them were found to be behind the massive Korean uprising and passionate public appeal for independence that would later be referred to as the March First Movement. The only religion to gain support from the Japanese authorities, at least financially, was Buddhism.

After the annexation, in an attempt to counter the growing popularity of Christianity, the Japanese government effectively revitalized Korean Buddhist orders. Claiming that Korean Buddhism was "in a decadent condition," the government-general assumed control of all Buddhist activities on the Korean peninsula. It legislated that resident or permanent priests had to be registered by the governor-general and pursued their adoption of Japanese practices, such as, from 1926, the ability for monks to marry and eat meat.[35] Although some Korean Buddhist orders ended up marginalized upon their refusal, many opted to compromise and follow the Japanese line.[36] Since they preceded the annexation by decades, Hwansoo Kim warns that it is wrong to label the many Japanese activities regarding Korean Buddhist orders as purely political, intent only on their assimilation into the Japanese empire.[37] Like their Korean counterparts, Japanese sects sought to promote their forms of Buddhism in Korea in part to counter Christianity, which was growing steadily, and in part to revitalize and modernize them using Japanese resources.

In Korea, both the legal measures to preserve what is today considered part of the national, cultural heritage and the categories under which properties would be listed were first set out during the period of Japanese colonial rule. The Japanese colonial government pursued a policy of vertical cultural assimilation aimed at encouraging colonial subjects to adopt the culture of the superior Japanese while carefully distinguishing nationalities based on race and traditions.[38] While many laws and regulations were enacted to protect the properties that now belonged to the Japanese empire, legislation showed a clear political agenda. The various measures regulated the transfer and management of Korean tangible cultural properties but showed no concern for intangible ones. In 1916, the Japanese began to protect old buildings and other state properties on the basis of them constituting cultural treasures, a novel notion, though not well developed at the time; it showed mainly a concern with the historical value of properties. Many cultural items were still easily removed from their original context, either by placing them in museums and representing them as part of the new culture, or by adding them to private collections in Korea or abroad.

The Japanese have often been blamed for the theft and destruction of many of Korea's cultural properties. Koreans estimate that during the colonial period more than fifty thousand items of historical or artistic value were shipped to Japan.[39] During the annexation, most of the treasures found in cities, such as the capitals of the ancient kingdoms Kyŏngju, Puyŏ, Kongju, and Kaesŏng, were shipped abroad, leaving the cities that had hitherto abounded with historical relics virtually empty; this, at least, is the contemporary Korean view. The vigor and enthusiasm with which the Japanese undertook the acquisition of Korean relics may account for the occasional use of explosives. Korean sources duly note that in 1904, in the chaos following the wars with China and Russia, the Japanese army used dynamite to open tombs in the region of Kaesŏng City and on Kanghwa Island, the contents of which—more than ten thousand pieces of ancient Korean pottery—were then shipped to Japan.[40]

From the turn of the nineteenth century, Japanese archaeologists and anthropologists began to come to Korea to conduct fieldwork and excavations. The Japanese government's ban on a wide range of domestic heritage excavations led many archaeologists to the colonies to further their academic pursuits.[41] Among them was Sekino Tadashi, an archaeologist from Tokyo National University, who in 1902 came to Korea at the invitation of the Korean imperial government to inspect Pulguk Temple outside Kyŏngju City. The temple has often been described as the hallmark of art of the Unified Shilla period (668–918), but it was partly destroyed during the Japanese invasions from 1592 to 1958, also known as the *Imjin waeran*. Yi Kuyŏl argues that Sekino's visit was intended to source materials to help justify the annexation of Korea.[42] Yi does not provide evidence for his view, but throughout the colonial period Japanese archaeologists did indeed interpret their findings in ways that supported Japanese imperialism. In their pursuit of the historical remains of Japanese ancestry and Japanese civilization on the continent, they highlighted the natural, scientific superiority of their race. They treated Korean history as subordinate to that of China and attributed all innovation on Korean land to its invaders.[43] Meanwhile, the Japanese politicians who supported the archaeologists were keen to introduce the notion of Japanese national treasures to Korea in an attempt to undermine patriotism and highlight the historical and biological superiority of the founders of the empire.[44]

In the year Korea was annexed, the Japanese began to undertake archaeological activities of a more serious nature.[45] The Japanese justified their actions by saying they were protecting historical treasures from the Koreans themselves. Sekino argued that this was necessary because of the Koreans' lack of concern for their own treasures and their rifling of many ancient structures. He also complained that the restorations Koreans had made to ancient structures violated their traditional form. But he conveniently overlooked how architectural changes made by the Japanese colonial government modified Buddhist and Confucian buildings. He himself revealed that, "with the inauguration of the administration of the Resident-General . . . it had become necessary to appropriate former shrines and other public buildings for government offices, post offices and school buildings etc., or to remodel them for such purposes."[46] Sekino's work and that performed by other Japanese archaeologists was comprehensive and detailed, and it was minutely recorded in annual reports published from 1918 to 1937 as Reports on Investigations of Ancient Sites in Korea (*Chōsen koseki chōsa hōkoku*).[47] In 1939, in what is a clearly pro-Japanese article, Edwin Reischauer stressed the value of the work conducted by the archeologists, saying, "The Japanese have continued diverse and geographically widespread excavations throughout Korea and Manchuria, which have been carefully planned to cover the most necessary fields, and which have yielded valuable, if not spectacular, results."[48] Reischauer reported the damage inflicted by Japanese troops as if it was collateral, and notes that in 1938 the work of archaeologist Oba Tsunekichi had been hindered by bandits. He deplores that Chinese scholars took relics with them when they withdrew from Nanking, but disregards the possibility that they may have done so in an attempt to prevent the relics from falling into Japanese hands.[49]

The Japanese archaeologists and anthropologists did not train the Koreans who served as their assistants and would publish their findings in Japanese, but they did have a profound impact on the development of the disciplines of archaeology and anthropology in Korea after independence, if perhaps in part because they inspired Koreans to seek a rectification of the colonial interpretations.[50] Those first taking up the discipline in the 1920s included a number of Korean cultural nationalists, who felt that their ideals could not be achieved through Western ideas and institutions and regarded it as important to maintain symbols of Korean historic achievements.[51] Ch'oe Namsŏn (1890–1957) and Yi Nŭnghwa (1869–1945), the forerunners of Korean folklore studies, chose to focus on shamanism in particular, because it did not exist in Japan, was indigenous to Korea, and represented the culture of the common folk.[52] While the two maintained a strong nationalist agenda, their work showed the influence of Japanese approaches and methodologies, including those developed by Yanagita Kunio (1875–1962), the founder of Japanese folklore studies, and possibly those of the aesthete Yanagi Muneyoshi/Sōetsu (1889–1961), who founded the folk crafts (*mingei*) movement and had a significant impact on the valorization of Korean folk arts and crafts.[53] In their attempts to celebrate a timeless culture untainted by Western modernity, Ch'oe and Yi were driven by nostalgia, much like Yanagita and Yanagi.[54]

The Temple Act (*Jisatsurei*) of September 1, 1911, was the first legislative measure to protect Buddhist temples and prevent further damage regardless of what was causing it. The authorities believed that positive measures could encourage Buddhists to support Japan, and restoring Buddhist temples was therefore something of interest to both Korean Buddhists and their colonial masters.[55] It stipulated that an inventory be made of all movable and immovable properties worthy of preserving. Once registered, the items could no longer be removed, disposed of, or repaired without prior approval from the appropriate Japanese authorities. The law made it obligatory for those who discovered relics to report them. Properties under its protection included all temples' estates, Buddha statues, tombstones, old documents, and temple bells. Although by 1923 the colonial government had listed as many as 385 historical relics, only 114 were eventually designated for repair due to a lack of funding.[56] Japanese statistics record, perhaps unsurprisingly, that between 1911 and 1928 the violators of the Temple Act were all Korean, but their number was small, not more than four per year on average.[57] Sekino claims that the Temple Act was aimed at enforcing regulations already set out in the Ancient Shrines and Temples Preservation Law (*Koshaji hozonhō*),[58] enacted in Japan in 1897, but Han Woo-keun believes the act was promulgated in order to suppress rebellion from the predominantly anti-Japanese monks. He argues that the Japanese used the act to sell off vast amounts of land that belonged to the temples and monasteries in order to prevent them from having funds to support resistance.[59] The law did indeed stipulate that temples and monasteries were to be used for religious purposes only and that any property in the possession of Buddhist organizations had to be minutely registered and could not be sold without prior approval from the Japanese governor-general.[60]

The Temple Act was superseded by the Regulations for the Preservation of Ancient Remains and Relics (*Koseki oyobi ibutsu hozon kisoku*) on July 4, 1916. With the promulgation of these regulations, the colonial government took charge of archaeological and preservation activities.[61] The committee that would manage the directives' execution was presided over by the vice governor-general and comprised of both academic experts and high government officials.[62] The regulations were primarily aimed at the proper registration of newly discovered relics, and considering the Museum of the Government-General of Korea was established a year prior, it is likely that they were born out of concern for the illegal appropriation of and trade in antiquities, especially in light of the burgeoning Japanese heritage tourism industry.[63]

A set of measures that broke down the already diminishing influence of Confucian institutions were the Regulations for the Management of Property of Schools Connected to Confucian Temples (*Kyōkō zaisan kanri kitei*) of 1920.[64] Han Woo-keun points out that these regulations were intended primarily to prevent local Confucian leaders from becoming too powerful.[65] Indeed, they did not specify procedures to safeguard the property of the Confucian schools but merely dictated measures to assume control over them. The schools were allowed to continue teaching, but property was effectively transferred to the colonial government, which charged Confucian adherents for its use whenever they organized an event or activity. Although Han makes the additional claim that the Japanese appropriated part of the schools' income to finance new public school programs,[66] the act stipulated that school income was to be used to finance the school's own running costs as well as the costs of maintaining Confucian shrines.[67] The regulations were nevertheless vague regarding the type of activities that would be exempt from taxation. Ironically, according to Article 3, the school facilities could be used free of charge except in case of activities of a cultural or educational kind.[68]

On August 9, 1933, the Regulations for the Preservation of Ancient Remains and Relics were replaced by the Law for the Preservation of Natural Monuments, Places of Scenic Beauty and Historic Interest, and Treasures in Korea (*Chōsen hōmotsu koseki meishō tennenkinenbutsu hozonrei*).[69] The new law not only provided for the protection of cultural properties; it was also the first to stipulate how to plan restorations or excavations and the first to dictate proactive measures to safeguard cultural properties.[70] While incorporating the cultural properties protected by the earlier 1911 and 1916 laws, it broadened the concept of cultural property to include scenic sites. Similar to the 1916 law, cultural relics were not listed in order of importance, but in groups, per province.[71] By August 27, 1934, 169 items had been selected, with Seoul's central Namdaemun (Great South Gate), Tongdaemun (Great East Gate), and the Poshin'gak bell pavilion making up numbers one to three respectively.[72] By 1940, the tally of recognized cultural properties stood at 377 treasures, 128 places of historical interest, 119 natural monuments, 2 places of scenic beauty and historical interest and the like, and 2 natural monuments and places of scenic beauty.[73] While in 1911 resident Buddhist monks could apply for funding for the repair of temple properties considered important, which they then had to carry out themselves, the 1933 law put the government in charge of repairs. By 1935, the Japanese claimed to have already restored various Buddhist structures, including the stone bridge of Pulguk Temple in Kyŏngju County, the hall of Pusŏk Temple in Yŏngju County in north Kyŏngsang province, and the Kŭmsan Temple pavilion in Kŭmje County in north Chŏlla province.[74]

Whereas the various laws were aimed at maintaining control over all kinds of properties, mostly for political purposes, the 1916 and 1933 laws suggest that the colonial government did consider the possibility of property being neglected or damaged by the Japanese. Anna Seidel argues that the similar laws promulgated in Japan between 1897 and 1933 were passed to protect Buddhist art that had been devalued following rigid Westernization during the Meiji period (1868–1910). Examples she provides include the pagoda of Kōfuku Temple in Nara, which was sold as firewood to a local bathhouse, and plans to melt down the large Buddha of Kamakura in order to sell its metal to foreigners.[75] The colonial government must have seen the need to pass the same protective measures in Korea, Japan's new territory, to protect local Buddhist art there too. The new legislation did not, however, imply that the Japanese would stop sanctioning the damage of properties that fell under its protection. Hyung Il Pai notes that in the 1920s and 1930s the Japanese undertaking of large-scale railway construction prompted considerable concern among Japanese scholars of the Society for the Study of Korean Antiquities (*Chōsen koseki kenkyūkai*).[76] Despite their persistent pleas, the scholars were only able to prevent a small number of the several thousands of tombs from being ruined, as railway tracks were laid with very little regard for whatever was in their way.

The relatively early enactment of the 1916 law could also reflect recognition of the threat posed by the antiques trade, which had been growing in East Asia since the end of the nineteenth century.[77] Many intellectuals and academics committed to the preservation of East Asian relics were also collectors, so it was often easy for them to acquire antiques and ship them abroad.[78] Japanese collectors regularly celebrated the great deals to be found in Korea.[79] A related problem that had been plaguing preservation efforts for many years, but was on the increase due to the steep rise in market prices, was looting. It coincided with a third, the growing trade in counterfeits. In 1912, *The North-China Herald and Supreme Court & Consular Gazette* began to report that due to the insatiable foreign demand for East Asian antiques, counterfeits were flooding the markets.[80] In Korea, in response to these market developments, the number of official registered antiques, or "second-hand" (*komul*) dealers, subsequently grew quickly, by no less than five hundred per year on average.[81] The 1916 law itself was not concerned with the protection of antiques,[82] but the number of violations of the associated Antiques Trading Regulatory Law (*Kobutsushō torishimarihō*) amounted to a rapid rise, with many Japanese among the perpetrators.[83] Realizing that it could not rely only on legal procedures to prevent theft and smuggling, the government-general decided to move important relics to the Museum of the Government-General of Korea.[84]

According to Pai, the system of designating national treasures (Jap. *kokuhō;* Kor. *kukpo*) began with the enactment of the 1916 law,[85] but while the term was already in use in Japan, neither this law nor any other promulgated by the Japanese colonial government would apply the term *kokuhō* to Korean cultural properties.[86] Although the 1916 law was the first legislation aimed primarily at the protection of cultural properties, it was the 1933 law that first categorized the most important ones as treasures (Jap. *hōmotsu;* Kor. *pomul*). Already in 1927, Yi Kyŏngnyŏl discussed the notion of cultural property in detail. In an article published in *Tonggwang* (Dawn) that year, he relates culture to civilization, emphasizing that both are connected strongly to nature. He argues that a cultured people are able to find good use for the cultural property they have acquired and to let it further develop. He also mentions the concept of cultural heritage (*munhwa yusan*), but does not elaborate on the notion.[87]

The cultural policy of the Japanese colonial government in Korea largely sought to justify Japan's colonization of Korea and to weaken potential sources of dissent and rebellion. It did not seek to establish an appreciation for heritage per se, but sought to preserve heritage for political purposes, and as sites for Japanese historical tourism.[88] The reinterpretation of Korean history, the manipulation of the Buddhist order, the destruction of dynastic symbols through the dismantling of tombs and the rearrangement and partial destruction of palaces, were nevertheless carried out by different parties, each of whom had its own set of interests. These actions reflected, besides cultural imperialism, a mix of archaeological, religious, and perhaps commercial interests, as well as individual ambition. As Roger Janelli suggests, it is unlikely that Japanese scholars' reinterpretation of Korean history simply followed from the dictates of the Japanese colonial government,[89] but such reinterpretation ultimately served the interests of imperial Japan and itself unquestionably benefited from colonial policies.

The Postwar Period: Adoption and Transformation

After liberation, on November 8, 1945, the provisional government renamed the Yi Royal Household Office to call it the Office of the Former Royal Household (Kuwanggung), operated under joint Korean and American jurisdiction. The office continued to oversee the enforcement of the 1933 law and the many treasures it aimed to protect, but because of economic and political instability, little was done. Economic rather than cultural programs had first priority in the post-Pacific War period and prevented major undertakings. On April 8, 1950, the Law for the Proceedings of the Property of the Former Royal Household (*Kuwanggung chaesan ch'ŏbunpŏp*) was enacted, which created three categories of cultural properties that had belonged to the royal household prior to Japanese colonial rule: (1) important palace buildings and their sites; (2) important works of art and historical souvenirs and documents; and (3) other items that require continuous preservation.[90]

The Korean War broke out on June 25, 1950, and raged until July 27, 1953. Although Eugene Knez, head of the US Information Service, was able to oversee an ingenious covert rescue operation that led to the safe evacuation of the Korean National Museum's collection to Pusan, many other cultural properties were severely damaged or lost.[91] Pai suggests the dramatic rescue effort may have come from a desire to prove the legitimate heir to the government of Korea through heritage, but she warns that some of the collectors of Korean art treasures, including Knez, were partly to blame for the plunder.[92] The involvement of the US Army Military Government in Korea (USAMGIK; 1945–1948) in securing the success of this operation would have also been grounded on this notion. The preservation law was renamed afterward, on September 23, 1954, and called the Law of the Property of the Former Royal Household (*Kuhwangshil chaesanpŏp*).[93] It was more specific about the cultural properties it covered, using these four categories: (1) important structures such as altars, shrines, palaces, parks, graves, and their sites; (2) important works of art, historical souvenirs, and written documents; (3) treasures, ancient remains, sceneries, and places of historic interest; and (4) matters resembling the hitherto mentioned cultural properties that require continuous preservation.[94]

In the early 1950s, no office had official responsibility for the types of cultural properties that fell beyond those specified in the 1954 law. Since 1948, however, the Education Department (Kyodokwa) of the Culture Bureau (Munhwabu) had taken on some of the heritage management-related duties. On February 17, 1955, a Department of Culture Preservation (Munhwa pojonkwa) was established and put in charge of protecting the national heritage.[95] On June 30, it redesignated 436 cultural properties that had been listed by the Japanese and renamed them "national treasures" (*kukpo*). Namdaemun and Tongdaemun thus became National Treasures nos. 1 and 2, respectively. The office also began to designate new cultural properties, and by 1960 it had listed a total of 606.[96] The department was superseded by the Cultural Properties Management Office (Munhwajae kwalliguk; CPMO), which was established on October 2, 1961, by merging the Department of Culture Preservation and the Office for the Management of Property of the Former Royal Household.[97] Located on the grounds of Tŏksu Palace, the office was put in charge of managing and overseeing all protection and preservation activities.

Japan's preservation laws continued to serve as models for Korea's heritage system even after liberation. The Korean government's adoption of Japanese ideas after liberation suggests that Koreans found the system's fundamental principles, including the establishment of national symbols, persuasive, and regarded them as useful tools to nurture nationalism. On August 29, 1950, the Japanese government enacted its comprehensive Law 214, the Cultural Properties Protection Law (*Bunkazai hogohō*). This incorporated the 1919, 1929, and 1933 laws promulgated in Japan and added two new categories of cultural properties, *maizō* (buried) and *mukei* (intangible).[98] Initially, folk performing arts (*minzoku geinō*) were to fall under the latter category, along with so-called manners and customs (*fūzoku*), but following a revision in 1975 they were separately categorized as important intangible folk cultural properties (*jūyō mukei minzoku bunkazai*).[99] The 1950 law divided cultural properties into five categories:

(1) Tangible cultural properties (*yūkei bunkazai*): buildings, artistic craft works, old documents, sculptures, etc.
(2) Intangible cultural properties (*mukei bunkazai*): plays, music, crafts, etc.
(3) Folk cultural properties (*minzoku bunkazai*): folk performing arts, manners and customs related to life necessities, occupations, beliefs, and annual events, etc. Properties in this category can be designated as *jūyō*

yūkei minzoku bunkazai (important tangible folk cultural properties) or *jūyō mukei minzoku bunkazai.*

(4) Monuments (*kinenbutsu*): flora and fauna, places of scenic or historical value such as gardens, bridges, and canyons.

(5) Groups of historic buildings (*dentōteki kenzōbutsugun*): fishing villages and villages under castle walls, etc.[100]

While the Japanese law recognized folk cultural properties (*minzoku bunkazai*), it was not until 1975 that it laid out legal measures for their protection, and not until the early 1980s that an amendment provided financial support for the performers of associated genres.[101] The Japanese system focused first and foremost on protecting those cultural properties considered in immediate danger of being lost. Well-established, iconic Japanese traditional performing arts, such as gagaku (court music and dance) and the theatrical drama genre of kabuki, were therefore initially omitted, though following much criticism they were placed under the law's protection through a revision in 1954. The new law also considered properties that were not necessarily in danger of being lost, but of significant "artistic or historical value" to the Japanese people.[102]

On January 10, 1962, the Korean government followed suit with the promulgation of Law 961, the Cultural Properties Protection Law (*Munhwajae pohopŏp*). Although it may seem odd that Park Chung Hee would enact a law of this scope no more than six months after his military coup, Chungmoo Choi posits that he may have pushed it in order to win the approval of the powerful nationalistic elite, who felt that there was an increasing need for government measures to preserve Korean traditions.[103] Among the politicians, scholars, and journalists arguing their importance, however, none was as effective as journalist Ye Yonghae (1929–1995). Between 1959 and 1963, Ye wrote a column for the *Han'guk ilbo* (Korea daily) entitled "In'gan munhwajae" (Human cultural properties), which demonstrated the dire state of many Korean traditions.[104] The new law placed cultural properties in four categories:

(1) Tangible cultural properties (*yuhyŏng munhwajae*): buildings, artistic craft works, old documents, sculptures, lacquer ware, etc.

(2) Intangible cultural properties (*muhyŏng munhwajae*): plays, music, dramas, crafts, etc.

(3) Monuments (*kinyŏmmul*): natural treasures such as animals and plants, and places of historic interest.

(4) Folk materials (*minsok charyo*): morals, customs, and beliefs.[105]

Its objective was to both "seek the cultural progress of the nation and at the same time contribute to the development of the culture of mankind by preserving and utilizing cultural properties."[106] It superseded earlier heritage-related legislation and adopted the properties recognized previously.[107]

The basic structure of the Korean Cultural Properties Protection Law was clearly based on the Japanese law. It incorporated the category of intangible cultural properties as part of the national heritage,[108] and used identical descriptions of the various categories of cultural properties. But it carried grander ambitions, highlighting the importance of cultural heritage not just for the Korean people's identity, but for the world as a whole.[109] Although it included performing arts related to the culture of the elite, it placed particular emphasis on folk traditions. Doing so avoided giving prominence to either Chinese influence or the culture of a privileged minority and helped remind the people of the Japanese oppression of Korean folk arts. Unlike the Japanese law, which considered only refined, classical performing arts and crafts as Important Intangible Cultural Properties (hereafter IICPs), it included folk music and dance, as well as martial arts, folk games and rituals, and even liquor distillation. Ironically, the prominence of folk arts and crafts may have been inspired by the work of Japanese folklorists and collectors, and the colonial-era *mingei* movement. While the activities of the aesthete Yanagi and his peers on occasion revealed a sense of cultural superiority over the Korean people and contributed to the smuggling of Korean antiquities,[110] they contributed significantly to the valorization of Korean folk arts and crafts, to which the establishment of a Korean folk art museum by Yanagi and Takumi Asakawa in 1924 and the fast growing antiques trade and tourism industry provided further impetus.[111] It seems odd, therefore, that when Koreans adopted the basic structure of the Japanese law, they omitted the subcategory of folk materials. It may be that, unlike Japan, where the term folk performing arts (*minzoku geinō*) had begun to be commonly accepted as a scholarly term after World War II, the term was not as widely in use in Korea even by the early 1960s. But it is more likely that the Park administration wished to either prevent folk religion from being foregrounded, like it was in Japan,[112] or play into the hands of those calling for reunification by emphasizing the culture of the common people (*minjok*).[113]

In Korea, the need to provide a basic income was recognized much earlier than in Japan. Following a revision of the Cultural Properties Protection Law on August 10, 1970, the designation of intangible cultural properties was tied not only to the designation of holders (*poyuja*), which largely due to Ye's column became commonly referred to as human treasures (*in'gan munhwajae*), but also to the provision of a basic income.[114] Financial support was regulated on the basis of Law 1417, the Special Accounting Law for the Management of Cultural Properties (*Munhwajae kwalli t'ŭkpyŏl hoegyepŏp*). It was enacted on October 21, 1963, but payments would not be made until November 1968.[115] In exchange for monthly support, holders were now expected to perform annually. The length and the conditions of performance had to meet certain requirements, for which the holders had to seek prior approval from the government. The law also required holders to pass on their art through teaching.[116]

The first cultural property to be redesignated under the new law was Namdaemun, on December 20, 1962. The order in which the Japanese had previously designated Korea's cultural treasures had already been adopted in 1955 and it was upheld again,[117] though the numbers had to be rearranged following the loss of many items over the course of the previous two decades. The law named and further categorized cultural properties as follows:

(1) National treasures (*kukpo*) and treasures (*pomul*), designated from among the tangible cultural properties (*yuhyŏng munhwajae*): buildings, artistic craft works, old documents, sculptures, etc.
(2) Important intangible cultural properties (*Chungyo muhyŏng munhwajae*), designated from among the intangible cultural properties (*muhyŏng munhwajae*): forms of art and craft that are of significant historical value.
(3) Important folk materials (*Chungyo minsok charyo*), designated from among the folk materials (*minsok charyo*): manmade implements used in all aspects of daily life in the past, including ritual implements, cooking utensils, and clothing.
(4) Historical sites (*sajŏk*), landmarks (*myŏngsŭng*), and natural monuments (*ch'ŏnyŏn kinyŏmmul*), such as animals, plants, and minerals, designated from among the monuments (*kinyŏmmul*).

The national treasures category reflects a value that is greater than that of the category of treasures. According to Article 2 of the Cultural Properties Protection Law, national treasures stand out because they are "rare and of great value from the standpoint of human culture."[118] Large structures in the capital were nevertheless ranked first. Indeed, many items from the same region continued to be grouped together despite significant differences in size, age, or historical significance.[119]

Until a revision in March 2015, unlike tangible cultural properties, all intangibles recognized were listed as "important." The current line-up of folksongs listed is shown in chronological order of appointment below:

No. 8: *Kanggangsullae,* a circle dance with songs, from south Chŏlla province, February 15, 1966;
No. 19: *Sŏnsori sant'aryŏng* (Standing Mountain Songs), from Kyŏnggi province, April 18, 1968;
No. 29: *Sŏdo sori* (Folksongs from the Western Provinces), from Hwanghae and P'yŏngan provinces, September 27, 1969;

No. 51: *Namdo tŭl norae* (Field Songs from the Southern Provinces), from south Chŏlla province, November 5, 1973;
No. 57: *Kyŏnggi minyo* (Folksongs from Kyŏnggi Province), July 12, 1975;
No. 84: *Yech'ŏn t'ongmyŏng nongyo* (Farming Songs from T'ongmyŏng-dong in Yech'ŏn County) and *Kosŏng nongyo* (Farming Songs from Kosŏng), from north and south Kyŏngsang province respectively, December 1, 1985;
No. 95: *Cheju minyo* (Folksongs from Cheju Province), December 1, 1989.
No. 129: *Arirang* ("Arirang"), the folksong in its myriad forms over time, September 22, 2015.

On April 17, 1975, the Cultural Properties Research Institute (Munhwajae yŏn'guso) was created under the umbrella of the CPMO for the purpose of conducting research on cultural properties. The institute concerned itself primarily with developing scientific approaches to preservation while also maintaining a library of all kinds of printed and audio-visual materials related to thc preservation of intangible cultural properties. In part because of the need to expand, the CPMO moved to Taejŏn City in 1998 and was renamed Cultural Heritage Administration (Munhwajaech'ŏng; CHA).[120] By the end of 2012, it had designated 315 national treasures and 116 IICPs. To maintain its duties, its budget was increased considerably, from 131.6 million wŏn in 1961 to 615 billion wŏn in 2012.[121]

The law established a Cultural Properties Committee (Munhwajae wiwŏnhoe; CPC) comprised of scholars from various fields of study, which would be put in charge of all measures necessary to protect Korea's national heritage.[122] In the first few years, the CPC was made up of a fair number of former classmates from Japanese academic institutions. The head of the subcommittee dealing with tangible cultural heritage was Kim Sanggi (1901–1977), a historian and former graduate of Waseda University. During the first three official meetings held between January and March 1965, he was joined by fellow Waseda alumnus Yi Sangbaek (1904–1966), a sociologist and historian, as well as historians Hwang Suyŏng (1918–) and Yi Hongjik (1909–1970), both Tokyo University alumni, archaeologist and art historian Kim Wŏllyong (1922–1993), a graduate of Keijō Imperial University, and Kim Tujong (1896–1988), a graduate of Kyoto University.[123] The head of the second subcommittee dealing with the intangible cultural heritage was Im Suk-jay (Im Sŏkchae, 1903–1998), an anthropologist and graduate of Keijō Imperial University. During the first two official meetings of his subcommittee he was joined by Sŏk Chusŏn (1911–1996), a historian and folklorist and former graduate of the Tokyo Dressmaking Graduate School, journalist Ye Yonghae, and three graduates of the Court Music Office of the Yi Royal Household (*Yiwangjik aakpu*), the government institute for court music and dance during the colonial period: musicians and musicologists Sŏng Kyŏngnin (1911–2008) and Pak Hŏnbong (1906–1977), and dancer and musician Kim Ch'ŏnhŭng (1909–2007).[124] Not all specialists were scholars, therefore, but the fact that apart from Ye all early committee members had been trained at Japanese-run institutes, including Keijō Imperial University where people such as Fujita Ryūsaku, the former director of the Museum of the Government-General of Korea, was a professor,[125] will have affected not only their candidacy and that of others, but also their modus operandi.[126] Howard finds that in the early years of the CPC academic expertise and the experience of training at a recognized historical institute such as the Court Music Office of the Yi Royal Household added significant weight to a member's expertise.[127] Indeed, as in all other walks of Korean life,[128] in the traditional music scene a degree from a reputable college will elevate people's status significantly.

Before a cultural property could be designated, one or two CPC members (*munhwajae wiwŏn*) would be commissioned to write a research report. Upon a positive review of the report by the committee, the CPC would submit it to the appropriate government minister—in 1962, the minister of education—who in turn could designate the cultural property. Separate committees were established for six specialized areas: (1) temples and traditional houses; (2) old texts and books, paintings, and sculptures; (3) historical sites, such as ancient tombs or shell mounds; (4) intangible items such as plays and music; (5) sceneries, animals and plants; and (6) museums. The committees have not convened according to a regular schedule, but they have met between four and ten times each year. In addition to its permanent members, the CPC may call on freelance "expert members" (*chŏnmun wiwŏn*) when a particular expertise, such as in folksongs or masked dance drama, is required.[129]

As laid out in Article 55 of the 1962 law, cultural properties not designated as national cultural properties can be listed by city or province as Municipal or Provincial Cultural Properties (*Shi-do chijŏng munhwajae*) if they are found to be deserving of preservation.[130] For this purpose, however, each major municipality and province establishes its own CPC. The state can only advise on regional cultural properties; although it may obstruct the initial research, it has no power to influence designations. Location and differences in budgets help explain the unequal number of municipal and provincial cultural properties. Because the capital has long been the center for entertainment, many traditional performing arts were developed there and are inextricably linked to the area. And since it is home to a third of the Korean population, the capital is able to financially support many local preservation activities. It should come as no surprise, therefore, that Seoul and the adjacent city of Incheon together have 365 tangible properties, 120 more than the combined total listed for the four other major cities of Pusan, Taegu, Kwangju, and Taejŏn. The differences in funding available to cities and provinces are also reflected in the financial support they are able to provide to their holders. Whereas Seoul currently pays its holders a monthly stipend of 1.3 million wŏn (roughly equivalent to US$1,120), most other regional administrations can pay no more than 800,000 wŏn.[131]

One category of municipal or provincial cultural properties that has gained prominence in recent years consists of folk arts transmitted from what are now North Korean regions. Korea's former military administrations would have resented promoting traditions that are associated as much with the north as with the south. Indeed, when they selected *Sŏdo sori* in 1969, masked dance drama from Pongsan and Ŭnyul (IICP nos. 17 and 61) in 1967 and 1978 respectively, and a shaman ritual from Hwanghae province's Pyŏngsan county (IICP no. 90) in 1988, they did so without highlighting their northern pedigree. As they sought to preserve traditions that were very much alive in South Korea and could intimate their demise in the north, in 2008 the government created a separate category of traditions that specifically considered their North Korean origin. Named Special Management Law Related to the 5 Provinces North of Korea (*Taehan min'guk ibuk 5 do-e kwanhan t'ŭkpyŏl choch'ipŏp*), this category of regional folk arts is rather unusual because it incorporates traditions preserved by people who have moved south from the north (Yi Inmuk 2009). One of the first traditions designated within this category was "Tondollari" (on November 2, 1998), a folksong and dance from south Hamgyŏng province. Another genre preserved under this category is *Sŏdo sŏnsori sant'aryŏng* (Standing Mountain Songs from the Western Provinces) from Hwanghae province; it was designated on August 26, 2009. It is somewhat similar to the *Sŏnsori sant'aryŏng* discussed in chapter 3 but has a smaller repertoire, and a less uniform appearance since each group member can wear his or her own color *hanbok*.

Inclusion on UNESCO's Representative List of the Intangible Cultural Heritage of Humanity has become an important proving ground for Korea's national heritage. International recognition of Korean culture has long been used to nurture national pride, but because the list is associated with an objective, international standard, the inclusion of items can have considerable impact on their national status. In 2009, many Koreans were offended when China officially recognized "Arirang" as part of its national intangible cultural heritage. The Chinese version of the song forms part of a Korean farmer's dance by residents from Yanbian, the Korean autonomous prefecture in China's northeast that borders on North Korea and is home to many Korean migrants.[132] In response, the CHA made additional efforts to see the Korean version of the song listed on UNESCO's list, and in 2012 and 2014 succeeded in having respectively "Arirang" and *nongak* (farmers' music) included. In 2014, the former was then listed a second time, though this time as a series of songs by that name from different provinces in North Korea. Since Japan's traditional papermaking craft known as Washi was added to the list in 2014, the CHA will likely make additional efforts to see the Korean tradition of *hanji*-making included in the near future.

Reports on Intangible Cultural Properties

Since the first study on *Kkoktugakshi norŭm* (Kkoktugakshi [puppet] play), more than 250 reports on important intangible cultural properties have been written. In some cases, several reports form the basis of a single designation. These so-called Research Reports on Intangible Cultural Properties (*Muhyŏng munhwajae chosa pogosŏ*) are published in small numbers and made available to selected universities and public libraries in Korea. Even though they form the basis of the discussions about designating IICPs, the studies are not so much new inquiries as summaries of the status quo regarding the general understanding of the cultural items concerned. Rather than questioning a consensus opinion about a cultural item, they seem to merely justify it. This is partly due to the fact that the process is rarely initiated by the Cultural Properties Management Office. It is initiated by a city or province. Bang So-Yeon of the Intangible Cultural Properties Division outlined for me the official procedure for designating IICPs:

> Proposal by an individual or group
> Cultural Properties Committee member or municipal/provincial CPC member
> Discussion by the CPC
> If positive: commission of *munhwajae wiwŏn* or *chŏnmun wiwŏn* (expert member)
> Fieldwork and research
> Report
> Discussion and subsequent recommendation by the CPC
> If positive: second deliberation by the CPC after no less than thirty days
> If positive: consideration by the minister of culture, sports, and tourism
> Appointment[133]

Until recently, the CHA could not designate an IICP without a holder. Because distinct talent was deemed important, if the skill required to perform a tradition was not considered unique it would not be designated as an IICP. Bang So-Yeon explained that this is why *sshirŭm*, Korean wrestling, had not been designated. However, because the CHA recognized the importance of such traditions, in 2012 the government began to work toward an amendment of the Cultural

Properties Protection Law in order to include traditions that have no holders. This allowed "Arirang," Korea's most common folksong, to also be appointed.[134]

Somewhat in contrast to UNESCO's Masterpiece Program, which recognizes the importance of securing approval from the community that holds a specific tradition,[135] the IICP reports do not reveal the opinion of the holders or their peer groups. The reports say where the holders of a candidate cultural property have been educated, whether they have a recording history, and what important awards they have won. Until recently, the most important award for folk performing arts was the *Chŏn'guk minsok yesul kyŏngyŏn taehoe* (National Folk Arts Contest). This contest was important for performers who wished to draw attention to themselves with a view to persuading the CPC to pursue research into their art, as well as for those whom CPC members were considering. "Kanggangsullae," a circle dance with songs, for example, had already been given the Minister of Culture and Sports Award in 1961 and had been performed five times at the contest before it was appointed as IICP no. 8 in 1966. *Kosŏng nongyo* won that same award in 1978, and singer Yi Sangsu garnered an individual award in 1979 when *Yech'ŏn t'ongmyŏng nongyo* won the Presidential Award at the contest.[136] These genres were collectively appointed as IICP no. 84 in 1985. Of note, the element of competition had a significant effect on folk traditions; due to the time limit of the contest and the distance between performers and audience participants, the performers began to focus on the most exciting part of their tradition, embellishing it with stage props and fancy costumes.[137] The late publisher and aesthete Han Ch'anggi told me that Ye Yonghae, who he considered a very close friend, had started the contests: "I blame him for the consequences. If the country supports folk art contests it should be done locally, but through competition they learn from each other; it creates uniformity, such as in clothing. They learn bad things there."[138]

The selection of traditions, the official deliberation, and concomitant hierarchy within them is affected by the relationships among CPC members and between members and practitioners. The musicianly and scholarly credentials of those involved bear heavily on those relationships. Building up one's profile by way of domestic and international performances and recordings, and establishing a good relationship with CPC members (or their allies), are common ways in which practitioners pursue the official appointment of their tradition. The process can be time-consuming and costly, especially if many practical arrangements have to be made so as to encourage and allow committee members to see a tradition in full.[139] Clark Sorensen, professor of Korean anthropology at the University of Washington, has related that when he visited a Pyŏlsin Kut on the east coast of Korea with an eminent Korean folklorist in November 1976, the troop of shamans insisted on paying the food and lodging costs of the folklorists and their guests.[140]

The CPC discussions, some of which have been recorded in *Munhwajae,* the annual journal of the CHA, at times indicate considerable differences in opinion concerning a designation or its cancellation. During one discussion, for example, the senior musicologist Chang Sahun successfully attacked a report on *Yangsan hakch'um* (Crane Dance from Yangsan Region) by his colleague Kim Ch'ŏnhŭng, saying, "Because Kim Ch'ŏnhŭng is not really a researcher and has only lent his name [to the report], I don't see why we should discuss [this] any further. We should bring an end to this research practice of simply lending one's name [to the report]."[141] The dance was never designated. Kim Ch'ŏnhŭng and Chang Sahun both studied at the Court Music Office of the Yi Royal Household. While Chang went on to become one of Korea's most respected musicologists, Kim became a senior member of the National Gugak Center (*Kungnip kugagwŏn;* until 2012 known as the National Center for Korean Traditional Performing Arts) and continued to perform. He was eventually appointed holder of two IICPs. Chang seemed not to regard Kim as a proper scholar and his own senior status allowed him to express this openly. Personal criticism like this has rarely been recorded; it is often leveled at the reports themselves. In 1978, when Kim Kisu was concerned about the quality of holder Han Kaptŭk of *Kŏmun'go sanjo* (Solo Pieces for the Korean Six-stringed Zither), he strongly criticized Hwang Pyŏnggi's report: "The research report has absolutely no substance to recommend it. I don't see any reason for keeping Han Kaptŭk's appointment."[142] This particular issue was not resolved, and Han Kaptŭk retained his appointment until his death in 1987.[143]

The IICP reports do not follow set criteria. All scholars perform research on their own terms, using their own methodologies. The research (including fieldwork) is usually conducted by two experts over a period of one or two weeks.[144] Because of this relatively short time frame, reports are often limited to information that is readily available, as there is no time to scrutinize the object of study from more than one perspective. In the case of folksongs, the emphasis has long been mostly on the folkloric importance of a particular genre. Other aspects, such as the music, dance, or costume, are rarely considered. The predominance of folkloric scholarship is not only evident in the government reports on folksongs but prevails throughout the history of folksong studies in Korea. Roger Janelli notes that studies of Korean history and culture were introduced under Japanese colonial rule, when the data were used to reconstruct history and justify the assimilation of Koreans. The study of folklore by Koreans, he says, was aimed at correcting the politically motivated interpretations of Japanese folklorists. The possibility of using their work to nurture cultural nationalism and to rid his administration of the stigma of collaboration may have led President Park Chung Hee to endorse the study of Korean folklore.[145] Efforts to construct the national identity would intensify in the 1970s, when Park's ongoing authoritarianism juxtaposed his patriotism.[146] The strong emphasis on justifying folk genres' importance may explain why data in regard to the sound and presentation of traditions were omitted in the past.

Very few of the reports on folksongs from the 1960s and 1970s contain musical transcriptions or analysis. This is surprising considering that the majority of the reports were written by Chang Sahun (1916–1992), a professor of music at Seoul National University. Sŏng Kyŏngnin (1911–2008), a former holder of IICP no. 1, *Chongmyo cheryeak* (Rite to Royal Ancestors), and head of the National Gugak Center from 1961 to 1972, also wrote reports (Sŏng Kyŏngnin 1966), and these equally focused primarily on lyrics. Musicologist and former CPC member Yi Pohyŏng told me that in 1971, when he joined the CPC, he was the only musicologist.[147] Folklorist Im Tonggwŏn (1926–2012), another former CPC member, contended that the lack of musical transcriptions came from the need to justify the preservation of folk music as opposed to court music.[148] The first musicologist to consistently include musical transcriptions in her reports was Yi Sora, who joined the CPC as an expert member in 1984. Yi has provided by far the largest number of musical transcriptions of folksongs using the Western notation system, but other members of the CPC have disputed her approach. Some of them blamed her alleged lack of expertise on the fact that she never studied folk music until she began working for the Cultural Properties Management Office.[149]

Koreans commonly find the standard Western notation system ill-suited for the many sliding notes, lack of a set tempo, and frequent use of overtones in Korean folk music. Yi Pohyŏng comments:

> The main problem lies in explaining Korean music using Western musical theory. It's not a method used by ethnomusicologists. Musicologists all know that the old [Western] method they used to explain Korean music. . . . was not good, and therefore new research based on several methods is now being conducted. So, likewise, I have also used the old method . . . I also studied Western composition techniques. I applied what I knew in the beginning, but when I carried my research out clumsily with this Western method it didn't come out well. . . . I wonder how I should explain Korean music, using which method.[150]

CPC members could have opted to record music for future analysis, but Kim Sam Dae Ja, who used to work for the library of the Cultural Properties Research Institute, told me that at least until the mid-1990s the library only held recordings of appointed holders, many of whom had sent in the recordings themselves.[151] Since then, however, the institute has actively collected recordings of a wide range of folk materials, including recordings made by scholars and performances by amateurs.

Hong Chonguk, a researcher working on tangible cultural properties at the institute, believed the system as a whole was too bureaucratic and should allow faster action. He recalled many cases in which the CPC's decision to execute protective measures came too late to prevent irreparable damage.[152] Because the number of informants who hold information regarding traditions inherited from the past is decreasing, most fieldwork should have ideally already been performed and many students promoted. Instead, the reports on IICPs often merely document prevailing repertoires, as sung by a very small number of professional singers, rather than studying a range of both professional and amateur versions. This is certainly the case with the reports written on the popular folksong genres from Kyŏnggi, P'yŏngan and Hwanghae provinces (discussed in chapters 3 and 4). Few reports combine different research perspectives, and they clearly lack standard criteria for recording and documenting.

In partial response to some of the issues outlined below, in March 2016 the government implemented the Act on the Preservation and Promotion of Intangible Cultural Heritage (*Muhyŏng munhwajae pojŏn mit chinhŭng-e kwanhan pŏmnyul*). While seeking to secure the global relevance of Korea's heritage program by adopting the broader categories of intangible cultural heritage applied by UNESCO, it centralizes the assessment and ranking of senior practitioners, recognizes specialist tertiary education as a form of transmission, and expands the number of specialists on the CPC to thirty. It also renamed all IICPs "National" Intangible Cultural Properties (*Kukka muhŏng munhwajae;* hereafter NICPs).[153]

Recognition of Intangible Cultural Properties

Throughout its forty-eight revisions, the Cultural Properties Protection Law has exhibited growing concern over environmental pollution and the illegal art trade. One significant amendment in 1970 (no. 2233) recognized holders of artistic crafts and established measures for the recording of "movable" (*tongsan*) cultural properties; another, in 1973 (no. 2468), established a licensing system for cultural property traders. Arguably the most comprehensive revision involved amendment no. 3644, in 1982. This amendment deleted the words *uri nara* (our country), used in defining all cultural properties, so that Chinese relics recovered off the coast of Shinan to the southwest could be included. Local tangible cultural properties that had not been officially designated but were deemed important for the preservation of local culture had before this amendment been designated "cultural properties outside designated cultural properties" (*chijŏng munhwajae-ioe-ŭi munhwajae*); but because this term was often interpreted as implying undesignated cultural properties, the revision changed the term to "cultural properties material" (*munhwajae charyo*).[154] In addition, amendment no. 3644 provided legal measures to enforce holders' education of students. Because lessons could be costly and prospects for a steady income dim, scholarships were offered to secure an appropriate number of students. The law recognized the need to appoint groups of holders in order to preserve folk genres that required multiple performers at the same time. Hence, from 1986 onward, for cultural properties such as IICP no. 75, *Kiji-shi chul tarigi* (Tug-of-War of Kiji City), and IICP no. 8, the folksong and dance "Kanggangsullae," groups of holders have been financially supported.

At the start of 2016, 129 IICPs were being transmitted by 174 holders, including 39 holders for 26 IICPs that fall under the category of music. The CPPL does not include a provision to prevent the double appointment of a holder. Kim Ch'ŏnhŭng (1909–2007), for example, was holder of both IICP no. 1, *Chongmyo cheryeak,* for which he was appointed in 1968, and IICP no. 39, *Ch'ŏyongmu* (Dance of Ch'ŏyong), a court mask dance honoring the spirit of Ch'ŏyong,[155] for which he was appointed in 1971.[156] Because holders are expected to represent and transmit their art, double appointments are a dilemma; these holders have to divide their time and efforts between different groups of students and possibly juggle conflicting festival seasons. The CPC can revoke designations and appointments. In the case of tangible cultural properties, where most revocations take place, the reasons are described in *Munhwajae.* For example, designation of a ginkgo tree was revoked because it had died, and in another case a specially designated area was canceled because, due to its large size, it was violating private property. In the case of holders and their students, however, the reasons for revocation tend to be obscure, being obvious only if the person concerned has died, married, or moved abroad.[157] For example, in the case of IICP no. 52, *shinawi,* a type of improvisational ensemble music, the holders moved abroad and their appointments were subsequently canceled. When a holder dies, his or her students may be grouped together under another, similar genre. This practice can control for anomalies and occurred in the case of two versions of *p'ansori,* IICPs nos. 36 and 59; which were integrated into one IICP no. 5, *p'ansori,* in 1973 and 1991, respectively.[158] The appointments of senior students are sometimes revoked in cases of ill health or because a holder asks for it, the latter of which happened with IICP no. 11, *p'ungmul* (farmers' music).[159] The CPC conducts regular reviews of all IICPs, but not annually. Based on a revision of the CPPL in July 1996, the CPC may now change the status of a holder into that of "honorary holder" (*myŏngye poyuja*) when an investigation concludes that he or she has become unable to consistently teach his art, due to, for example, old age or poor health. In those instances, a senior student will in principle be promoted to replace the mentor lest the NICP is dropped. In practice, however, holders always retain their status among their students and peers, regardless of their physical condition, making it highly unlikely that a senior student will seek to replace his or her mentor against the latter's wishes.

According to Articles 18 and 19 of the Cultural Properties Protection Law Enforcement Ordinance (*Munhwajae pohopŏp shihaengnyŏng*), students can be recognized and financially supported in several ways. At the bottom of the list are special scholarship students (*chŏnsu [changhak]saeng*).[160] Once these students graduate, they become graduates (*isusaeng;* more commonly referred to as *isuja* [*cha*/-*ja* = person]). From among these students, a holder can select an assistant teacher of graduates (*chŏnsu kyoyuk chogyo;* usually abbreviated *chogyo*) or a musician (*aksa*) to assist with the teaching or performance.[161] The best student could also be selected as a future holder (*poyuja hubo*),[162] but this category no longer exists. Future holders were supposed to replace holders upon their death, but such appointments were not guaranteed, as the status was often awarded merely to avoid antagonism. For instance, report no. 236, published in 1996, discusses the succession of holder Han Yŏngsuk (1920–1989) for IICP no. 24, *Sŭngmu* (Monk's Dance). Although future holder Yi Aeju was eventually appointed, presumably based on the recommendation of senior CPC member Shin Ch'an'gyun, expert member Kim Munsuk advised against her succession because, or so the report says, he thought that her art differed too much from the original form; yet the possibility must be considered that her political activism was a factor.[163] In 2000, the government canceled the future holder and musician categories, bringing them together under the banner "assistant teacher of graduates" (hereafter assistant teacher). This coincided with the formalization of the evaluation process for a senior student's suitability as holder, which examines his or her activities, reputation, and physical condition.[164]

Hierarchy, Age, and Finance Matters

Folk musicians appointed for group performances are ranked according to how vital their skills are to the preservation of the tradition. Im Tonggwŏn told me that in the case of farming songs, singers are considered to be of a higher rank than those who play instruments;[165] for NICP no. 3, *Namsadang nori* (Male Temple Group Play), on the other hand, musicians playing the *kkwaenggwari* (small gong) are ranked higher than those who perform acrobatics. It is not, however, usually the government that determines the hierarchy but the groups themselves; the government office merely copies how the group members rank themselves.[166] Even so, in a 1992 interview with Keith Howard, Im Tonggwŏn explained that the government rankings can lead to antagonism within groups: "The government only gives money to the top few [group members]. . . . The person who just misses nomination is very unsatisfied and tends not to want to work together with those who are nominated. . . . This is a big problem, so in the future, we must give money to the whole group so that the group can work together. This also entails a contradiction, though; somebody who has really excellent skill might abandon his responsibility."[167] Im stressed that the rankings alone do not preclude those who do acrobatics in *Namsadang nori,* and who have less valued specializations in other genres, from being appointed.[168] But without financial support, students may choose to focus on other things and abandon a career in the art form. The hierarchy has a negative influence on students' willingness to learn a certain aspect of a given tradition. Practicing acrobatics, for example, is likely to be less popular among special scholarship students than learning how to play the lead instrument. This, in turn, is bound to result in a lack of senior performers of the less prestigious parts of a tradition, a situation that may be exacerbated by the increasing number of women performing folk music traditions.[169]

Age is a major determinant within the ranks of traditions. In the past there was a consensus among CPC members that holders should be at least sixty years old, but in recent years many younger holders have been appointed.[170] In the 1990s, the CPC began to appoint younger holders when it recognized that in the case of traditions that require athletic strength, such as *chul t'agi* (tightrope walking) or the martial art *t'aekkyŏn,* appointing old people would be impossible, if not sadistic. While on a few occasions, such as in the case of Yun Chongp'yŏng for *Sŏnsori sant'aryŏng,* prospective holders die before they can be appointed, very old holders have nevertheless been appointed for some traditions. Ha Pogyŏng, holder of IICP no. 68, *Miryang paekchung nori* (Ghost Festival of Miryang), for example, was appointed in 1987 at the age of eighty; and in 1993, Kwŏn Yongha was appointed for IICP no. 13, *Kangnŭng tanoje* (Tano Festival of Kangnŭng) at the age of 75.[171] Old age often affects performers' energy and voice, as well as, presumably, their ability to teach. In October 1995, at the *Nongak myŏngin chŏn* (Show of Celebrated Farmers' Music Performers) at the *Seoul nori madang* (Seoul Playground) near Lotte World, two senior performers apologized to the audience for being too weak to finish their performance.

The monthly stipend has steadily grown over the years, but holders have complained that it is insufficient, which suggests that the increments remain unsatisfactory.[172] Many holders and senior students are nevertheless able to ask for additional funding from the government for specific activities, including overseas performances, and they can use their official status to charge considerable fees for private lessons. In 1995, for example, Kim Suyŏn, a senior student of the holder of *Kyŏnggi minyo,* Muk Kyewŏl, charged 50,000 wŏn per hour. Rates have since quadrupled. Kang Ŭn'gyŏng, a graduate student of Ahn Sook-sun (An Suksŏn), holder of NICP no. 23, *Kayagŭm sanjo mit pyŏngch'ang* (Solo Pieces with Song for the Korean Twelve-stringed Zither), pays between 500,000 and 800,000 won per month for private lessons, in addition to the fee for group lessons.[173] Considering private lessons usually occur once a week, this amounts to an hourly rate of approximately 200,000 won (USD167). Because income from group performances is often shared, however, students may use it to offset the cost of their tuition. Private sponsors are a potential third source of income. On various occasions over the years I have accompanied a senior musician at a dinner or late-night drink hosted by one or more businessmen. It appears that female musicians, in particular, are able to add to their income by liaising with sponsors privately, somewhat reminiscent of the *kisaeng* tradition discussed in chapter 3. The status and opportunity that come with an official appointment may thus lead to forms of corruption in the selection process. Some holders, for example, complain that the government is biased in its selection of cultural properties and holders, while others complain that their disapproval of the appointment of future holders was ignored.[174] In chapters 3 and 4, I relate the cases of respectively Kim Okshim and Pak Chunyŏng, whose failure to be appointed holder cannot be easily justified on the basis of a lack of skill, pedigree, or experience.

Clearly, Korea's national heritage preservation system is founded on the Japanese system. Although it has gone through many revisions ever since it was first established, key components and notions, such as the categorization of properties and the leverage from training at a Japanese institute, affected the range of properties and their deliberation until recently. In terms of scale and complexity, however, the current system can certainly hold its own. And yet the number of measures it provides to ensure the authenticity of intangible cultural properties is limited. Whereas it acknowledges authentic forms and seeks to maintain them as much as possible, they are not intended to preserve performance genres in amber without change, since it is recognized that certain adaptations need to occur. The CPC continues to judge the performance of traditions based on their alleged original form, but it does not seek to freeze them. It accepts that traditions will evolve as a result of sociopolitical and economic developments and in order to secure the successful transmission of genres in this way, it makes compromises. It reviews the activities of holders to ensure they do what is within their power to preserve their art, but the holders maintain a degree of freedom. The system does not, therefore, stipulate that traditions must be preserved exactly as they were at the time of designation, but it merely proscribes a few straightforward measures that can be taken when the CPC believes that traditions deviate too much from their original form.

Because of the system I have described, each National Intangible Cultural Property has come to represent an authentic form with one or more representatives. To practitioners and audiences, holders have come to represent important distinct lineages (and hierarchies) that appear to hold as much sway as the authentic forms they are meant to preserve. Students study the versions and styles that are passed on to them by their mentors as faithfully as possible. To deviate in favor of an earlier version recorded in the past could be perceived as a denial of their mentor's authority, and thus jeopardize their advancement in the ranks. As the age and gender and social class of performers and audiences change, so do costumes, lyrics, voices, and performing styles. These issues will be dealt with in more detail in chapters 3 and 4.

CHAPTER 2

Defining Korean Folksongs

CHARACTERISTICS AND TERMINOLOGY

A category of folksongs often comprises a very broad range of musical expressions. Because of the myriad possible interpretations of a single song, it is easier to deliberate the signifiers of such a category than to define the songs in it, though doing so still requires delineations of application, content, time, and music.[1] Even if one were to consider all transcribed collections available, it is, as Dave Harker notes, very hard to determine what the songs that antiquarians, scholars, and folklorists have passed down to us tell us about the feelings or thoughts of a majority population.[2] In 1954, the International Folk Music Council defined folk music (a category incorporating both dance and song) as "the product of a musical tradition that has been evolved through the process of oral transmission." Such a tradition, it considered, was shaped by three main factors: "(i) continuity which links the present with the past; (ii) variation which springs from the creative impulse of the individual or the group; and (iii) selection by the community, which determines the form or forms in which the music survives. . . . The term does not cover composed popular music that has been taken over ready-made by a community and remains unchanged, for it is the re-fashioning and re-creation of the music by the community that gives it its folk character."[3] As Keith Howard rightly points out, the definition is Eurocentric and anachronistic.[4] It considers communities as having a distinct culture that somehow naturally retains its connection with the past, and it prioritizes authenticity and the re-creation of music by the group, even though this rules out composition, which may be the only part of the definition capable of creating meaningful links to the present.

The term "folksong" connotes tradition, country life, and particular instruments that are not used in other forms of music. A folksong is passed on by people who, individually or in a group, often sing it to support a specific activity on a particular social and sometimes seasonal occasion. Beyond that, it may be easier to say what a folksong is not, or probably is not. A folksong is not a pop song; it is rarely composed by a known composer and its rhythm is unlikely to suit popular dance. Much like modern American rap, folksongs freely use music and text from other songs, and so their specific origins are often lost. Similarly, as appropriation and substitution occur, so a folksong's relationship to activities or social occasions is blurred or lost. In Korea, where many folksongs have been given new meaning by the Cultural Properties Protection Law, that relationship is often emphasized in vain, as many traditional activities and occasions have been forgotten. Even though pop music has become dominant and left a wide gap between itself and folk music, this has not obscured the genre of folksongs. To define them may be difficult, but they remain an easily distinguishable genre that manages to occupy a comfortable niche in society.

What has come to be regarded as a folksong (*minyo*) in Korea is that which was once sung by lay people during work or on special occasions. Many songs have since acquired different functions, but they occasionally still hold clues to their original context. While the lyrics of many songs relate to work such as weaving and farming, others relate to religious or sociopolitical affairs. Although not necessarily separate from the latter categories, some songs serve primarily as an emotional outlet and would be sung, for example, at times of mourning. Folksong lyrics can, however, be vague and indirect, so there are times when music and rhythm are better indicators of a song's original or current function. The rhythm of songs to accompany the pounding of rice, for example, varies according to whether the work was done by hand or foot, the former faster and the latter slower. Working songs are usually in perfect sync with the movement and the breathing required of a specific task.[5] An interesting case in this regard is the opening scene of the 1994 movie *Story of Two Women* (*Tu yŏja iyagi*). Inspired by the national appeal of farmers singing "Arirang" during hard work, in the scene *Minjung* director Lee Jung-Gook lets farmers sing the Chindo version (from Chindo County in South Chŏlla province)—in the movie presented as a working song—during harvesting, as though it is a source of energy and inspiration.[6] The rhythm of the song, a turgid 12/9-beat, clearly prevents them from getting on with their work, as the farmers are shown pausing repeatedly in order to finish performing (as opposed to merely singing) a line.

The type of folksongs that first emerged remains unclear. Because folksongs are usually transmitted orally, one can only guess at their origin, but some folklorists, including Ko Chŏngok and Kim Muhŏn, believe the first folksongs were composed for or during work. They believe that other songs, such as those sung to lament the loss of a relative or to complain about aspects of life, were composed by adjusting and altering those earlier songs.[7] Im Tonggwŏn disagrees on the grounds that there simply is not sufficient evidence for this. He finds the earliest written remnants of folksongs among *hyangga* (songs of home), a broad range of songs of written poetry from the time of the three kingdoms period (57 BCE–668). The latter include songs about work, the relationship between men and women, and religion. Although they constituted polished expressions of the experiences of the elite, composed in Chinese, Im believes they were influenced by folksongs, like many other forms of Korean literature.[8] Since folksongs can be interpreted in various ways, the same song may have been sung for different purposes, such as for commercial profit or personal entertainment. To rely entirely on semantics when establishing a folksong's reason for existence is unwise, because lyrics can be misleading. Songs with a controversial meaning are, after all, more likely to hide or twist their actual intent. Although the function of a folksong may change ahead of the lyrics over time, in general one must assume that meaning and function are largely identical at the time of its creation. Scholars therefore usually analyze lyrics, music, and rhythm when searching for the original function of a song.[9]

Before recordings of folksongs began to appear in the early 1900s, Korean folksongs served as accompaniment for all kinds of manual labor, rituals, and other aspects of the daily life of the lower classes, or sung by working-class entertainers on special occasions. Raymond Williams argues that in the West, after 1870, folksongs came to be associated with the preindustrial, pre-urban, and preliterate as opposed to the popular, working class, or commercial.[10] The Western definition of folksongs, he notes, changed continuously; by the mid-twentieth century, distinctions were further blurred when orally transmitted country and industrial songs were recorded and adapted to new composition and performance. In Korea a similar process of commercialization began in the early 1900s, when recordings of folksongs helped thrust the latter into the limelight. The notion of rurality to which Williams alludes, on the other hand, does not hold in Korea, where from the late nineteenth century itinerant folksong singers came to perform increasingly in urban areas. When in the early 1900s the first commercial gramophones of Korean folksongs appeared, however, they were still associated with tradition, in part because they were recorded without much musical accompaniment, and in part because the *sorikkun*, the professionals who sang them, continued to perform mostly "live." The distinction between folk and popular songs was nevertheless obscured by both categories, including songs that became widely cherished as uniquely representative of the Korean colonial experience, such as the popular songs "The Tear-soaked Tumen River" and "Tears of Mokp'o."[11]

The new media had a significant effect on the sound, length, and variety of folksongs. Whereas phonograph technology improved fast, it allowed only a limited duration and tonal range, which led to a preference for certain repertoires and sequences, as well as specific voices. Since the majority of recordings were carried out in Japan, Japanese musical standards influenced the quality of the final sound on records. The influence of the phonograph industry extended to the lyrics as well. All record companies operating in Korea were Japanese-owned, and the Koreans working for their lyrical departments had all been trained in Japan.[12] Not only through phonograph records, but also through the radio and school music curricula, Koreans became very familiar with the sound of Japanese music. But whereas Japanese music was part of the Japanese cultural policy, it could not replace Korean music. Indeed, while an elaborate system of censorship ensured that all entertainment was in line with Japanese colonial policy, those interests often conceded to commercial demands. Korean customers remained king. The first folksong recordings censored on the basis of "disturbing public order," for example, were versions of the theme song of Na Un'gyu's popular film "Arirang" (1926) by the same name, sung by Ch'ae Tongwŏn, Kim Taegŏn, and Yi Aerisu. It is believed that because the movie had strong patriotic undertones, when film narrators made the audience sing along to a modernized, "new" version of the song during the end credits it acquired a nationalist flavor, which the music and lyrics did not otherwise support. Subsequent recordings were therefore censored, until the Japanese authorities realized the song's popularity was unlikely to wane and was, in fact, growing even among Japanese. Using the song's momentum, they commissioned the production of several pro-Japanese versions of the song instead.[13] Although radio broadcasts were intended as a mechanism of information control—and to this end, toward the late 1930s they came to include Japanized Korean popular songs as well as patriotic songs in Korean—it was important to recognize the interests of Korean radio service subscribers for them to have the desired impact.[14] In 1933, those interests forced the government-general to create a separate Korean channel with a distinct Korean flavor. Much of the programming focused on the study of the vernacular language, as well as on Korean traditional music and radio dramas.[15] While the channel was established to facilitate the assimilation of Koreans into the colonial empire, it would ultimately not only reinforce the notion of Koreanness, but also place it within modernity. The music industry thus merged both political and commercial objectives.

In the early 1930s, the radio began to increasingly use gramophones as opposed to live performers for their music broadcasts, and this, along with the decreasing cost of the medium for private use, led to a significant growth in record sales.[16] Korean intellectuals were concerned about the influence of popular music on traditional Korean music. And Japanese folklorists, fascinated with the notion of an untainted, authentic Korea that provided a marked contrast with that of Japan, agreed with them. In February 1932, Takahashi Jun, a frequent contributor to the government-run monthly *Chōsen* (Korea), expressed his concern with the standardizing effect of urbanization on the regional diversity of Korean folksongs, urging for immediate efforts to collect them to prevent further loss.[17] In 1935, in a series of columns on musical entertainment in farming villages for the Tonga daily, folklorist Song Sŏkha singled out the negative effects of gramophone culture on folksongs: "They shamelessly and without hesitation call these nauseating pop songs [*kayo*] with their backward lyrics and excruciating melodies 'folksongs,' even using the poor expression 'new folksongs,' and by simply using people's instinct to like novelties, they make them numbingly sentimental and cold without any opportunity for artistry."[18] But the process of standardization was irreversible. By the end of the colonial period, traditional folksongs were drowned out by the sound of foreign and Korean popular music.[19]

After liberation, pop music continued to harbor the aspirations of Koreans keen to express themselves freely, and emulate the idyllic, romantic lifestyles they had grown familiar with through cinema. During the Korean War (1950–1953), Koreans began tuning in to the American Forces Network Korea (AFKN), a radio channel that constantly played the latest Western pop hits. And when they were forced to seek refuge in Pusan, they were able to pick up the signals of Japanese radio channels. For a while, folksongs were rarely performed in public. A small number of musicians composed or performed folksongs on behalf of the Department of Defense, sometimes as part of small military entertainment troupes,[20] but most of them were forced to abandon their profession, and would struggle to pick it up again after the war. Modern dance was a powerful expression of individualism and a significant facilitator of social interaction. Many of the records sold in the 1950s and 1960s therefore showed on the back cover or inside sleeve what type of dance would suit the songs included. Folksongs lost their appeal with the younger generations, who keenly followed the latest developments in Western popular culture. Radio stations incorporated traditional music, including *Kyŏnggi minyo* and *Sŏdo sori* in their programming, but foreign music grew in popularity unabatedly.[21]

Underpinned by the establishment of the Cultural Properties Protection Law (1962) and the *Minjung* movement that began approximately a decade later, folk art was reevaluated and a clear picture of the lower and middle classes established.[22] Folk arts and crafts became the proud heritage of all social classes. While Koreans are often eager to point out which honorable or aristocratic lineage their family belongs to, most of them regard folksongs as a collective heritage, as though they originally belonged to the lower social classes that sang them. A significant divide nevertheless persisted between the city and the countryside at least until the 1990s: journalists and scholars who went out to the countryside often found that rural singers were embarrassed by their local culture, which they regarded as inferior to that of urban areas. This no doubt affected people's active participation in folk arts in urban areas as well.[23]

While some students of folksongs may study at a conservatory and dream of a professional career in music, the majority of students study folksongs as a pastime only. They are not obsessive about folk life and tradition and keenly follow the latest trends and fads, including K-pop. These days, people who learn to sing folksongs come from a wide range of backgrounds, both in terms of their parents' occupation and financial position. In my explorations of the Korean folksong scene, I have not, however, come across students from very wealthy families, which may be because they choose to dedicate their spare time to activities more suitable to a career in business. Because they have considerable free time, middle-aged housewives make up the majority of folksong students. Even among the elementary and middle school students learning folksongs, female students comprise the vast majority. This predominance of female singers is largely the result of Confucian norms: while men are expected to dedicate their time and energy to their occupation, and to ensure that they can support their family through it, women may dedicate themselves to pastimes without such pressure, as long as their children and household matters are well looked after.[24] The possibility that the dominant presence of women in folksongs is driven at least partially by a preference toward a more effeminate representation must be entertained, though both male and female performers continue to express their concern over the general lack of male practitioners. The gender imbalance significantly affects the presentation and the music of a number of genres, as I will demonstrate in chapter 3.

Korean Folksong Characteristics

A Korean folksong is typically sung along a pentatonic scale and a free three-beat cadence with a wide range of vocal ornaments and relatively clear diction. A single definition would, however, deny the wide range of styles and variations that have long existed. Every large region in Korea has its own cultural, linguistic, and geographical characteristics, all of which are represented in local folksongs. To tie regionally specific folksongs to a particular region would have been easier in the past, before recording and broadcast media began standardizing them. But such songs rarely refer to a particular locale these days. This is in part because due to rapid urbanization many have lost the connection to their hometown, and in part because of the increased use of standard Korean. It was nevertheless a distinction based on location that the Academy of Korean Studies used to categorize its comprehensive collection of oral literature in South Korea, the *Outline of Korean Oral Literature* (*Han'guk kubi munhak taegye*), published between 1979 and 1990. Although the collection, which consists of 82 volumes, is useful in that it collects oral literature from different regions in Korea, it provides very little background information and is based on poor methodology and rushed fieldwork, leaving the regional distinction of much of the collected data opaque.[25]

To refer to a particular regional melodic characteristic or mode, Koreans often use the Sino-Korean suffix *-cho*/*-jo* or the pure Korean term *t'ori*. Although it is widely used for Korean traditional music these days, Korean music practitioners and scholars agree that the system of staff notation is problematic. Despite being comprehensive, it is based on metrical partitions of time and relatively set pitches, and therefore does not correspond well with the sound and performance of Korean traditional music.[26] Han Manyŏng recognizes five main melodic characteristics in Korean folksongs that correspond with music staff notes as follows: (1) the mode of Kyŏnggi province, also known as *Kyŏngjo,* a pentatonic mode equivalent to the pitches C, D, F, G, and A (or B♭); (2) the melody of the P'yŏngan and Hwanghae provinces' representative song "Sushimga" (Song of Sorrow), based on a tritonic mode consisting of the relative pitches D, A, and C; (3) the tritonic—E, A, and B—melody of the song "Yukchabaegi" from the southwestern *namdo* (lit. "southern provinces") part of the peninsula, which covers north and south Chŏlla provinces and south Ch'ungch'ŏng province; (4) Kyŏngsang provinces' tritonic mode known as *menarijo,* based on the folksong "Menari," consisting of the relative notes E, A, and C; and (5) the song "Odolttogi," representing Cheju province's central mode, made up of tones equivalent to E, A, and C.[27] Given the wide range of songs and the many different singing styles, it is not surprising that Han's definitions somewhat differ from those of other scholars. Keh Chung Sik, for example, argues that the melody of *namdo*'s "Yukchabaegi" is quadratonic, made up of A, D, E, and F,[28] while Yi Pohyŏng and Chang Sahun regard B, E, and F as the dominant tones of that mode.[29]

The vocal timbre common among professional folksong singers is husky, occasionally raspy, as well as intense and seemingly unpolished, a quality that in the West might be described as "broken." Professional singers make wide use of chest, head, and falsetto registers, in addition to considerable dynamics. Whereas voices may have overtones and be praised for them, it is not a planned or manipulated quality. To ornament and express their phrases singers use a wide range of vocal techniques, such as appoggiaturas, exaggerated fricatives, and vibratos of different width and speed.[30] The essence of Korean traditional music is found in the raw, natural beauty of the sounds of the elements that help produce the tones, as well as in the emotion and spontaneity with which they are performed. Since the voice is considered no different from an instrument, the production of sound effects is more or less made visible. Joshua Pilzer argues that a small number of folksongs have been standardized so much that singers' vocal timbres have become the only remaining avenue for personal expression.[31]

As with most Korean traditional music, a pitch-perfect tone is not the ideal: sliding from one pitch to another is a fairly common ornament. Although laymen often attempt to maintain a particular pitch, professional singers may noticeably adjust it during singing, at specific instances.[32] Shin Taech'ŏl finds that due to the influence of Western classical music, singers have come to increasingly adopt the pure tone and vocal clarity typical of bel canto. He attributes the influence in part to the predominance of Western music in education, and the use of Western music notation and Western classical music instruments in teaching Korean music.[33] As I demonstrate later, the church has been a major factor in the spread of Western classical music in Korea. Christians now make up more than half of the population of Korea, and church and Western classical music are therefore likely to affect the way in which folksongs are sung.

When they sing, musicians do not keep to a strict beat; instead, they follow set rhythmic cycles, *changdan* (*chang* = long, *tan*/-*dan* = short), which tend to stretch one measure and are regularly repeated. The use of these circular patterns, which are named, allows the singer to speed up or slow down endlessly, though it is vital to follow set accents in order to demarcate and identify the cycles and to allow the listener to anticipate a specific accent. Each of the patterns effectively creates a mode that can be conducive to a sad, spirited, or joyful mood.[34] Examples of these patterns are the moderate *chungmori* (12/4), the livelier *kutkŏri* (12/8), and the faster *chajinmori* (12/8).[35] In Western musical notation, these cycles are commonly transcribed using 12/4, 12/8, as well as 15/8, 9/8, 6/8, and 3/4 meters, with an indication of the exact tempo,[36] but as mentioned earlier, many Koreans find the system unsuitable for Korean traditional music because of the frequent sliding, "imperfect" tones and the rhythmic cycles that do not follow a regular tempo. On many occasions singers perform to the accompaniment of the hourglass drum. It is commonly played with the hand on one side and a stick on the other to produce both warm beats and sharp little accents. The basic pattern of the three cycles is as follows:

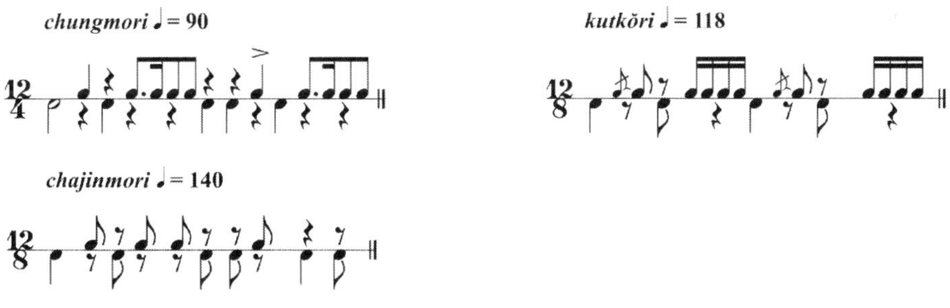

Im Tonggwŏn notes that the musical aspect of a folksong is more constant than its lyrics.[37] Many folksongs, and farming and funeral songs in particular, follow a call-and-response structure. Because the chorus of such songs is constantly repeated, singers can endlessly extend the song through single-line improvisation. The improvised part does not necessarily have to make sense in the context of the song, and many singers use common exclamations instead to incite participation. Many such songs were likely invented during drinking parties. A well-known example of this type of song is "Kanggangsullae," the name of which constitutes the four syllables sung at the end of each phrase. Other examples can be found among the *Sŏnsori sant'aryŏng* (see chapter 3), which have a shorter chorus. In either case, the potentially improvised lines tend to be sung solo (*sŏnch'ang, tokch'ang,* or *apsori*), while the repeated parts at the end of each phrase are sung by two or more singers (*hapch'ang* or *chech'ang*).[38] A good example of solo lines followed by the chorus of a group in a funeral song (in this case a bier carrying song, *sangyŏ sori*) can be seen in Im Kwon-taek's 1996 movie *Festival* (*Ch'ukche*).[39]

Another important characteristic of Korean folksongs is that only a few, including NICP no. 8, "Kanggangsullae," and the repertory of the *Sŏnsori sant'aryŏng,* are still accompanied by dance. As elsewhere, in Korea many folksongs were originally associated with dance. The influence of both Buddhism and Confucianism presumably led to the decline in dance early on. According to Im Tonggwŏn, Buddhism and Confucianism both prohibited the expression of emotion. While Buddhism regarded singing as a form of meditation or relaxation and generally considered dance disorientating, Confucianism required a static, near-motionless performance.[40] Although this appears to contradict the common idea that folksongs are a direct expression of emotion,[41] it is possible that such moral codes influenced public performances in this way, as they also historically led to women being banned from traveling entertainment groups (see chapter 3). Such social constraints, on the other hand, have had little effect on private singing occasions. Im does point out that during the Chosŏn dynasty those in the higher echelons of society considered it improper for women to sing folksongs,[42] but this view was probably uncommon among the rural farming communities where women were expected to take part in labor and ritual activities outdoors. A movie in which village women are shown fishing and diving (as well as doing all the cooking and housekeeping while still duly dreaming of heteronormative romance) is Kim Suyong's 1965 *The Seaside Village* (*Kaenmaŭl*). The untitled theme song for the movie was included on Jigu Records LM 120076, a compilation of theme songs that was brought out in the same year and has a jacket with the image of women dressed in a white *hanbok* dancing in a line on the banks of a river, which typically associates the folksong tradition of "Kanggangsullae." Curiously, the song and dance do not feature on the album or in the movie, but they were appointed an IICP in the ensuing year.

Korean folksongs are rarely tied to a specific costume. But, at least from the early years of the Chosŏn dynasty until the end of the colonial period, professional singing groups—such as those that developed the *Sŏnsori sant'aryŏng* repertoire—often wore combinations of color in order to stand out from the crowd of commoners traditionally dressed in plain white. From the early 1980s onward, competition at major folk events such as the National Folk Arts Contest led to further embellishment. While many groups added colorful garments and accessories, others focused on enhancing the impact of their presentation by making their white costumes and the performers' movements entirely uniform. In the 1990s, the iconic success of the women's circle dance song "Kanggangsullae"—which itself introduced various uniforms over the years—inspired a group from the Pukch'ŏng Folk Arts Preservation Society from south Hamgyŏng province (Hamnam Pukch'ŏng minsok yesul pojonhoe) hoping to emulate the anti-Japanese prestige of the tradition to adopt a similar costume. As discussed in the previous chapters, the group's efforts were successful and led to the official recognition of their main song, "Tondollari," in 1998.[43]

Thematically, Korean folksongs differ from those of neighboring countries in one major aspect: the predominance of Confucianism. Although the initial intent of songs often remains obscure, many folksongs relate to the difficulty of abiding by strict Confucian moral codes and hardship caused by social and gender stratification.[44] Im Tonggwŏn's 1984 *Yŏsŏng-gwa minyo* (Women and folksongs) includes many songs that express the hardship that women suffered as a result of Confucianism. The following example condemns the hard work that was commonly expected of a wife by her parents-in-law:

> You're getting married, you're getting married.
> Don't get married into a countryside household.
> The spinning wheel that your father-in-law made creaks.
> When you fall asleep during work all spent, you use the spinning wheel as your pillow.[45]

Another song describes the burdens imposed by married life in a more comical manner:

> The fart of my father-in-law is an ordering fart.
> The fart of my mother-in-law is a nagging fart.
> The fart of my sister-in-law is a snitching fart.
> The fart of the male servant is an airy fart.
> The fart of my husband is an unconcerned fart.
> My fart is a stealthy fart.[46]

A quality that many South Koreans believe can be found in folksongs across virtually all possible categories, including the two songs transcribed above, is *han*. This feeling of bittersweet melancholy, which is believed to lie at the core of the Korean disposition, is commonly regarded as an essential element of

Korean traditional music. It is a mode born out of the suffering of an individual, or of the Korean people as a whole as victims of foreign aggression, but because it is not entirely negative, it can coexist with humor.[47] *Han* has often underlain scholars' interest in folksongs, and many works on folksongs either refer to the term or argue its significance.[48] Some have argued that it has roots going back as far as the three kingdoms period,[49] but Werner Sasse found that while the term *han* was barely used in publications in the 1950s, it became strongly endorsed during the *Minjung* movement in the 1970s and 1980s.[50] It would, however, be wrong to dismiss the term's relevance on the basis of it having been invented. Words will always have their limits in describing a mode and style of performance, but in Korea today, *han* has fairly clear connotations. Folksongs that associate the quality typically reference daily toil, grief over the loss of a loved one, or the homesickness of women forced to live with their in-laws.

Despite the prevalence of Confucian themes, in the past few decades a growing number of Christians have made attempts to obscure or erase Confucian, Buddhist, or shamanistic elements from traditional customs and rituals, either by interfering with them directly or by replacing them with Christian alternatives.[51] Yi Kyŏngyŏp's 2006 study of local rituals on Chŭngdo Island shows that although the impact of Christianity on folk rituals may be subtle and may necessitate a fair degree of compromise and adaptation on the part of the Christians, it is nevertheless substantial.[52] Although Christians who perform adaptations of traditional music in church occasionally face criticism from fellow Christians,[53] the practice is growing. Usually the changes affect only the lyrics, such as in the case of Pak Minhŭi. Pak released two folksong albums in March 2012, one a selection of standardized traditional folksongs, the other a selection of Christian variations on traditional folksongs. The latter CD, *Kugak ch'anyang* (Korean traditional songs of praise), comprises seventeen traditional folksongs with traditional accompaniment but with new lyrics.[54] The first song is "Hyo arirang" (Pious Arirang). Whereas the music and chorus are identical to "Arirang"—Korea's most prevalent folksong and the first song of Pak's other album, *Chŏnt'ong minyo* (Traditional folksongs)[55]—the verses are different. The first verse of Pak's Christian version bears little resemblance to the traditional one:

> *Hananim abŏji sŏmginŭn nara pumonim ŏrŭshin-do chal konggyŏnghase.*
>
> Blessed be the country of the Lord, our father; let us honor our parents and children.

Even though this verse is very similar to a psalm, the singer's voice and fairly heavy accompaniment on this Christian version seem identical to the traditional one, which makes it seem as though the traditional song was recorded only to demonstrate the singer's credentials.

The *Kugak ch'anyang kasu hyŏphoe* (Association for Singers of Praise in Korean Traditional Music), established in July 2011, fosters the creation and performance of songs that are based on traditional folksongs but with new lyrics. Recordings of these songs sometimes betray a vocal style reminiscent of choir-style singing and a greater emphasis on melody. The arguably more traditional elements constitute the core repertoire and vocal style, as well as the selection of musical instruments and costume. The association includes two church ministers, one of whom is singer Yi Munju. Yi was appointed holder of *Sŏdo sŏnsori sant'aryŏng* (Standing Mountain Songs from the Western Provinces) on September 2, 2009, at the age of fifty-four.[56] He has actively promoted the use of traditional Korean music to proselytize and has composed approximately fifty gospel versions of folksongs in the northwestern tradition of *Sŏnsori sant'aryŏng* (Standing Mountain Songs), including "Sŏnggyŏng sant'aryŏng" (Mountain song from the Bible) and "Hallelluya sangsadiya" (Hallelujah sangsadiya). According to Yi, it is important to include gospel in traditional music: "There is way too much music that sidelines Christianity in the name of tradition. That's a real shame, you know. I am going to put all my efforts into fusing traditional music with Christian culture."[57]

Even with the ardent efforts of singers like Yi, the potential threat of Christianity to the authenticity of Korean folksong traditions remains negligible, at least for now. Although the scale of Christian activities in this regard is increasing, the number of singers involved is still small. Very few people are likely to mistake the gospel folksongs for traditional folksongs, and many will continue to sing traditional folksongs, including people such as Pak Minhŭi and Yi Munju, whose efforts may serve to promote traditional folksongs as much as their own adaptations. What is more, Christians sing adapted forms of traditional music not only because of their spiritual faith, but, rather, because of a range of sociopolitical pressures, some of which are intermixed with Confucian norms.[58]

Folksong Terminology

In Korea, many terms have been used to refer to folksongs over the years. While the relatively new term *minyo* (*min* = the people, *yo* = song) is now commonly used by both scholars and non-scholars to indicate either specific genres or folksongs in a general sense, many songs are also—sometimes exclusively—referred to as *sori, norae*, or *t'aryŏng*, the latter, however, mostly in direct relation to a specific song or repertoire. In literature, other terms, mostly Sino-Korean, such as *sogyo* (popular song), *tan'ga* (short poem), and *kukp'ung* (national custom), have been used in the past but are no longer in use.[59] The term *minyo* was first used by Korean scholars in the second decade of the twentieth century. One of the first collections of folksongs that used the term was Ko Wimin's 1916 *Classification of Korean Folksongs* (*Chosŏn minyo-ŭi pullyu*).[60] The term was borrowed from Japan, where Mori Ogai (1862–1922) is believed to have coined it around 1890. Ogai, who studied in Europe, is said to have composed the term by literally translating the German word *Volkslied* (people's song).[61]

Philip Bohlman contends that Johann Gottfried Herder's (1744–1803) narrow conception of "Volk" as pertaining to the rural, illiterate European peasantry has long marred definitions of folk music.[62] As it served to deepen the culture of a uniform, sovereign people, folk music was essential to Herder's Eurocentric view of a nation as culturally and linguistically distinct—"es hat seine National Bildung wie seine Sprache." Indeed, the view rejects the notion of (socio)cultural pluralism and ignores the myriad differences in age, class, or region.[63] Ko Wimin and his peers presumably chose to use the Korean word for Volkslied to highlight the culture of Koreans who for centuries had been deprived of self-ownership, be it due to China's past suzerainty over Korea or Japanese colonial rule. The Korean notion of the folk, *minjok,* was similarly born of opposition to colonial aggression by imperial powers such as China, Russia, and Japan around the turn of the nineteenth century.[64] Rejecting Confucian historiography on the basis that it was preoccupied with the lives of the elite, Shin Ch'aeho (1880–1936), a frontrunner of Korean nationalism, rewrote Korean history from the viewpoint of the Korean *minjok* as an ethnically and culturally unique people, independent from the cultural yoke of Sinocentrism. And true to the vernacularization that is central to Anderson's conception of "imagined communities,"[65] linguist Chu Shigyŏng (1876–1914) found the essence of the Korean spirit to lie in the vernacular script of *han'gŭl,* which he regarded as key to "ending the habit of aristocratic cultural slavery to Chinese culture."[66] The need for a pure Korean historiography also inspired Ch'oe Namsŏn, one of the main founders of Korean folklore studies. According to Yi Tuhyŏn, Ch'oe played a pivotal role in developing recognition of the Korean people's unique identity. Following the annexation of Korea, he set out to study the history of the *minjok* "to advocate Koreanism and resurrect the Korean spirit" (*Chosŏnjuŭi purŭjikko, Chosŏn chŏngshin-ŭl puhwalshik'inŭn-de*).[67] The study of folklore (and folksongs) thus sought to establish a body of knowledge that demonstrated Korea's cultural independence, even though, ironically, the field of study itself was influenced by the work of Japanese scholars, who like the Koreans had been keen to adopt Western ideas and methodologies including the Eurocentric notion of Volk.[68]

In the 1980s, scholars began using the terms *t'osok* and *t'ongsok* to distinguish between local, regional songs and refined, professionalized songs, respectively.[69] The distinction between regional and national is a potentially contentious one. Many Koreans care greatly about the region with which people are associated, whether by birth or by choice. That association affects their potential for success in finding employment in the private sector, or, at least since 1987, voters in the public sector. Among the primary reasons often given for the regional divide are the fairly recent Kwangju incident, the regional conflicts from the time of the Three Kingdoms period, and the logistic disadvantage of, in particular, the southwestern provinces located away from major economic trading networks.[70] The term *t'osok* (Jap. *dozoku*) was first introduced by the Japanese colonial authorities, who used it to refer to the many primitive, uncivilized aspects of Korean culture.[71] By the 1980s, however, following major urbanization, *t'osok* had begun to shed its negative connotation and come to represent a unique, local quality. Since regional associations also imply specific cultural and linguistic specificities, the distinction may have signaled a concern that government regulations regarding folksongs would lead to homogenization and the dilution of their expression of unique, regional identities.[72]

According to Keith Howard, the two terms were originally used to distinguish between professional and amateur entertainers. He argues that their continued use is not always helpful, because professional and regional, popular (or amateur) folksongs have often influenced each other.[73] Hwang Yongju, holder of *Sŏnsori sant'aryŏng*, uses the terms as measures of folksongs' regional characteristics: "When they are limited to a certain region, you must call them *t'osok minyo*, but if the region is quite large, then all the songs that are handed down must be called *t'ongsok minyo*" (pers. comm., November 18, 1995). Im Tonggwŏn, on the other hand, disliked the terms: "*T'osok minyo, t'ongsok minyo*, terms like that are used by people who play traditional . . . or court music, but I have always warned people who play court music about the negative aspects of the terms. *Minyo* are *minyo*, and there are no *t'osok minyo* or *t'ongsok minyo* within *minyo*. All *minyo* are both *t'osok* and *t'ongsok*."[74] Song Minsŏn, who worked as a folk materials archivist at the Cultural Properties Research Institute, agreed with Im. She argued that the songs should all be called *minyo* because both professional and regional songs are sung by "the people" (*minjung*).[75] The genres I discuss in chapters 3 and 4—*Sŏnsori sant'aryŏng*, *Kyŏnggi minyo*, and *Sŏdo sori*—have arguably retained their local flavor but are also refined and professionalized, so I avoid relying on the terms *t'osok* and *t'ongsok* exclusively. What is more, some folksongs that would once be considered *t'osok minyo* now belong primarily to the repertoire of professional singers.

The term *minyo* is commonly used by those who do not sing folksongs—often to distinguish them from other types of music. When referring to specific songs, singers tend to use *sori* or *norae*. The pure Korean term *sori*, like its Sino-Korean equivalent *yo*, is mainly found in compound names of folksongs. According to Kim Muhŏn, *sori* implies a particular function, such as in the numerous *kimmaegi sori* (weeding songs) and *maettol sori* (milling songs). He believes that because the term *norae*, which Ko Chŏngok and Im Tonggwŏn have used, derives from the verb *nolda* (to play), it is not always appropriate.[76] The meaning of the term *sori* (sound or song), on the other hand, is broad and may have been used in the past to indicate other forms of oral literature. While the word *norae* can indicate genres such as *kasa* (narrative songs), *shijo* (sung poems), and *kagok* (lyric songs), *sori* can describe the genres of *minyo*, *chapka* (described below), and *p'ansori* (folk dramatic song).[77] Hwang Yongju told me that he used to pronounce *sori* as *sorae*, but he adapted to the modern *sori* for pedagogical reasons:

> If . . . you wonder what they would sound like if we sang the words of the songs the old-fashioned way. . . . the *sori* in songs such as '*Chŏng sori*' (Song of Affection) and '*Yŏmbul sori*'[78] was pronounced *sorae*, you see, because our language was like that in the past. Nowadays it's *sori*. We now use standard Korean for things like this. We preserve the melody and the rhythm as they were, but it must be a general rule that as far as the language [is concerned], we follow the standard Korean.[79]

Although the more common term *t'aryŏng* (song) can still be found in the names of many folksongs, *t'aryŏng* is not commonly used to indicate folksongs on their own, unlike *minyo* or *sori*. Singers from Inji village on the island of Chindo province once told Howard that the term related to songs from the mainland, but according to Chang Sahun the term originally related to songs specifically from the Hwanghae and P'yŏngan provinces.[80] Today, it is easy to find it in the names of folksongs from other regions of Korea.[81] Well-known examples include songs such as "Arirang t'aryŏng"[82] and "Panga t'aryŏng" (Milling Song). Joshua Pilzer argues that the term refers to songs with a shaman origin,[83] though this is inconsistent with the consensus that the genre of *Sŏnsori sant'aryŏng*, discussed in the next chapter, was developed by itinerant Buddhist entertainment troupes.

Another term often used to refer to specific folksongs is *chapka*. Although the origin of this word is unknown, in written literature its first known appearance, in *Kwanuhŭi* (Watching the Comic Folk Play) by Song Manjae, dates from the early nineteenth century. At that time it appears to have been commonly used to refer to *p'ansori*. It was not until the late nineteenth century that *chapka* began to be used to refer to local folksongs.[84] *Chapka* literally translates as "miscellaneous songs," but the first character, *chap*, has a slightly negative connotation. Folklorist Yi Pohyŏng believes the term should no longer be used because the expression *chamnyŏn* (*nyŏn* = bitch/tramp) is equivalent to the

British word "slag." Today, *chapka* is commonly used to describe the twelve refined songs from Kyŏnggi province, which as a whole are designated National Intangible Cultural Property no. 57. These so-called *shibi* (twelve) or *kin* (long) *chapka* are sung by seated performers and are thus at times described as *chwach'ang* (*chwa* = sitting, *ch'ang* = singing). Because *chapka* can also refer to *Sŏnsori sant'aryŏng*, a genre of professional group songs from the Kyŏnggi provinces sung standing and occasionally referred to as *ipch'ang* (*ip* = standing), *chapka* does not designate a specific singing posture.[85] Kim Hŭnggyu's definition of *chapka* as "expert" songs, as opposed to folksongs for amateurs,[86] is somewhat useful in that it avoids defining the singer or region; but this usage is problematic in that it unnecessarily distinguishes *chapka* from folksongs on the basis of their alleged degree of complexity. Many folksongs, including the *Sŏdo sori* discussed in chapter 4, are generally considered very difficult to sing.

One sometimes comes across other terms that denote folksongs, such as those that use the Sino-Korean suffixes *-yo* and *-ka/-ga*, which both imply "song" in a general sense and are part of the compounds *minyo* and *chapka*. However, perhaps in part due to the impact of Im Tonggwŏn's extensive collections of folksongs, published in seven volumes as *Collections of Korean Folksongs* (*Han'guk minyo chip*) between 1961 and 1995, it appears that the suffix *-yo* now implies that a song is specifically a folksong. Im explains that, at least in the first volume of his *Collections of Korean Folksongs*, he uses *-yo* whenever he believes that the song is not very well known, while he calls songs that are more widely known *norae* or *t'aryŏng*.[87] The suffix *-ka/-ga*, meanwhile, can be found in the names of well-known folksongs such as "Sushimga" (Song of Sorrow) and "Sabalga" (Rice Bowl Song), as well as in the general term for shaman songs, *muga*.

The Modernization of Folksongs

Various factors have played a role in the modernization of folksongs, including Japanese education policy, modernization, and commercialization. Around the time of the annexation of Korea by Japan, the Protestant Church constituted a fourth. When the Japanese police began to strictly enforce restrictions on freedom of speech, the church, which openly renounced the new government, albeit not all from the outset, came to constitute one of few places where people could voice their opinions.[88] The musical style of hymns was a prime source of inspiration for what would eventually be known as *ch'angga* (*ch'ang* = singing, *ga* = song), songs based on either European or Japanese melodies that were sung along an eight-bar scale and 4/4 beat that became very popular from around 1905. Yi Yusŏn argues that although the songs were already taught at missionary institutes in Korea in 1886, the term *ch'angga* was copied from Japan, where the term *shōka* (=*ch'angga*) was first used in the *Collection of Songs for Primary*

Schools (*Shōgaku shōkashū*) from 1881.[89] "Haktoga" (Student Association Song), which was written by Kim Inshik (1885–1962), Hong Nanp'a's former teacher, may have been the first *ch'angga,* though the exact date of its composition is unknown.[90] The songs eventually became sung at Protestant homes and primary schools as well. However, as they came to be developed further by Korean writers and composers, many of whom had studied in Japan or the West, their mode and intent changed from edifying to romantic.[91]

Ch'angga reflected the rapidly changing times, and from the early 1920s, following the patriotic March First Movement of 1919, songs that covertly criticized the Japanese quickly gained popularity. Many of these newly composed songs were called "Aegukka" (Song of Patriotism).[92] They expressed patriotism and often glorified the nation, much like "Arirang" and "Han obaengnyŏn" (Five Hundred Years of Sorrow). Yi Yongshik argues that aside from the rhythm and the Japanese pentatonic *yonanuki* (lit. "omitting four [*re*] and seven [*sol*]") scale typical of *enka,* the influence of *ch'angga* on the folksong "Tondollari" is demonstrated by its patriotic content.[93] Realizing that the patriotism did not extend to the Japanese empire, the Japanese colonial government eventually prohibited many of them. It also removed them from school music books or replaced them with pro-Japanese versions.[94]

From the early 1930s, following the decline in popularity of *ch'angga,* nonpolitical *shin minyo* (new folksongs) were brought out by Japanese-owned local record companies such as Victor and Okeh.[95] While the majority of *shin minyo* were about romance, including "Kashiryŏmnikka" (Are You Leaving?), the subjects of the songs recorded were diverse, ranging from a woman's view on married life, as in "Ch'oriptong" (A Young Man with a Straw Hat), to descriptions of sceneries, such as in "Sŭri sŭri pom param" (The Soft Spring Breeze) and "Nodŭl kangbyŏn" (The Nodŭl Riverside).[96] The lyrics of the latter song, performed by *kisaeng* Pak Puyong, were written by the acclaimed singer and comedian Shin Pulch'ul (1906–1976?):

> Should I try to tie the waist of fleeting time around the branches that circle down from the spring willow that stands by the Nodŭl[97] riverside?
>
> E-he-yo, you cannot trust the spring willow either. That blue water there just keeps flowing.
>
> Our traces in the sand by the Nodŭl riverside have been wiped away so often by all kinds of severe rains and wind.
>
> E-he-yo, you cannot trust the white sand either. That blue water there just keeps flowing.
>
> Blue water of the Nodŭl riverside, did you take with you the precious bodies of talented men and beautiful women? E-he-yo, please come to your senses, and take away all the resentment built up in this world.[98]

Noted male singers of *shin minyo* included Kim Yonghwan (1912–1948) and Kang Hongshik, while acclaimed female singers included Wang Subok (1917–2003), Yi Ŭnp'a, Sŏn Uilsŏn (1918–1990), and Yi Hwaja (1917–1949).[99] They have been rereleased in recent years, for example, on Seoul Records SRCD-1232 (1995), *30-nyŏndae shin minyo* (New folksongs from the thirties).

Although the songs were still sung in compound meters (6/8, 9/8, or 12/8) using the vocal timbre typical of traditional folksongs, the lyrics and music of *shin minyo* were composed by individuals and performed in a relatively fast tempo to the harmonic accompaniment of Western instruments. Chang Yujŏng finds that the term *shin minyo* is problematic, because it is a poorly defined category that includes a number of *yuhaengga* (pop songs) and (traditional) folksongs. An example she provides is Kang Hongshik's song "Ch'ŏnyŏ ch'onggak" (The Virgin and the Bachelor) from 1934, which according to the lyrics sheet included in the sleeve was a "folksong," but was actually a newly composed *shin minyo*.[100] Since it was already in use in Japan in the 1920s, albeit for a different type of song,[101] the latter term is likely to have been imported. Another issue complicating the term is that contrary to the basic definition, the composer of songs labeled *shin minyo* is not always known. Chang Sahun and Yi Pohyŏng believe, for example, that well-known folksongs such as "Han obaengnyŏn" and "Ch'ŏngch'un'ga" (Song of the Bloom of Youth) are both *shin minyo* that were composed during the colonial period.[102]

Referring to the version brought out on records since the late 1920s, Yi Pohyŏng also includes "Arirang" in this category, in the popular and standardized (*t'ongsok*) form developed from a local (*t'osok*) song from Kangwŏn province, "Chajin arari" (*chajin/chajŭn* = fast).[103] The basic melody of the song as it is widely known today is as follows:

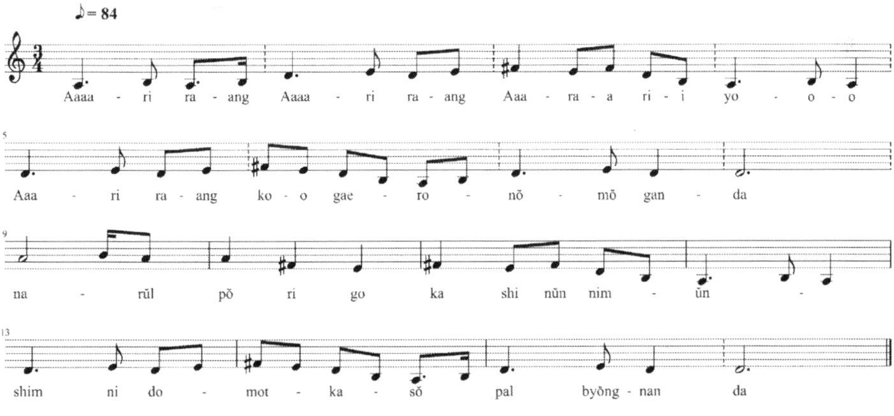

Arirang Arirang, Arariyo. Arirang kogae-ro nŏmŏganda. Na-rŭl pŏrigo kashinŭn nim-ŭn shimni-do mot kasŏ palbyŏngnanda (Arirang, Arirang, Arariyo. We cross over the Arirang pass. My husband who abandons me will get sore feet before he has walked ten li [4 km]).

He finds the necessary evidence in the distinctive style of the songs: the use of little vocal vibration, often following a duple subdivision of the beat, rather than the more common triplet subdivision of traditional music, which indicates to Yi an adjustment to Western popular songs that began to occur toward the end of the nineteenth century, when missionaries came to Korea and introduced Christian chant. He believes that many singers changed the melodic style because Koreans regarded Western music as more modern, and therefore preferable: "The origin of 'Han obaengnyŏn' is actually 'Arirang.' Kangwŏn province's '*Kin arirang*' (*kin* = long) goes like this: *A-ri-rang, han-o-baeng-nyŏn sa-ja.* But they changed the beat into a two-beat. As for *A-ri-rang,* this has become a two-beat, a *shin minyo.*" Yi sang the first phrase for me while loosely clapping four beats per measure:

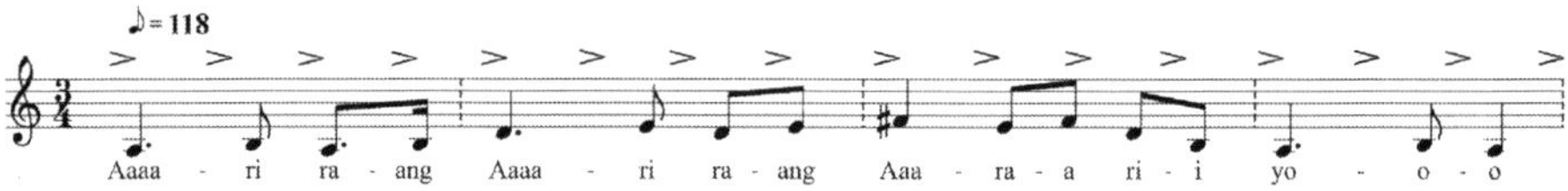

"The melodic line has a Western 'smell,' doesn't it? That's because something like a Christian vigor, a Christian chant, seeped into it" (pers. comm., September 26, 1995). The influence of Christian hymns on the music of both *ch'angga* and *shin minyo* was first argued by Ko Chŏngok. Because *shin minyo* reflected the times of their composition, an intrinsic feature of folksongs, Ko believed the genre was still representative of the "folk."[104] Despite having been Ko's student, Im Tonggwŏn would disagree. He believed that folksongs should be defined as songs that have been composed by a group of people with no particular musical skill and not by a single talented person.[105]

Although most *shin minyo* have been accompanied by Western instruments during and shortly after the colonial period, when Okeh brought out Pak Puyong's rendition of "The Nodŭl Riverside" in 1934, the accompaniment on the hit record was comprised of both Western and traditional Korean instruments for the first time.[106] Since then, *shin minyo* began to be "reinvented" by recording companies who increasingly favored ensembles that used traditional Korean instruments. Of great importance with regard to this change are *Kyŏnggi minyo* singers An Pich'wi, Yi Ŭnju, and Muk Kyewŏl, who adopted a series of *t'ongsok minyo,* and, arguably, *shin minyo* such as "Han obaengnyŏn," "Nodŭl kangbyŏn," "Arirang," "Yangsando," and "Ch'ŏngch'un'ga," into their standard repertoire from the time they started working for recording companies in the 1940s. By doing so, they arguably followed in the footsteps of Wang Subok, Yi Ŭnp'a, Sŏn

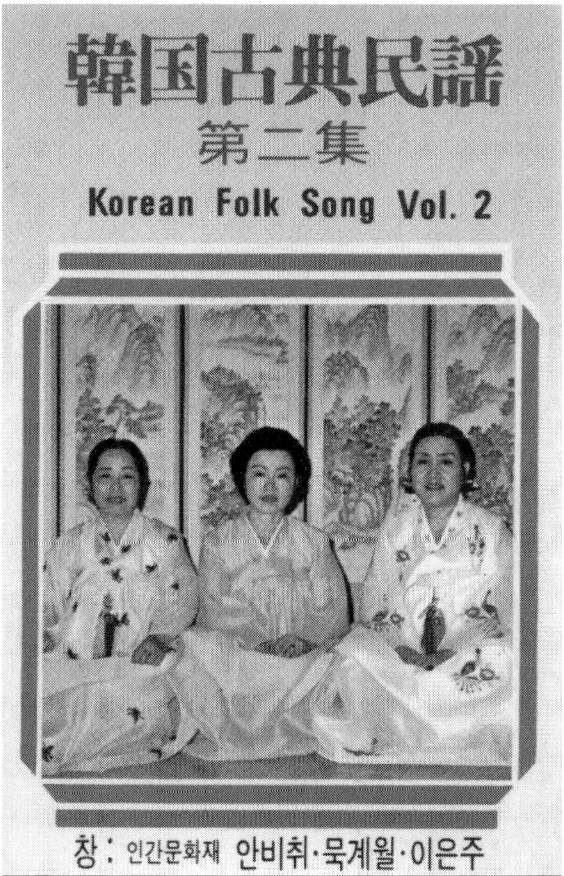

Front cover of Han Kook Record Co. HC-200055 (1979; cassette tape), *Korean Folk Song Vol. 2,* featuring, from left to right, Muk Kyewŏl, Yi Ŭnju, and An Pich'wi.

Uilsŏn, and Yi Hwaja, who because of their training in traditional folksongs as *kisaeng* were able to gain great popularity through recordings of *shin minyo* in the final decade of the colonial period.[107]

Because Japanese and Koreans trained in Japan were very much involved in the writing and arrangement of music at record companies, it was only a matter of time before *shin minyo* became influenced by the similar Japanese *enka.*[108] The first Korean adaptations of Japanese *enka* were called *yuhaengga* (*yuhaeng*= popular), *yuhaeng ch'angga,* or trot (*t'ŭrot'ŭ*), a term that derived from the Western dance music of foxtrot, with its relatively fast two-beat rhythm.[109] The song "Hŭimangga" (Song of Hope) from 1923, which is also known by its opening line, *I p'ungjin sesang-ŭl* (This world the wind has covered in dust), is regarded as one of the first examples of this style.[110] Yi Yusŏn argues that the genre consists of songs that maintain the direct character of *ch'angga,* but are more refined.[111] Pro-Japanese versions of this type of song would be taught at schools from the 1930s, particularly in the lower grades. Like *ch'angga,* they are characterized by a two- or four-beat rhythm, but have more melancholy in the lyrics and are often imbued with grief over the loss of autonomy and forced relocation.[112] The titles of some of the most popular *yuhaengga* reflect this: "Aesu-ŭi soyagok (Serenade of Sorrow), "Nunmul chŏjŭn Tuman'gang" (The Tear-soaked Tumen River), and "Mokp'o-ŭi nunmul" (Tears of Mokp'o).[113] *Yuhaengga* further developed into contemporary pop ballads, often simply known as *kayo* (lit. "songs"). They are similar to Western pop ballads in terms of instrumentation, singing style, and presentation, and have been broadcast widely on television and radio since the 1950s.[114] Since they involve a light vocal style (with a slightly exaggerated vibrato) and are often accompanied by the simple 2/4 beat of a Western drum set or synthesizer, they are often pejoratively—and at times fondly—called *ppongtchak* (boom tchak), after the sound of the bass and snare drum.

In this chapter I have described the various forms of folksongs and their terminology, and discussed how a combination of modernity, colonialism, and Japanese music impacted Korean folksongs during the colonial period. In the next two chapters, I deliberate the ways in which the three major folksong NICPs have developed over the years, both before and after their appointment. I explore the history of the folksong genres *Sŏnsori sant'aryŏng, Kyŏnggi minyo,* and *Sŏdo sori,* including the tradition of *Paebaengi kut.* I describe the musical and lyrical elements of the genres as well as their representatives over the years, paying particular attention to how the government has either prevented or encouraged change in the three genres. In chapter 3 I focus in particular on the genders with which the representation of *Sŏnsori sant'aryŏng* and *Kyŏnggi minyo* have been associated. In chapter 4 I argue that the tradition of *Sŏdo sori* will not be broken by the impending loss of native representatives and place, but sustained instead by its ability to evoke nostalgia.

CHAPTER 3

Masculinity in Demise

SŎNSORI SANT'ARYŎNG AND *KYŎNGGI MINYO*

On April 18, 1968, *Sŏnsori sant'aryŏng* (Standing Mountain Songs) became the first folksong genre to be officially recognized as an Important Intangible Cultural Property (IICP). Although another folksong genre, *Sŏdo sori* (Folksongs from the Western Provinces),[1] was recognized in the same year, it was placed ten items lower on the IICP list (no. 29). Holders for both genres were appointed in the following year. *Kyŏnggi minyo* (Folksongs from Kyŏnggi Province) was designated a year later, and numbered 57, but holders were not appointed for that genre until 1975. That *Sŏnsori sant'aryŏng* (hereafter *Sant'aryŏng*) was designated ahead of the other two genres may seem odd considering it has a shorter history than its two counterparts and was always less prominent in the recording and broadcast media. The primary reason for the genre's early recognition was that its foremost representative, Yi Ch'angbae, was a central figure within the national folksong scene and a former teacher of those eventually appointed holders of *Kyŏnggi minyo*. The early recognition of *Sant'aryŏng* has nevertheless failed to prevent it from changing noticeably since. Today, the genre is no longer sung almost exclusively by men, as it was when it was designated. The result has been a change in the look, performance, and sound of the genre. While *Kyŏnggi minyo* and *Sŏdo sori* have also come to be predominantly represented by women, this has had much less impact from the viewpoint of tradition since the genres already had many noted female representatives before they were recognized as IICPs.[2]

Itinerant Entertainment: *Sŏnsori sant'aryŏng*

A performance of *Sant'aryŏng* commonly entails a group of female singers holding small hand drums and one male leader carrying a large hourglass drum, all of whom stand in a line facing the audience, swaying slightly, and singing with dynamic intensity. Although no harmonizing takes place, both the synchronicity and the gradually increasing intensity of the singing and drumming add considerable impact to the performance. In the past, when the majority of groups originated from provinces along the west coast of the peninsula, the singers would take the audience along on a virtual journey across the country, using lyrics describing the landscapes they would encounter. Today's lyrics still describe scenery that extends well beyond the capital, but the genre has nevertheless come to be associated exclusively with Seoul. It is said that the second and third songs of the core repertoire describe the mountains in the southern and northern parts of the city, respectively.[3]

In contrast to the songs from the midwestern Kyŏnggi, and northwestern P'yŏngan, and Hwanghae provinces, where until the early twentieth century *Sant'aryŏng* constituted a major form of vocal performing art, in the southwestern region (*namdo*) songs in the *Sant'aryŏng* genre were usually sung by performing troupes known as *kwangdae,* which specialized in *p'ansori* (folk dramatic song).[4] Because in this region *p'ansori* has long been considered a higher art form, the folksongs are not often sung on local stages.[5] Yi Pohyŏng comments:

> Female performers of *p'ansori* are therefore able to sing the songs well, but they only came up during the colonial period. During the Chosŏn dynasty, *p'ansori* singers did not sing *Sant'aryŏng,* but at the end of the dynasty, when city theaters sprang up and they needed a repertoire as a vocal troupe, the *kwangdae* troupes learned those [songs] and performed them. So during the colonial period . . . all those studying *p'ansori* also studied *Namdo sŏnsori.* So it may be that only those who perform *p'ansori* are able to understand *Namdo sŏnsori.* . . . Although it was men who sang them first, [nowadays] only women are able to sing them well. There may have been some influence from the *p'ansori* singing style, but only very little.[6]

What the term *sŏnsori* means here is unclear. Although *sŏn* could signify "standing," like the character *ip* in *ipch'ang* (standing songs), Yi Pohyŏng warns that *sŏn* also means "first," or "front," just like the character *ap* in *apsori* (solo singing).[7] In this way, *sŏnsori* could signify solo singing, such as that performed by the leader before the group sets in with the refrain. But since this type of song is commonplace, *sŏnsori* is usually interpreted in spatial terms instead, referring to the position of the singers on stage.[8] This would correspond with the practice of distinguishing repertoires based on whether they are sung seated (*chwa*) or standing (*ip*). Even so, the actual position of singers is not set. It is often determined by the conditions—the venue—of a particular performance.

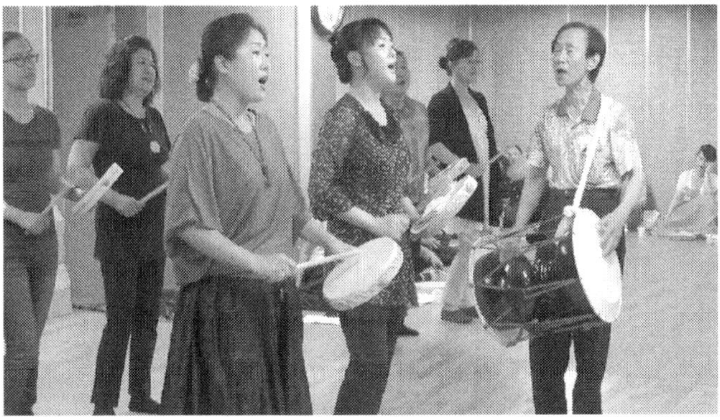

Hwang Yongju teaching at the Seoul Training Center for Important Intangible Cultural Properties on December 19, 2012.

Sant'aryŏng are sung predominantly by groups of singers, but their number varies considerably. In the last few decades, the group surrounding the current holder, Hwang Yongju, numbered between six and sixty on formal occasions.[9] Singers stand in formation beating a plain, white version of the *sogo,* a small and flat handheld double-headed drum.[10] One or two leaders, known as *mogap,* stand sideways and initiate songs or verses by singing a solo couplet beating an hourglass drum that is slung by a strap over their shoulders. The group then joins in to sing the remainder of the introduction or verse. During performance, the formation of the group changes frequently. A couple of singers regularly take turns stepping forward and singing stanzas, known as *apsori.* After the group has fallen in to sing a refrain, *twit* (back/rear) *sori,* the two singers step back into line. During the songs, the singers rock gently from left to right, but they may become animated when a song reaches a climax. The dance steps, known as *pallim ch'um* (*ch'um* = dance), are simple and imply no more than a sequence of slow formation changes.[11] The meaning of *pallim* is unclear; but the fact that the term is also used to indicate the movements of *p'ansori* performers when acting out a scene suggests that it comes from the verb *pallida,* which can mean "to expose."[12] The songs are energetic and cheerful, and the audience is more than once enticed to clap along to the rhythm. As the performance progresses, the vigor with which the singers beat their drums increases and the singing becomes significantly louder and more expressive.

In general, *Sant'aryŏng* require a wide vocal range. Paek Taeung argues that the difficulty of the singing style lies in the fact that the voices do not slide by gradual progression from octave to octave but rather jump beyond what he calls the "fourth octave."[13] Other particularly demanding aspects of the Kyŏnggi repertoire are its constantly changing rhythmic structure and strong dynamics.

Since the songs include many different stanzas and must be sung with considerable expression, singers need to be well trained lest the songs end up sounding joyless and convoluted. Chŏng Tŭngman, former holder of *Sant'aryŏng,* once described the songs as "light, just like the food in Seoul, and straightforward like spice."[14]

In 1968 the *Sant'aryŏng* of Kyŏnggi province were designated IICP no. 19, along with holders Kim Suhyŏn (real name: Kim T'aebong, 1898–1970), Yu Kaedong (1898–1975), Kim Sunt'ae (1914–1978), Chŏng Tŭngman (1907–1992), and Yi Ch'angbae (1916–1983). Perhaps because the repertoires from the southwestern (*namdo*) or northwestern (*sŏdo*) regions are relatively short, they were not initially considered for designation, though as discussed in chapter 1, in 2009 the latter were designated as a separate, regional folk art. The core of the official Kyŏnggi repertoire comprises four songs: "Nollyang" (also known as "Nollyŏng"), "Apsan t'aryŏng" (Song of the Front Mountain), "Twissan t'aryŏng" (Song of the Rear Mountain), and "Chajin sant'aryŏng" (Fast Mountain Song). According to Hwang Yongju,[15] "Kaeguri t'aryŏng" (Song of the Frog) could be considered part of the core repertoire as well, as it is always sung at the end of Fast Mountain Song. Other songs that are often included are "Tohwa t'aryŏng" (Peach Blossom Song); the standard, narrative (*sasŏl*), and fast (*chajin*) versions of "Panga t'aryŏng"; "Kyŏngbokkung t'aryŏng" (Song of Kyŏngbok Palace); and "Yangsando."[16]

Although the singing style is similar for both the Kyŏnggi and northwestern repertoires, the latter are sung considerably faster. In the southwestern region, where local folksongs have a distinct sound, the two central songs are sung in a style very similar to that of the Kyŏnggi genre, presumably because they derive from it.[17] A performance of the southwestern repertoire would typically start with the song "Poryŏm," which although designed to rid the performance space of evil spirits,[18] would in the past be performed while enticing the audience to donate money. It first follows the moderate rhythmic cycle of *chungmori* (12/4) but then moves to the faster *chungjungmori* (12/8), *kutkŏri* (12/8), or *chajinmori* (12/8). A song that routinely follows is "Hwach'o sagŏri" (*hwach'o* = flowering plant),[19] which has a rhythmic pattern much like that of "Poryŏm." The two songs are commonly followed by songs such as "Sagŏri," "Hŭng t'aryŏng" (Sighing Song), Song of the Frog, and the common version of the popular "Yukchabaegi," a slow lament to a six-beat (18/8) rhythmic pattern, which Han Manyŏng defines as "a song of lost love, of poverty, life and desertion."[20]

Presumably because the Kyŏnggi province repertoire is believed to be the origin of the northwestern repertoire, the Kyŏnggi version of "Nollyang" is sometimes referred to as "Ku nollyang" (*ku* = old) and the northwestern version as "Shin nollyang" (*shin* = new).[21] What *nollyang* itself means, however, remains unclear. The song's lyrics convey the thoughts of a person walking through the countryside on the way to a temple as part of a troupe, with the northwestern version also expressing a yearning for a lover. The Kyŏnggi song is divided into two parts: a long, relatively fast first part (one beat = 275~330/min) and a short, slightly slower second part (one beat = 216~240/min) that consists of approximately three verse lines starting with the term *yukkuhamdo* (wide road), referring to the main road leading from Hanyang county in south Kyŏngsang province to China via Seoul.[22] The first part is very similar to the northwestern version and starts with a long introduction called *ch'omogi* (trees and plants),[23] which Han Manyŏng describes as partially incoherent Buddhist incantations.[24] This introduction is sung to a slow rhythmic pattern, but as the song gradually quickens it occasionally shifts to the rhythmic cycle of *semach'i* (9/8). Apart from shifts in rhythm, "Nollyang" includes many high-pitched notes.[25] Chang Sahun argues that because of this complexity few people can sing the song properly.[26]

Below are translations of the lyrics of both the Kyŏnggi and northwestern versions of "Nollyang" as transcribed by Hwang Yongju:[27]

(KYŎNGGI)

Introduction:

The landscape is dense, but we enjoy the sightseeing.
Ee. .ehe naha-a-ŏ ŏ-ŏya-a-a e-ehenaha-a toneroguna ma nŭn-nehe eheeya.
Ee. .ŏ ti-i-i-i-i-i-iŏ-ŏ-ŏlleroguna ti-i-i-i-i-i-i. .eradiyŏ ŏ-ŏ-ŏyana illeroguna-e yŏ-ŏ ŏdi-i-i ŏlshiguna chŏlshiguna, amuryŏdo neroguna, eŏdi-i-i-i-i. .eŏdi-i-i-i-i ti-i-i-i-i-i-i-i-iŏ-e naha-a-a aha-aŏ iŏlleroguna.

Verse 1:

Ee. ., Listen, the road along which the willows stand stretched leads straight to the office of the governor of Pyongyang, *ee. .ehe-e-e iŏ-iŏlleroguna.*
The spring trees are in full blossom and the wild geese fly with a steady flap of the wings. A tall pine tree with heavy branches has cracked with a snap and the dead branches are all that's left.
Chijihwajaja, wouldn't that be nice.
Chijihwajaja, wouldn't that be nice.
Ŏlshiguna, all right, listen up, *ee. .ehe-e-e iŏ-e naha-a-a aha-aŏ iŏlleroguna.*

Verse 2:

Even if we walk all day, Ch'ŏngnyong Temple will still be in Ansŏng. Still dreaming of a forest in January, and a small fish in March, [second part begins here], the wide road now has monks of all levels, *ŏlshiguna chŏlshiguna, amuryŏdo ne.*
The day all green willows, fragrant plants and love plants darken, *e. .aha iŏlleroguna.*

(SŎDO)

Introduction:

Eradiyŏ ŏ-ŏ-hŏya yo-oho-olleroguna, the road that stretches toward the green willow leads us straight onto Mount Pukhyang, *ee. .ehe-ehe-ie-ŏ-ŏhŏya yo-oho-olleroguna.*

The spring trees are in full blossom and the wild geese fly with a steady flap of the wings. A tall pine tree with heavy branches has cracked with a snap and the dead branches are all that's left.

Chihwajaja, wouldn't that be nice.

Chihwajaja, wouldn't that be nice.

Verse 1:

Ŏlshiguna, good, listen up, we leave the life of mortals behind us and climb the blue mountain, *ee. .ehe-ehe-ie-ŏ-ŏhŏya yo-oho-olleroguna.*

The twilight persists while the tailed cuckoo sits on a tree, and another sits on the ground.

Where did you suggest we go?

Where did you suggest we go?

When you cross this mountain you will find the tailed cuckoo.

When you cross this mountain you will find the tailed cuckoo.

Verse 2:

The picture of a young face and beautiful body keeps entering and leaving my sight. Her whispering is ringing in my ears.

I pray, I pray, I pray for my wishes to be fulfilled.

In March, the wide road has monks of all levels, *ŏlshiguna, chŏlshiguna.*

My love is like piles of grain, my love.

When I open the south-facing window and the north-facing window and look, my love deepens like piles of grain.

My love crawls over the rocks by the pine tree.

A wooden roller, the vines of love plants and tobacco plants, the vines of a gourd, they are as thick as the love that has become entangled in my chest, *ee. .nae-e-elleroguna a-aha-a.*

The differences between the Kyŏnggi and northwestern versions of "Nollyang" are fairly small overall, both in terms of the music and the lyrics. The same can be said about the song that is usually sung next, Song of the Front Mountain. Both versions of this song describe the mountains around Seoul, but the northwestern version's sixth and final verse may have been added later, as it rather suddenly refers to scenery around Pyongyang.[28] As in the case of "Nollyang," both versions of the song convey the thoughts of a person traveling to a temple, with the northwestern song adding a yearning for a lover. Singers use many high-pitched notes and strong articulation. The music and lyrics of the northwestern version are virtually the same as those from Kyŏnggi, but it is sung approximately a third quicker (one beat = 176~184/min as opposed to 116~126/min) and follows a set rhythmic cycle, *semach'i*, while the Kyŏnggi version follows a triplet-based beat that does not follow a particular cycle.[29] Hwang Yongju transcribes the first parts of the Kyŏnggi and northwestern versions of the song as follows:[30]

(KYŎNGGI)

Introduction:
Nanŏ ninano-ho oho-o-o e-ehŏ ehŏ ehe-eya-ehŏ-ŏ ehŏ iŏ-ŏhŏru, it's a mountain.

Verse 1:
The hermitage for Buddhist chant on Mount Kwanak in Kwach'ŏn is located on [the mountain's highest peak, called] Yŏnjudae. At Pulsŏng Temple on Mount Tobong [the road] turns toward Sammak Temple.
Ee. .eŏ ŏdi-i ihŏ-ŏhŏ ehe-eya-e hŏ-ŏ-ŏ-ŏ ehŏihŏ ŏru, it's a mountain.

Verse 2:
The phoenix of Mount Tan comes flying in with a bamboo fruit in its beak. The Naktong River in Sangju surrounds Mount Taebaek in Kyŏngsang province while Mount Chiri in Chŏlla province is only surrounded by the Sŏmjin River in Ha-dong.

(SŎDO)

Introduction:
Nane noni na ehe-e ehe-e no-o nahe-e hero, it's a mountain.

Verse 1:
Yŏmburam Temple on Mount Kwanak in Kwach'ŏn is located on Yŏnjudae. At Pulsŏng Temple on Mount Tobong [the road] turns toward Sammak Temple.
Ehe. . ehero chi-i chiroguna mar-ŭlleya nae-ehero, it's a mountain.

Verse 2:
The white horse stamps his four hoofs clang clang, while you just sigh wringing your white hands. Don't cry, don't cry, don't cry such heavy tears. Even if you cry endlessly, there's nothing I can do.

The northwestern version of Song of the Front Mountain closely follows the Kyŏnggi version in terms of music and lyrics, even borrowing the latter's first and fifth verse; but with as many as eleven verses the Kyŏnggi version is considerably longer.

Of equal length is Song of the Rear Mountain. In Kyŏnggi province, the song is also known as "Chunggŏri" (*chung* = center/middle), which Chang Sahun explains as deriving from being the second of the three core songs.[31] The lyrics and the singing style are very similar to those of Song of the Front Mountain, but the tempo of the northwestern version (one beat = 264~276/min) is almost twice as fast as the Kyŏnggi one (one beat = 144~162/min). Like the previous song, it is usually sung to a triplet-based beat but without following a particular rhythmic cycle.[32] The introductory first line is identical in both the Kyŏnggi and the northwestern versions:[33] "It's low, but it's a mountain, *ee.* ., there are azaleas on the plateau too, it's a mountain." Hwang includes a second and third introductory line for the northwestern version that are omitted from other transcriptions, because these lines are not regularly sung: "One, Nonsan, two, Kangyŏng, three, Poju, four, Pŏpsŏng. They all enclose Yŏsan Port. *Ee. .eheyo eheyo e-ŏ ŏhŏya,* [there are azaleas] on the plateau too, it's a mountain."[34]

The fourth song of the core repertoire, "Chajin sant'aryŏng" (Fast Mountain Song), is also known as "Toraji t'aryŏng" (*toraji* = bellflower).[35] According to former holder Yi Ch'angbae, his teacher Pak Ch'unjae told him that the reason for this was that at the end of the song there used to be mention of a bellflower in a line that has since disappeared.[36] Unlike the other songs in the core repertoire, neither the Kyŏnggi nor the northwestern version, which is called "Kyŏngballim" or "Kyŏng sagŏri" (A Sunny Crossroads), has an introduction, but singers sometimes sing the introductory line of Song of the Rear Mountain instead. It describes scenery and makes references to Buddhism by naming temples and alluding to reincarnation, by pondering over the spirits of a fallen tree and a bird. Hwang transcribes the first verse of Fast Mountain Song as follows:

> Why have you lain down there on the blue mountain, old pine tree? Is it because you snapped, unable to withstand the wind and the snow? Who knows whether the wind has blown? In the meantime, who knows about the accident? The tree trunk sways and the summer rain is about to pour as clouds gather on Mount Mansu.[37]

Hwang's version of the first verse of "Kyŏngballim" is as follows:

> In the region bordering on China [i.e., Korea] these are noisy times. Half of the three mountains stretch beyond the blue sky. On the sand bank in the middle of a division of two streams sits a white egret. You just hassle me by saying "where shall we go?" You just tag after my heels saying, "where shall we go?" [So] I suggest we go to Ch'ŏngnyong in Ansŏng.[38]

Like other *Sant'aryŏng,* Fast Mountain Song starts slowly but gradually quickens and becomes more cheerful as it starts to follow a six-beat (6/8) rhythmic cycle (one beat = 126~132/min). The Kyŏnggi and northwestern versions of the song are not only nearly identical—Han Manyŏng recalls Yi Ch'angbae once telling him that the slightest error could make them sound indistinguishable—but their melody is very similar to that of Song of the Rear Mountain.[39]

Shin Ch'an'gyun argues that a song called "Homi kŏri," the title of which he says derives from *homi* (hoe) and *kŏllida* (to hang),[40] should be added to the Kyŏnggi repertoire.[41] Since the song shares many thematic and structural aspects with the four basic songs of the repertoire, Yi Ch'angbae also supports the song's inclusion in the official *Sant'aryŏng* genre. The song was often sung in the Kyŏnggi countryside around mid-July as part of a folk play to celebrate the completion of the rice weeding, but it was eventually incorporated into the repertoire of courtesans/entertainment girls (*kisaeng*) and thus was performed seated as well. Shin reports that the song was transmitted by Kim Hyŏn'gyu (1942–2004), who was born in Koyang City.[42] In the early 1990s, after doing some teaching at the school of the then holder of *Sŏdo sori,* Yi Ŭn'gwan, Kim set up his own institute, the Institute for Folksongs from Kyŏnggi Province and Standing Mountain Songs (Kyŏnggi minyo sŏnsori sant'aryŏng hagwŏn). His school looked out on Tansŏngsa Theater, just off Chongno 3-ga in central Seoul, and was located in a building across from where Hwang Yongju had his institute until the late 1990s.[43] When I asked Hwang Yongju, holder of *Sant'aryŏng,* and Yi Ŭnju, holder of *Kyŏnggi minyo,* about Kim's activities, both singers were rather dismissive of his skills, but in 1998 he was nevertheless appointed as holder of Kyŏnggi Province Intangible Cultural Property no. 22, *Koyang Songp'o Homi kŏri*, which comprises music and ritual from Songp'o-dong in Koyang City. Because of the separate designation, and its strong emphasis on farming, the song can no longer be included in *Sant'aryŏng*'s standard repertoire.

The Early Years

There is a consensus among scholars that *Sant'aryŏng* are based on the songs sung by itinerant Buddhist entertainment troupes called *sadangp'ae* (temple group troupes; *p'ae* = troupe) or *yŏsadang* (female temple groups). The troupes go back as far as the early Chosŏn dynasty (1392–1910), when just like two other major types of troupes, *kwangdae* and *kŏllipp'ae,*[44] they traveled across the country to earn their living by performing music and dance at market places and town squares. Until the nineteenth century, the troupes had semiformal ties to Buddhist temples, on whose behalf they are said to have performed.[45] In exchange for the earnings they passed on, the temples provided them with food, lodging, and patronage. But the ties the troupes had with temples were controversial. At the start of the long dynasty in which Confucianism became the dominant state religion, King T'aejo (r. 1392–1398) banned the establishment of new Buddhist temples and set up a registration system for monks in order to prevent the religion from growing further. Many Buddhist temples were subsequently destroyed and their properties and slaves confiscated. Buddhism was given some chance for recovery from the late fifteenth to the mid-sixteenth century, but the religion was fervently suppressed after that and eventually turned into a faith practiced primarily by women.[46] Although they were not officially tied to the Buddhist institution, *sadangp'ae* were not exempted from government prosecution. Yi Nŭnghwa cites a government ordinance from the True Record of the Chosŏn Dynasty (*Chosŏn wangjo shillok*) that was allegedly sent out to the governors of all provinces in August of the eleventh year of King Sejo (1465): "The so-called *sajang* [*sadang*] falsely claim a connection with Wŏn'gak Temple and they beg for offerings while carrying writings with the seal of Wŏn'gak Temple on it. They go around all regions and because they often collect valuables, we inform the governors of all districts and order them to immediately arrest and imprison the people who behave in this way, whether they are monks or not, and report to the court."[47] Possibly because of continued government interference, by the nineteenth century the troupes' connection with temples was lost.[48]

Sadangp'ae consisted of between one and five women, with whom the term *sadang* became associated, and between four and ten men, the *kŏsa* (lit. "Buddhist devotees").[49] The men wore trousers and jackets, and towels around their heads, while the women wore brightly colored skirts, jackets, and, occasionally, a fur cap known as an *ayam*.[50] The troupes' repertoires consisted of songs, Buddhist chant, dance, and acrobatics. Yi Pohyŏng told me:

> Initially, these troupes sang Buddhist songs, but many people disliked them so they started singing [a sequence of] cheerful folksongs called "P'an yŏmbul" [staged Buddhist chant]. The women just sang while the men [sang and] accompanied the singing by playing small drums and dancing. The singing was antiphonal, or call and response. The *sadang* did the call part [*apsori*] and the *kŏsa* would respond, with the drums as well, followed by another woman singing a call part. Because they performed for a long time, they had to sing various songs. They first sang some Buddhist songs and then many folksongs.[51]

Because very few sources describe the troupes' activities during the Chosŏn dynasty, scholars generally rely on the work by two folklorists active during the colonial period, Yi Nŭnghwa and Song Sŏkha (1904–1948). Song briefly discusses how the troupes staged their performances,[52] but even though he, unlike

Yi, based his analysis partly on fieldwork,[53] neither scholar offers a clear insight into the style and content of performances in the earlier centuries of the Chosŏn dynasty.

The temples that had a connection with *sadangp'ae* were able to use the earnings the latter passed on to cover their building and repair costs,[54] but they were not always able to provide lodging within their perimeters. Some of them arranged lodging at a cabin in a nearby village, which was nicknamed *sadanggol* (*sadang* camp). A famous one, near Ch'ŏngnyong Temple, was located in Ansŏng City, in Kyŏnggi province. It appears in the lyrics of "Chat'an'ga" (Song of Lament), which Yi Nŭnghwa included in his 1927 study as part of the repertoire of *sadangp'ae*:[55]

> I put on a pretty dress made of the finely wrinkled ramie from Hansan and go to Ch'ŏngnyong Temple in Ansŏng to perform.
> Is my hand a door-ring? This fella grabs it; that fella grabs it.
> Is my mouth a wine cup? This fella sucks it; that fella sucks it.
> Is my stomach a ferry? This fella rides it; that fella rides it.

Sim Woo-Sung, a scholar and performer well known for his work on itinerant performing troupes, argues that the *sadangp'ae* were little more than bands of prostitutes and the performance merely a pretext.[56] Although the troupes made money by performing and selling Buddhist amulets (*pujŏk*) from the temple they had a connection with, he believes that prostitution was their primary source of income and that they dedicated only a portion of their income to their patron temple. Sim is not the first academic to have held this view of the troupes' primary service. On the back cover of the October 1940 issue of the partly Korean-run journal *Korean Folklore* (*Chosŏn minsok*), in which Song Sŏkha's study on *sadang* was first published, the title of his article "Sadang go" (Scrutinizing *sadang*) is translated into English as "On 'Sadang' or Wandering Prostitute Singers." Although each woman formed a pair[57] with one of the *kŏsa*, Sim believes that the latter were merely "parasites," as they did not perform any major part in the act.[58] While the *mogap* (leader) took care of management, the other men made themselves useful by looking after the women, either by acting as their pimps or by doing small chores for them, including carrying heavy luggage.[59]

According to Sim, *sadangp'ae* began to disappear toward the end of the Chosŏn dynasty, with the last troupes performing in the 1930s.[60] Yi Pohyŏng argues that their disappearance may have been occasioned by people's dislike of women singing in marketplaces,[61] but because the troupes had always belonged to the lowest social class, there may be another explanation. Kim Sung Soon posits that the abolition of palace and municipal slavery in 1801 removed the incentive for many commoner women to join itinerant performing troupes,[62] but they nevertheless persisted for at least another century until they eventually transformed into their predominantly male counterpart, the *namsadangp'ae* (*nam* = male).[63] For various aspects of their performance, these *namsadangp'ae* used boys in their preteens or younger, called *mudong* (dancing boys).[64] Their small weight allowed the group to perform complex acrobatic routines. But although the boys were able to reach higher octaves relatively easily, they had inferior voices and were unable to sing more elaborate Buddhist chants. The troupes therefore performed mostly masked dance dramas, farmers' music, and puppet plays.[65]

Like the *sadang*, the boys were often used for prostitution, so having good looks was important.[66] Sim is therefore rather cynical about the image painted by the *Sant'aryŏng* lyrics. Rather than seeing the *sadangp'ae* and *namsadangp'ae* as followers of some Buddhist order, he regards them as troupes of lesbians and homosexuals, respectively, who, given the strict moral codes of Chosŏn society, needed to roam over the peninsula in order to live independently.[67] The 1991 Great Dictionary of Korean Folklore (*Han'guk minsok taesajŏn*) also makes note of the male troupes' homosexuality but does not mention if this was a private matter, merely related to the troupe members, or commercial, born out of a need to survive, or both.[68] A former member of a *namsadangp'ae* has, however, commented that when he and others performed sexual acts with other men it was for purely commercial reasons.[69]

In the early twentieth century, apart from these types of itinerant troupes, a new kind of singing formation emerged, called *sant'aryŏngp'ae* or *sŏnsorip'ae*. The troupes, which comprised up to eight members, were mostly active in Seoul, where they busked standing at marketplaces and town squares and, on some occasions, though mostly in a seated position, in theaters and at the houses of aristocrats.[70] Their repertoire and stylistic pedigree are traced back to the first known singer of *Sant'aryŏng*, Ŭit'aek (1780–?), who headed a troupe named after him. The singer Hŏ Tŏksŏn and his pupil Kim Pangul from Pyongyang are credited with having used the *Kyŏnggi sant'aryŏng* of Ŭit'aek and his student Chongdae to create a northwestern repertoire, but Seoul continued to offer the primary venues for the troupes.[71] Chongdae passed on his repertoire and style of singing to Shin Nakt'aek,[72] who became a noted singer around the end of the nineteenth century and at the start of the colonial period joined a *sant'aryŏngp'ae* in Seoul that included the renowned singers Kim Pyŏnggyu, Kim Ŭngnyŏl, and the female singer Wŏlsŏn. Although it was officially named the Hojo Tari Troupe (*tari* = bridge)—named after the Hojo Bridge in Seoul's central Chin'gogae area, today known as Ch'ungmuro—it was also known as the Chin'gogae Wŏlsŏni Troupe due to Wŏlsŏn's popularity.[73]

Several *sant'aryŏngp'ae* from Seoul were named after a bridge because of their involvement in the national folk festival known as *Tapkyo* (*tap* = to tread;

kyo = bridge). Celebrated on the fifteenth day of the first month of the lunar calendar, the festival is believed to date back to the early days of the Chosŏn dynasty.[74] Regardless of age, sex or social status, people would gather on this day to cross twelve bridges, or, presumably, any bridge as many as twelve times, in order to avert any illness of their legs and feet—the word *tari* also means leg(s)—throughout the year. In Seoul, everyone would participate in the celebrations, though according to Chang Sahun, the aristocracy performed on the preceding day in order to avoid mixing with the common people. Im Tonggwŏn argues that they performed on the day after the event as well, though not so much because of the commoners per se, but because on the actual day, popular bridges in the city center were simply too crowded to cross.[75] Indeed, the physical demands of performing on the day of the festival may explain the large number of female performers on the following day.[76] Sometime before the start of the official parades, residents of Seoul would come to the Poshin'gak bell pavilion on "Bell Street" (Chongno) in the center of town to await the sound of the bell before heading off to their favorite bridge accompanied by the music of a troupe.

Among the most prominent *sant'aryŏngp'ae* from the Seoul area were the Ttuksŏm Troupe, which included the noted singers Hwang Kiun, Yi Tongshik, and Yi Tongun; and the Kwach'ŏn Panga Tari Troupe, named after a bridge by a water mill (*panga*), which included the well-known singers Han Int'aek and So Wanjun (b. 1870), the teacher of later holder Chŏng Tŭngman. Other well-known troupes included the Nalt'ang Troupe from Pyongyang;[77] the Paeogae Majŏn Tari Troupe, which included the noted singer Pak Samsoe; the Ch'ŏng Troupe from Ch'ŏngp'a-dong; the Tchanji (=pickled radish) Troupe, made up of the singers Kim T'aeun, T'ak Pongman, Yi Myŏngsan, Yi Myŏnggil, and Paek Naktang;[78] and the Wangshimni Troupe from Seoul's Wangshimni District, which included the eminent singers Ha Sunil and Yi Myŏnggil (1890–1960). Besides these famous troupes, there were the Han'gang Troupe, presumably named after one of the bridges across the river (*kang/gang*) Han in Seoul; the Soebunggu Troupe, from Sŏbinggo; the Chamunbak Troupe; the Yongsan Samgae Troupe, from Yongsan District and the adjacent Map'o District; the Tongmak Troupe, from Kongdŏk-tong; and the Sŏngbuk-tong Troupe, named after the area northeast of central Seoul.[79]

Because *sant'aryŏngp'ae* often had female members, many scholars believe they originated from *sadangp'ae*.[80] Indeed, there is sufficient evidence for a historical link between today's *Sant'aryŏng* and *sadangp'ae*. Perhaps the strongest argument is provided by the numerous references to Buddhism in the lyrics of the former. The inclusion of the songs "Nollyang," "Sagŏri," and Song of the Frog in the repertoire of both troupes provides further evidence, as does the shared practice of performing standing and playing the *sogo* drum.[81] There may have also been a connection between the song repertoires of the *sant'aryŏngp'ae* and the *sadangp'ae*'s eventual successors, the *namsadangp'ae,* but Yi Ch'angbae strongly rejected the notion. When he asked holder of *Namsadang* Nam Unyong about his troupe's "P'an yŏmbul," the latter allegedly confirmed that there was no relation with that of *Sant'aryŏng* whatsoever.[82]

Since it continued to develop after it was officially recognized, the official *Sant'aryŏng* repertoire has come to differ considerably from that sung by troupes approximately a century ago. Not only has it now lost its connection with Buddhist practice, but its lyrics have changed, and as discussed later in this chapter, it is performed increasingly by women. Unfortunately, although commercial recordings of *Sant'aryŏng* have been produced since the early 1910s,[83] the first complete sound recording of the official genre was not produced until 1993, so discussion of any changes made to the tradition during the decades prior can be based on lyrical transcriptions and images only.[84] Compared to the lyrics of Kyŏnggi *Sant'aryŏng* as transcribed by Chang Sahun in his 1966 government report, the current ones are shorter and appear to have replaced a significant amount of vernacular with Sino-Korean terms. It is possible that some embellishment took place, probably at the hand of a highly respected singer such as Yi Ch'angbae, who had vast knowledge of Korean traditional song genres and held a job teaching *kisaeng* for many years.

Whereas the sequence called "P'an yŏmbul" was part of the repertoire of the early troupes, it disappeared as a separate song sometime between 1916 and 1966. Han Manyŏng and Yi Pohyŏng believe that "P'an yŏmbul" is an old version of "Nollyang," but lyrical transcriptions of the two songs differ considerably.[85] Only a few phrases appear in both transcriptions, albeit in slightly altered form due in part to the application of different Korean orthographies. A comparison of a transcription of "P'an yŏmbul" published in Pak Sŭngyŏp's 1916 collection *Hyŏnhaeng ilsŏn chapka* (Japanese and Korean Songs of Today) with a 1966 version of "Nollyang" as sung by Yi Ch'angbae—one of the first transcriptions of "Nollyang" published after the Korean War—reveals, among other things, that the first begins with a long introduction that is missing in the latter (which is almost identical to that by Hwang Yongju, translated above).[86] The first verse of this introduction is similar to that of "Chin'guk myŏngsan" (The Famous Mountains Buttressing the Nation), a *tan'ga* (*tan* = short; *ga* = song) that was used as a warm-up song by *p'ansori* singers in the past.[87] The verse also appears in a version of the Kyŏnggi folksong "Ch'angbu t'aryŏng" (*ch'angbu* = husband of a shaman), which is believed to have developed out of a shaman song: "From the lofty peaks of famous mountains buttressing the nation, one peak covered in yellow flowers stands out in the blue sky."[88]

One characteristic found in both "P'an yŏmbul" and "Nollyang" is the mention of *ch'ŏngnyong*. In an earlier transcription of "P'an yŏmbul" that was first published in 1915 and is included in Chang's CPC report,[89] one finds the passage, "*Ansan-ira chusan-ira chwau-rado ch'ŏngnyong*," which can be translated as "whether it's Ansan or Chusan, Ch'ŏngnyong will be on either your left or right." In this case, Ansan (Peaceful Mountain), Chusan (Main Mountain), and Ch'ŏngnyong (Blue Dragon) are geomantic concepts referring to the three mountains crucial to containing vital, positive energy within a specific site, for example, for burial or construction. According to geomantic practice, the four most important mountains are the tallest Main Mountain north of the favorable site, White Tiger (Paekho) to the west, Blue Dragon to the east, and Red Bird (Chujak)—made up of the two mountains Ansan and Chosan (Morning Mountain)—to the south.[90] The association of *ch'ŏngnyong* with Ch'ŏngnyong Temple would have been made after "P'an yŏmbul" was replaced with "Nollyang."[91] The current version of the latter song includes the reference, but the oldest surviving textual transcription of the northwestern version of "Nollyang," from 1914, does not; nor do transcriptions of Kyŏnggi versions from 1921 and 1922.[92] A contemporary transcription by Hwang Yongju of the northwestern version of "Twissan t'aryŏng" includes a final, ninth verse that more strongly relates the current *Sant'aryŏng* genre to *sadang*.[93] Since the verse does not appear in any other transcription, it is likely to have been composed by Hwang Yongju, presumably in an effort to support the historical legacy of his tradition: "The East Gate road in Ha-dong, in Kyŏngsang province, leads to Ch'ŏngnyong Temple in Kyŏnggi province, but in Hwanghae province many *kŏsa* and *sadang* gather in front of Sŏngjubŏp Temple on Mount Kuwŏl in Munhwa and night and day, day and night they learn how to dance and sing "Nollyang" to the beat of the *sogo*, suggesting they go on a boat trip to Chilp'odae by the five rivers, eh . . ."

Two Personal Stories

Chŏng Tŭngman

The last two active holders of *Sant'aryŏng* have been Hwang Yongju and his predecessor, the late Chŏng Tŭngman. Chŏng was born in the township of Sŏbinggo, in central Seoul's Yongsan District, on October 27, 1907. Although Chŏng was born as the eleventh child, with four brothers and six sisters, his brothers all died early, leaving him as the only remaining son with the obligation to look after his parents in their old age. Chŏng showed a great passion for singing from early on. He disliked school and preferred going to places where folk music was performed. Since it was located at a point where traffic from five important branches of Seoul's Han River converged, his hometown was an important trading place. It was usually crowded with sailors from different parts of the country, so many troupes of entertainers came to the town in the hope of earning good money both at the open markets and at the sailors' frequent parties.[94] Chŏng fell in love with the music and often watched the performances while quietly moving his shoulders up and down to the beat. At other times, when wealthy young aristocrats (*yangban*) took boat rides accompanied by young girl entertainers, Chŏng would follow the boats by walking along the river shore to listen to the girls' singing.[95]

When Chŏng turned fifteen, his family moved to the township of Amsa in Kwangju County, southeast of Seoul. But some five years later a major flood forced them to move back to the capital, to the township of Huam-dong.[96] Around 1928, Chŏng took lessons in the *p'yŏng* (common) and *chirŭm* (yelling) types of *shijo* (sung poems) with the singer Mun Segŭn. After one year, when he felt he had nothing left to teach Chŏng, Mun introduced him to the well-known folksong singer Ch'oe Kyŏngshik.[97] One day, when he and his new teacher were sitting in a public bath and Chŏng confessed that his voice could not reach the tones he heard his teacher sing, Ch'oe reacted with delight: "Well, now your ears have opened up! There are people who've studied for decades and still haven't opened their ears."[98] Yet when Ch'oe told him that he had found a successor in him, Chŏng felt the responsibility weigh heavily on him. He therefore began studying with Kim T'aebong, a later holder of *Sant'aryŏng*. During this time, Kim introduced Chŏng to Yi Ch'angbae, who at the time was working as a civil servant conducting land surveys. Chŏng and Yi would eventually become close friends and fellow holders of *Sant'aryŏng*. After studying with Kim for one year, Chŏng took lessons with Cho Tŏkkyŏng, who had established himself as a performer of both *Sant'aryŏng* and the *t'aep'yŏngso* (conical oboe). It was Cho who taught Chŏng how to sing the *Sant'aryŏng* repertoire.

By the late 1920s, Chŏng had begun to lead a very busy life, selling fruit and vegetables at Namdaemun market during the days and spending most of his evenings singing folksongs. From the age of twenty, Chŏng also worked as a gardener, mostly for Japanese customers. Once he learned how to tend Japanese-style gardens, this provided him with an easy way to earn a living.[99] To help look after his parents, Chŏng eventually moved back to his native township,[100] where, at the age of twenty-five, he met So Wanjun, the lead singer of the Kwach'ŏn Panga Tari Troupe. So had moved to the township of Sŏbinggo when his son took a job working as a civil servant for the local railroads. He found employment teaching folksongs at a local community center for the elderly (*kyŏngnodang*), and it was there that he would help Chŏng hone his skills.[101]

Before liberation, Chŏng became a member of the Korean Research Committee for Song and Dance (Chosŏn kamu yŏn'guhoe), which had been established by Ch'oe Kyŏngshik for the purpose of bringing together singers of both the Kyŏnggi and the northwestern repertoires of *Sant'aryŏng*. The committee, which included well-known singers such as Ch'oe Chŏngshik and Pak Ch'unjae, acted as a society of friends rather than an agency, as it did not offer performances or teach up-and-coming singers.[102] Shortly after the end of the Pacific War, Chŏng joined the newly established Korean Traditional Music Entertainment Company (*Kugak yŏnyesa*). Because it included noted folksong singers such as Yi Ŭn'gwan and Chang Sop'al, the troupe was fairly successful and was frequently broadcast on the radio. As a result, Chŏng's income from singing increased considerably. While the monthly salary of singers in most other troupes was approximately 30,000 wŏn, equivalent to a little below today's minimum wage, Chŏng was paid almost twice as much.[103] He was never, however, able to rely on his income from singing and was forced to continue to take gardening jobs until he was in his fifties.[104]

Despite the relative popularity of *Sant'aryŏng* during the colonial period, the status of the performers remained low. Chŏng Tŭngman said, "Even though I studied *Sant'aryŏng*, I didn't really want to. In those days, people who performed *shijo* or *kasa* [narrative songs] were given the honorable title 'Sir' and they were invited to sing by the aristocracy [*yangban*], but those who sang *Sant'aryŏng* were called 'balladeers' [*t'aryŏngkkun*] and were treated with contempt."[105] Chang Sahun quotes the noted *p'ansori* singer Shin Ŭnhyu as saying that before the Korean War, *p'ansori* singers avoided singing songs from the *Sant'aryŏng* repertoire on the radio because they were considered to be below their status. He notes that the low status of the *sadangp'ae* is reflected in the explicit lyrics of some of the songs.[106]

When the Korean War broke out, the Traditional Music Entertainment Company fell apart. For a period of approximately four years, Chŏng lived in the township of Yanghwa, in south Ch'ungch'ŏng province, from where he commuted to the city of Kongju to sell fish. When he moved back to Seoul not long after the war, Chŏng joined Yi Ch'angbae's private school, the Korean Institute of Traditional Vocal Music (Ch'ŏnggu kojŏn sŏngak hagwŏn), which had moved from one of Seoul's central neighborhoods, Tonŭi-dong, to another, Kyŏnji-dong, where it had originally been located. Lessons included *Sant'aryŏng* and *Kyŏnggi minyo*, and they were offered free of charge. Yi had taken over teaching from another later holder of *Sant'aryŏng*, Chang Haksŏn, immediately after the Korean War. Although Yi managed to complete his comprehensive work on traditional Korean song styles, A Compendium of Vocal Music in Korea (*Han'guk kach'ang taegye*) in 1976, his physical condition was weak. Chŏng ended up doing all the teaching, from the late 1960s onward, not long before he was appointed holder of *Sant'aryŏng*.[107]

Some time after his appointment in 1968, Chŏng re-established the Korean Folksong Research Society (Han'guk minyo yŏn'guhoe), an organization that under the management of Wŏn Ch'unghŭi set out to propagate the many folksongs passed on in Kyŏnggi province apart from *chapka*.[108] An earlier organization by the same name had existed since 1962 and is noted for having organized a folksong festival at the National Theater in March 1967.[109] It is possible that Wŏn's lack of experience prompted noted singer An Pich'wi to once again re-establish the organization only a year later. She assumed the position of director, with Kim Ch'ŏnhŭng as a permanent advisory member.[110] Since Kim was a member of the CPC, he may have had a hand in the relatively early recognition of *Sant'aryŏng* as IICP. Although it lacked sponsors for large-scale projects, it managed to organize major annual events such as *Kugag-ŭi hyanggi* (The Fragrance of Traditional Korean Music), *Minyo paegilchang* (Folksong Composition Contest), and *Ridŭm '81* (Rhythm '81). Although the activities came to a stop in 1979, An's senior students re-established the organization once again in 2006 and it remains active today.[111]

Chŏng spent much of his time teaching special scholarship students, including the current holders Ch'oe Ch'angnam and Hwang Yongju. He established the Society for the Study and Preservation of Standing Mountain Songs (Sŏnsori sant'aryŏng yŏn'gu pojonhoe) on the fifth floor of the Hansŏng building just north of Chongno 3-ga, in Myo-dong, and was able to rely considerably on Yi Ch'angbae for help with management and paying bills.[112] Chŏng meanwhile became the director and departmental chairman of the Society for Korean Traditional Music (Han'guk kugak hyŏphoe), an organization consisting mainly of folk musicians, including CPC members Pak Hŏnbong and Kim Ch'ŏnhŭng, as well as Yi Ch'angbae and An Pich'wi.[113]

Chŏng Tŭngman died on October 30, 1992, leaving behind his wife, Ch'oe Pobae, two daughters, and a son. A few months earlier, on July 1, his students Ch'oe Ch'angnam (b. 1935) and Hwang Yongju (b. 1937) were appointed to replace him. Although Ch'oe was two years senior to Hwang and had been appointed future holder (*poyuja hubo*) a year prior to his peer, Hwang was appointed holder first because he concentrated on singing *Sant'aryŏng.* Not long before his death, Chŏng explained his preference for Hwang as holder: "I hope my "assistant teacher," Hwang Yongju, will be appointed soon, before I die. It seems that only then the songs will be transmitted. Actually, "future holder" Ch'oe Ch'angnam may be well known because of his many appearances on radio stations, but since he emphasizes only the *Kyŏnggi minyo* [genre] he neglects *Sant'aryŏng.* However much talent you have, the cultural property only has value if you know how to teach students."[114]

Hwang Yongju

Hwang Yongju was born in Changgil-dong's Songsŏlli, in Kongju City, south Ch'ungch'ŏng province, on December 3, 1937. Hwang recalls that when he was seven years old, his family moved to Ch'uksalli, Kŭmnam-myŏn, in nearby Yŏn'gi County. He lived there until he was twenty years old and during this period he attended Yŏngmyŏng High School.[115] When he was twenty-three years old, Hwang took lessons in *shijo* with Yi Chuhwan at the National Gugak

Center in Seoul. After one week, however, on October 14, 1960, he moved to Yi Ch'angbae's institute. While continuing his day job, he studied with Yi every night, enjoying private lessons over a period of eight months. For four hours at a time, Yi taught *kasa, shijo, Sant'aryŏng,* and other folksongs.[116] Sometimes Yi also encouraged him to perform, but there were not many opportunities to do so:

> There was no house where we could sing. And what is more, in our case, the seniors who had no levels left to study, as well as those who had learned a lot and were [very] active, performed at traditional music events a few times a year and also on the radio, but other than that there was nothing. In addition, during the course, the teacher would perform on the radio a couple of times a year, but there was little opportunity to go and watch it, or [to] try singing, you see. To sing as often as we do nowadays was impossible then. That's because, at the time, the situation in Korea wasn't as globalized as it is now. But it was fixed likc this after the Pacific War and before and after the Korean War, and because foreign culture came in, it was a period during which the Korean culture was forgotten for a moment. The people were like that and they were concerned with foreign culture. During that period, therefore, traditional music performers didn't get on the radio or things like that, just like now, and although they did perform, there weren't many traditional music performances.[117]

According to Hwang, opportunities for folk singers to perform on stage generally came after the introduction of the Cultural Properties Protection Law in 1962. Indeed, in the 1970s, soon after the first holders of *Sant'aryŏng* were appointed, senior *Sant'aryŏng* singers began to be regularly asked to perform on television and even overseas.[118]

Having graduated from Yi Ch'angbae's institute in February 1965,[119] in 1968 Hwang set up the Institute of Korean Folk Artistry (Taehan minsok yesul hagwŏn) on the premises of the Society for the Study and Preservation of Standing Mountain Songs. In 1982, Hwang renamed it the Society for the Preservation of *Sant'aryŏng.*[120] Because the number of students steadily increased, the single large room and small adjacent office eventually became too small to be shared by both the institute and the society. Despite Hwang's good health, the lack of an elevator made it difficult for him to easily reach the premises. Around the turn of the millennium, therefore, Hwang moved his preservation society to the Seoul Training Center for Important Intangible Cultural Properties (Seoul chungyo muhyŏng munhwajae chŏnsu hoegwan) in Samsŏng-dong, in Kangnam District, which offers much more practice space as well as facilities on the

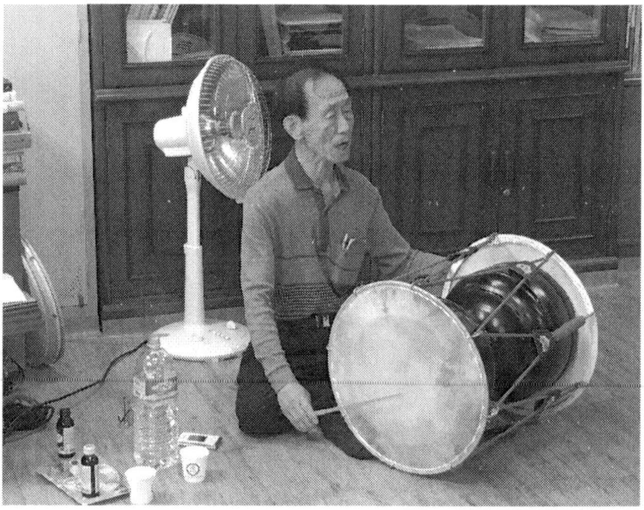

Hwang Yongju teaching at his institute in Myo-dong, on December 14, 2015.

ground floor. In 2015, however, Hwang relocated back to Myo-dong, to the fourth floor of a building alongside Tonhwamun Road.

Today, students join the society to learn all kinds of folksongs. Hwang used to teach five days a week, but he has had to cut back due to his old age. In 1993, Hwang had approximately twenty students, including four female special scholarship students—Paek Aejin (b. 1954), Hong Yŏnsun (b. 1955), Yŏm Kyŏngsuk (b. 1969), and Kang Migyŏng (b. 1967). In 2009, holder-elect Ch'oe Ch'angnam (b. 1935) was also appointed holder. But while his assistant teachers used to be all male, they now include apart from Pak T'aeyŏ (b. 1924), Yŏm Ch'angsun (b. 1945) and Pang Yŏnggi (b. 1958), the women Ch'oe Sukhŭi and Yi Kŏnja (b. 1960).[121] The number of students has almost tripled, but in all classes, across generations, female students far outnumber their male counterparts.[122]

Changes in the Status Quo

One of the genre's most striking features is the uniformity of the performances in song, movement, and appearance. Even so, the actual dress of *Sant'aryŏng* singers has changed considerably since the 1970s. A picture of a formal performance from 1976 shows the lead singers with "normal" hairstyles and wearing plain white folk costumes, while in the back singers can be seen wearing what are presumably silk waistcoats.[123] Pictures published from 1984 until the late 1990s, however, show all singers wearing blue silk waistcoats.[124] If singers performed in a style faithful to the genre's origin—the itinerant entertainment troupes at the end of the Chosŏn dynasty—then silk waistcoats ought not to be worn, because only aristocrats had traditionally worn the fabric.[125] Because of this, Yi Pohyŏng did not approve of the shirts,[126] but he and Han Manyŏng point out that a *p'ansori* text written down by Shin Chaehyo, includes a passage on *sadangp'ae* in which the *sadang* as by some miracle come out of a gourd with their hair covered by "purple silken" towels. And in a small study of the *sadang* first published in 1936, Paek Hwarang speaks of "silk in five bright colors." Although the former story is fantasy, and the latter unsubstantiated, it is likely that *sadang* wore brightly colored pieces of cloth in order to stand out from the crowd and add color to their performances.[127]

In the 1970s and 1980s, two other attributes were added to the formal costume of male *Sant'aryŏng* singers. Those surrounding the holders of the genre began to tie their hair up in a knot, around which they tied a version of the traditional hair band made of horsehair called the *manggŏn*.[128] The use of the hairband is curious, as there are no signs of it ever having been used by any past itinerant entertainment troupe. Since the 1970s, straw sandals (*ch'ohye*) have become another new addition, presumably in an effort to return to a more traditional costume. The image on the cover of this book shows the Tchanji Troupe from Seoul performing in leather shoes in May 1938. Such footwear is likely to have been considered a luxury and regarded as an improvement, but its use in performances would have been uncommon. Similarly, between the 1970s and 1990s, many folk musicians wore white sneakers, even at National Folk Arts Contests. Although this may have been a purely financial matter at first (sneakers are not expensive), it is possible that the shoes were considered a style improvement. Straw sandals, on the other hand, may not be comfortable in the municipal areas where *Sant'aryŏng* are now mostly performed, though they are well suited for rural, unpaved terrain.

The drive toward uniformity also led to the temporary exclusion of female singers from formal performances, resulting in a more masculine overall sound.[129] Although a female singer appears in Yi Ch'angbae's 1976 *A Compendium of Vocal Music in Korea,*[130] from then until the late 1990s female singers were absent in all formal pictures of the official group of *Sant'aryŏng* performers, despite the fact that their number had grown considerably during that time. The particular attraction of *Sant'aryŏng* to the many women who have taken up studying the genre in recent decades lies, aside from the social, performance and musical aspects, in the practical and social implications of their involvement. Unlike some other genres of traditional performing arts, *Sant'aryŏng* is based in the center of Seoul and it is not strongly associated with Buddhist or shamanistic practices. Participation therefore does not require too much free time, and does not contradict Christian beliefs.[131]

The number of female students now exceeds that of male students, making the *Sant'aryŏng* genre once again appear "female."[132] This phenomenon has occurred in many other forms of folk art too, including *Kyŏnggi minyo* and *Sŏdo sori,* and as discussed in chapter 2 derives in most cases from the Confucian pressure on men to support their family; folk music rarely guarantees a sufficient income so the majority of those involved are amateur women.[133] Although studies on *Sant'aryŏng* acknowledge that the genre's origin is both female and male, Im Tonggwŏn was nevertheless unhappy with the development:

> *Sŏnsori sant'aryŏng,* like *nongak,* has always been something that men do, not women; even *nongak* is nowadays dominated by women. And even masked dance dramas, which were things that men did, not women, is now performed by a large number of female university students, so there is no proper relation with the transmission of culture. We have in such cases never appointed women as *in'gan munhwajae* [human cultural properties]. We look for things that are practiced in their original forms, the old ways, unchanged. Yet, this—let's call it the "exchange of roles" nowadays . . . —this is now all changed and Korean women are now boldly getting into what men should do. They go out playing the hourglass drum and the *puk* [barrel drum], don't they? We cannot change that situation, but we don't appoint them as human cultural properties.[134]

A contemporary female performance of *Sant'aryŏng* is certainly different from a male one from a few decades ago. Until the mid-1990s, official performances of *Sant'aryŏng* were carried out mostly by men, who lay great emphasis on the dynamics of their singing and drumming and on rousing their audience. Because the volume would go up considerably at times, the singers' voices often ended up sounding raw and emotional toward the end of the performance. But there was a lot of humor: the singers contorted their faces during the solo parts and expressed much delight during the riotous drumming climaxes, when they seemed determined to finally break the skins of their handheld drums, often with mischievous looks on their faces. They would hold their drums in their left hand in such a way that it seemed like an anvil they were hammering a hot sword on.[135] The groups that have since represented the *Sant'aryŏng* tradition, on the other hand, focus on the elegance of the performance. A group of mostly women now stand dressed in elegant *hanbok,* swaying softly left and right, with composed facial expressions and their hair tied back with a long hairpin. Although their voices are powerful, there is less depth in their voices, and rather than on the dynamics of their music, the emphasis lies on the melody of the songs and the spectacle of the brightly colored line-up. It is nevertheless unlikely that many people will recognize the changes, or even care. At the public performances of *Sant'aryŏng* I attended in the early to mid-1990s, the average age of the audience was well above sixty. Younger generations will grow up with the new version of this tradition and become accustomed to the new standard.

Sedentary Entertainment: *Kyŏnggi minyo*

The genre of *Kyŏnggi minyo* (Folksongs from Kyŏnggi Province), which usually involves one or two women performing seated on a stage floor dressed in a standard *hanbok,* has arguably been institutionalized the longest of all folksong traditions. When in the late nineteenth century many professional folk arts began to converge in Seoul, folksongs from Kyŏnggi province and the northwestern Hwanghae and P'yŏngan provinces were turned into professional art forms suited to the growing number of indoor stages. A large number of singers came from male singing groups, while young women were trained, by men, at institutes for hired female entertainment. Because the genre of *Kyŏnggi minyo* was already recognized as a set repertoire by the turn of the century, it became standardized long before the IICP system was established. Even so, during the first few decades of the colonial period, sound recording technology and radio broadcasting influenced the style of the genre and the status of its singers, allowing some to become household names despite being from working-class or lower middle-class backgrounds. Although these representatives were both male and female, in the 1940s and 1950s a relatively greater number of male singers fell away from the entertainment scene. Whether this was because they had died during warfare, had ended up on the North Korean side of the demilitarized zone, or had chosen a different occupation for their livelihood, the result left more opportunities for female performers. The shift in gender representation in *Kyŏnggi minyo* thus set in before the genre became an IICP, but it was consolidated by the subsequent designation of only female holders for the genre in 1975.

Unlike *Sant'aryŏng* and *Sŏdo sori,* the *Kyŏnggi minyo* genre is not only transmitted by holders and their students but also by a fair number of trained singers in and around the capital with whom they are only loosely associated. During the colonial period, record companies and radio stations helped create recognizable, set repertoires. *Kyŏnggi minyo* began to include popular *t'ongsok* songs from across the country, which led to a degree of diffusion of regional characteristics into the polished songs from the capital.[136] The influence of professionalized *t'ongsok* songs on local (*t'osok*) songs was equally significant, though it is impossible to determine its exact extent. Beginning in the early twentieth century, folksong recordings increasingly featured singers from the capital, and so the Kyŏnggi style undoubtedly left its mark on the style of folksongs outside the province. Many songs from Kyŏnggi province have become interchangeable with the professionalized *t'ongsok minyo,* including the well-known songs "Arirang," "Ch'angbu t'aryŏng," and "Sach'ŏlga" (Song of the Four Seasons). Like other *Kyŏnggi* folksongs, they exhibit the homogenizing effect that resulted from the mingling of myriad folk music styles in the city, which in general entailed a loss of regional vocabulary, a faster and less complex rhythm, and a lighter vibrato.

It is possible that the negative connotation of *chap* (=miscellaneous) in *chapka* (see chapter 2) led the government to settle for the rather broad, existing term, *Kyŏnggi minyo,* to signify the genre of refined folksongs from Kyŏnggi province. Another reason may be that the government did not expect to designate another major genre of folksongs from the province. *Kyŏnggi minyo* could, after all, be expected to comprise all songs sung in the province of the capital, including, for example, unpolished (*t'osok*) local songs, the polished (*t'ongsok*) folksongs from other provinces that were introduced to Seoul by itinerant entertainers, and the lighthearted *hwimori* (fast) *chapka* (*chap* = miscellaneous, *ka* = song). Officially, however, the term *Kyŏnggi minyo* came to define only the twelve refined folksongs, known as *shibi* (twelve) *chapka* or *kin* (long) *chapka.* The songs, which resemble sung poetry and use a considerable number of Sino-Korean words, are sometimes categorized as *chwach'ang* because they are commonly sung while seated.[137]

The *Kyŏnggi* repertoire of *shibi chapka* can be further subdivided into a core of eight (*p'al*) *chapka* and four *chapchapka* (miscellaneous *chapka*). In the past, around the early eighteenth century, performances tended to focus on the first eight. Holder Muk Kyewŏl recalls that when she was young, she only heard the term *p'al chapka,* not *shibi chapka.*[138] In both music and lyrics, these eight songs are considered more graceful than the remaining *chapchapka,* which are likely to have been composed later, at the end of the nineteenth century. These later songs were presumably added to reach a total repertoire of twelve songs, which corresponded with the number of songs in the *p'ansori* and *kasa* genres, with which the folksongs have much in common musically and lyrically.[139] The lyrics of five of the *shibi chapka,* for example, are based on the story of the *p'ansori* piece *Ch'unhyangga* (Song of Ch'unhyang).

The eight core songs of the *Kyŏnggi* genre are "Yusan'ga" (Picnic Song), a song comparing the beauty of a number of Korean mountains and streams with scenic spots in China; "Chŏkpyŏkka" (Song of the Red Cliff), a song depicting a scene from the popular Chinese war novel *Samgukchi yŏnŭi* (Romance of the Three Kingdoms) in which the defeated Cho Cho (Chin. Cao Cao) begs Kwan U (Chin. Guan Yu) for his life; "Chebiga" (Swallow Song), a song describing the scene from the *p'ansori* piece *Hŭngboga* (Song of Hŭngbo) in which Nolbu tries to find a swallow; "Chipchangga" (Grabbing the Stick Song), a song from *Ch'unhyangga* about the beating of Ch'unhyang as she is punished for refusing to bend to the wishes of the corrupt magistrate; "So [short] Ch'unhyangga," a song relating the scene in which Ch'unhyang meets Yi Toryŏng and describes the surroundings of Ch'unhyang's house; "Hyŏngjangga" (Song of the Torturing Stick), describing Ch'unhyang's imprisonment; "P'yŏngyangga" (Song of Pyongyang), a song recounting how a local playboy tries to spend the night with Wŏlsŏn, a *kisaeng* from Pyongyang; and "Sŏnyuga" (Boating Song), a song about the joy of boat trips.

In comparison to *Sant'aryŏng*, the lyrics of *Kyŏnggi minyo* are more melancholic and sorrowful, though they retain some humor. Consider, for example, Yi Ch'angbae's transcription of "Chebiga":

> Deep inside the mountains, an old tiger plays with a fat bitch by biting it and letting it go.
> Like falling leaves in a storm, floating through the blue sky.
> While the sun sets abruptly behind the hills in the West, the moon rises above the peaks in the East. The wild geese fly past high in the sky, honking.
> I am going to net a swallow, I am going to net a swallow. I go out with the net that Fu Xi[140] tied thrown over my shoulders. I go to Mount Mangdang, uiyŏ. . ŏ. . ŏ-ŏ-ŏ-ŏ-ŏ-ŏ-ŏ-ŏ-ŏ-igo, hey, you swallow, where are you flying off to?
> They kick away the white clouds and defy the black clouds flying off high up in the sky, uiyŏ. . ŏ. . ŏ-ŏ-ŏ-ŏ-ŏ-ŏ-ŏ-ŏ-ŏ-ŏ-ŏ-igo, why are you flying away? Come, all of you, flutter to my house.
> Thinking it's a swallow I net an oriole sitting on a willow.
> Aha i-ei ehei eheya ne, where do you go? At midnight, when the moon that stands in the center of the sky is bright, but the sad sound of the common cuckoo can be heard, which lover will come for me?
> In spring, all the birds that fly in the dense woods form pairs and they play together and sing to each other in harmony flying off and on.
> The sky is full with the parrot that speaks well, the crane that dances well and the beautifully marked peacock. Flutter, flutter, flutter, the ruddy kingfisher, the cuckoo and the cicadas [all] come.
> Wild geese come fluttering, goldfinches come tingling, they all come, except for the swallows; where have they all flown off to?[141]

The remaining four *chapchapka* are "Talkŏri" (Monthly Matters), a song about the special characteristics of each of the twelve months; "Shipchangga" (Song of Ten Sticks), another song depicting the scene in which Ch'unhyang is beaten; "Pangmulga" (Song of Fancy Goods), in which women's merchandise items are used one by one as metaphors to express the sorrow felt by a married woman left behind; and "Ch'urin'ga" (Boating Song), a song with little narrative content but in which the initial part derives from the farewell scene of *Ch'unhyangga.* These four songs have all appeared on recordings since the late 1920s, performed by singers such as Song Man'gap, Cho Moran, Pak Puyong, and O T'aesŏk, but they constitute only 15 percent of the total number of *chapka* recordings from the colonial period, suggesting they were less popular than the eight core songs of the *Kyŏnggi* genre.[142]

Unlike the *shibi chapka,* the *hwimori chapka* are relatively short and comical. Although they are not part of the official repertoire, holders of *Kyŏnggi minyo* may sing one or two *hwimori chapka* depending on the occasion. These *chapka* comprise approximately ten songs, including "Kombo t'aryŏng" (Song of the Pockmarked One), "Pawi t'aryŏng" (Song of the Rock), "Saengmae chaba" (Catching a Falcon), and "Yukch'irwŏl hŭrin nal" (Cloudy Days in June and July). Although the songs are believed to originate from *sasŏl shijo*—narrative, sung poems set to a four-tone scale and a five-beat rhythmic pattern—their singing style has come to resemble that of the *shibi chapka,* though they follow a slightly faster (12/8) three-beat pattern and are usually performed standing.[143] Both the *shibi chapka* and *hwimori chapka* are marked by relatively fast rhythmic patterns, many accented notes, and somewhat hasty vibration. They are sung with much power, but the relatively fast overall tempo precludes strong emotional expression.[144] Singers are virtually motionless when they perform sitting down, and they merely sway gently left and right when standing.

The *shibi chapka* are all sung in a 6/4 rhythmic pattern called *todŭri.* Whereas "Chebiga" and "Hyŏngjangga" double in pace at the start, and "Talkŏri" does so at the end, "Chipchangga" is sung at a double pace throughout.[145] Unlike that of *Sŏdo chapka,* the meter of *Kyŏnggi chapka* is set. The melodic style of most songs is similar to that of the northwestern region, but "Sŏnyuga," "P'yŏngyangga," "Talkŏri," and "Ch'urin'ga" follow a pentatonic system common to the Seoul region. Because the songs are sung in the vernacular, unlike the otherwise relatively similar *kasa,* they are more direct in their expression of emotions. Hwang Yongju notes that although the genre's rhythmic structure and singing style resemble those of *kasa,* the two genres are easily distinguished.[146] *Kasa* are sung much slower than *Kyŏnggi chapka,* with little vocal ornamentation except for a slow if slightly crescendo vibration at the end of most notes. The notes of *Kyŏnggi chapka,* on the other hand, are sung with vibration from beginning to end, and because the songs are sung much faster, the lyrics can be easily understood. Singers of either genre may be accompanied by a drummer, but the role of the latter is smaller in the case of *kasa.*

During the first few decades of the twentieth century, the professional repertoire of Folksongs from Kyŏnggi Province came to include not only *chapka* but also a number of *t'ongsok minyo* from other regions in Korea. Most of the *t'ongsok* songs were set to orchestral accompaniment and arranged to suit short three- to four-minute time slots, ideal for gramophone records and radio broadcasts. The resulting *shin minyo* came to share several musical characteristics with *Kyŏnggi chapka,* which long retained their melody, singing style, and rhythmic cycles: an emphasis on lyricism at the expense of emotion in what may, in relative terms, be seen as a fast, straightforward singing style in which the quality and length of vibrato are sacrificed in order to keep the pace of the ornamented melodies.[147] Singers use a combination of the chest, head, and falsetto registers, occasionally quickly jumping from one to the other within phrases. The vibrato is most noticeable at the end of each phrase, but during singing quick rhythmic accents at times resemble glottal-stop-like acciaccatura. The late holder of *Sant'aryŏng,* Chŏng Tŭngman, commented on the difficulty of singing *Kyŏnggi* folksongs: "They say that *Kyŏnggi* songs are easier than *p'ansori,* but that's not true. With *p'ansori* there is room to breathe, but there is none with *Kyŏnggi* songs. That's why, in the end, they cannot sing solo, but they have to sing in chorus. In order to sing *Kyŏnggi* songs, you have to know how to take a 'secret breath.' Even among famous *Kyŏnggi* singers, there's hardly anyone who can sing solo."[148]

As with other folksongs, the ideal vocal timbre is a husky one. Yi Ŭnju, holder of *Kyŏnggi minyo,* told me, "The way to get a hoarse sound is not simply to compress your voice [*mog-ŭl tchalpke hada*], but to pull your voice up [*mog-ŭl ppopta*], so it's extremely difficult."[149] Below I provide a transcription of the first phrase of "Yusan'ga" by Muk Kyewŏl from 1997 that shows the fast vibratos and long, sustained notes:[150]

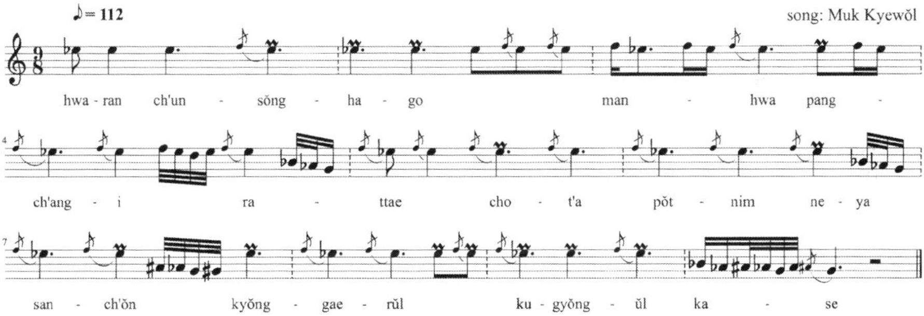

Hwaran ch'unsŏng-hago manhwa pangch'ang-ira ttae chot'a pŏt[/n]nim ne-ya sanch'ŏn kyŏnggae-rŭl kugyŏng-ŭl kase (With flowers blossoming vibrantly and all things growing lushly, this is the perfect time. My dear, let's go enjoy the sight of the mountains and streams).

Having worked on more than a few hundred folksong records, singer Pak Ch'unjae (1881–1950) was one of the most prolific recording artists of the colonial period. On an early standard-play (SP) recording of the song from 1911,[151] Pak sings the very same lyrics, but he follows a tempo that is almost double overall. The much higher pace may account for the fairly basic tonal ornamentation and lack of grace notes.[152] Another difference is that in Pak's version the main pitch drops half a tone from F to E in the last few measures (see below). The greater speed is likely to have been caused by the very limited recording time. SP recordings generally provided no more than three-and-a-half minutes of playing time per side. What is more, the recording technology did not allow small nuances nor great dynamic shifts, which left most recordings from this time sounding flat by today's standards:[153]

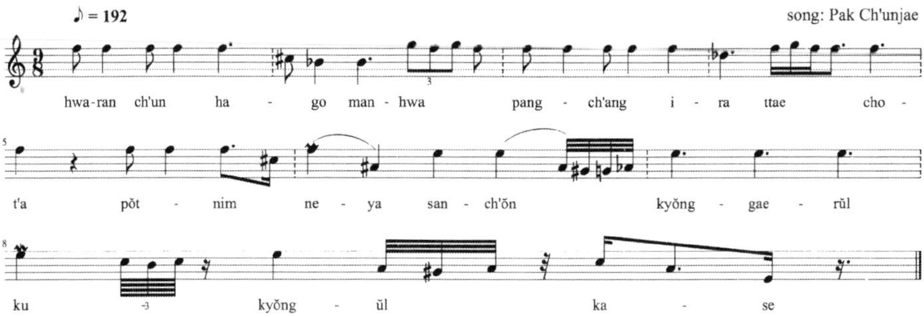

The first phrase of "Yusan'ga" on Pak Ch'unjae's 1911 recording has virtually identical lyrics, but much less ornamentation.

History of the Genre

The exact origin of the *Kyŏnggi chapka* repertoire is unclear, but the genre is believed to have developed and been passed on from around the early 1800s by a succession of four prominent male singers, starting with Ch'u Kyoshin, a talented *kagok* (lyric songs) singer born in 1814. His student Cho Kijun (1835–1900), a renowned singer of both *kagok* and *kasa,* in turn taught Pak Ch'un'gyŏng (1850–1920?), who became a specialist of *kasa, shijo,* and *chapka,* and instructed, among others, Yu Kaedong and Pak Ch'unjae. Pak Ch'un'gyŏng was a member of the successful male singing group Sagyech'uk, which was presumably named after the hometown of its main members, which stretched from today's Malli-dong to Ch'ŏngp'a-dong just south of Seoul Station. The group performed at marketplaces and town squares, while also regularly meeting in a so-called *kip'ŭn sarang* to perform, teach, and practice.[154]

A *kip'ŭn sarang* (*kip'ŭn* = deep, *sarang* = reception room for men), sometimes referred to as an *umjip* (dugout), was a hole roughly three by nine meters wide and one-and-a-half to two meters deep, dug into the side of a field with a simple roof placed over it.[155] The dugout would have looked poor from the outside but would have been nicely decorated on the inside, usually with wallpaper, a folding screen, a table, and basic furniture.[156] When farming work became impossible because of the winter cold, occasionally as many as thirty commoners, including handicraft traders and farmers, comprising both amateur and semi-professional singers, would gather in tents like this to enjoy folksongs, *kasa* and *shijo*. The songs they sang in the *kip'ŭn sarang* were sometimes referred to as *pangan sori* (room songs).[157] Before they disappeared in the 1950s, there were many of these hangouts scattered around Seoul, in townships such as It'aewŏn, Sŏbinggo, Wangshimni, Majang, Ch'ŏngp'a, Ŭngbong, and Ttuksŏm.[158] In summer, folk music enthusiasts would also regularly gather to sing and play music in the naturally air-conditioned summer version of the *kip'ŭn sarang*, the *kongch'ŏng* (public posts). The *kongch'ŏng* looked like the lookouts that can still be found in farming fields today. They had a roof over an elevated wooden floor built on pillars a few feet above the ground, and like the *kip'ŭn sarang*, they were often furnished with chairs and floor mats.[159]

Both the *kip'ŭn sarang* and the *kongch'ŏng* served primarily as practicing and performing spaces for male students. At the end of the nineteenth century, most female singers of *Kyŏnggi chapka* and other folksongs from the region were trained at professional *kisaeng* schools. For a long time three classes of *kisaeng* had existed: members of the first (*ilp'ae*) belonged to a government office, and although a number of them may have served as courtesans, they studied dance, the refined arts of the aristocracy (*yangban*) known as *p'ungnyu*, and *kagok* as their sole vocal art. Some of the women in this class studied medicine as well, so they could treat women at the palace. The performers were either trained at government institutions called *ch'ang hagwŏn* (singing institutes) or at provincial government offices at small, local posts called *kyobangch'ŏng* (deputy offices).[160] The second class (*ip'ae*) of entertainment girls consisted of retired first-class *kisaeng* who usually ended up as concubines or ran their own entertainment establishment, while the third class (*samp'ae*) comprised working-class hostesses who sold wine, sang folksongs, and occasionally performed sexual services.[161]

Businesses dealing in prostitution and young female entertainment would persist well into the twentieth century, but the legal foundations of the long-existing class distinction between the aristocracy and commoners, including *kisaeng*, were abolished in the mid-1890s as part of the major social and political changes made to the Korean government known as the Kabo Reform.[162] Reputations and traditional notions of class would, however, long persist, leaving the social status of those at the lower and upper echelons of the social hierarchy largely unchanged. Even a 1908 police ordinance abolishing the distinction between the various classes of female entertainers did little to ameliorate the women's position, especially when in March 1909 it was decided that like prostitutes, *kisaeng* now also had to be examined by a designated doctor each month to determine whether they had any contagious illness.[163] Over the following years, the Japanese nevertheless implemented social reforms that sought to bring an end to the low status of certain social groups, such as Buddhist monks, butchers, and entertainers.[164] The rising market economy they helped usher in meanwhile served to expand the middle class and change social markers, enabling those considered working class to buy items that symbolized a degree of sophistication not previously associated with their station.[165] Although popular *kisaeng* may have had some power in the form of social capital, as they appeared on recordings and the radio, the majority remained firmly locked in the lower echelons of society.[166] The burgeoning Japanese tourism industry may have focused on the girls' artistic talents, but it made little attempt to hide their association with sex work. Widespread contempt, social isolation, and the duty to perform sexual services drove many to suicide or, like the celebrated *p'ansori* singers Yi Hwajungsŏn (1898–1943) and Pak Nokchu (1906–1979), drug abuse.[167]

The Japanese closure of the state schools for *kisaeng* in the early 1910s created possibilities for private entrepreneurs, some of whom had already established schools for *kisaeng* in and around Seoul and Pyongyang.[168] While the smaller establishments in the countryside would only engage a handful of girls, including former prostitutes, those in central Seoul took on as many as 180 girls, including former first-class *kisaeng*. Most of the girls came from poor families, a small, but notable percentage of which were shaman households.[169] While the students and teachers were all Korean, management of the schools would eventually come to include a number of Japanese. The girls, who were mostly in their mid- to late teens, were trained over a period of three years in a variety of skills. Although the range of skills covered differed between schools, they included calligraphy, *kasa, shijo, kagok, Kyŏnggi minyo,* traditional Korean instruments, Japanese and Western dance, as well as etiquette and the Japanese language. As part of etiquette, the girls were taught how to walk and sit, and how to greet and engage in conversation with their male clientele.[170]

The establishments outside Seoul were mostly known as *chohap* (associations). From 1914 onwards, however, those in Seoul began to adopt the term *kwŏnbŏn* (Jap. *kenban*), the Japanese equivalent of which was used for geisha agencies.[171] In Seoul, one of the first schools was the *Ta-dong chohap* (Ta-dong Association), which was established in February 1913 by Ha Kyuil (1867–1937). Located in Seoul's central Ta-dong area, between Ŭlchiro 3-ga and Ch'ŏnggyech'ŏn, the school trained many girls from the northwestern region, but it changed its name to *Taejŏng* [Jap. *Taishō*] *kwŏnbŏn* in 1919 when it set up a separate school for girls from Pyongyang called *Taedong kwŏnbŏn,* presumably named after the Taedong River that ran through their hometown. It was located nearby, in Sŏrin-dong, on the northern side of Ch'ŏnggyech'ŏn below Chongno

5-ga.[172] In 1923, three years before taking charge of teaching vocal art at the Court Music Office of the Yi Royal Household, Ha renamed the original association *Chosŏn* (Korea) *kwŏnbŏn* and adopted all the students from the *Kyŏnghwa kwŏnbŏn,* which had been located in Shi-dong in the south of Seoul. It was at the *Chosŏn kwŏnbŏn* that later holders An Pich'wi and Muk Kyewŏl, and nominee Kim Okshim, would eventually come to study *Kyŏnggi chapka* with Ch'oe Chŏngshik. Other schools in Seoul's Central District included the *Kwanggyo kwŏnbŏn*—later renamed *Hansŏng kwŏnbŏn*[173]—in Mugyo-dong, where *chapka* were taught by a former student of Pak Ch'un'gyŏng and eventual holder of *Sŏnsori sant'aryŏng,* Yu Kaedong, and the *Hannam yegi kwŏnbŏn* (*yegi* = *kisaeng*), better known as simply *Hannam kwŏnbŏn,* in Kongp'yŏng-dong.[174] They were joined by the *Chongno kwŏnbŏn* in Nagwŏn-dong, where *chapka* were taught by another of Pak Ch'un'gyŏng's former students, Pak Ch'unjae. In 1940, the *Chosŏn kwŏnbŏn, Chongno kwŏnbŏn,* and *Hansŏng kwŏnbŏn* merged to form the *Samhwa kwŏnbŏn.*[175]

The schools did not only provide professional training in a variety of skills, but also created possibilities for the girls to perform for the media. Although it is not clear exactly what it broadcast between 1924 and 1927, the year in which the Kyŏngsŏng Broadcast Corporation's radio service went "live," newspaper announcements show that at least from July 12 to September 23, 1926, it employed only *kisaeng* from Seoul's main schools, primarily to sing folksongs.[176] Due to the popularity of a number of *kisaeng,* the association with third-class *kisaeng* began to fade. Yet despite the fact that they had all been trained at one, the first generation of *Kyŏnggi minyo* holders remained reluctant to discuss their experiences with *kisaeng* organizations, and it is perhaps therefore left out of the CPC's report.[177] An Pich'wi, for example, referred to the stigma when she commented, "I know that in the past *kwŏnbŏn* were places where commoners and *kisaeng* [female entertainers] were trained, but that was not absolutely so. The study substance and atmosphere were more strict and diligent than at today's art schools."[178]

Three Personal Stories

An Pich'wi

An Pich'wi was the most celebrated of the first three holders of *Kyŏnggi minyo.* She was born the youngest of three siblings on March 21, 1926, in Hyoja-dong, in Seoul's central Chongno District. Her parents had had two boys and four girls but decided to have one more child when they lost all of their daughters. Due to the ill fate of her sisters, her father, An Yŏngsu, named her Pokshik (blessed child).[179] An first started to dream of singing and dancing professionally some time after finishing Ch'ŏngun Primary School. Although she was not a very good student, her teachers recognized her talent for the performing arts. Her mother and grandmother were devout patrons of shamanism, and once every three years they invited a shaman (*mudang*) to their house to conduct a ceremony, even when there was no impending misfortune. An would watch the ritual day and night, and mimic the singing and dancing of the shaman. Using her father's record player, she often listened to recordings of famous *p'ansori* singers such as Song Man'gap (1866–1939), Chŏng Chŏngyŏl (1876–1938), Yi Tongbaek (1867–1950), Yi Hwajungsŏn, and Pak Nokchu, as well as to recordings of *Kyŏnggi minyo* by professional singers such as Yi Chinhong (1892–?) and Yi Chinbong (1896–?).[180]

When An told her family about her plans to become a professional singer, her father and brothers were strongly opposed. Because her father was a merchant, the family was relatively well off. Singing folk music as a profession was associated with a low social status and with sex work, so those who could avoid it did so. She recalled her father being irate and her brothers pledging to commit suicide and saying she would bring shame on the house, but she was determined. The commotion that followed was so great that at some point An thought they were going to cut her throat. She finally fled the house and, together with a friend who also wanted to sing and dance, went to look for a homestay in the neighboring area of Ch'ŏngjin-dong. When An's mother eventually found out where she was, she secretly provided her with clothes and money to pay for rent and tuition.[181] Although even her landlady tried to persuade her to return home, An remained headstrong. She desperately wanted to sing, and pleaded for her help instead. The landlady then introduced her to Ha Kyuil, who persuaded An to join the *Chosŏn kwŏnbŏn,* where he worked both as a teacher and superintendent. It was there that she would meet Muk Kyewŏl, one of An's future co-holders of *Kyŏnggi minyo.*

An had to get up every morning at five o'clock to do vocal exercises before leaving her room to study with her teacher, who sometimes kept her busy until nine o'clock in the evening. It was Ha who nicknamed An "Pich'wi" (jade/kingfisher), a name he reportedly gave her because of her beauty. Most *kisaeng,* however, appear to have had nicknames, many of which, like Pich'wi, were common.[182] Ha taught An several court dances as well as *kagok* and *kasa,* genres long popular with the aristocracy. Because she was much more interested in folk music, however, An began to take lessons in traditional dance with Han Sŏngjun, a leading authority on folk dance, and in the *yanggŭm* (dulcimer) with Kim Sangsun.[183] In 1937, two years after An had joined his classes, Ha Kyuil died. His best pupil, Yi Pyŏngsŏng, took over the teaching of song and dance, but because no teachers at the school knew folk music, An decided to take evening lessons in *kin chapka* with Ch'oe Chŏngshik, a noted singer of folksongs from Kyŏnggi and the northwestern provinces who would eventually take up a teaching position at the *Chosŏn kwŏnbŏn* as well.[184]

When she had turned fourteen, Ch'oe introduced An to the professional folksong scene by taking her to a local *kip'ŭn sarang.* An recalls her first visit:

> When I went there with my teacher and my seniors, old men had laid down fancy mattresses and set up a folding screen. They were sitting in a circle. We would sit up all night singing songs there. As for those men, they were people from Seoul who had a profound knowledge of folksongs. They were truly esteemed singers. I was put to the test in front of them. After bowing, I sat down neatly, and after I sang *shijo* with a male and a female *tessitura,* I sang *kin chapka* and *chapchapka.* They sat there listening motionlessly and then took a short break. They smoked cigarettes and after they had opened the window above to let out the smoke, they again sat down motionless. We just ate tangerines and raw eggs with salt, bit by bit, and sang with our backs straight up, unable to turn around.[185]

Eventually, the old men complimented her on her talent. Having passed this test at the *kwŏnbŏn,* An went through a proper initiation ceremony and became a member of the select group of professional folksong singers that frequented the *kip'ŭn sarang.*[186] She would nevertheless continue to study with Ch'oe until she was approximately twenty-five years old.

In 1940, at the age of fifteen, An became a member of a traditional music group that performed court and folk dances across the country. In addition, she regularly performed for the Seoul Broadcasting Company (the present Korea Broadcasting System, or KBS).[187] However, the Pacific War eventually put her career on hold. As warfare intensified, the number of work opportunities became significantly limited. The Japanese authorities forbade folk and popular entertainment and even ordered some of the folk musicians to work in the coal mines. Others, including An's group, were forced to pay so-called sympathy visits (*wimun*) to the Japanese military, either in Korea or on tour in Japan.[188] Because many of the songs had to be sung in Japanese, the experience was often demoralizing for the performers, but few if any were in a position to opt out.

After 1945, An began performing in a new group brought together by Shin Pulch'ul, a famous singer and stand-up comedian who was responsible for the lyrics of the popular trot "The Tear-soaked Tumen River." Shin's group offered a variety of performing arts, including folksongs, *p'ansori,* and dance, as well as a form of stand-up comedy called *mandam* or *chaedam* (lit. "witty chat") that had strong roots in traditional folk performing art. An described Shin as "an ugly man with glasses, but incredibly talented," and said he spent a lot of time in jail during the Japanese occupation because he made a habit of boldly inserting patriotic comments in his comedy routine.[189] Despite being employed, An's financial situation remained poor, as she was often not paid for performances. On a few occasions she was even held hostage by a hotel manager because she was unable to pay her bill. It was around this time, at the age of nineteen, that An met Kang Kijun, a bank clerk. The two fell in love and married in the same year. Her husband supported her career, which meant she was able to carry on with it despite also mothering five children. When her husband died at the early age of thirty, she continued to sing while singlehandedly raising three sons and two daughters.

In the years following the Korean War, An took part in a traditional music program, the predecessor of the later national folksong singing competition, alongside noted singers such as Kim Sohŭi, Yi Ch'angbae, and Kim Okshim. It was not until 1959, however, that she was able to go overseas for the first time; she went as part of a tour of Japan and performed for audiences comprised mostly of overseas Koreans. An performed in the role of a *kisaeng* in a *ch'anggŭk* (traditional Korean opera) version of one of the *p'ansori* pieces, *Ch'unhyangga*, alongside, among others, the famous *p'ansori* singer Im Pangul, actress Pok Hyesuk, and actors Pak Chin and Ch'oe Sangdŏk. At home, throughout the late 1960s and 1970s, An Pich'wi dedicated much of her time to organizing folksong events in her role as director of the Korean Folksong Research Society.[190]

On July 12, 1975, An Pich'wi was appointed holder of *Kyŏnggi minyo,* along with her peers Muk Kyewŏl and Yi Ŭnju. An remembered that by the time she was appointed, the IICPs had acquired considerable status. She recalled that in 1964, when the Cultural Properties Management Office began announcing the first holders, many artists avoided being appointed:

> In those days we lived under constant supervision and nobody wanted to be appointed because this meant extra supervision. . . . Back then, all the well-known singers of *Sŏdo sori* died without being appointed. Singers such as Paek Unsŏn, Chang Haksŏn, and Yi Pandohwa were excellent singers, but they died after nothing but hardship. You won't find singers like that any more.[191]

An added that mere appointments would not guarantee the preservation of traditional music:

> Nowadays, you can no longer go out at night to sing at some workplace or party. Although my income has decreased as a result, I think that it is a very good thing. I am not in favor of people who are called to some place to sing for a petty amount of money. The problem is that they [the CHA] just appoint cultural properties without there being any countermeasure.

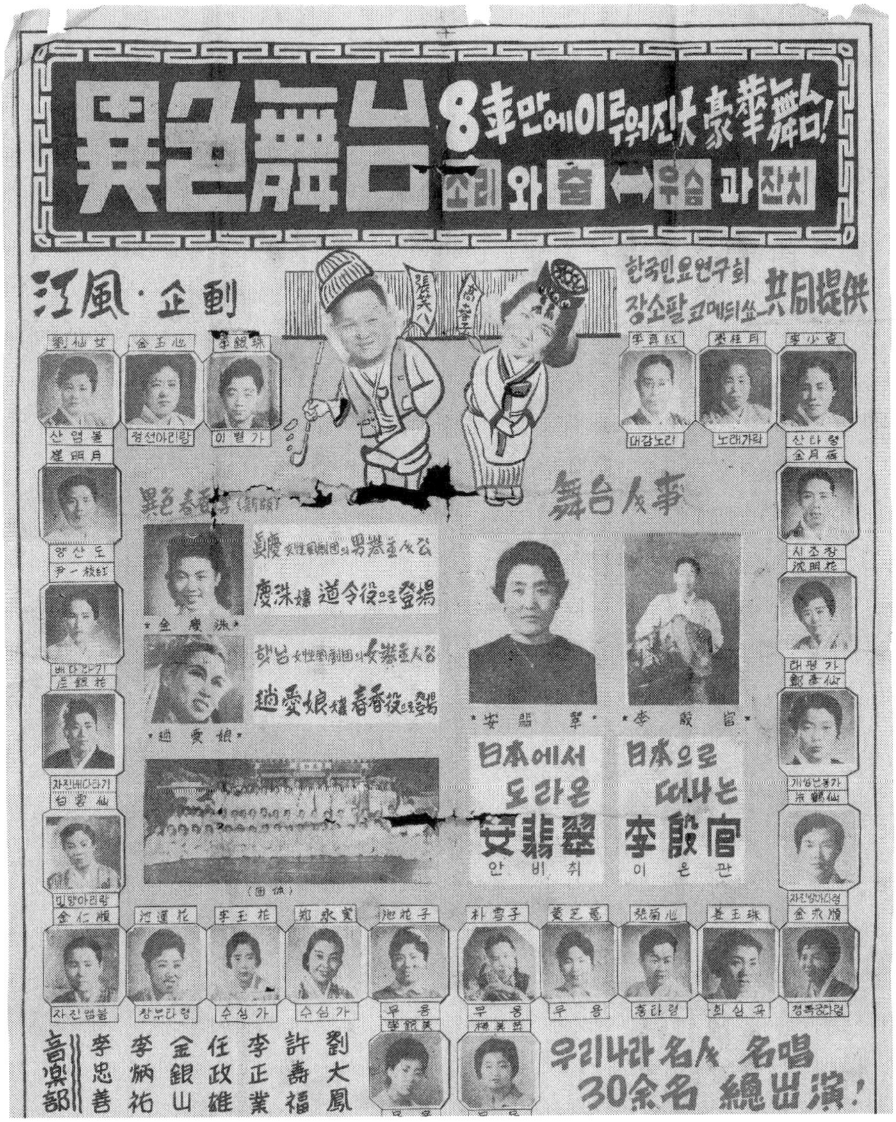

Poster of the Korean Folksong Research Society (Han'guk minyo yŏn'guhoe) from around 1962 featuring An Pich'wi, "who has returned from Japan," and Yi Ŭn'gwan, "who is heading off to Japan," in the center. Shown also in second and third position from the top left are respectively Kim Okshim and Yi Ŭnju, and, from the top right, Yi Sohyang, the society's director, and Muk Kyewŏl. (Poster reproduced courtesy of the National Gugak Center.)

Don't they say that nowadays only those who are well dressed and attractive are suitable for appointment? Traditional music programs have been given the cold shoulder by the broadcasting stations. When you go to a national broadcasting station such as KBS and try to talk to them, they say that there's no sponsor for such programs. How can a national broadcasting company that runs on account of our taxes say that it disregards traditional music because it has no sponsor?[192]

An Pich'wi remained active until the early 1990s, when she became terminally ill. In performance and in teaching she always sang the lyrics as they appeared in Yi Ch'angbae's 1953 *Song Compilation* (*Kayo chipsŏng*). She noted that popular singers and teachers had a responsibility to immediately correct students' "wrong" habits: "A number of popular Korean singers have hits by singing 'Han obaengnyŏn,' 'Nodŭl kangbyŏn,' 'Sae t'aryŏng' [Bird's Song], or other folksongs, but somehow there should be supervision. Even when I myself teach students at university, not only do they pronounce *sarang* (love) as *ssarang,* but the melody is also very wrong. This has become fixed by habit and to change it is very difficult. We have to sing folksongs that have character."[193] Yi Ch'unhŭi (b. 1947) described her teacher as someone who focused much on decorum: "She always says that women have to behave like women and provide what women are meant to provide. She says that we have to know and follow what are the right and proper ways to dress and prepare food . . . and despite the fact that there are neither husband nor relatives in her house, the ceremony and formalities remain unchanged during meals. We students respect her for her discipline."[194] By 1995, An was no longer able to teach. Because her husband had died and all her children had moved to the United States, she lived alone until she passed away on January 3, 1997. Yi Ch'unhŭi and fellow future holder—now assistant teacher—Kim Hyeran (b. 1951) had regularly come to An's house to study, and they helped look after her when she became ill. On November 11, 1997, Yi replaced An as holder.

Muk Kyewŏl

Muk Kyewŏl, one of An Pich'wi's former classmates at the *Chosŏn kwŏnbŏn,* was born as Yi Kyŏngok on November 18, 1921, in Kwanghŭi-dong, in central Seoul, across from where the Kyerim Theater used to be. Her father, Yi Yun'gu, made a modest living tying silk decorations. Muk was the second youngest of five daughters. She developed a passion for singing from the age of eleven while attending Pangsan Primary School. A singer who heard her voice went to Muk's house to ask permission to teach her. When her father refused, the man was able to persuade Muk's mother, and so, in 1931, to further her development as an entertainer, Muk was allowed to move out of her home to live with a foster mother, a certain Ms. Yi, who owned a large house in Nagwŏn-dong just north of Chongno 2-ga.[195]

Ms. Yi was one of the special adoptive mothers (*suyang ŏmŏni*) for *kisaeng*, who advanced fees for the girls and housed them while they studied at a *kwŏnbŏn*. Until the early 1910s at least, many *kisaeng* also had a *kibu* (male partner/agent). The *kibu*, who was often a few years older, provided protection and often advanced tuition fees.[196] The word *kidungsŏbang* (pimp) has been used to describe the role of the *kibu*, but although some *kisaeng* performed sexual services, the *kibu* will have been able to protect them and others, including those whose primary role it was to provide musical entertainment, from having to perform any sexual act or being sexually assaulted. The role of the *kibu* could be compared to that of the *kŏsa* of *sadang* described earlier in this chapter.

From the moment she moved in with her foster mom, Muk stopped going to school and contact with her real parents was practically cut off. Most *kisaeng* were given new names, and because Ms. Yi's late husband had had the surname Muk, Yi Kyŏngok changed her name to Muk Kyewŏl. Muk first took lessons in *shijo* and *chapka* with Yi Kwangshik, who managed a small private singing school in the area. But when Muk found him to be a poor teacher, her foster mom told her not to go back and enrolled her in the *Chosŏn kwŏnbŏn*. Although Muk expected to be taught *kagok*, her teacher Ha Kyuil found that her voice was better suited to *chapka*, and so she ended up studying with *chapka* specialist Chu Subong (1870–?). There were twenty to thirty students in her class, and because she had enrolled late, Muk was seated at the very back of the classroom; she and her teacher could barely see each other. Muk therefore left the school after less than a year. Her foster mom took her to teacher Kim Yunt'ae, who taught students privately and was able to give Muk extensive feedback. She also studied *songsŏ*—a genre of sung excerpts of prose, a particular piece of which each *kwŏnbŏn* considered obligatory—with Yi Munwŏn, an itinerant singer who sang in exchange for money and lodging.[197] Another teacher with whom she studied for a while was Ch'oe Chŏngshik, a specialist in "new folksongs" who was renowned for the hits he had with his modern renditions of "P'ungdŭngga" (Great Harvest Song) and "Kŭmgangsan t'aryŏng" (Ballad of Mount Kŭmgang).[198]

By the time she turned sixteen, Muk was fast making a name for herself, performing at many public and private occasions, inside rich people's homes and at *kip'ŭn sarang*, but she remained socially isolated. Muk passed on all her earnings to her foster mom, who was always suspicious that her protégée was holding back money and discouraged Muk from entertaining friends at home. When Muk turned twenty, she could no longer bear living with her foster mom and moved back to her parents' home. A few years earlier, at the age of eighteen, she had made her first recordings of Western-style popular songs of the day, *kayo,* for Victor Records. But although this signaled the start of a breakthrough, her career came to a virtual halt when she married a few years later, in 1942. Her husband, Kim Koin, a miner, had Muk stay at their home in Tonam-dong, in Seoul's northern Sŏngbuk District, to look after their son and two daughters while he paid back the debt owed to Muk's foster mom. When he lost his job after a few years, the family—which included children from her husband's previous marriage[199]—had to rely on Muk for their livelihood, and life became very difficult. Ryu Ŭiho records that Muk's parents died before liberation,[200] which suggests that Muk was unable to ask her parents for support and may have had to carry the additional burden of looking after them for some time. She eventually found work again singing for the *Samhwa kwŏnbŏn.* It was not a place where she could make a name for herself, but it did provide a more secure income and allowed her to send both her own children and those of her husband to school.[201]

The Korean War forced the family to move south, to Pusan, where Muk was eventually able to make a little bit of money singing. When the family returned to Seoul in May 1953, only the four outside walls of their house remained. By borrowing money from her sisters and taking any singing job she could find, Muk was able to support her family and little by little finance the reconstruction of their house. After 1957, when she was first invited to perform for KBS-TV, the family's living conditions began to improve, but the prospect of paid work in folk music remained bleak at least for another decade. Even Muk's appointment as holder in 1975 did not immediately provide much relief from financial strain. Because she had been told unofficially prior to her appointment that her performances at sixtieth birthday parties jeopardized her position as a candidate, Muk made up her mind not to continue such activities after her appointment, despite the fact that this implied a significant loss of income.[202]

Upon becoming a holder, Muk Kyewŏl selected two special scholarship students, Im Chŏngja (b. 1943, stage name Chŏngnan, then a future holder as well) and Ko Churang; one female assistant teacher, Chi Hwaja (1942–2001); and seven graduates, both male and female.[203] One of Muk's students, Yu Ch'ang (b. 1959, original name Yu Ŭiho), who was another of Hwang Yongju's graduates for *Sant'aryŏng,* was appointed assistant teacher for *Kyŏnggi minyo* in 2001 and holder of Seoul City Intangible Cultural Property no. 41, *songsŏ,* in 2009.[204] About teaching, Muk said:

> I tell my students to study hard, but that's all I do. When we were young, there were no books and we learned by just looking at our teacher's lips. . . . We worked hard day and night, but nowadays people don't work that hard. And even after you've become fairly comfortable with the notes after studying for a few years, you have to constantly touch it up and do your own thing by way of research. If you don't, then you can only copy the

typical sounds. It's like when you make diamonds and you must cut the stone and make it smoother to get a really nice ball [*kong*].[205]

According to Ryu Ŭiho, Muk, like her fellow holders, had trouble teaching her special scholarship students. This was for the most part because they had graduated from Yi Ch'angbae's institute, which taught styles that differed musically from those of the three *Kyŏnggi minyo* holders.[206] Although Kim Yŏngim (b. 1953) and Yu Ch'ang (b. 1959), the only male senior professionals of the genre, replaced Chi Hwaja in 2001, Kim's position has remained fairly weak, which may be because she also studied with Yi Ch'angbae and thus lacked the full support of her teacher. In an article for OhmyNews, Kim Munsŏng compares Kim Yŏngim to singer Kim Okshim, described below, whose talent and accomplishments appear to have been ignored at the time the first three holders of *Kyŏnggi minyo* were appointed.[207]

Besides singing and teaching, Muk was chairman of the folksong committee of the Society for Korean Traditional Music, which in 1968 honored her with an award at the first National Contest for Korean Traditional Music (*Chŏn'guk kugak kyŏngyŏn taehoe*). In addition, she served as vice-chairman of the Korean Folksong Research Society.[208] On September 16, 1995, Muk gave her last public performance,[209] but she continued to teach at her institute, the Muk Kyewŏl Institute for the Preservation of Kyŏnggi Folksongs (Muk Kyewŏl Kyŏnggi sori pojonhoe), despite her deteriorating health. The institute was first located on the fifth floor of a building opposite Seoul's central fire station and eventually moved to a small office on the second floor of a rundown building in Sŏdaemun District. It finally moved to the space used for teaching by her student Yu Ch'ang, in the basement of a small office building in Pongik-tong in Seoul's central Chongno District. Because of her old age and frailty, Muk's status was changed into that of honorary holder on April 20, 2005. She died approximately nine years later, on May 2, 2014.

Yi Ŭnju

Yi Ŭnju, the youngest of the first generation of holders of *Kyŏnggi minyo*, was born Yi Yullan in the township of Changhang in Yangju County, northwest of Seoul, on October 6, 1922.[210] Yi said that when she went to primary school she already desperately wanted to study singing and she listened to records of famous singers as often as possible. Pak Kyŏngsu reports that because Yi's father was a poor farmer, he decided to send her to a *kwŏnbŏn* at the age of eight;[211] but Yi told me the decision to go to a *kwŏnbŏn* was her own and had been prompted by the lack of singing teachers in the area. Her mother took her to Seoul, where an acquaintance introduced them to Wŏn Kyŏngt'ae[212] at the *Chongno kwŏnbŏn*.

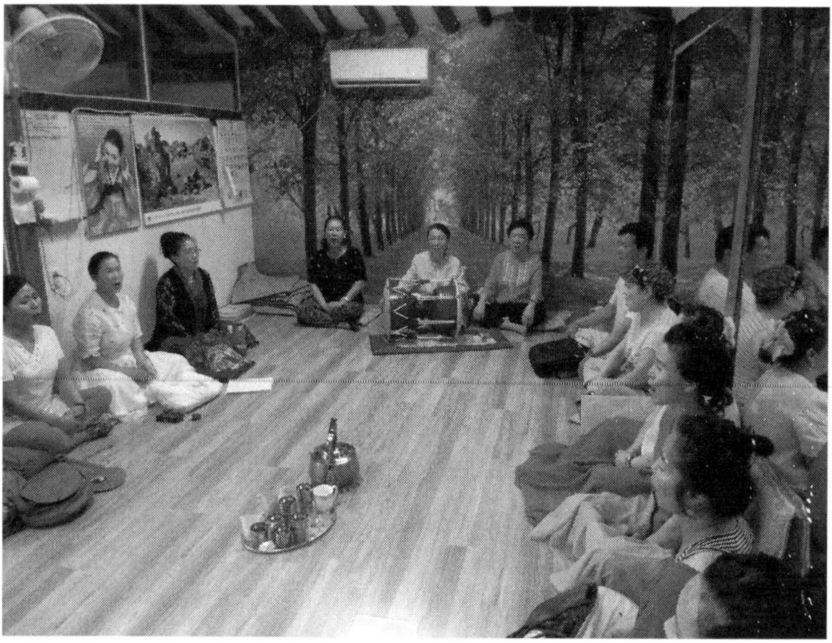

Yi Ŭnju teaching at her home in Kwŏnnong-dong on July 8, 2013.

Yi would study for five years with Wŏn, learning *chapka, shijo,* and *kasa.* Wŏn was a very stern teacher and Yi recalls being beaten, sometimes to the point of bleeding. Pak reports that during those years Yi lived with a foster mother, like her peer Muk Kyewŏl, and that at the age of eleven she was already an *aegi kisaeng* (*aegi* = child) who performed in front of customers; but Yi insisted that she was not a real *kisaeng* and only took private lessons.[213]

In her late teens, Yi moved to Taegu City, where for one year she was unable to find employment. She was encouraged to try composing instead, which shortly after liberation led her to create a revised version of the *shin minyo* "T'aep'yŏngga" (Song of Peace) for inclusion in the standard *Kyŏnggi minyo* repertoire.[214] Finally, around 1939, Yi's teacher suggested that she participate in a singing contest held at Hŭngmyŏng Theater. At the occasion, Yi not only won first prize, but also met her future husband, with whom she would have a daughter and a son. At the age of eighteen Yi subsequently began working for the theater for a while, singing songs in front of the ticket booth in order to lure in customers.[215] To reduce the amount of time and money spent traveling, the family moved back to Seoul, but her husband soon fell ill and died. Although in order to make ends meet she ran a small eatery, her teacher had recommended her for radio work, which would soon offer a significant secondary source of income. Yi recalls her first appearance: "In those days there were no recording methods available, so radio was [all] live broadcasts. I sang, beating the *changgu* [hourglass drum] in a room with tatami mats on the floor. It wasn't, like, 'sing this,' but I had to sing what I knew. And, because it was live, it would come out the way I sang it, good or bad."[216]

When she was twenty-two years old, Yi participated in a competition called *Myŏngch'ang taehoe* (Great Singers Convention), held at Tansŏngsa Theater. Because she once again won first prize, her career began to really take off. She became a prolific artist, performing songs from several regions for radio and TV stations and appearing on more than eighty records, almost twice as many as the other holders of *Kyŏnggi minyo*. In 1947, Yi found work as a folksong teacher for the *Taehan kugagwŏn* (Korean Traditional Music Institute) in Seoul's central Taok-tong. In 1955, she returned to Tansŏngsa Theater to compete in the first Korean traditional music contest and won first prize yet again, this time for singing *Kyŏnggi chapka*.[217] In the 1960s and 1970s she often joined her peers at events organized by the Korean Folksong Research Society.

Despite Yi's reputation, however, she was told she would only become a holder if she could sing *shibi chapka*. The deliberation regarding her appointment initially led her to freeze her singing style and stick to a set repertoire: "Before I was appointed I was an 'assistant teacher.' Because I was still young, I couldn't sing that many songs, but as I grew older I realized that this song has to be sung like this, that song like that, and so on. In those days teachers would just sit down and teach and I was never able to sing in a different way, but I thought of how I could sing the songs my own way and I changed them all."[218] Ever since Hwang Yongju's book, *A Compendium of the Vocal Music from Korea's Kyŏnggi and Western Provinces* (*Han'guk kyŏng/sŏdo ch'angak taegye*), came out in 1993, Yi has used it for all of her teaching. Due to the availability of recordings and books, she feels that students have it much easier now than she did when she started out. Yi had to memorize everything and her teachers would whip her on the calf whenever she made a mistake. Even so, she believes the standard has much improved because students all genuinely want to learn to sing.[219] Around the early 2000s, she still provided guest lectures at Ehwa Women's University, but now she teaches at home, in her relatively spacious traditional-style house in central Seoul's Kwŏnnong-dong. Because of her very old age, her status was changed to that of honorary holder on July 12, 2013, though she continues to be involved in the teaching and performance of her art.

Yi has one female future holder and five assistant teachers, Kim Kŭmsuk, Kim Yŏngim, Kim Changsun, Kim Hyeran, and Yi Yŏnhwa. She also has fifteen to twenty graduates, both male and female, but she told me she tried to avoid taking on male students.[220] Her relationship with Kim Kŭmsuk (b. 1949), another former student of Yi Ch'angbae's song institute, has been poor. In 1997, she told me: "Now I have one [graduate] too, but the relationship between us isn't good, so I don't teach her. She cannot sing very well. So, I worry a lot. I tried to get the *Munhwajae kwalliguk* to drop her, but that was no longer possible because she's already appointed."[221] In 2013, Yi Ŭnju said the relationship was still bad and that they rarely met.[222] Perhaps unsurprisingly, in an interview back in 1991, Kim refrained from praising Yi. While senior students commonly tend to express admiration for their mentors, Kim's praise for Yi was rather dispassionate: "As a housewife she's thorough, as a Christian she's devoted, and as a singer she's of course a talented artist."[223]

Pedigrees Ignored

Hong Hyŏnshik and Pak Hŏnbong, the compilers of the 1969 government report on *Kyŏnggi minyo,* left much unexplained. On March 18, 1970, the Cultural Properties Committee therefore agreed to disregard the report, saying that it "contain[ed] too many deficiencies." They commissioned Pak Hŏnbong to compile a new report under the name "Kyŏnggi chapka."[224] But even this second report fails to explain why Kim Okshim (original name Kim Aehŭi) was not appointed despite being nominated. Her rejection—she was appointed future holder—has fueled suspicion that the preservation system is corrupt.[225] Kim Okshim was born on August 30, 1925, in Insa-dong, in the township of Changhŭng in Yangju County, north of Seoul. Like Muk Kyewŏl and Yi Ŭnju, she studied at the *Chosŏn kwŏnbŏn* with Chu Subong and Ch'oe Chŏngshik.[226] After her training she often appeared on stage, alongside her folksong peers, as well as with the noted court musicians Kim Ch'ŏnhŭng, Kim Kisu, and Sŏng Kyŏngnin. Kim also joined her peers An Pich'wi, Muk Kyewŏl, and Yi Ŭnju at the Korean Folksong Research Society.[227] She was a prolific recording artist and performer, and appeared on more records than An and Muk. Having earned a status equal to that of the three *Kyŏnggi minyo* holders before their appointments, in 1968 she even beat them to win the Prime Minister's Award at the first National Contest for Korean Traditional Music.[228] It seems she stopped performing some seven years before her death in January 1988. On April 29, 1975, shortly before her departure from the scene, the CPC agreed not to consider Kim for appointment as holder of *Kyŏnggi minyo,* because it had been too long since she withdrew from the arts world,[229] but reports of her performing can be found in the *Munye yŏn'gam* (Yearbook of culture and arts) for 1975 and 1978 and the *Han'guk yesulchi* (Record of Korean arts) published in 1980.[230] Folksong enthusiast Kim Munsŏng, who spent many years trying to raise money and resources to see Kim Okshim's full oeuvre preserved, believes that she was not appointed as holder because she suffered from high blood pressure and was

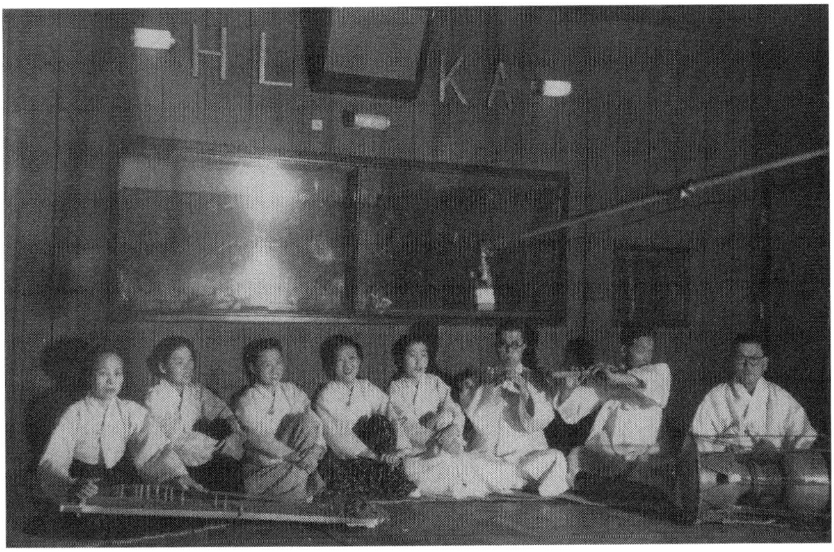

A 1954 recording session at the Seoul Central Broadcasting Station (later renamed KBS Radio 1). Yi Ŭnju and Kim Okshim sit in third and fourth positions from the left, respectively. (Photo reproduced courtesy of Korean folk music critic Kim Munseong.)

unable to perform regularly.[231] There may be more to the story. According to Yi Ŭnju, Kim became very depressed over having been passed over, and it was her subsequent heavy drinking that caused her early death.[232]

In their CPC report on *Kyŏnggi minyo,* Hong Hyŏnshik and Pak Hŏnbong acknowledge that the genre was originally dominated by male singers in the late nineteenth century and that each of the five men they nominated for the position of holder of *Kyŏnggi minyo* had at some point taught one of the four female nominees.[233] Eventually, however, the men were appointed for *Sant'aryŏng* instead. Although they could have been appointed for both *Sant'aryŏng* and *Kyŏnggi minyo,* it was presumably considered best to appoint others for the latter genre, in order to divide up the large number of students between both. Yi Pohyŏng once told me it was wrong to appoint only women as official representatives of *Kyŏnggi minyo,* but it would have been hard to avoid, considering Yu Ch'ang is currently the only man among the official graduate students and assistant teachers.

For the reasons discussed in chapter 2, the current number of female students of folk arts, and folksongs in particular, has begun to affect the association of traditions with specific genders. While they are mostly practical, the idea that women are better seen singing songs while they are sitting rather than standing (as in *Sant'aryŏng*) may have also played a part in their inevitable appointment as *Kyŏnggi minyo* holders. Martin Stokes notes, "The boundaries that separate male and female and assign to each other proper social practices are as 'natural' as the boundaries which separate one community from another. Musical practices are no exception—it is as 'natural' that men will make better trumpeters as it is 'natural' that women will make better harpists."[234] Related to this is the iconic image of geisha, whose performances have long represented the summit of elegance and perfection, at least in Japan and Korea's patriarchal societies, and the Orientalizing West. The idea that women's femininity often affects what is expected of a piece of music implies that certain forms of music, especially those that are traditionally associated with boisterousness and physical power, like *Sant'aryŏng*, are considered less ideal for female musicians.[235] Rather than their musicianship or artistry, it is their visual performance that set a standard of presentation that the recording industry and other media in colonial Korea would endorse from early on and encourage *kisaeng* to emulate. This standard was not abandoned upon liberation, but would continue to serve as an important point of reference to those involved in *Kyŏnggi minyo*'s preservation.

CHAPTER 4

Embodying Nostalgia

SŎDO SORI

Sŏdo sori (Folksongs from the Western Provinces), a broad genre of songs from the now North Korean P'yŏngan and Hwanghae provinces, were designated IICP no. 29 in 1968. Unlike *Kyŏnggi minyo,* which consist of only a subgenre of refined folksongs composed largely in Sino-Korean, *Sŏdo sori* include both *chapka* and colloquial, once vernacular folksongs composed for *kisaeng.* Because *Sŏdo sori* have been sung and recorded by professional singers in the capital, at least since the beginning of the colonial period, the tradition has become very much associated with Seoul: not only do many *Sŏdo sori* singers also perform songs from Kyŏnggi province, but they improvise in standard (South) Korean and they wear Seoul's latest *kugak* fashion. Determining how *Sŏdo sori* have come to differ from how they originally sounded is nevertheless difficult. Apart from the fact that only few early recordings survive, entailing somewhat "sterilized" excerpts of poor sound quality, the genre is now predominantly studied and performed in Seoul by locals who are cut off from the environment that spurred its creation and early development. In this chapter I contend that the genre will not be broken by the impending loss of native representatives and place, but sustained instead by its ability to invoke nostalgia.

Keith Howard writes that after initiating the Galloping Horse Movement in 1957, North Korea developed a homogenized singing style based on *Sŏdo sori*: "Folksongs were collected, assembled, published and promoted after texts had been approved or revised . . . . In the DPRK, folksongs now sound very different. The musical structure relies on western diatonicism enhanced and encouraged by a piano accompaniment. The voice features constant *metallo di voce* shading a steady vibrato, much like western *bel canto.*"[1] Many songs that were considered incongruent with socialism, be it lyrically, musically, or both, have been left out of songbooks, including those with romantic or spiritual contents.[2] Indeed, when the late O Pongnyŏ, a holder of *Sŏdo sori,* visited North Korea in

October 1989, she found that her traditional style of *Sŏdo sori* had lost its appeal to the North Korean people. According to O, there was hardly any sign of professional activities in the field of *Sŏdo sori,* and when she asked a local singer why all the songs appeared to have been modernized, he replied, "What if the masses don't like it?"[3] Singer Ch'oe Sŏngnyong (b. 1972), who lives and teaches *Sŏdo sori* in Yanji, the capital of Yanbian, which borders on North Korea, confirmed that in the North the tradition of *Sŏdo sori* had developed differently from that preserved in South Korea. Arguing that the southern tradition is more authentic—and thus, I surmise, of greater interest to potential students—he has regularly traveled to Korea to study with Pak Chunyŏng, an assistant teacher of the genre.[4] It seems, therefore, that the preservation of the genre now depends on the singers who work and live in and around Seoul, where they are likely to be influenced by the regional Kyŏnggi style of singing and performing.

A degree of nostalgia will always drive those involved in the preservation of Korean folk performing arts, in particular those directly affected by the division of the peninsula. Songs are given meaning as much by their sound and music as by the conditions in which they are performed, and considering that chances of reunification appear slim, the conditions for nostalgia are positive in South Korea, where the government has successfully revitalized folk traditions over the last half-century. *Sŏdo sori* may have originally been associated with features of everyday life in the northwestern provinces, but a fair if declining number of Koreans born in the North now live south of the border, and they will appreciate the nostalgia the songs have come to evoke. Some may disagree with the genre's aura of authenticity because the pronunciation and diction these days inevitably follows the South Korean vernacular, but the genre is not intended for them only. Due to their relatively plaintive tone and powerful but restrained performance, *Sŏdo sori* are a strong symbol of the country's division. Equally, those born below the 38th parallel can easily relate to the feelings of loss and injustice that they stir and cherish them as their heritage.

The genre has long maintained a strong presence in the Korean music scene, but the area known as Sŏdo used to carry a negative connotation. Several musicologists point out that after Yi Sŏnggye founded the Chosŏn dynasty in 1392, it was believed that many of the traitors had come from the northwestern area, and people from this area were therefore prevented from becoming officials in the dynasty's governing apparatus. These scholars contend that it is because of such discrimination that many songs from these provinces express feelings of grief and resentment.[5] Indeed, most *Sŏdo sori* are both thematically and tonally melancholic and sorrowful, especially when compared to the quicker and relatively more light-hearted *Kyŏnggi minyo.* Two of the genre's most characteristic songs, however, "Sushimga" and "Nanbongga," express great passion, even sexual desire, for a loved one. They were presumably developed by the courtesans and itinerant entertainers who transmitted the genre into the twentieth century. Rather than out of sympathy for the plight of unsuccessful upper-class public office hopefuls, the lower-class singers would have maintained the plaintive quality as a musical tradition to which their lives offered ample inspiration.

Songs from the P'yŏngan provinces are relatively restrained, while those from the Hwanghae provinces are a little more ironic and optimistic. The musical characteristics appear to contradict the local character of the people as described by the Confucian scholar Yi T'oegye (1501–1570). Describing the provinces' different traits on his travels through Korea, he portrayed the people of P'yŏngan as loud, fierce, and aggressive, like a "brave tiger coming out of the forest" (*maengho ch'ullim*), and those of Hwanghae as slow, diligent, and suffering, like a "cow ploughing in a stony field" (*sŏkchŏn kyŏngu*).[6] Singer Kim Chŏngyŏn has argued that although the songs from P'yŏngan province still follow Yi T'oegye's characterization, some change must have occurred: "Like the saying 'a brave tiger coming out of the forest,' *Sŏdo minyo* have a melody that is even better than the natural conditions of the northwestern provinces, as it makes us feel the spirit of brave men, but there must be some historical reason for the fact that they have such a sad feel nowadays."[7]

The best-known folksong from P'yŏngan province is "Sushimga" (Song of Sorrow), a melancholic, sorrowful yet passionate love song that is sung slowly without a set rhythm.[8] Until the 1910s, many versions of the song existed. The American company Victor Talking Machine Co. produced the first recording of the song (Victor Records 13550) sometime between 1908 and 1910, but the record has been lost.[9] When the song began to frequently appear on gramophone records, it was shortened and rearranged to follow contemporary developments in music while still enabling people to recognize the song's core.[10] Because lyric sheets did not appear until the mid 1920s,[11] the first textual transcription of the song was not published until 1914, in the collection *New and Old Chapka* (*Shin'gu chapka*).[12] Although numerous textual transcriptions of the song have since been passed on, it appears as though Yi Ch'angbae's transcription has become the standard, because it has been widely republished for research and teaching.[13] Much like "Arirang," the song has a simple structure that allows it to be easily extended by adding on phrases: each new phrase is followed by one of a small set of standard chorus lines. One transcription by Han Kisŏp, for example, includes as many as eighty-one phrases.[14] However, neither the great variety of versions available nor the rich use of symbols embedded change the theme of the song. The following is a translation of the first nine phrases of Yi Ch'angbae's transcription:

> Life is but an empty dream, in which our name means nothing.
> When I think about it, time runs so fast; I so need to know what I should do.

If I could visit my beloved in my dreams as often as I'd like, the stone road before her gate would turn to sand.
The more I long for her beautiful face, the less I know what to do.

Rivers and mountains don't change, and they meet again in spring. But I have not heard from her since she left.
When I think about it, time runs so fast; I so need to know what I should do.

When the sun sets behind the western hills, the moon rises above the eastern peaks.
The more I long for her beautiful face, the less I know what to do.

While the willows on the riverside are a striped green, the peach blossoms of the hereafter are a spotted red.
When I think about it, time runs so fast; I so need to know what I should do.

When you board a big ship in that blue dress, then the autumn waves of Lake Tongjŏng will be [blue] like heaven.[15]
When I think about it, time runs so fast; I so need to know what I should do.

On a lonely mountain on an autumn night at sunset, the peonies and yellow chrysanthemums have all blossomed.
Let us not mourn the rosiness of our youthful cheeks and play as much as we want.

Oh heartless train, go without a sound. I am immediately reminded of my lover who left without a word.
Whether you're male or female, once you leave this life, there's no coming back.

The tears I cannot withhold become cloudy white rapids that clatter in the Taedong River. As I heave a sigh another peak is added on the peony mountains.
One day we will also become a gush of rain and rock back and forth.[16]

In performance, "Sushimga" is usually followed by a lyrically more elaborate and rhythmically faster and more complex version, called "Yŏkkŭm sushimga." The term *yŏkkŭm* can be found in traditional *kagok* and *shijo* too, where it usually indicates a version of a song with more words. When the term is used for songs with fewer lyrics, it may, on the other hand, refer to a more complex rhythm. Because the melody of "Sushimga" was historically used at the end of many other famous *Sŏdo sori*—including the refined songs "Kongmyŏngga" (Song of Kongmyŏng), "Ch'ohan'ga" (Song of the Ch'o and Han), and "Chejŏn" (Making a Sacrifice)—the song is widely regarded as the basis of *Sŏdo sori*.[17]

Famous *chapka* from P'yŏngan province include "Yŏngbyŏn'ga" (Song of the Peaceful Border); the *shich'ang* (poem written in the style of traditional Chinese literature that is sung without a set rhythmic pattern) "Kwansanyungma" (The Kwan Mountain Where Horses' Hoofs Clatter Loudly), a song about a man who in his later years decides to climb Agyang Pavilion; and the *songsŏ* piece "Ch'up'unggam pyŏlgok" (Special Song of the Feeling of the Autumn Breeze), the music and lyrics of which are credited to No Saengwŏn and Kim Kwangju, respectively. Finally, a slow (*kin*) and fast (*chajin*) version of the song "Ari" are incorporated into the official repertoire of *Sŏdo sori* as well. Although the title of this song suggests a relation to the popular folksong "Arirang," the word *ari* does not appear in the lyrics of the song—while it does in the refrain of "Arirang", where it carries no particular meaning—and there seems to be no similarity between either the lyrics or the melody of the two songs.[18]

Well-known songs from Hwanghae province include the fast version of "Yŏmbul" (a Buddhist chant), and the slow and fast versions of "Nanbongga," the first two syllables of which mean "difficult to meet" in Chinese. "Nanbongga" contains many nonsense phrases and is not easy to translate, but it includes several comic one-liners about sex and love. A relatively large number of folksongs from Hwanghae and Kyŏnggi are collectively called "Nanbongga," and many songs from Hwanghae use the specific song's melodic contour.[19] Other popular songs are "Monggŭmp'o t'aryŏng" (Song of Monggŭm Port) and "San yŏmbul" (*san* = mountain). Despite its Buddhist connotation, the latter song lost most of the Buddhist characteristics in its lyrics, rhythm, and melody, presumably when it became a popular folksong. It is a relatively lively song that follows the rhythmic pattern of *ŏtchungmori* (12/4), a pattern more common in the southwestern (*namdo*) region.[20]

In general, *Sŏdo sori* are sung with a relatively slow, slightly nasal resonance in a low register. The first note of each new phrase is produced strongly, much like a wail. It is forced up from the abdomen, usually at a high pitch. The pitch then slides slowly down with a wide, somewhat hiccup-like vibrato, while the tempo decelerates and the volume is reduced. Accomplished singers jump between scales to pick very different pitches of the same note. All of this is conducive to an ornamented but somber, plaintive tone. Whereas many songs, including "Sushimga," have a free rhythm, the most commonly used rhythmic patterns are *todŭri* (6/4), *semach'i* (9/8), and *kutkŏri* (12/8).[21] Although the hourglass drum may be used, the songs are usually sung without accompaniment. Han Manyŏng has surmised that this may be because the songs often contain many irregular pauses, which instrumentalists would find difficult to follow.[22]

Performers of *Sŏdo sori* typically move very little. Much like *Kyŏnggi minyo,* they perform standing, but with more restraint. They sway gracefully, and the women sometimes use their arms to carry out a slow pellet drum–like movement, which amounts to a toned-down version of the "shoulder dance" (*ŏkkae ch'um*).[23] But a performance of *Sŏdo sori* does not just visually resemble that of *Kyŏnggi minyo.* While singers of either genre use very similar modes,[24] singers of *Sŏdo sori* also use rhythmic patterns from Kyŏnggi province for several songs. When singing "Monggŭmp'o t'aryŏng" or "Paekkot t'aryŏng" (Song of the Pear Blossom) from Hwanghae province, for example, they use the rather slow *chungmori* (12/4) pattern, which is common throughout Korea, as well as the more distinctive *chajin kutkŏri* (12/8) pattern, a relatively fast and light rhythm typical of the *Kyŏnggi minyo* style.[25] Musical influence is likely to have occurred in both directions. Yi Pohyŏng points out the similarities between "Sangyŏ sori" (Bier Carriers' Song) from Hwanghae province and "Obongsan t'aryŏng" (Song of Mount Obong) from Kyŏnggi province. Since the latter appears to have been composed later, no earlier than the late nineteenth century, it was probably influenced by the northern song.[26]

Key Figures

Since the end of the Chosŏn dynasty, many professional singers of *Sŏdo sori* have come to reside in Seoul. It was there that they kept the tradition alive even after the Korean War, which separated them from the source of the songs, from the songs' provincial home, and from the singers of old. Chang Sahun argues that *chapka,* the more refined songs, only became popular around the time of King Kojong's reign (1863–1907). During this time, folk festivals became particularly popular, and many singers performing there were also invited to royal banquets, where they competed with other singers to win prizes.[27] The events encouraged singers to broaden their repertoire and master the singing styles of several regions. Since regional repertoires were not yet set, singers often adapted songs to suit a particular style.[28] Because *Kyŏnggi minyo* and *Sŏdo sori* became the most popular genres during the ensuing period of colonial rule, a great number of singers specialized in singing both.[29] Examples are Ch'oe Chŏngshik (1886–1951), Pak Insŏp (1898–1951), Yu Kaedong, and Pak Ch'unjae (1881–1950),[30] as well as Paek Moran (1900–1945), Yi Kyewŏl, and Yi Yusaek (1896–?).[31] These singers had all been taught by Ch'oe Kyŏngshik (1876–1948), who had himself studied with Chang Kyech'un (1868–1946), a former student of Cho Kijun who had taught *kagok* and *kasa* at the Hansŏng training school for *kisaeng* in Seoul. Recordings of folksongs from either genre began to regularly appear in the 1920s. Singers such as Pak Ch'unjae and Kim Hongdo (1877–1948), who was famous for *Kyŏnggi*-style singing, were among the first recorded. Both singers appear on what is probably the first recording of the long (*kin*) versions of "Sushimga" and "Nanbongga" on Nipponophone 6001/2.[32]

In the early twentieth century, Pak Ch'unjae had perhaps the best reputation as a singer of both regional repertoires. He is nevertheless known more for having been the first professional performer of a genre of stand-up comedy known as *chaedam.*[33] Apart from specializing in folksongs and stand-up comedy, Pak Ch'unjae had a special talent for the comic folktale *Changdaejang t'aryŏng* and the folk play *Palt'al* (Foot masks). Born in Seoul, he studied *shijo* and *chapka* with Pak Ch'un'gyŏng and *kasa* with Cho Kijun. In 1900, he was given an official appointment as the Royal House's Special Inspector for Music and Dance (Kungnaebu kamubyŏlgam), despite the fact that he was only twenty years old. Eventually he would teach *chapka* to the later holders of the genre of *Sant'aryŏng*, Yi Ch'angbae, Chŏng Tŭngman, and Kim Sunt'ae.[34] This, again, demonstrates the close relationship between *Sŏdo* and *Kyŏnggi* songs.

In the 1940s, another important singer of *Sŏdo sori* and one to foster a line of female practitioners was Kim Milhwaju. Kim, who managed a *kwŏnbŏn* in Pyongyang, was the main teacher of several celebrated singers, including the first holder of *Sŏdo sori*, Chang Haksŏn (1905–1970), as well as Yi Chŏngnyŏl (1919–?) and Yi Pandohwa (1920–1973). Another noted singer from Pyongyang was Han Kyŏngshim. Han specialized in both *Sŏdo sori* and *Sŏdo sant'aryŏng*. She first took part in a regular collective performance at the *Kŭmch'ŏn taejwa*, a cinema in Pyongyang's central Kyŏngnim-dong (renamed the March First Cinema after liberation), which included Chang Haksŏn, Mun Myŏngok, and Kim Ch'unhong. She then moved to Seoul, where in the late 1930s she appeared on several recordings put out by Regal and Columbia Records, performing songs such as "Sushimga," "Pyŏngshin nanbongga" (*pyŏngshin* = irregular), and "Miryang arirang" (Arirang from Miryang). After liberation, she is reported to have taught singing at the Pyongyang Music and Dance College.[35]

Chang Haksŏn, Han's former colleague, was appointed the first holder of *Sŏdo sori* on September 27, 1969. Chang was born Chang Hyŏn'gil in Pyongyang in 1905. She did not attend school and instead, from the age of ten, learned *Sŏdo sori* in what was known as a singing room (*soribang*), a place akin to a *kip'ŭn sarang* where future *kisaeng* and amateur singers could hone their skills.[36] When she was fourteen, Chang joined Kim Milhwaju's *kwŏnbŏn* to continue her study of folksongs, and in 1924 she won first prize at the *P'alto myŏngch'ang taehoe* (National Convention of Great Singers) for her performance of "Sushimga."[37] Some time later, she won first prize at a contest for famous singers (*myŏngch'ang taehoe*) sponsored by the newspaper *Chosŏn ilbo*. Despite her success at such contests, Yi Ch'angbae reports that Chang was becoming too weak to teach students in the 1960s, which suggests that her activities became limited to special occasions. As her condition deteriorated further, Yi Ch'angbae took over teaching her students until her death on September 6, 1970.[38] Chang's inability to teach did not preclude her nomination as holder of *Sŏdo sori*. Considering poor health may have stood in the way of *Kyŏnggi minyo* singer Kim Okshim becoming holder, Chang's appointment was possibly related to her close relationship with Yi Ch'angbae, who was very influential both as a singer and music scholar. It may, however, also be related to the very large number of commercial recordings on which Chang appeared.

Another former holder of *Sŏdo sori,* who was appointed to replace Chang Haksŏn, was Kim Chŏngyŏn. Kim was born in Pyongyang's Sangsuri District on June 26, 1913. She was the fifth daughter and tenth child, but she was one of only five children in her family who reached adulthood. She excelled at learning and continued to attend school after her family moved to Kaesŏng when she was nine. Although her ancestors had been wealthy, her father had squandered the family fortunes, so her older sister Kim Chuksa, who shared her passion for folksongs and would later become a noted singer in her own right, suggested sending her to the local *kwŏnbŏn.* Despite a schoolteacher's efforts to dissuade her parents and Kim Chŏngyŏn's own resentment, her family was unable to support her staying home. Kim therefore moved to the *kwŏnbŏn,* where she studied *kagok* and *kasa* with Yi Sŭngch'ang, folk dance with Yi Changsan, and *Sŏdo sori* with another pupil of Hŏ Tŏksŏn, Kim Ch'ilsŏng, an old friend of her father. Because her dance teacher found that despite having talent she was a little too short to become a professional dancer, Kim decided to focus more on singing.

In 1930, Kim married a businessman at the age of seventeen, but the marriage was without passion. Although her husband did not support her continuing her career as an entertainer, he went bankrupt and fled to Manchuria two years into their marriage, which led Kim to return to performing. Soon after she had joined the *Chosŏn kwŏnbŏn* at the age of twenty-five, her husband returned, but in part because she was now the mainstay of her family she gave him the silent treatment for years. When he eventually turned to heavy drinking, Kim took him with her to Seoul and had him hospitalized. He eventually regained his health, but Kim's career was taking off and he refused to accept her late-night performance schedules. He eventually left her, not long before he died in 1945, a few years after Kim was enlisted by the colonial government to perform for Japanese troops in Korea and Japan alongside other Korean performers.

After liberation, and inspired by the loss of her homeland, Kim made many efforts to preserve traditional arts, putting out recordings and publishing five books on song and dance. In her final years she also volunteered for the Youth Education Association (Ch'ŏngsonyŏn kyohwa yŏnhaphoe), visiting juvenile penitentiaries and reform schools. Kim's nomination as a holder of *Sŏdo sori* on January 8, 1971, was owed partly to her many efforts toward education and the great concern she showed for maintaining Korea's traditional culture. She died at her home in Ch'angjŏn-dong, in Seoul's Map'o District, on February 26, 1987.[39] Her main student, Yi Ch'unmok (b. 1953), replaced her as main teacher, but she was not appointed holder until more than a decade later, when she was forty-eight years old.[40] As discussed in chapter 2, one of Kim's former graduate students, Yi Munju, was eventually appointed holder of a folksong tradition from the northern regions, *Sŏdo sŏnsori sant'aryŏng.*

Two Personal Stories

O Pongnyŏ

Among the "first-generation" holders of the genre, O Pongnyŏ and Yi Ŭn'gwan had the longest careers. O was born in Pyongyang's Sangsuri District on December 17, 1913. She showed a talent for singing from a very early age, and whenever she came to the bank of the Taedong River in spring or summer, people going on boat rides would ask her to join them onboard to sing. The other children in her neighborhood would tell her not to go along, but O enjoyed the opportunities to practice singing in front of a wide range of audiences. She remembered vividly how the old people in her neighborhood would dance and play the hourglass drum while she sang: "Those boat rides along the Taedong River, during which people would tie up the boat at a small island . . . opposite Nŭlla-dong and eat gourd soup and play, were [like] a big party that made the whole town move up and down."[41]

When O reached the age of sixteen, her family moved to Seoul, where at Kyŏnggi High School she became close friends with Chang Okchŏng. Chang's parents taught folksongs in one of their house's spare rooms, and because O often came to their house to play, she started to become interested in taking lessons herself. Because O's own parents did not consider learning folksongs a worthwhile pastime, she had to try very hard to persuade them.[42] Within days after O began to take lessons, her teacher Chang Kŭmhwa recognized her talent and allowed her to continue her training free of charge. Having merely relied on her ability to copy the sound of other singers until then, O was now able to learn the foundations of vocal technique. In 1929, she went to study *kasa* and *kagok* with Chŏng Hakki, who was teaching at the *Chosŏn kwŏnbŏn* in Ta-dong, Seoul,[43] but after one year she returned to her former teacher, Chang, to study *Sŏdo sori*.[44]

Although O eventually married and had four children, the Korean War brought her great hardship. In addition to losing three of her children, her husband was kidnapped and taken to North Korea. O had to give up singing in order to raise her only remaining son. She moved to Taegu, where for some fifteen years she sold quilts, fruit, and vegetables.[45] In 1966, she decided to return to Seoul, where she first went to see her old companion from Pyongyang, Kim Chŏngyŏn. With Kim, she took part in a folk art festival called I Still Want to Sing Folksongs (*Kŭjŏ soriga hago ship'ŏ*), which marked her return to the folksong scene.[46] In 1971, O Pongnyŏ was appointed holder of *Sŏdo sori*, alongside Kim Chŏngyŏn.

From the time she was appointed until her death on January 8, 2011, O was a very active instructor and performer. From the early 1970s onward, she was a regular instructor at Chung-Ang University, after *Sŏdo sori* became a major

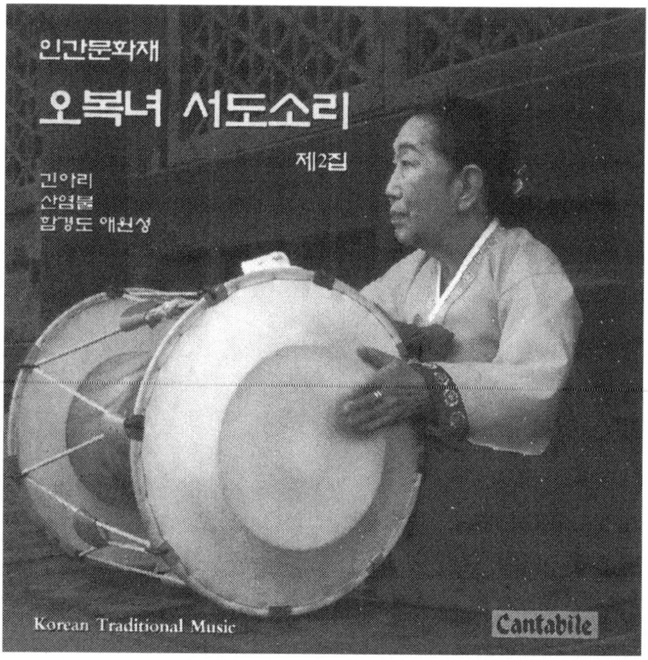

Front cover of Seoul Records SRCD-1171 (1994; CD), *O Pongnyŏ Sŏdo sori che-2-chip* (O Pongnyŏ's Folksongs from the Western Provinces, Volume 2). (Courtesy of Tony Jung.)

there. She even taught special classes at Yongin University at the age of eighty-one. Among her first students at Chung-Ang University was Kim Kwangsuk (b. 1953), who in 1981 became O's assistant teacher and was appointed holder in 2001. In 1991, O had eleven pupils, four special scholarship students and five graduates.[47] O Pongnyŏ once commented that while Kim Kwangsuk was "solid" (*tŭndŭnhago*), Yu Chisuk, one of her special scholarship students, was "promising" (*hŭimang-i issŏyo*).[48] Yu Chisuk (b. 1963), who like Kim Kwangsuk was born and raised in Seoul, began teaching at O's *Sŏdo sori hagwŏn* (Institute for Folksongs from the Western Provinces) near Kwanghwamun in Seoul from the time of its opening, in January 1994. Since 1997 she has regularly performed at the National Gugak Center, while also lecturing at institutes such as the Gugak National High School and Ewha Woman's University.[49]

Over a period of ten years, O Pongnyŏ taught Yu Chisuk approximately fifty songs, all without using musical notation, as she strongly believed in oral transmission: "The way you use your throat is naturally difficult, so you don't find many people studying [*Sŏdo sori*]. It has to come out by putting pressure on the stomach and you have to use different singing techniques. But you cannot sing old songs unless you learn them by rote."[50] Her belief lay partly in the fact that she considered Western musical notation to be inappropriate for *Sŏdo sori.*[51] In 1978, she therefore published a book in which she transcribed songs using a modified system of notation. With this system, O attempted to indicate the exact current of her voice, using a graphic line that goes up and down a ten-bar scale. Apart from detailing the lyrics and the voice, the notation also showed how she used the hourglass drum.[52] Yet despite O maintaining that oral transmission was the only way to learn how to sing, she did not believe that you could teach someone to become a good singer: "You don't need a special teacher. If you have talent, then even if you haven't been taught the quality of your voice will show when you hum."[53]

Yi Ŭn'gwan

On October 15, 1984, at the fairly late age of sixty-seven, Yi Ŭn'gwan became holder of *Sŏdo sori.* Yi was born in the township of Ich'ŏn, in Ich'ŏn County, Kangwŏn province, on November 27, 1917. He grew up in a farming household as the oldest of seven siblings. From when he was very young, Yi had a good ear for songs and enjoyed singing folksongs at school or with his friends. He disliked heavy farming work, and whenever his father, Yi Yunha, made him help out with the farming chores, he did so reluctantly. After finishing the local public school, Yi went to Ch'ŏrwŏn High School and in the same year married a girl two years his senior named Nam Sangok.[54] In his third year, at the age of nineteen (1937), he participated in a contest held at the local Ch'ŏrwŏn Theater and won first prize.[55] In addition, Yi appeared on Seoul Radio, an experience that brought him instant fame back in his hometown. Because of his success, Yi decided to drop out of school and focus on becoming a professional singer. Since his voice was high pitched and soft by nature, he decided it was best to concentrate on *Sŏdo sori.* For that purpose, he went to Seoul, where he roamed around searching for a teacher until he heard about the possibility of studying with Yi Insu, a noted singer who trained *kisaeng* at the *Hwangju kwŏnbon* in Hwanghae province.

Yi Ŭn'gwan's father could not afford the two-wŏn teaching fee, so Yi Insu allowed Yi Ŭn'gwan to help out in the house and to sleep on the poorly heated part of the floor. While commuting between Hwangju and Seoul, Yi studied with Yi Insu for a period of three to four months. Besides the one-man operetta *Paebaengi kut,* he studied the singing and performance style of *Sŏdo sori,* such as the slow and fast versions of "Yŏmbul"; "Ŏrang t'aryŏng" (Fishermen's Song),[56] from the northeastern Hamgyŏng province; and a *shin minyo,* "Chang t'aryŏng" (Field Song). Yi eventually incorporated all these songs into his *Paebaengi kut.*[57] In addition, Yi took lessons in *shijo* with Ch'oe Kyŏngshik in Seoul.

And, to increase his chances of being employed by a record company, he also began studying with Yi Myŏnggil, a well-known member of the Wangshimni Troupe. From him, Yi Ŭn'gwan learned *Kyŏnggi minyo* such as "Ch'ŏngch'un'ga," "Ch'angbu t'aryŏng," and "Sabalga" (Rice Bowl Song).[58]

Having learned the basics of folksongs from both the Kyŏnggi and northwestern provinces, Yi landed a job teaching folksongs to *kisaeng* at a *kwŏnbŏn* in Changyŏn, Hwanghae province. After a while, however, he returned to Seoul to study with Kim Pongŏp, who was famous for tightrope walking and a skilled player of the Korean fiddle. From May 1942 onward, Yi performed in a group called the *Chosŏn kamudan* (Korean Singing and Dancing Group), which was managed by the well-known singer Kim Tuch'il. In that group, Hyŏn Ch'ŏl took on the role of leader, and Yi Ch'angbae that of music director; the remaining singers included Pak Ch'ŏnbok, Yi Ch'unok, Ch'oe Kyŏngshik, Ch'oe Ilsong, Chŏng Tŭngman, and Ŏm T'aeyŏng. The group performed in many different places, including Pyongyang, Haeju, Shinŭiju, and Wŏnsan.[59] Because the other members were well-established singers, Yi Ŭn'gwan was not given much opportunity to sing, but the experience of working with them must have been a good learning opportunity and likely added significantly to his credentials.

Yi Ŭn'gwan told me that Pak Ch'ŏnbok arranged a job for him at the *Chosŏn kwŏnbŏn,* where he then worked for some time. Pak also introduced him to the famous Shin Pulch'ul.[60] After an audition, Shin asked Yi to perform in his group, which at that time included, besides Pak himself, the comedian Song Hongnan and the singer Kim Kyech'un. It appears that many of the members of this group were also part of the Korean Traditional Music Entertainment Company (Kugak yŏnyesa), including Yi Ŭn'gwan. Kim Kyech'un, with whom Yi ended up performing *Paebaengi kut,* was usually the opening act.[61] Her version of *Paebaengi kut* was different from that of Yi in that it contained many sad, narrated parts, while Yi's was much funnier overall. Yi wished to establish his own name, but because Kim was well known, he found it difficult to compete with her. During one of his performances, he therefore had a close friend clap his hands, stamp his feet, and shout "*chal handa*" (bravo) in order to win the approval of the audience, and as a result he was allowed to perform *Paebaengi kut* on his own at their next show in Taegu. Even so, the success that Yi enjoyed in Taegu did not immediately win over his colleagues. Yi remembers the disappointing reaction of Kim Kwangsan of the group's management, who warned him not to overdo it.[62]

In the 1940s, Yi Ŭn'gwan started to appear frequently on the radio and his popularity led to his participation in many folksong recordings in the 1950s. It was through several recordings of this time that Yi became known as a specialist of *Paebaengi kut.* In addition, he performed at shows organized for the Japanese military, presumably for quite a while, but not voluntarily: "In those days, if you were young, in order to avoid being drafted you either had to follow [performing] troupes and cooperate with the Japanese, or, if you didn't want that, walk around hiding in the mountains."[63] By the end of the colonial period, when the Japanese started to enforce more and more regulations aimed at undermining Korean nationalism, both Shin's group and the Korean Traditional Music Entertainment Company began to fall apart and Yi came to depend largely on invitations to sing at private occasions.[64] Although both groups briefly resurfaced in the late 1940s, they disbanded following the outbreak of the Korean War.[65]

In May 1946, after leaving Shin's group, Yi became a member of the folksong society of the Korean Traditional Music Institute (Taehan kugagwŏn). A few years later, approximately two months before the outbreak of the Korean War, the Bureau of Public Information (Kongboch'ŏ) drafted Yi to perform for servicemen stationed in rural areas. Yi Ŭn'gwan subsequently participated in several propaganda activities as part of a group that included a few other singers from the folksong society, namely Pak Ch'ŏnbok, Chang Sop'al and Yi Ŭnju.[66] At the time, the only way to travel was by truck, and Yi spent most of his time in the back of pickups, traveling from village to village, preparing for his next performance. Because there was little time to rest and because the performers often had to sit out in the cold and rain, Yi eventually lost his voice. When war broke out, Yi took his family with him to a shack in Yŏngju-dong, in Pusan, where they lived a very desolate life for a while. It was not until 1952 that Yi was able to sing again.[67]

In 1956, Yi's role as the charlatan in Yang Chunam's film *Paebaengi kut* led him to become a household name throughout the country, a condition to which he ascribed his later popularity.[68] A record released along with the film sold an astounding 60,000 copies. According to Yi, it is because of this film that *Paebaengi kut* is now well known throughout Korea.[69] Later, Yi played both the narrator and a male shaman in Kim Ki's 1973 movie *Paebaengi*.[70] He also appeared in the movies *A Henpecked Husband* (*Kongch'ŏga,* 1958), alongside Chang Sop'al, Pak Hŭngsu, and Paek Kŭmnyŏ; *Blossoms Fall, Water Flows* (*Nakhwa yusu,* 1958), in which he sings "Paennorae" (Boat Song); and *The Village Where the Cuckoo Calls* (*Tugyŏnsae unŭn maŭl,* 1967), in which he sings "Sangyŏ sori." In the 1960s and 1970s, Yi Ŭn'gwan began performing abroad, visiting Japan, the United States, and Vietnam. In the mid-1990s, he told me that he was asked to perform in Japan as part of a celebration of Korea's independence almost every year. Despite all his travel, he remained a prolific recording artist and appeared on more than thirty recordings.[71]

In March 1970, Yi began to run his own institute, the Yi Ŭn'gwan Institute of Folk Artistry (Yi Ŭn'gwan minsok yesul hagwŏn). It was first located on the third floor of the Seun Sangga business block in Changsa-dong, in Seoul's central Chongno District, but it moved to Sŏdaemun District in 2012.[72] A widower for many years, Yi lived alone in Hwanghak-tong, in downtown Seoul, but spent much of his time in his office. The sorrow of losing touch with his relatives in his hometown in the north weighed heavily on him,[73] and it would have been compounded by the growing unlikelihood of reunification. In part due to his very old age, Yi regained considerable popularity within the Korean folk music scene. In 1993, he had six special scholarship students, two of whom were women, and one male assistant teacher, Kim Wansu (b. 1945).[74] They comprised his first two students of *Paebaengi kut,* the twins Kim Kyŏngnyŏl and Kim Kyŏngsŏn, as well as Pak Chunyŏng, Ch'oe Pyŏngmun, Pak Kiok, and Kim Kyŏngbae, who had moved to Yi's institute following the death of his mentor Kim Chŏngyŏn in 1987.[75] Back in 1997, Yi felt the talent of his students left much to be desired: "I have students studying with me, appointed by the CPMO [Cultural Properties Management Office]. They get scholarship money to learn it. The country provides them with the money to learn traditional Korean songs, but there is no one of real merit among them. If I live for ten more years, there has to be one that will be good, or even five years, but I don't know if I can live that long."[76]

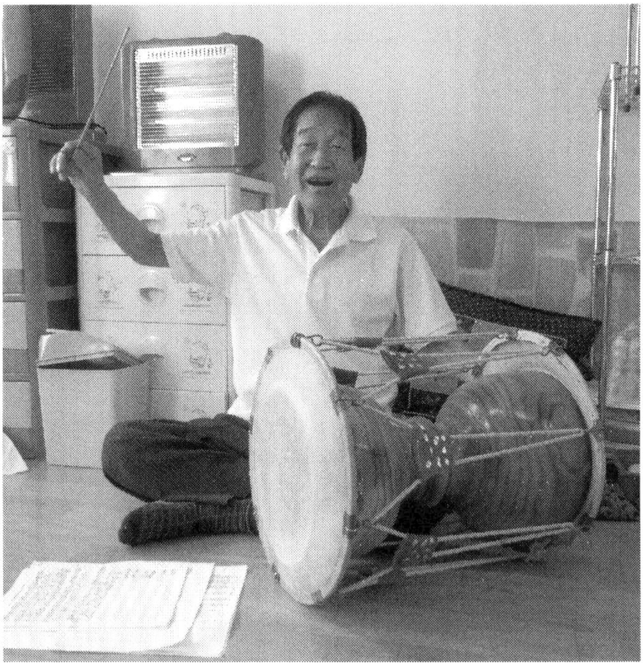

Yi Ŭn'gwan teaching at his institute in Sŏdaemun District on September 11, 2012.

When I visited Yi again in 2001 and asked him about the transmission of *Paebaengi kut,* he recommended that I go see Pak Chunyŏng (b. 1957), who had become his assistant teacher in February 1996. Pak currently runs the Pak Chunyŏng Traditional Music Institute (Pak Chunyŏng kugagwŏn; named Institute for the Preservation of Folksongs from the Western Provinces [*Sŏdo sori pojonhoe*] until 2014) in Incheon's Pup'yŏng District. He told me that when he first approached Yi to enquire about the possibility of becoming his student, Yi asked him to sing for him first. He then just looked at him intently for a moment and said, "Hmm, you do have the face for it" (*Mm, ŏlgur-ŭn twaenne*). Before taking him to his institute for further auditioning, he explained to Pak that the radio era was almost behind them, and because TV was now important, they needed to focus on visual performances.[77] Pak chose to specialize in singing *Paebaengi kut,* but despite his efforts, it was his junior Kim Kyŏngbae (b. 1959) who on March 14, 2013, approximately a year before Yi's death on March 12, 2014, was selected as holder.

Paebaengi kut

All holders of *Sŏdo sori* have so far mastered a wide range of the genre's most popular songs, but Yi Ŭn'gwan's special skill in performing the operetta *Paebaengi kut* was officially recognized at the time of his appointment in 1984. *Paebaengi kut* constitutes a dramatic performance by one performer and an accompanying musician. Although the story pokes fun at a senior government minister and his wife, as well as at monks and shamans generally, it equally elicits empathy for the couple by emphasizing their emotions by way of both the length of specific sequences and their performance. As with *p'ansori,* the performance space used is small, not exceeding a few square meters.[78] Despite the spatial confines, the piece includes many different scenes and characters. *Paebaengi kut* is made up of approximately fifty sequences that are either narrated (as *aniri*) or sung (as *ch'ang*). Most of the sung parts follow the melody of "Sushimga." Occasionally, however, Yi also uses the style of "Kangwŏndo Arirang" in the *menari* mode.[79] Some songs in the operetta are introduced by name, such as "Tungdung t'aryŏng" (Boom Boom Song) and "P'yŏngyang mudang sori" (Song of the Shaman from Pyongyang).[80]

The length and selection of the operetta's narrated and sung parts vary depending on the occasion.[81] Like other *Sŏdo sori,* the sung parts convey a sense of melancholy, and consist of a number of high-pitched exclamations that slide down in a wide tremolo while the tempo slows. The rhythmic patterns used include *semach'i* (9/8) and *kutkŏri* (12/8), both typical of the northwestern style, as well as the common *chungmori* (12/4) and *ŏnmori* (10/8). On a few occasions the songs are cut short when the character Yi acts out and is overcome by emotion. Although Yi's accompanying musician mostly plays the hourglass drum, he may switch to other instruments, such as the *p'iri* (bamboo oboe), the *taegŭm* (large bamboo horizontal flute), the *para* (cymbal), or the *haegŭm* (Korean fiddle).[82] As in the case of regular folksongs, more musicians may be employed for a recording.[83] On three recordings from the 1950s,[84] for example, Yi performed the piece to the accompaniment of either a Western-style or a traditional Korean orchestra.

Over the years, Yi has performed in a *hanbok,* sometimes with a traditional tall horsehair hat (*kat*). He often holds a large and brightly colored shaman fan,[85] which he uses to visually support his gestures (*ch'uimsae*) throughout the performance. Underneath his costume he usually wears traditional silk shoes, but he occasionally opts for the folk culture-related traditional straw sandals.[86] The use of the sandals, which connote the peasantry, is somewhat peculiar, considering that Yi does not represent farmers or farming at any point in his performance of *Paebaengi kut,* nor when he merely sings folksongs. Yi is likely to have worn sandals when he was young, and may have felt encouraged to use them again when they began to be widely introduced in the folk music scene following the *Minjung*-supported drive to revalorize farming culture in the 1980s.

The protagonist of the story is a wealthy minister named Ch'oe, who along with his wife and two close friends lives in the capital, Seoul.[87] Yi Ŭn'gwan's present version reveals little about Ch'oe's past (see the appendix for a translation of a full performance from 1980), but based on Yi's earlier performances the late musicologist Chang Sahun elaborated on the minister's identity, saying that he lives at the bottom of Mount T'aebaek in north Kyŏngsang province. Having become wealthy through his work as a shaman, the minister decides to take the state examination, which he passes with the highest score in the capital. He is appointed a royal archivist and is given the opportunity to become a government inspector for Kyŏngsang province. Yet four days after he arrives at his new office, his shaman background is discovered. This makes it difficult for Ch'oe to focus on his work, and he therefore decides to move to Hwanghae province, taking his wife and parents with him. It is there that he meets the retired ministers Kim and Yi, with whom he forges strong friendships.[88] Two other versions appear to corroborate this account. One is the first part of a recording of the operetta by Yu Inman, of a performance by an unknown singer, entitled *Mudang kwahak kŭpche* (The shaman passes the civil service examination). Another is that by Yang Soun, who used to perform an introduction called *Mudang satto* (The Shaman-Governor).[89]

According to the 1980 version, the Ch'oe, Kim, and Yi households are all childless and the three wives decide to pray for a child at a large temple on a noted mountain over a period of one hundred days. Only two older transcriptions of Yi Ŭn'gwan's version mention that the three wives decide to pray at a large temple on a noted mountain for that particular length of time.[90] In a version of *Paebaengi kut* by Kim Chuho, on the other hand, the decision to pray at a temple comes from the idea to follow the actions of Confucius's mother, who equally prayed at a temple prior to giving birth.[91] Im Tonggwŏn commented that in Korean folklore one can find many examples of people praying for a child at a temple, such as in the *p'ansori* tale *Ch'unhyangga*.[92] One can also find the idea in *Changdaejang t'aryŏng,* a comic folktale from the Seoul area, which, like *Paebaengi kut,* has many sung parts and may also be loosely related to *p'ansori*.[93]

The wives of Kim and Yi subsequently have a dream in which moons fall from the sky into their laps. Because the Korean word for moon (*tal*) is similar to that for daughter (*ttal*), the moons are a positive omen. Ch'oe's wife, on the other hand, dreams of an old white-haired man who descends from the sky to give her a pair of decorative false hairpieces (*talbi*), which she then twists and folds away tightly in her skirt's pleats. Immediately after the dream, the three women turn out to be pregnant and, soon after, they all give birth to girls. Since her mother dreams of receiving three moons, the character Yi's daughter is named Sewŏlle (*sewŏl* = three moons), and because her mother dreams of receiving four moons, Kim's daughter is named Newŏlle (*newŏl* = four moons)—the ending *-(l)e* derives from *ae* (child). Because *sewŏra newŏra* is also a colloquial expression that indicates the idle wasting of time, the girls' names are somewhat ironic. The shaman's daughter, meanwhile, is named Paebaengi.

Chang Sahun argues that the name Paebaengi must come from the word "hundred" (*paek*), which, he conjectures, the shaman and his wife would have chosen to honor the successful outcome of the one hundred days of prayer.[94] But Yi Ŭn'gwan's version explains the origin of the name this way: "because the wife of minister Ch'oe said she gave birth after dreaming that a white-haired old man gave her a pair of false hairpieces, which she had then folded tightly [=*paebae*] into the plaits of her dress, it was called Paebaengi."[95] An almost identical description appears in a transcription of a performance by Kim Yonghun (1917–1992).[96] In a version by singer Kim Sŏngmin, on the other hand, it is a pair of pigeons that come flying down into the woman's lap.[97] In still another variation, Detlef Nolden has found a North Korean transcription of the operetta in which the family's surname is Pae, and Pangi[98] is the name of a lovely female servant in whose honor the parents name their child, Pae Pangi.[99]

The three daughters all grow up quickly, and both Sewŏlle and Newŏlle move out to their in-laws' houses, where they give birth to their own children. When Paebaengi is eighteen years old, she falls in love with a Buddhist monk who comes to her house to beg for money.[100] The monk, who has equally fallen in love with Paebaengi, cannot stop thinking about her and falls ill from love sickness (*sangsapyŏng*). To help him, his fellow monks hide him inside a deep wicker basket, which they carry to the door of Paebaengi's house. They tell her father that the basket contains flour, which they plan to use for a Buddhist ceremony the next day. Saying that it is too late for them to return home, they ask him if they can store the basket in the most sacred place of the house for the night. Trusting the monks' good intentions, the father cannot refuse and allows them to place the basket in Paebaengi's room.

The monk and Paebaengi are therefore able to secretly spend some time together, but after a while, the monk has to return home. According to Pak Chunyŏng, the monk feels trapped when Paebaengi gets too serious about their affair.[101] He promises to return for her in several months' time, but when he fails to come, Paebaengi cannot overcome her sadness and falls ill. The situation worsens and one day, when her father has gone to town to get medicine for her, she suddenly dies. The parents are overcome with grief. In order to placate the spirit of the young girl, the shaman and his wife call upon noted shamans from all provinces and have them perform rituals. They promise that the shaman who allows them to once more speak to their daughter will receive all their possessions. A vagrant learns about the circumstances surrounding Paebaengi's death from an old lady who serves him at a small tavern. Later recordings of Yi Ŭn'gwan's *Paebaengi kut* suggest that the old lady learned about the circumstances from Paebaengi's father when he drank himself into a stupor on his way home to his dying daughter, while two older versions of Yi's performance tell us that the old lady used to be Paebaengi's nanny.[102]

Because the vagrant is broke and unable to pay his tavern bill, he pledges to fake a ritual and win the reward in order to pay back the old lady. He goes to the parents' house and manages to convince them that Paebaengi's spirit has taken possession of his body, but the other shamans are not impressed. They decide to test him by making him pick out Paebaengi's father's horsehair hat from among others. When the shaman impersonator begins to tear up every hat that is not that of Paebaengi's father, carefully observing the shamans' reactions, they soon all jump in to retrieve their hats leaving little doubt that the exceptionally large hat remaining is that of the father. The charlatan thus earns his reward and returns to the tavern to pay back the old lady.[103]

The birth of the three daughters, the love affair between Paebaengi and the monk, and the scenes in which the shaman's authenticity is tested are strongly reminiscent of the fertility ritual *Sejon kut* (Ritual of Lord Buddha). In this ritual, a girl gives birth to three sons after spending a night in the same room with a visiting monk. The boys grow up the objects of much ridicule and set out to find their father, who then carries out a number of tests to determine if they are related. After the sons and their mother have turned into deities, the ritual moves to a second act in which two monks unsuccessfully pretend to be shamans in order to cheat villagers into giving them money.[104] It is impossible to determine the age of *Sejonkut*, but it is likely much older than *Paebaengi kut* and may therefore have served as a source of inspiration for the latter. Sŏng Kyŏngnin and Yi Pohyŏng report that there is a theory that *Paebaengi kut* developed out of the "Tongi kimil" song, which used to be performed during shaman rituals.[105] Although the meaning of "Tongi kimil" is unknown, the title suggests that a water jar (*tongi*) was used as a drum during singing. A shamanistic origin is also suggested by the passage dealing with the love affair between Paebaengi and the Buddhist monk, because it bears a resemblance to the narrative *muga* (shaman song) named "Tanggŭm aegi," after its protagonist.[106]

Theories that link *Paebaengi kut* to shamanism leave open the possibility that the piece is related to *p'ansori*, which, according to some scholars, has strong shamanistic roots as well.[107] Because of the many similarities between *p'ansori* and *Paebaengi kut*, Kim Tonguk, Sŏng Kyŏngnin, and Yi Pohyŏng regard the latter as a northern equivalent of the southern *p'ansori*, which, unlike *Paebaengi kut*, is listed as a separate NICP.[108] Yi Pohyŏng considers that, like *p'ansori*, *Paebaengi kut* should be designated separately because it is not a folksong nor a genre of folksongs, and the frequent use of *Sŏdo sori* clearly distinguishes the operetta from the *p'ansori* genre: "In the southern regions, in the past, *p'ansori* singers couldn't sing folksongs because they were sung by the common people. Professional singers all thought like that and didn't sing folksongs, but in the western provinces there was no such idea. Because there wasn't such a concept, they also sang folksongs."[109] Yi believes that *Paebaengi kut* was created by a type of itinerant singer, *kwangdae*, in the north of the country. He believes that these singers may have already turned *Paebaengi kut* into the performance that Kim Kwanjun first became known for: "In the south they made the epic drama song, *p'ansori*, and *kwangdae* in the northwest created *Paebaengi kut*. There they didn't only have *Paebaengi kut*, but singers from the south performed there too, so I think they too would have wanted to create something of their own."[110]

P'ansori and *Paebaengi kut* nevertheless share similarities. Both are performed by one male or female singer and an accompanying musician. The latter usually indicates the rhythm and highlights specific phrases, playing the *puk* while exclaiming short words of encouragement in reaction to the singer's words. The performances constitute partly sung, partly narrated stories, performed with significant changes in mood and concomitant dynamics depending on the story line. In a commercial recording of Yi Ŭn'gwan from 1979, for example, one at first hears the narrated parts (*aniri*) performed in an energetic and occasionally ironic or tragic manner; but the performance as a whole, including both the sung and spoken parts, turns into a rather expressive tragedy as soon as the story reaches the point where Paebaengi is about to die (see Hyundai Records, *Chŏngt'ong paebaengi kut*).[111] *P'ansori* and *Paebaengi kut* both contain several linguistic styles. While some passages are taken from Chinese sources that only the upper classes would have understood in the past, others may be Buddhist,[112] or uncomplicated and explicit, reflecting the sentiments of the illiterate masses. The mix of linguistic styles supports the theory that *Paebaengi kut* was, like *p'ansori,* performed by itinerant travelers for whom, out of commercial necessity, it was necessary to be entertaining for as wide a range of audiences as possible.

There are nevertheless considerable differences between *p'ansori* and *Paebaengi kut,* including that of duration. While a *p'ansori* piece may take up to six hours and is therefore seldom performed in its entirety, a full performance of *Paebaengi kut* lasts under an hour. Because the rhythm of many *Sŏdo sori* is free, the role of the accompanying musician tends to be less prominent in *Paebaengi kut.* The vocal style is different too, as *p'ansori* singers excel in picking notes from low and high octaves within phrases, while Yi Ŭn'gwan's performance of *Paebaengi kut,* for example, moves across octaves more smoothly. The language used throughout the operetta is on the whole easier to comprehend than that of a *p'ansori* piece. Cho Tongil argues that *p'ansori*'s relative complexity in terms of both lyrics and vocal technique comes from the need for singers to constantly embellish their art.[113] It is, on the other hand, also possible that the relative simplicity of the words of *Paebaengi kut* are a recent development. Because the Korean people have long been less familiar with the story of *Paebaengi kut* than with *p'ansori* stories, this may have led singers to filter out the relatively more difficult passages from the operetta over time. Yi Ch'angbae claims, for example, that when in the 1930s Yi Ŭn'gwan joined an entertainment troupe led by Shin Pulch'ul, Shin asked Yi to make changes to *Paebaengi kut* in order to maximize its commercial appeal.[114]

P'ansori and *Paebaengi kut* differ in one more important aspect: the nature of the protagonist. In *p'ansori,* the main character is usually a hero, an embodiment of the good, such as the pious daughter Shimch'ŏng who sacrifices herself for her father in "Shimch'ŏngga" (Song of Shimch'ŏng). Characters like her may display traits such as wit and audacity, but they remain examples of filial piety and loyalty, partly in order not to offend the elite. Even so, this does not imply that *p'ansori* are incapable of ridiculing moral standards set by the elite; indeed, singers were the only ones among the lowborn whose outspoken criticism of the elite was tolerated.[115] In *Paebaengi kut,* on the other hand, the main character is a no-good charlatan. Although he honors the commitment he makes to the old lady in the tavern, he has no qualms about deceiving and upsetting people in order to achieve his goals.

Because the acts of deceit it portrays are clearly cynical and at times undeniably humorous, Yi Ŭn'gwan's *Paebaengi kut* is best considered a form of picaresque folk drama. It illustrates the possible benefits of breaking moral strictures and ridicules the establishment. Although it develops empathy for the parents, it tells us more about the charlatan's motivations than about Paebaengi or her parents. As is common in picaresque stories, wit is an important factor, as in the scenes describing the love between Paebaengi and the monk: the monks show their cunning by tricking Paebaengi's parents into allowing a basket concealing their lovesick companion to be placed in their virgin daughter's room. Wit also plays an important role in the final scenes, when the shaman imposter has to improvise in order to win over his scrutinizing audience. The fact that the piece ends with a passage highlighting the charlatan's triumph shows how important the charlatan's view on life is to the story of *Paebaengi kut* as a whole.

The strong picaresque element, as well as the story line that sees a witty man pretending to be a shaman in order to fool a child's mourning parents, supports the notion, first posited by Kim Tonguk, that *Paebaengi kut* derives from the folktale about a young man named Tongyun, which is included in Yu Mongin's (1559–1623) compendium of tales called *Ŏu's Historical Tales* (*Ŏu yadam*).[116] Yet another theory is that *Paebaengi kut* was created by An Ch'angho, a prominent member of the independence movement, in 1907. According to this theory, An wrote a scene that criticized superstitious beliefs in spirits, for the famous singer Kim Kwanjun, who then used this as the basis for *Paebaengi kut*.[117] There is, however, no evidence to support this, and because An's other compositions follow entirely different lyrical and musical styles, it is difficult to support. What is more, on a few occasions in the version that survives today, the currency "*yang*" is mentioned (see Appendix). It is possible that it was included much later, to support the ancient setting portrayed, but the currency came into existence only in 1892 and went out of use again in 1902, no more than five years before An would have created the piece, at which point the defunct coin would not have been associated with a faraway past. The true origin of the narrative and the performing style of *Paebaengi kut* will likely remain as elusive as the charlatan in the story.

Paebaengi kut's Lineages and Interpretations

In contrast to the origin of *Paebaengi kut*, tracing the pedigree of its performers is relatively straightforward. Kim Kwanjun, one of Hŏ Tŏksŏn's pupils who belonged to the professional folksong scene from Ryonggang County in south P'yŏngan province, is believed to have been the first to perform the operetta on stage. Yi Ch'angbae argues that after Kim adjusted the story of *Paebaengi kut* and began to sing "appropriate lyrics," he passed on his art to his son, Kim Chongjo, who in turn passed it on to well-known singers such as Ch'oe Sun'gyŏng (1902–?) and Yi Insu.[118] Ch'oe Sun'gyŏng would become widely recognized for the piece due to a set of 1934 recordings for Chieron (200–202) and another for Okeh (1631A/B) in 1936.[119] The only other gramophone records of the piece produced during the colonial period were recordings by Kim Chongjo and Kim Chuho. Yi Ŭn'gwan once noted that although Ch'oe Sun'gyŏng and Kim Chongjo were quite successful, he himself "was funnier, moved better, had a more powerful voice and could sing very high for a man."[120]

Yi Insu was born in Ryonggang County, in south P'yŏngan province. Having made a name for himself in the region, he moved to Hwangju City, Hwanghae province, in the 1930s to take up a teaching position at the local *kwŏnbŏn*. He taught approximately fifteen people, most of whom were *kisaeng*, and Yi Ŭn'gwan. Two other performers of *Paebaengi kut* active in Hwanghae province, Chang Yangsŏn and Mun Ch'anggyu, who was from T'aet'an near Haeju City, passed on their art to the female singer Yang Soun.[121] Yang Soun, who in 1967 became holder of IICP no. 17, *Pongsan t'alch'um* (Pongsan Mask Dance), was born in the village of Kuyang, in Hwanghae province's Chaeryŏng County, on July 12, 1924. When she was twelve years old, she took lessons in a variety of folk dances and songs, including mask dances, Buddhist dance, and *Sŏdo sori*. She also studied *Paebaengi kut* with Chang and Mun for a period of one or two years beginning in 1937.[122] In 1974 the Cultural Properties Research Institute made a recording of her performing *Paebaengi kut* (MICD-1847/8), but it was unavailable to the public until it was reissued on CD in 2000.[123] Kim Kyech'un, another female performer of *Paebaengi kut,* alongside whom Yi Ŭn'gwan once performed, disappeared from the scene in the late 1930s. According to the latter, Kim was born in Hwanghae province in 1913 and died of alcohol abuse in Yŏngdŭngp'o in the southwest of Seoul shortly after the Pacific War.[124]

When the Korean War broke out, many singers of *Paebaengi kut* found themselves in disputed territory and were either killed or forced to flee far from their native villages.[125] Besides Yi Ŭn'gwan, several other noted singers of the piece nevertheless remained active in South Korea after the Korean War.[126] Among them was Kim Yŏngt'aek, but he admitted to having only studied the piece for a short while; in 1982 he was officially recognized as an accompanying musician for another folk performing art, the Ŭnyul mask dance from Hwanghae province.[127] Another singer of *Paebaengi kut* was Ch'oe Sun'gyŏng's pupil Paek Shinhaeng. Paek was known for both "Sushimga" and *Paebaengi kut,* and he appeared on a few radio shows and recordings in the 1950s. He also won the Award for Merit (*Kongnosang*) for a performance of *Paebaengi kut* at the National Folk Arts Contest on October 14, 1963, but there is no record of him performing after that. Yi Ch'angbae reports that Paek never committed himself solely to singing and eventually made a lot of money in the mining industry.[128]

Three other singers of *Paebaengi kut* active after liberation are Yi Mansŏk, Kim Yonghun, and Kim Sŏngmin. Yi Mansŏk released a recording in 1991 at the age of forty-four (Shinsŏng Records SSL-053), but he lacked recognition and appears to have left the entertainment scene not long afterward.[129] The first transcription of the piece by singer Kim Yonghun was made by Kang Yonggwŏn in March 1974. Again, few details are given, but Kim is said to have been born in the township of Sŏhwa in Ryonggang County, south P'yŏngan province. Sŏng Kyŏngnin and Yi Pohyŏng divide Kim's version of the operetta into nine scenes, which at least in terms of the narrative differs little from those of Yi Ŭn'gwan.[130] According to Han Kisŏp, who transcribed the lyrics of one of his performances, Kim was born in 1917 and died in 1992.[131] Unfortunately, no more information about the singer is available, which suggests that Kim's main career was not in entertainment.

In 1942, folklorist Ch'oe Sangsu went to Pyongyang to record a version of *Paebaengi kut* by Kim Sŏngmin. Little is known about this singer other than that he was ten years older than Yi Ŭn'gwan and was born in Kirim village near Pyongyang, where he allegedly studied the piece at the age of seventeen with a teacher from Ryonggang County, whose name Ch'oe could not recall but was mostly likely Yi Insu. The Cultural Properties Committee (CPC) reports on *Paebaengi kut,* published in 1980 and 1984, merely note that this singer was still alive after the Korean War. In Ch'oe's transcription, there is no love affair like the one in Yi Ŭn'gwan's versions, and Paebaengi ends up dying because of an unexplained disease. The love affair between the monk and Paebaengi is replaced by an equally long account of Paebaengi's mother giving birth.[132] At the start of Kim's performance and that of Yi Ŭn'gwan as transcribed by Ch'oe in the 1950s, the full version of "San yŏmbul" is sung first, as a prologue to the story.[133] In other versions transcribed, however, performers start with an abbreviated version of the song or no song at all.

In the third volume of his monumental folksong compendium, Im Tonggwŏn includes what he calls "Paebaengi kut yo" (Song of the Ritual for Paebaengi).[134] He gives no information other than that the song was recorded in the Seoul area, but in November 1997 he told me that the song was sung to him by an old woman from Hwanghae province (where the song had been popular) who had fled to the south during the Korean War. The song essentially summarizes the operetta's story, closely following Yi Ŭn'gwan's version, but with small differences such as the absence of the birth of the girl Newŏlle. Paebaengi's name is not mentioned until the mother cries out when her daughter dies. The humor, meanwhile, seems to be slightly more earthy than it is in Yi Ŭn'gwan's version, so that, for example, when the three girls are born, Paebaengi's father says, "In our house it came out of that thing, and in the house in the back something was born out of some kind of shellfish." A few lines farther on, the father picks up the baby, saying, "Hello, baby! Where would you like to go . . . Argh, it's weeing!"[135]

In 1982, a partly illustrated textual transcription of a *ch'anggŭk* version of *Paebaengi kut* was published in Yanbian, called *The Folk Epic Ritual for Paebaengi* (*Min'gan sŏsashi Paebaengi kut*), intended for the local population. Unlike other versions examined here, all is arranged in stanzas consisting of four lines, each of eight syllables. Compiled by Chang Tongun using the recollections of a number of senior Korean Yanbian citizens, the storyline is no different from the brief outline given above, but, in the absence of narration, humor is lacking. While the names of Sewŏlle and Newŏlle are not explained, Paebaengi's name is said to derive from the word "tight" (*paebae*).[136] Because the old minister relies on Buddhist and shaman beliefs, while the charlatan makes off with so much money, Chang suggests this indicates the piece was composed around the late nineteenth century, when the *yangban* aristocracy was weakening and capitalism was becoming more central.[137]

Besides these variations, a theatrical version of *Paebaengi kut* exists. This was performed, but not sung, by several actors and was based on a transcription of an oral recording made by Kim Hŭngsŏp from Unsan City in north P'yŏngan province. This *Ritual for Paebaengi Drama* (*Kŭkpon paebaengi kut*) subsequently became known as *Unsan paebaengi kut*.[138] It was first published in the journal *Korean Script* (*Han'gŭl*) by Kim T'aejun in 1934 and was republished later that year in Chungang University's journal *Korean Folk Materials* (*Han'guk minsok charyo*) in a slightly altered form, and again in the magazine *Historical Tales Monthly* (*Wŏlgan yadam*) in 1938. The latter text includes no background information. It is based on the third act of the story in which the charlatan hears about the reward offered to the shaman who can allow Paebaengi's parents to bid their daughter a proper farewell, and subsequently pretends to be one in order to get his hands on the reward. It opens with a list of the central characters and their age, and then breaks up the piece into four chapters, providing the lines for each character with some basic information on the sequence between brackets, but without any indication of how the lines are supposed to be performed.[139] In 2007, special scholarship student Pak Chunyŏng arranged and performed a new *ch'anggŭk* version of this piece along with his senior students with financial support from the city of Incheon.

Reputation versus Authenticity

On March 14, 2013, Kim Kyŏngbae was selected as holder. An assistant teacher since March 2001, Kim had won a number of major awards between 1996 and

2002. Pak Chunyŏng, his senior, on the other hand, had been an assistant teacher since 1996, and had won a similar number of awards of comparable prestige, including the KBS Grand Prize for Korean Traditional Music in 2008.[140] It was nevertheless Kim who managed to win over the four judges when he and Pak carried out a trial performance of a full version of *Paebaengi kut* on October 30, 2012. The CPC report on the decision dismissed claims of bribery due to a lack of evidence.[141] Pak believed that Professor Ch'oe T'aehyŏn from Chungang University, who attended the trial performance as a CPC member, had favored his former student Kim. When he asked the Cultural Heritage Administration to investigate, representative Bang So-Yeon informed him on January 23, 2013, that based on an enquiry the administration had come to the conclusion that his claim was unfounded due to Ch'oe not having been present at the final meeting in 2013 where the decision was made.[142] In 2015, in order to increase his status among peers (see also chapter 1), Pak entered Dankook University's graduate school.

Similar to Kim Okshim for *Kyŏnggi minyo,* the decision to pass over Pak Chunyŏng as Yi Ŭn'gwan's successor brings the legitimacy of the preservation system into question. While Kim Chuksa and Yang Soun equally failed to be appointed despite being considered for the position of holder of *Sŏdo sori,* their cases appear less contentious. Like her sister Kim Chŏngyŏn, Kim Chuksa was a well-known singer. She was born Kim Suyŏng in Seoul's Central District, on September 25, 1905, and soon developed an interest in music. She took lessons with one of Kim Kwanjun's students, Kim Ch'ilsŏng, in *kagok, kasa,* and *shijo,* while also practicing the *yanggŭm* (dulcimer). Eventually, she became the first singer to be recorded singing "Ch'up'unggam pyŏlgok," "P'yŏngyang kyŏnggaega" (Sketch Song of Pyongyang), and "Ip'al ch'ŏngch'un'ga" (Sweet Sixteen), a *shin minyo* from Kyŏnggi province.[143] Although Kim Chuksa and Chang Haksŏn were regarded as the sole contenders for nomination, Kim was not appointed and she subsequently disappeared from the records. There is a mention of her in a newspaper from May 6, 1976, five years after O Pongnyŏ and Kim Chŏngyŏn were appointed to replace Chang.[144] Yi Pohyŏng reckons that Kim may not have been appointed because she did not perform very often, or because she was too old.[145] Meanwhile, although Yang Soun's previous appointment as holder of *Pongsan t'alch'um* in 1967 did not legally prevent her from being appointed again, the CPC preferred not to burden holders with the responsibility of teaching two types of performing art to more than one body of students.

Yi Ŭn'gwan's appointment as holder of *Paebaengi kut* was not without a degree of controversy. Although Ch'oe Sangsu claimed that Yi's *Paebaengi kut* was a recent composition,[146] the two government reports on *Paebaengi kut* noted that Yi had made some small changes to his art since the mid-1950s.[147] Yi was aware of the criticism around the time he was appointed: "Initially [this CPC

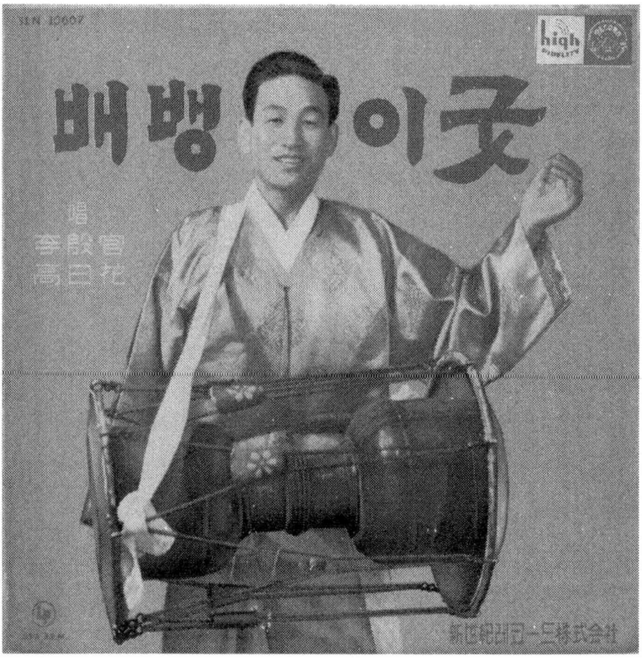

Front cover of *Paebaengi kut,* featuring Yi Ŭn'gwan (Sinseki Record Co., Ltd. SLN-10607; early 1960s LP). Muk Kyewŏl, Yi Ŭnju, and Kim Okshim are also featured on this recording.

member][148] didn't consider *Paebaengi kut* as having any artistic value. Many among the songs that have now been appointed were initially considered by the CHA as lacking in value."[149] Yi claimed *Paebaengi kut* as his own creation and freely improvised in various ways, including the use of unorthodox musical instruments such as a saxophone.[150] When I discussed this with Yu Chisuk and Pak Chunyŏng on July 11, 2011, they said that the use of the instrument was inappropriate but something Yi could get away with because of his age and position. Another form of improvisation involves lyrical change: whereas in the past a performance lasted approximately two hours, a contemporary version is less than an hour long.[151] Since Yi Ŭn'gwan's work for recording companies began in the mid-1950s and peaked at the end of the decade, it is likely that he condensed his performance around that time. The ten-inch LP that was the standard in Korea throughout the 1950s, when he began to put out records, can only hold up to thirty-five minutes divided over two sides.

Pak Chŏnghong claims that although Yi Ŭn'gwan's *Paebaengi kut* is for the most part similar to the "original form" (*wŏnhyŏng*), there used to be no passage dealing with Paebaengi and the Buddhist monk's mutual love. Pak does not specify which original form he means, but he specifically notes that he once lived in what he believes to be the place of origin of *Paebaengi kut,* Ryonggang County, where he was acquainted with many folksong singers. He makes a convincing argument that Yi created the passage about Paebaengi's love affair because love as a theme became so popular and it enabled Yi to expand the number of songs in the operetta, thus changing the balance between song and narrative.[152] Since the passage in question does appear in transcriptions of his performance by Ch'oe Sangsu and Kim Tonguk from 1957 and 1961 respectively, Yi likely created it around the mid-1950s, shortly after the Korean War.[153]

When designating professional folk performance genres, a state preservation system can sometimes benefit from such genres having already gone through a process of restructuring for the contemporary stage. Performance arts like Yi Ŭn'gwan's *Paebaengi kut,* staged by one or two performers and lasting less than an hour, can easily be promoted and marketed through recordings and other media. Although there are more amateur folksongs than there are these staged genres, folksongs usually have no connection to professional singers and have rarely been performed on stage, hence few have been refined to appeal to a commercial audience. Several groups of holders have been appointed for amateur folksongs, but the number of professional genres appointed as NICPs is greater. Amateur folksongs are more difficult to promote when sung by people with varying talent. Their texts can be difficult to understand because many are sung in dialect, and shortening their length to suit a commercial stage can be awkward.

The earliest recording of Yi Ŭn'gwan's *Paebaengi kut* I have found is from the early 1960s,[154] when Yi would have already made some changes to his art. When comparing this with a 1993 recording,[155] it is important to consider not only the smaller recording time allowed by the former format, a ten-inch LP playing at 33 rpm with a maximum recording time of approximately seventeen minutes per side, but also that Yi would have been seventy-six years old at the time the CD was produced. Yi would record his last full performance a year later for Jigu Records.[156] The use of Western notation to transcribe Boom Boom Song, which in both versions starts at around two minutes into the piece, is complicated. Because Yi regularly changes his tempo considerably within measures, the latter are useful only as an indication of the structure of the melodic line, as opposed to a representation of the rhythmic structure. Ideally, therefore, a transcription like this would be combined with a notation of the *changdan.* Rather than trying to indicate the changes in tempo through the measures, I give an indication of the average tempo for each of the two transcriptions in the figures on pages 144 and 145.

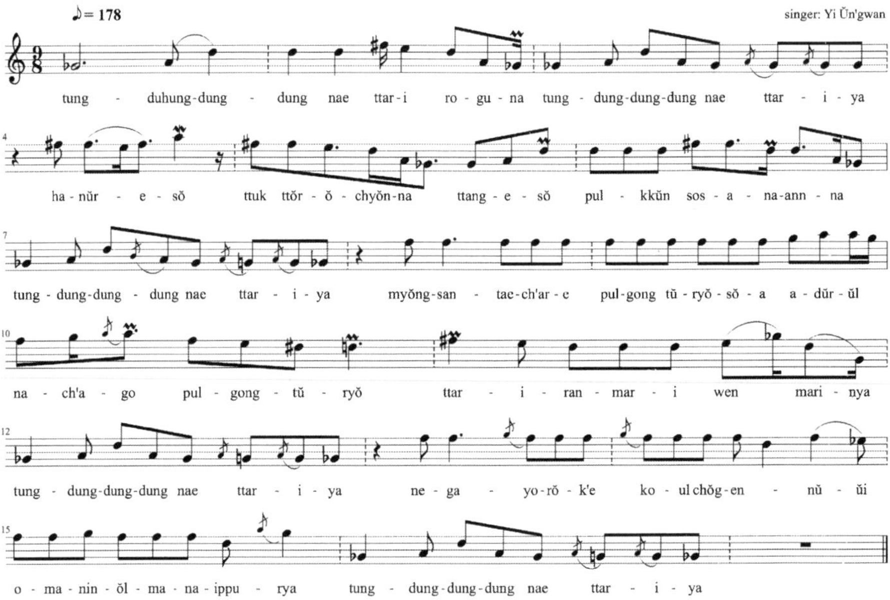

A transcription of Yi Ŭn'gwan's 1960 recording of *Paebaengi kut.*

Boom Boom, Boom, Boom, you're my daughter. Boom Boom, Boom, Boom, you're my daughter. Did you drop from the sky; did you spring up from the ground? Boom Boom, Boom, Boom, you're my daughter. We carried out a Buddhist ritual at a large temple on a noted mountain because we wanted a son, so how come we got a daughter? Boom Boom, Boom, Boom, you're my daughter. If you are already this beautiful, how pretty your mother must be! Boom Boom, Boom, Boom, you're my daughter.

Boom Boom, Boom, Boom, you're my daughter. Boom Boom, Boom, Boom, you're my daughter. Where have you come from, where have you come from? Boom Boom, Boom, Boom, you're my daughter. Did you drop from the sky; did you spring up from the ground? Boom Boom, Boom, Boom, you're my daughter. You were born with the vital energy of all four mountains, Mount Kŭmgang, Mount Chiri, Mount Kuwŏl and Mount Myohyang.[157] Boom Boom, Boom, Boom, you're my daughter. If you are already this beautiful, how pretty your mother must be! Boom Boom, Boom, Boom, you're my daughter. I will raise you well even though you're a girl. Let's see whether your descendants offer to their forebears. Boom Boom, Boom, Boom, you're my daughter.

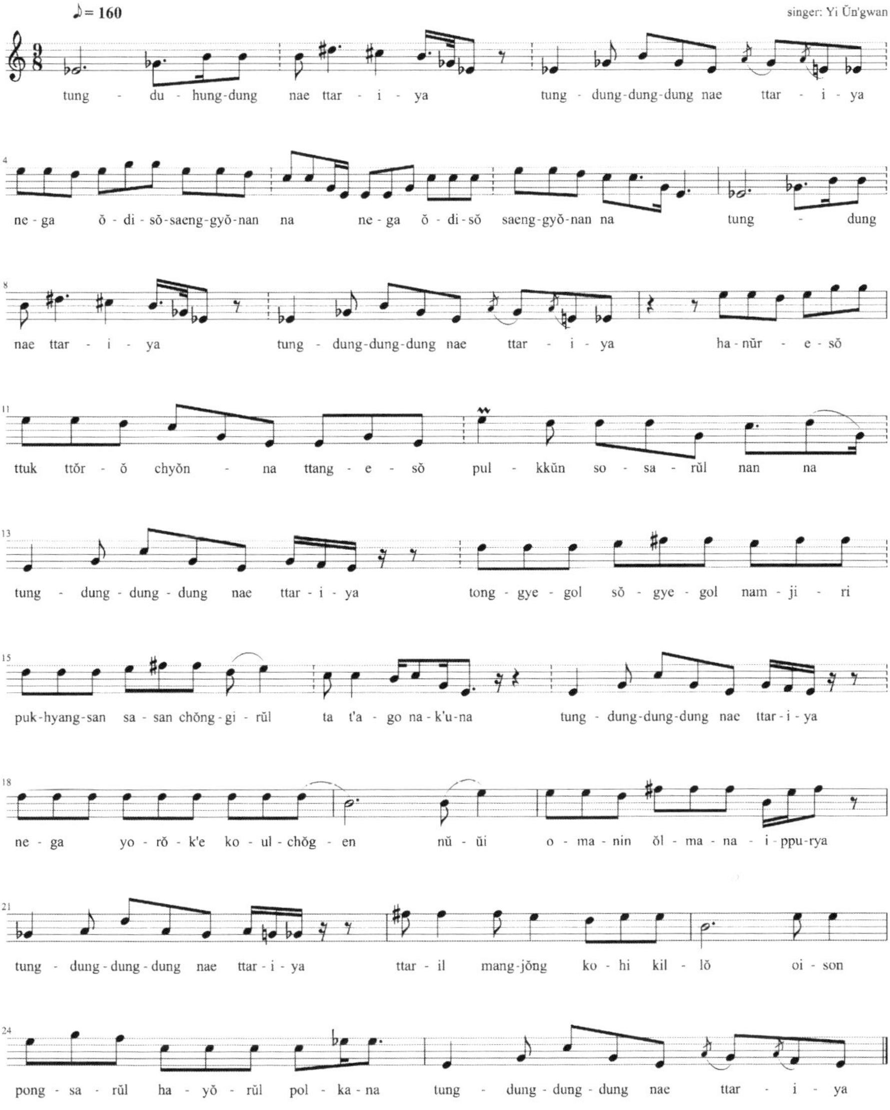

Transcription of Yi Ŭn'gwan's 1993 recording of *Paebaengi kut.*

The transcription of the earlier recording shows that despite the faster tempo, Yi sang with a greater number of acciaccatura and a more defined vibrato while alternating between chest and falsetto registers more noticeably. The difference in finesse and ornamentation are presumably caused by the difference in Yi's age, while the difference in speed may be the result of the different playback media the recordings were made for. Although the verses are similar, the later version includes a phrase I have not found in any of Yi's earlier recordings. The phrase that begins with "Tonggyegol" and ends with "t'ago nak'una" appears in Yi's compendium too,[158] but it is not included in the version sung by his student Pak Chunyŏng, who uses an unpublished booklet called "1970-nyŏndae Yi Ŭn'gwan sŏnsaengnyu: Paebaengi kut" (Paebaengi kut in the style of Yi Ŭn'gwan from the 1970s), which he noted contained a number of errors.[159] It is likely that Yi added the phrase later when he no longer had to consider time constraints.

The appointment of *Sŏdo sori* as an IICP did not have much impact on the tradition of the genre as a whole. Even though the CPC may have been aware that Yi Ŭn'gwan made some changes to his art shortly before his candidacy as holder, the committee considered that Yi would come to represent an important tradition that had a strong pedigree as an art form both on stage and in other media. His elevated status arguably led Yi to take a little too much artistic freedom in performance. His emphasis on the importance of improvisation not only exaggerates this aspect of his work but also draws attention away from other traditional performing arts that have actually shown a greater disregard for authenticity. Yi's *Paebaengi kut* is in principle ideal for a preservation and promotion system that seeks to show both the refinement of Korean performance arts and their variety. The operetta is wonderfully diverse, with references to religious practices and rural customs of old and to the various dialects of Korea. Because it is both sung and narrated by a single standing performer and a single seated musician, and ranges from the deeply dramatic to the very humorous, it continues to be compared to *p'ansori,* a genre now designated as both NICP no. 5 in Korea and as a UNESCO Masterpiece of the Oral and Intangible Heritage of Humanity.

Even so, Yi's attitude raises the question of whether holders should perform as they did at the time of their appointment or if they should be asked to go back in time and perform according to what they, and perhaps other performers or scholars, think the art once was. This would imply a rejection of variation as an essential element of folksongs, as it denies an art its "human" factor, namely improvisation. Although he must be aware of the changes he has made to his art over time, Yi Ŭn'gwan himself did not feel any constraints. He freely adapted his art according to the length allotted for his performance and to the region in which he performed (or from which the shaman he impersonated was supposed to come) by adjusting to the local dialect. To him, being able to adjust to the needs and expectation of audiences was imperative:[160] "Because of the system, many things have been preserved, but you have to think of the populace. Traditions have to be kept, but new things have to be developed out of them."[161]

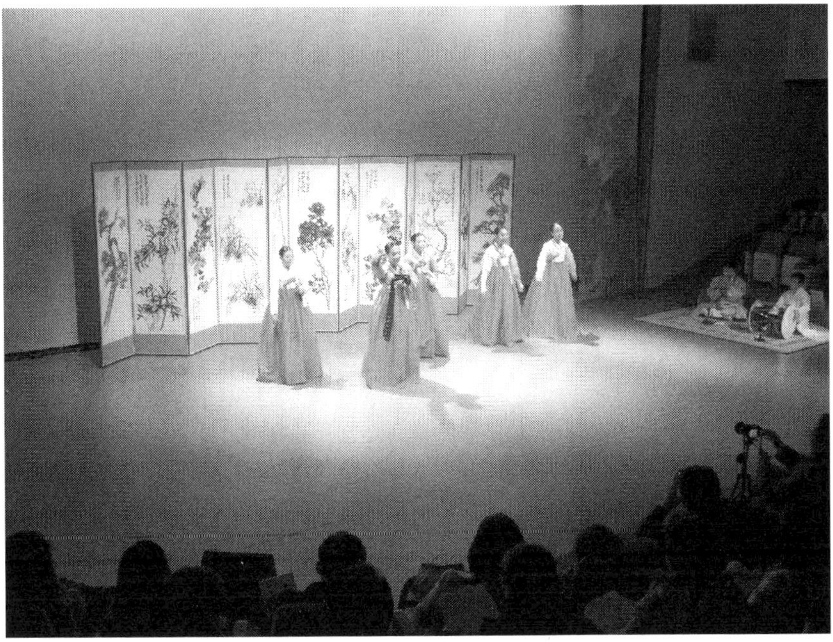

Pak Chunyŏng's students perform at the Seoul Training Center for Important Intangible Cultural Properties on November 21, 2008.

The government supports previously staged performing arts by designating them as cultural properties based on their likelihood of becoming extinct, the personal artistic skill of the performers, and the degree to which the properties represent a tradition it considers important.[162] The reports on the designation of *Paebaengi kut* stress the urgency of the first point in particular. Although they acknowledge that the tradition has gone through a number of changes in the recent past, they emphasize that Yi Ŭn'gwan's art is unique and in need of trained successors.[163] By publicly recognizing Yi as the sole holder of *Paebaengi kut,* the piece attracted and nurtured new talent. This, in itself, justified Yi's suitability as holder.

The fact that Yi was appointed and given the discretion to adapt his performance according to what he believed were the needs of his audience illustrates that the NICP system is intended to promote cultural icons and present them as objects of cultural nationalism. Indeed, despite the changes Yi made, one must consider that in 2013, at the age of ninety-six, he was still performing at home and abroad, making his status as the holder of something old and worth preserving only that much stronger. Another issue that could be raised in Yi's defense is that during his professional life, Korean society changed much more dramatically than did Yi's rendition of *Paebaengi kut*. Today most people appreciate his music through recordings and broadcasts—most young people have neither the time nor the interest in folk music to attend a live performance. Modernization and the spread of Christianity in Korea have also affected how *Paebaengi kut* is perceived: a few promoters have, according to Pak Chunyŏng, asked that the piece's name be changed from *Paebaengi kut* (where *kut* denotes a shaman ritual) to *Paebaengi sori* (where *sori* denotes "song").[164]

Further complicating the transmission of *Paebaengi kut* is the future lack of singers born in the *Sŏdo sori* genre's native land. Former holder of *Sŏdo sori* Kim Chŏngyŏn said that in order to be able to sing in the northern style, one had to have been born there or have at least one parent from the region.[165] She later added, "Folksongs will no longer be formed naturally out of the customs or the life that are characteristic of the *Sŏdo* region. If so, can we then correctly understand and transmit these songs here in Seoul, which is not in the western provinces?"[166] Yu Chisuk found that a few older students who were born in what is now North Korea picked up the *Sŏdo sori* technique much quicker than other students.[167] None of the professional *Sŏdo sori* singers currently active on the professional scene, however, grew up in the northwestern provinces, which means that they cannot genuinely represent the living conditions and sceneries of old. And yet, although the North Korean lands and customs that the tradition is associated with may eventually be considered lost for good, this is likely to strengthen the ability of *Sŏdo sori* to summon nostalgia. Reunification may prove a greater "threat" to the appeal of the genre in the south than the Korean Demilitarized Zone. Although a desire for continuity will support existing traditions or foster the creation of new ones, "the loss of nostalgia—that is, the loss of the desire to long for what is lost because one has *found* the lost object—can be more unwelcome than the original loss itself."[168]

As Korean society continues to evolve, many—both young and old—will likely come to appreciate the genre for the cultural heritage it represents. With this in mind, the idea that a cultural preservation system should seek to fully preserve the version of a performance art as it existed at the time of its NICP designation, although this is commonly stated in print, cannot be carried through. While doing so would aid historical memory, the appointment of Yi Ŭn'gwan as holder and the discretion he was since allowed shows the importance of weighing such historical elements against an individual's or group's ability to nurture interest in the performance art, which was long Yi's prime concern.[169]

Conclusion

MIMICRY AND ADAPTATION

LOCATED in the East and West wings of Incheon Airport's departure terminal stand the Korea Traditional Cultural Experience Centers. They are fairly large galleries that offer Korean traditional handicrafts for sale and, albeit "free only for foreigners," do-it-yourself workshops. Young ladies dressed in *hanbok* scurry through the narrow aisles offering assistance and information, while tourists seated at large tables concentrate on their crafts. In the corner there used to be a small raised platform for music recitals, but they have been replaced with theme park-like processions in traditional costume. Although the galleries pipe traditional music through their speakers, no such CDs are for sale. One can, on the other hand, buy miniature versions of a small range of musical instruments, such as flutes, drums, and zithers. The centers represent the scope of the Korean government's heritage management scheme, while revealing some of its challenges at the same time. A fair amount of what is on offer is indeed created by artistry and craft passed down through generations, and their assorted display and commercialization may serve to sustain traditions and nurture an interest in them.[1] But displayed here, surrounded by images of a global economy and popular culture, the objects take on new meaning. Critics would label them "airport art" for being kitsch,[2] but judging by the large number of workshop participants, few of the visitors care. The items offer them a unique experience, one that may allow them to pass time or add a measure of cosmopolitanism to their travel experience. They will expect the traditional items to have been somewhat manipulated, but are not concerned by this as long as their presentation of Korean traditional culture is unique and holds its own in comparison to other iconic Asian airport art.

An important feature of airport art is its representation of culture in a way that allows consumers to recognize it as iconic, and relate it to that of other cultures. Whereas it may be akin to a romantic orientalism to deny the importance of comparison and seek, like Arthur Phillips did, recognition of one's art as it is,[3] such would deny it a wider audience and crucial testing ground. For decades, Korea has promoted local tourism and Korean cultural events overseas not only as a way of generating direct revenue or soft power, but also to foster nationalism domestically, through the foreign endorsement they receive.[4] Eclipsing the impact of Japanese icons has been an important motive. Throughout the colonial period, Japanese traditional performing arts impacted the sound, performance, and presentation of Korean folk music. Even after liberation, decades of strong nationalist propaganda and censorship of Japanese cultural expressions did little to erase the iconic standards that they set. In response to the colonial experience, Koreans long maintained Japanese standards as their benchmark.

The Korean cultural preservation system has nurtured Korean national pride and benefited from it. Even the desire of performers of intangible cultural properties to adapt their art to changing sociopolitical and economic conditions can benefit the system and help them maintain their relevance. The degree to which the system achieves this will remain the subject of debate, but the alternative, a perfectly preserved set of cultural activities, would likewise require regular adjustment of the public information that promotes the significance of such activities, as well as many efforts to secure their transmission. Nevertheless, the many developments in Korean society have arguably led to less desirable changes in folksong traditions, such as those in which personal status, commercialism, or loyalty to peers have come into play. Many of these factors are not new, but they are playing out in novel ways and are often exacerbated by the preservation system. It could, therefore, be useful to distinguish which major forms of change were induced or implemented by the preservation system and which were not. In order to determine the most significant factors, one must go back to the end of the nineteenth century. The personal stories of the holders I have related show that several factors that affected the folk performing arts around that time continued to effect change in Important Intangible Cultural Properties at the time they were appointed.

From the turn of the nineteenth century, Seoul began to rapidly grow and modernize. Urbanization led to the demise of many folk genres that could only be performed in marketplaces and village squares. As opportunities for folksong singing decreased, songs were adapted to suit indoor stages and to fit the limited six- to seven-minute recording time of gramophone records. In the 1920s and 1930s, gramophones and the radio served to widely promote individual singers. While the technology remained ill-suited for group performances such as *Sant'aryŏng,* it allowed *Kyŏnggi minyo* and *Sŏdo sori* to be turned into two of Korea's primary music genres.[5] Some singers, such as former *kisaeng* Kim Okshim and Muk Kyewŏl, were therefore able to make a living as recording artists, while *Sant'aryŏng* singer Chŏng Tŭngman had to continue to support himself working as a gardener for Japanese clients. The medium of film affected the professional folksong landscape as well. By being performed in the final scenes of Na Un'gyu's 1926 controversial silent film of the same name, a version of the song "Arirang" gained such popularity that it became an integral part of the repertoire of *Kyŏnggi minyo* singers in the later years of the colonial period, and of that of the genre's eventual holders.

The colonization by the Japanese had a significant impact on Korean folk performers and their art. While slowly removing all symbols of the Korean traditional hierarchy by way of an extensive cultural policy that laid down the foundations for Korea's own system of cultural preservation, the colonial authorities promoted the notion that Koreans were now important subjects of a new order. They ushered in several new media, but maintained control of both their content and consumption. They also established local subsidiaries of major record companies and set up a radio network for Japanese and Korean listeners. Responding to the growing presence of Japanese, schools for young female entertainers taught both Korean and Japanese forms of music and, on occasion, Western music,[6] and it is likely that some blending of styles occurred. Although regular schools would eventually teach pro-Japanese popular songs, the Japanese had little interest in meddling with Korean folk music. Since radically changing existing forms of Korean music merely to meet Japanese standards would jeopardize their commercial potential, especially among Korean consumers, the colonial authorities sometimes relied on their censorship apparatus to weed out subversiveness. A few of the later holders of folksong traditions, such as An Pich'wi, Kim Chŏngyŏn, and Yi Ŭn'gwan, managed to make the best of the new order, though they were ordered by the Japanese to perform for troops around the time of the Pacific War.

The print and broadcast media contributed to performing arts becoming standardized and associated with a certain style of representation and performance. When *Kyŏnggi minyo* was finally designated as a genre in 1975, for example, it was in principle open to both male and female singers, but it had in the previous decades become an exclusively female domain, as shown by the large number of female solo recordings released from the 1940s to the 1960s. During those decades, many record jackets showed a Korean woman singing, seated on the floor with her hair tied up and dressed in a colorful traditional costume. The image was reminiscent of Japanese geisha, a likely inspiration, because when the songs first appeared on recordings in the 1930s not only were virtually all record labels Japanese owned, but Japanese comprised a significant percentage of the *kisaeng*'s clientele. Maintaining such an image would allow Koreans to compete with the internationally dominating cultural icons of Japan,[7] a factor that may have led those involved in the designation of *Kyŏnggi minyo* to give preference to female singers.

The fact that the official recognition of folksong properties boosts the status of the designated traditions and that of its main practitioners can have undesirable results. It can grant someone like Yi Ŭn'gwan great liberty to improvise, despite criticism. Like other holders, he became the arbiter of authenticity. Practitioners of *Kyŏnggi minyo, Sŏnsori sant'aryŏng,* and *Sŏdo sori* have all begun to use the transcriptions published by the first-generation holders Yi Ch'angbae (1976; first published in 1959), Hwang Yongju (1993), and O Pongnyŏ (1978). Yi Ŭn'gwan finished his musical and lyrical transcriptions of *Sŏdo sori* in 1999, and they too will likely become the standard for his students for the foreseeable future, at least lyrically. In his own compendium of songs, he includes many new compositions, most of which are fairly unknown, except "Changhanmong" (Long sorrowful dream), which has existed at least since the 1940s.[8] Because the compendia are comprehensive, they assume a certain authority that the holders' successors may never transcend. Another negative outcome of the elevated status is the pressure it exerts on those senior practitioners hoping to become professionals. Since there are very few enviable positions to award, competition among performers is fierce. As shown, the importance of the special status may have even led to Kim Okshim's death back in the late 1970s. Still another problem is that intangible cultural properties can overshadow folksongs that have not been designated, or even others that have. *Kyŏnggi minyo* exemplify this. The genre has become so popular that holders of *Sŏdo sori* and *Sŏnsori sant'aryŏng* spend a considerable amount of time teaching *Kyŏnggi minyo.* They may never turn away students of their own genres, but such a situation cannot be conducive to either style of singing taught.

Because of their increasing prominence in everyday life, it seems that most intangible cultural properties are successfully promoted. Despite the success of Korea's preservation scheme, however, it is difficult to compete with the lure of popular culture. The popularity of folk music as the main attraction has waned. Usually several folk performing arts are combined as part of a show or offered as accompaniment to a fancy dinner or fine arts exhibition. The younger generations, in particular, show little interest. In addition to promoting them as intangible cultural properties, the government has therefore included many folksongs in school music books since the 1970s.[9] In 1997, the National Gugak Center produced an elaborate folksong music book for elementary and secondary schools that included working songs from all regions in South Korea.[10] At public schools, folksongs now make up a considerable part of the music curriculum. Because the government recognized that to teach traditional music often requires special skills,[11] a 2007 revision of the school curriculum incorporated new methods for teaching traditional music. It compares Western and traditional Korean musical notation and emphasizes, among other things, the importance of involving physical movement for working songs. Some problems

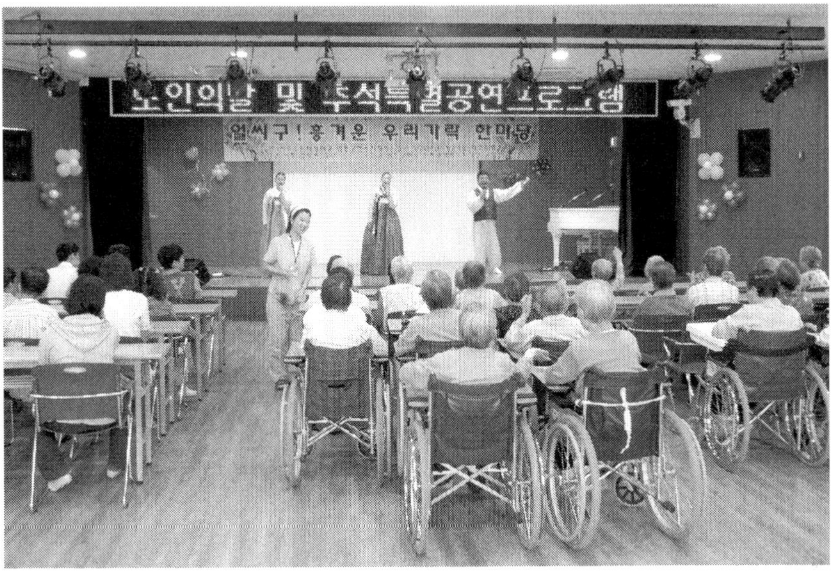

Pak Chunyŏng and his teaching assistants perform *Sŏdo sori* at a retirement home in Incheon on September 29, 2009.

persist, in part due to the pervasiveness of Western music and the negative effect it can have on students becoming acquainted with the grammar and sound of traditional Korean music.[12]

In addition to schoolteachers, the broadcast media have also been urged to help sustain the popularity of folk music. In 1973, the Korean government revised broadcasting legislation in order to improve the quality of programming. The new law stipulated that no less than 30 percent of a broadcast station's radio and television programs had to be dedicated to education, and so in 1974 the Korean Broadcasting System dedicated 49.1 percent of its radio programs to culture and education, while commercial stations allotted an average of 35 percent. Korea was a military dictatorship at the time, and so it was obviously considered better to be safe than sorry. A survey conducted in 1975 by the Committee on the Ethics of Broadcasting pointed out, however, that the programs were usually broadcast at times when only very few people were tuned in.[13] The policy regarding folk music did not change much throughout the 1980s, but in 1989 the Munhwa (Culture) Broadcasting Corporation (MBC) commissioned the *Great Compilation of Korean Folksongs* (*Han'guk minyo taejŏn*) series. According to producer Ch'oe Sangil, the aim was to record as many folksongs as possible to prevent them from being lost. He said he initiated the series because he believed that neither the efforts made by private scholars nor those prompted by the Cultural Properties Protection Law would prevent a vast number of folksongs from disappearing. Ch'oe's recordings were broadcast daily on MBC radio for several years. In addition, books with lyrics, photos, and maps with geographical detail accompanied CDs provided to museums in Korea and overseas. But the listener ratings were low. In 1995, no more than 2.5 percent of the population listened to the program.[14] The continued lack of interest in traditional music led the government to set up a separate channel dedicated to traditional Korean music in 2001, Kugak FM. At the time, many of my peers in Korea argued against the move, fearing that it would not serve an educational purpose: only those who already wanted to listen would tune in to the station, while others would simply ignore it.

The lack of an audience for traditional music as a form of entertainment has also affected the size and composition of audiences. At the 1995 National Folk Arts Contest in Kongju City I noticed that on the first day the half-filled stadium was made up of mostly middle-school students who were required to attend. Pictures of the contest in other years sometimes show an even smaller audience, and an equally large proportion of students.[15] Although the printed program of the 1995 contest includes a picture of a packed Kongju Stadium, the event shown is not actually one of the National Folk Arts Contests, but the 73rd National Athletics Contest (Chŏn'guk ch'eyuk taehoe).[16] At other events in 1995, at several of the regular Saturday afternoon performances of Korean music and dance that I observed at the National Gugak Center, young students were standing at the exit collecting the used tickets for their friends as "proof" of their obligatory concert visit. The interest in folksong performances has not much improved since then. Folksong groups continue to perform around the country, as well as abroad, but the number of special concerts of traditional folksongs for paying audiences has dwindled. Most of them are sponsored by the government and are part of gratuitous festivals that include other forms of folk art as well.

Even so, folksongs still constitute a successful element of the Korean heritage management scheme, and they remain a source of entertainment for many. Despite the dominant presence of other forms of music in everyday life, a large number of people enjoy folksongs for their music, their lyrics, and their expression of emotions. Because folksongs are not appreciated as much as they were in the past, they have lost their direct commercial value. But they serve other important purposes: they offer diversity and remind people of what it means to be Korean. They also support the Korean Wave, and not only by featuring in some of the related products. Because folksongs by definition represent the common folk, as well as the people's diversity and unique history, they offer an important contrast to the image of South Korea as a highly competitive, economically powerful, high-tech nation geared toward global expansion. The fact that the traditions have undergone changes does not, therefore, affect their national importance—and provide an incentive for the government to intervene—as long as they serve those purposes. Indeed, although *Sant'aryŏng* and *Kyŏnggi minyo* have, among other things, become almost exclusively female genres, while *Sŏdo sori* is now represented exclusively by people born outside the genre's native land, to resist change would ultimately result in the traditions' absolute demise, making the compromises not only understandable but ultimately unavoidable as well.

I have pointed out that a few of the decisions made by those involved in the preservation of intangible cultural properties have been unjustified. The appointment of only women for *Kyŏnggi minyo,* for example, and the passing over of several performers cannot be justified on the grounds of the successful candidates having superior performing talent or teaching skills. What is more, in a few cases, the appointments may arguably lead to a further loss of authenticity. Although the government affected both the state and the scope of Korea's intangible cultural properties when it first selected them, I have shown that it has allowed them to be subjected to some degree of adaptation since. It is possible that a number of adaptations are nevertheless reversed in the future: *Sant'aryŏng* may, for example, become represented by a majority of men again; and although it is not likely, *Sŏdo sori* may again be performed by people born in the tradition's native land. A drive toward greater authenticity could, on the other hand, lead to unwelcome changes. True authenticity cannot be achieved; the responsibility to make changes for specific older versions of songs would lie with a small minority of performers who would perform in front of very different audiences from those of old. Because the look and sound of many early versions of folksongs have now been recorded on audiovisual media, this information will be available for people wishing to revisit them. The thorough collecting and reporting by people such as Ch'oe Sangil and former Cultural Properties Committee member Yi Sora have been of great importance. Ko Chŏngok once put forth a plan to establish a "museum" for all folksong-related materials, a plan that was promoted again by Im Tonggwŏn.[17] But although the vast collection of materials currently held by the Cultural Heritage Administration would provide fertile soil for such an undertaking, a museum has yet to be created. The collection of field recordings is often considered to be of the utmost importance in preventing folksongs from disappearing forever, but in Korea we may have already arrived at a point where the songs most lively in the minds of old people are the songs that were the most popular at the end of the colonial period, the genre of popular songs called *yuhaengga.* On December 24, 1995, Han Ch'anggi, founder of the aesthetics magazine *The Deep-rooted Tree,* told me, "As for the spread of mass culture, we are slaves of what we see most, repeatedly: Western notation, pop songs [*yuhaengga*]; Western singing is easy. I believe in cultural saturation. If I have had a full dinner I can eat no more; there's a limit. The same thing happens in culture. When I sing pop music I forever lose the chance to sing a traditional song."

Modern Korean pop is making ample use of the sounds and images of traditional folk music. The sampling and borrowing of folksongs, as well as their use in popular entertainment, will help expose them to a wider audience. The idea of allowing a small degree of change in folk music properties on the basis of enabling singers to appeal to contemporary audiences need not and should not be promoted, because adaptations will occur regardless. It is important to recognize the challenges folk music faces in trying to regain the appreciation of people whose palates have come to expect different flavors, but society will continue to affect what folksongs represent and how they are performed. Because folksongs can no longer strongly reflect the conditions that originally gave them their significance, they are appreciated less for their music and lyricism. That their appeal has come to rely more strongly on their visual presentation and nostalgia may be regrettable, but it is an unavoidable development; and it would be wrong to dismiss the possibility of folksongs being popular with audiences on account of those particular qualities in the past. Folksongs belonged to specific social groups, and they had strong regional characteristics and associations as well as applications. They were a kind of outlet as much as they were forms of entertainment, often as part of special occasions. Preserved folksongs retain some regional elements, but they are promoted as the valuable property of all rather than of a particular social or regional community. They can still summon feelings of belonging, just like they did in the past, but as Korea becomes demographically more diverse and the memory of the social conditions and native lands fades, the reasons for people to preserve the traditions will change. The songs will only maintain their use as expressions of postcolonialism as long as personal aspirations or Korea's position in the region demand it.

It is possible to compare the role of the Korean government in the institution of folksong properties with that of the entertainment companies behind the majority of today's K-pop idols. The two institutions play a major role in the representation and promotion of their acts, but must carefully adjust their approaches to the sociopolitical and economic status quo. Those factors remain of foremost importance as they affect the preferences and opportunities of both the performers and their audiences. As the realm of popular culture increases, so does the prestige of traditional performing arts, irrespective of their alleged authenticity. Developing the broken voice of professional Korean folksong singers requires years of practice and hard work (and many a coarse throat). The considerable personal investment necessary and the timbre it produces serve to shield the traditions from the perception of being broken themselves. It is ironic, perhaps, that although K-pop dominates domestic entertainment with its strong reliance on celebrity, individualism may be more strongly associated with folksong traditions. And yet, the beauty preserved in the folksongs and their musicianship is lost on many Koreans today. Although they once made up a genre of music by and for the people, the metaphor "broken" now applies to some degree to the direct relationship between the song and the singer. The traditions still captivate, but for arguably less practical and more political reasons, such as tourism, nostalgia, and community pride. Folksongs that were once meant merely to entertain or serve as an outlet of emotion have thus gained broader significance, undoubtedly to the delight of both professional performers and policy makers.

APPENDIX

PAEBAENGI KUT

THE following translation is based on Sŏng Kyŏngnin and Yi Pohyŏng's transcription of a performance by Yi Ŭn'gwan in or shortly before 1984.[1] Sung parts are shown in italics.

The sun that at night sets over the mountains in the west will return once again in the morning, but the realm of the dead is so far away that once you go there, there's no coming back. Oh Buddha Amitabha.

In the past, a minister Yi, a minister Kim, and a minister Ch'oe lived in the capital Seoul. They were wealthy, but had no single child to care for, so they proposed going to a large temple on a noted mountain to try to get a son or daughter by carrying out a Buddhist ritual, and off they went.

We thoroughly wash and purify ourselves and when we, with waists thin like a willow, have piled a full load on our heads, we go pray between the mountains and streams; we go pray between the mountains and streams. What time is this? It is the pleasant time of spring. All the different trees are growing lavishly. Now and then we see a paulownia, and now and then a bristle-tooth oak. We pass by a handful of flushing honey locusts. This tree, that tree, the juniper, the rhododendron, the azalea; they are all in full bloom. When we look up, we see ten thousand valleys and a thousand hills. When we look down, the sandy path is white.

While singing like this the three wives went to a large temple on a noted mountain and every day they prayed together for a son.[2] They say that sincerity moves heaven, and so from roughly that month onward the three wives had a feeling inside their stomachs as if they were pregnant. One day, the three wives sat down together and started talking. At first the wife of minister Yi said, "Oh my, I had a dream the other day in which the sky suddenly opened and three moons fell down. I wrapped the three moons in my skirt and woke up. Since this dream only a couple of days have gone by, but now I keep having this annoying headache and I keep craving for a bowl of rather sour and bitter wild apricot." The wife of minister Kim then said, "I had a dream the other day too. When suddenly the sky opened, four moons fell down and I tried to catch them." Now the wife of minister Ch'oe said, "I had a dream the other day as well. An old man with white hair gave me a pair of false hairpieces. I took them and twisted them tightly into my skirt. That was my dream and now somehow I also keep having this annoying headache while craving for a bowl of pickled pumpkin." From this month on, the wives of the three ministers showed signs of pregnancy. Within one or two months blood was formed, in the fifth and sixth month the intestines, and in the ninth and tenth month it came to the point where the babies were ready to come into the world all perfectly. The bellies of the three women were no smaller than Namsan.[3] At first the wife of minister Yi gave birth, but she acted pathetically and so gave birth like this:

> *"Oh my stomach, oh my stomach! It's nice when at night my husband thinks that I'm pretty and says that he loves me, but at times like this it's horrible. Oh my stomach, oh my stomach! Oh honey, my stomach. Waah, waah, waah."*[4]

So each of the three houses saw the birth of a baby, but when the minister who had been standing patiently outside realized that his wife had just given birth to a child, he thought she might be somewhat embarrassed if he went inside, so he went to see the old lady next door. "Hello, old lady, are you home?" "Oh my, who is it?" "Ma'am, my wife has given birth to something. Could you please come have a look?" The old woman came over quickly. "Oh my, it would have been great if you had given birth to a boy and a girl just like that, one after another. I may be blind even with my eyes wide open, so I can only tell whether it is a boy or a girl by closely examining it with my fingers. It would be nice if something would hang from this little one, but you got one with a spot along the Han River where boats pass by." In this way a child was born at each of the three houses, but they weren't very fortunate because at one house they gave birth to a daughter, at another to a little lady, and at another to a girl. If you wonder how they were named, then minister Yi's daughter was called Sewŏlle because his wife said she received three moons in her dream, minister Kim's daughter was called Newŏlle because his wife said she received four moons in her dream, and because the wife of minister Ch'oe said she gave birth after dreaming that a white-haired old man gave her a pair of false hairpieces, which she had then folded tightly into the plaits of her dress, the child was called Paebaengi. Sewŏlle, Newŏlle, and Paebaengi grew up so quickly, they were like well-watered cucumbers. And one day, after several months, the ministers were so happy they sang the "Boom Boom Song":

> *Boom Boom, Boom, Boom, you're my daughter. Boom Boom, Boom, Boom, you're my daughter. Where have you come from, where have you come from? Boom Boom, Boom, Boom, you're my daughter. Did you drop from the sky; did you spring up from the ground? Boom Boom, Boom, Boom, you're my daughter. We carried out a Buddhist ritual at a large temple on a noted mountain because we wanted a son, so how come we got a daughter?*[5] *Boom Boom, Boom, Boom, you're my daughter. If you are already this beautiful, how pretty your mother must be! Boom Boom, Boom, Boom, you're my daughter. I will raise you well even though you're a girl. Let's see whether your descendants offer to their forebears. Boom Boom, Boom, Boom, you're my daughter.*

They raised them in this way, and Sewŏlle from the house in front and Newŏlle from the house in the back grew up well, moved out to their in-laws, had both a boy and a girl, and had good lives. But Paebaengi from the house in the middle was long unable to move out to her in-laws. When she eventually got engaged to a man, she was given a lot of silk for her trousseau, which she sewed during the day and spun at night. When she was about to finish her preparations and move in with her husband-to-be, a handsome monk from a Buddhist monastery on Mount Kŭmgang came to the door of her house to beg:

> *With my whole heart, I passionately pray to Buddha Amitabha on the top of paradise. When praying to Buddha, there are virtuous benefactors everywhere. White-haired old men whose spirits have ripened through their lifelong thoughts live well and play well throughout their life and go to Nirvana after death. Young and old walk on the road to death. Whether young or old, the old go first and the young go later. The impartiality of heaven and earth, even the water that flows below heaven has a now and then, and it flows only when its time has come like the turquoise water that flows off the high peak of Sumi Mountain. Please bless us in the hereafter, oh Buddha Amitabha.*

Just as he had begun to recite this prayer, Paebaengi heard it and stopped sewing. When she looked outside, she saw a handsome student monk singing.

He prayed well and was truly handsome. Paebaengi threw down her needlework and began staring blankly at the student monk. When the student monk looked inside he realized that a pretty girl was looking at him. Finding her extremely beautiful, the student monk looked back at Paebaengi and just melted right there on the spot. He no longer prayed but was head over heels in love.

Benefactors everywhere, please lend me your ears! Because we're born with empty hands and empty bodies, please donate, please donate, please, please, please.

Because he was very much in love, he stopped praying and begging and returned to his monastery on Mount Kŭmgang in Kangwŏn province, where he thought about her day and night. Unable to stop thinking about this girl, Paebaengi, the student monk eventually became so sick he was close to dying. When one day the priest of the monastery asked him about his condition, the monk replied, "Somehow, I got this illness because by a twist of fate I went to some village and saw some girl there." "Well, if that's the case, we have to help you out of your misery." They set up a plan to heal his pain by going to the mountains, cutting down a clover tree, and weaving it into a wicker box for begging, and off they went.

Let's cut down a clover tree, let's cut down a clover tree. Let's cut down this thick clover tree and that thick clover tree and try to save our student monk. Let's cut down a clover tree.

After they had stripped the clover tree and made a wicker box, they laid the suffering student monk inside and covered the surface properly with leaves. They then lifted it onto their shoulders and went to visit Paebaengi's house.

We go, we go, we go to visit Paebaengi's house. Come on, let's go, let's hurry to Paebaengi's house.

The monks had now arrived at Paebaengi's house: "Is the master home?" "Yes, what brings you here?" "The thing is, we're all monks here. But we have been given a wicker box full of wheat flour. Since we intend to use it for a Buddhist ritual at our temple, would you mind keeping it in the purest room of your house?" Unaware of the monk inside the box, Paebaengi's father believed that there was really wheat flour inside and placed it in the purest room of his house. Because the room where his daughter slept was pure, he placed it in the room of Paebaengi, his daughter. Around midnight, blinking with his eyes, the student monk inside the box could see the figure of Paebaengi, who was spinning for her trousseau. And while Paebaengi thought of the day the student monk had come and gone, and how fate had led him to her house to beg, she spun cotton, sang a song, and spun cotton:

Three measures, eight measures, twelve measures. I make a costume for some husband, but I want to see him, I want to see him, I want to see that student monk.

When he heard that from inside the wicker box, he thought, "Ah, she's singing. Having heard this one song, living or dying is now all the same for me." While contemplating his fate, the monk inside the wicker box also sang a few lines:

You want to see me, don't you? I've come so you'll see me. Who do you desire this much?

Oh my, Paebaengi was shocked; a song was coming out of the wicker box, but they had said it was wheat flour, so how very strange that a song was coming out. Paebaengi was both afraid and surprised, so she walked around it and said,

Please just sing one more line if you really are a person.

The student monk inside the box then sang once again:

It's really me. You want to see me, don't you? So just lift the lid of the box.

Paebaengi then took out a silver-decorated knife and with it she lifted the lid of the box. There sat a monk with ears like a bat. She took him out immediately and when she looked closely it was definitely the student monk who had that one fateful day come to her house to beg. So now the two people enjoyed themselves, with her laying the monk in the box at daytime and taking him out at night. But one day the student monk said, "Hey you, since we cannot live hiding from your parents like this, why don't I go and do a lot of busking at Pongsan in Hwanghae province and come back in February or March next year? Let's try to find a good way to live then." The student monk made a solemn promise and then headed off to Pongsan in Hwanghae province. Paebaengi waited until February, March the year after, even several years, but there was no sign of the student monk. Paebaengi could wait no more and fell ill from longing, having lost all will to live:

Student monk, where have you gone on Mount Kŭmgang in Kangwŏn province, and why can't you save me? You said you would come in February or March the following year; where are you? Don't you know I am dying?

Paebaengi's illness was getting worse by the day, and one day, when only Paebaengi's mother was home looking after her because her father had gone out for medicine in an attempt to save her, Paebaengi said, "Mother, mother, I am dying. Please go to the kitchen quickly and prepare three pairs of shoes and three bowls of rice. I'm dying. Mother, I'm dying. Mother . . ." She whimpered a couple of words, blinked once with her eyes, and died. Paebaengi turned stiff instantly. Her mother was distraught:

Paebaengi, Paebaengi! Why did you die? Why did you go on your own, leaving your mother and father behind? Your dad went out to get medicine. Paebaengi, Paebaengi, why, why did you go alone?

She cried like this and then rushed out to see if her husband had come back. But on the way back from some stinky herbal medicine store Paebaengi's father had gone to a rice beer tavern and drunk himself into a stupor. When he returned home inebriated and staggering, he yelled, "Honey, honey!" "Oh no, darling, what are we going to do?" "Hey, what's the matter? What's happened to Paebaengi? Honey, what's happened to Paebaengi?" "Darling, Paebaengi or someone else may have sold her small lifeboat to buy us a ship. Come on, go in and look, go in and look!" "What's happened to you, Paebaengi? Hey, Paebaengi, Paebaengi, I got you medicine. Paebaengi, take your medicine. Did somebody kill you by feeding you a piece of firewood? You're stiff from top to bottom. Oh my, oh my . . ."

"Paebaengi, Paebaengi, oh Paebaengi, what are we going to do with this bag of medicine now. The medicine I brought is of no use."

They picked up the medicine pipkin next to them, threw it away, and burst out in a lament to heaven. Now that Paebaengi had died, they tied twelve straw ropes around her torso. Twenty-four workers carried her away on a bier to her place in the hereafter.

Let us, let us, let us cross the road and go. Look at how Paebaengi's mother behaves: she puts an apron to her eyes and comes out of the house hastily, saying,

"Hey Paebaengi, you listen to me! Why do you go off alone leaving your mummy and daddy behind? If you go now, when will you return? If you go now, when will you return? Will you return when Mount Odae is flat, when the oceans and rivers have dried up and turned to dust? Will you come back when the chickens on the folding screen stretch their short necks and cackle?"

Let us, let us, let us cross the road and go. The realm of the dead is far away for us, but for you today, your place in the hereafter is just outside the gate. Come on, let us cross the road and go. When I travel 3,700 li in this world there are 33 rivers, but in that world there are 33 rivers too, and even the stars have 33 rivers, so when I cross 99 rivers, my hands and feet are so painfully cold on the soft sand of the white shores that I cannot go any further. The daytime messenger drags her by the hands, and the nighttime messenger slaps her on the back. Let us say goodbye to the old ancestral shrine and perform a ritual for the new one. For people living far away so they can hear it well, and for people nearby so they can see it well. Let us sing the "Bier Carriers' Song" and walk in line. High places become low, shallow places become high, and when we go up hastily we reach the realm of the dead.

Singing like this, the workers carried Paebaengi to her grave in the midst of the mountains and streams and, having buried her deep down, her parents returned to their house where they lived tearful, solitary lives. One day one of them said, "Say, dear, what are we going to use all our wealth for? Now that Paebaengi, the only thing we had, has died, let's summon shamans from all provinces and see if we can hear the spirit of Paebaengi one more time." They put out the word that they were having a ritual. Shamans gathered, and it is said that the number that gathered was 5,782 and a half. When Paebaengi's father thought about it for a moment, he realized they would end up as beggars if they paid all the shamans for a ritual. He called a young friend who was the roughest in the area and a good fighter and said, "Hey, we are having several shamans perform a ritual. You must leave the ones who are performing well, but immediately throw out those who don't." So they now had to pick their shaman. A young shaman from Pyongyang, was first:

Oh Buddha Amitabha.

Having watched her for a while, they felt she was too dignified: "What ritual is as dignified as that? Hey, that ritual can't be right!"

If it's autumn today, you want to look at spring, and if it's spring, you want to look at autumn. It's offensive.

"Ah, that's the way to do it! It's wrong when it's too dignified." Saying that this shaman was too well behaved they had her leave. Because the next shaman had seen the shaman performing in a dignified manner being thrown out, she decided to perform in a boisterous manner:

Oh Buddha Amitabha, when she says she's coming, she apologizes, and when she says she's going, she's embarrassed. Having come this way, she'll go like that. Why did she say she'd come in the first place? Oh Buddha Amitabha.

"Hey, you're much too boisterous; you're out!" "I thought it was passable."

The woman was thrown out for having performed too frivolously. The next shaman came from Haeju in Hwanghae province. She tried a cleansing ritual.

Cleanse her, cleanse her, lady Kamŭng,[6] *cleanse her. The high trees carry yellow fruits and the low trees carry blue ones. Seasonal fruits such as yellow chestnuts and jujubes belong to the earth spirits. Cleanse her, cleanse her, lady Kamŭng, cleanse her.*

"No, the spirit of Paebaengi has to come; how can she just cleanse her . . ." She was also expelled. The next shaman came from a secluded place in the mountains of Kangwŏn province.

Long live the King, long live the King. This world that you long for today, that you long for today, the world of the living, this country east of the sea. Long live the Korean King, our King. Today, this family will have great fortune. Long live the King, long live the King.

This shaman was also thrown out. Then, a shaman from Seoul tried a Seoul ritual.

One day, damn it, we fell into this decrepit rattrap, but after a glass of milky-white rice beer, no post stood up on the Wŏn mountain[7] *and we felt lonely. However, because we suddenly lost our grace, Your Almighty came down. We went to a silver mountain to get silver, and to a gold mountain to get gold for you. We will serve you for good fortune and the fulfillment of our wishes.*

Several shamans performed rituals like this, but Paebaengi's spirit did not once appear. Paebaengi's elderly parents, who were lying in the living room, were becoming increasingly fatigued. They were no longer looking at the ritual space and were burning up inside.

Then, finally, that charlatan friend of ours from Pyongyang, who was of rich descent but had blown his fortune on entertainment girls and who had taken traveling money to go around the country, happened to pass by the town where the ritual for Paebaengi was being performed. He went to a road with taverns and when he sat down, he noticed next to him a tiny grass hut selling rice beer. Because our charlatan friend had spent all his money and was hungry, he was out on a limb: "I'm so hungry I'm about to die. I'm just going in, order a glass and once I've emptied it I'll take the punishment or whatever." With this plan in mind, he went in. "Oi, anybody there?" "Eh, who's there?" "Could I have a cup of that, please?" "Certainly." The lady brought him one cup of rice beer. She served him from a calabash and that no-good emptied his glass in one gulp. He then wanted to drink more but had to withstand the urge. He was so thirsty, it was as though he had only caught and eaten a mosquito or a whale a shrimp, but he had to withstand it. When he looked around there was nobody else. He decided to wheedle more drink out of her. "Ma'am!" "What is it?" "What I drank up until now was on credit; can I have some more bowls on credit, please?" "No, what credit? Damn you! You'd die a rich old man. Wine on credit, on credit?" "Eh, ma'am, surely you're going to give me some wine on credit? If you don't give me credit it won't be fun any more." "My God, go on, drink everything, drink it all, go on! The way those veins in your eyes flicker, you'll end up catching somebody and devouring him, you blood-shitting git. Go on, drink it all!" As our charlatan friend drank the beer, he began to behave like a drunk. "Ma'am, goodness, what's all this about? When I drink, you see, it's all about the moment. Ma'am, when people drink a glass, they drink, when they play, they play, and when they dance, they have to dance." As he talked gibberish like this, he suddenly looked up to the sound of the barrel drum, the hourglass drum and the sound of commotion coming from a large tile-roofed house in a large neighborhood in the back. "Ma'am, why are they making such a noise banging the barrel drum and the hourglass drum over there?"

"Oh, you no-good! It makes me cry just talking about it. As for that house, they say that when the ministers Yi, Kim, and Ch'oe from the capital Seoul prayed on a noted mountain, a Sewŏlle was born in the house in front, a Newŏlle in the house in the back, and a Paebaengi in the house in the middle. Sewŏlle and Newŏlle moved out to their in-laws, had a son and daughter and lived well, but Paebaengi from the house in the middle was for long unable to move to her in-laws. She was finally engaged to a man, and even received silk for her trousseau and wedding accessories, but she suddenly died. It's so sad she died, it's so sad." "Eh, ma'am, you seem to know all about her getting a trousseau." "Paebaengi was given several kinds of silk for her trousseau." "What kinds then?" "There were many kinds. Silk like a rising moon, silk like a rising sun, three rolls of winter silk from Kilju, Myŏngch'ŏn, and Hoeryŏng, Hŭkkong silk, Mokkong silk, silk with misty, overgrown mountains, silk from Zhuge—Fairness—Liang, the Sleeping Dragon,[8] purple, deep purple silk from Yŏnan, and purple, bright purple silk from Haeju. There were many kinds such as these. It is said that she also had as many as 100 calico socks."[9] "Really, ma'am? It's hard to believe there would be more." "Why wouldn't there be? And when Paebaengi was three years old, her grandfather said she was cute and gave her a penny when she went out to play, a penny for not crying, and a penny for playing well. She bound 99 yang, 7 ton, 7 pennies, and 5 li tightly together, put it in a string-knit wicker basket and died. It's so sad she died, it's so sad. Hey, you have such a good way with words, that's right, you go to that house, perform a ritual and make some money. And when you come back, you can repay me for the beer, okay?" "Good-bye ma'am. I'll repay you for the beer when I return."

The no-good charlatan had listened carefully to the words of the old lady. He quickly went to Paebaengi's house and shouted, "Hey there, let me perform a ritual!" But because he was a male shaman, there was no way the female shamans in the house would let him perform a ritual. Our young charlatan thought for a moment. Having learned all about Paebaengi's history from the old lady in the tavern, he was sure that they would make him perform as long as he sang the song of a shaman from Pyongyang. So, he ran to the ritual ground and as he walked on, he began to perform the song of a shaman from Pyongyang:

> *What kind of shaman, what kind of holy spirit did you think had arrived? Tell me that a shaman came who stuck a knife into the front and back legs and chest of an ox and danced to the music.*

They looked at him for a while and felt he was singing a real shaman song. A female shaman then sang a prayer:

> *There are many things that people who eat cooked food with brass spoons don't know, and there is nothing that they know. Please forgive us for not having come to meet you, Spirit General, on your way here.*

Hearing the prayer, he felt confident he could pull it off. So, our charlatan friend responded:

> *If you really think like that, and give me the cap of a monk's robe and a fan, I will perform a ritual in my own style.*

When they gave him the cap of a monk's robe, our friend put it on and suddenly looked like a true shaman. He was aware that if he continued and said that Paebaengi's spirit had come, he would have to confront her parents and prove that her spirit had come, so he first had to find out which of those watching were Paebaengi's mother and father. The no-good then thought of a trick: If he said that Paebaengi's spirit had come, then he would be able to make out who was crying sadly and go up to that person. Having made up his mind, he began to cry, saying that Paebaengi's spirit had come:

I have come, I have come, I have come. I, Paebaengi, who sadly died and went to the hereafter, have come borrowing the body and voice of a male shaman from Pyongyang. Mother, mother, where's my mother gone? I tell you that your daughter Paebaengi has come, but you pretend you don't know me. When I was alive, you would come jumping as if you saw a flower in the eleventh or twelfth month of the year, but am I of no use to you now that our paths have split upon my death? Do you realize that I'm here when I have come, and that I'll be gone when I go? Mother, where are you, mother?

At that point, an old lady from Hamgyŏng province believed she had come and said: "My dear, you've come, you've come after all. Paebaengi's spirit has come. She will go after she has said all she wants to say." When he heard the old lady speak, it was in Hamgyŏng dialect. He knew this wasn't Paebaengi's mother. Keeping a close eye on his audience, he sang on:

Mother, where are you? This old lady from Hamgyŏng province has come forward. Old lady from Hamgyŏng province, were you always healthy? I died and my body was buried deep, deep in the hereafter. As for my soul, after I died, the room where I slept will surely have changed. When I was about to move out to my in-laws, the loads of silk I was given for my trousseau, silk like a rising moon, silk like a rising sun, three rolls of winter silk from Kilju, Myŏngch'ŏn, and Hoeryŏng, Hŭkkong silk, Mokkong silk, silk with misty, overgrown mountains; lay it all down in front of the shamans, so I can see it, as Paebaengi's spirit has truly come. Mother, mother, if you could just lay down here the silk I got for my trousseau, then before I return to the hereafter I'll look at it as if I am looking at you. Quickly, quickly, bring it out!

When the old lady from Hamgyŏng listened again and heard her even revealing details about her ceremonial dress, she believed that Paebaengi had truly come. She went into the living room and said to Paebaengi's mother, "Oh my, quickly go outside! Paebaengi's spirit has truly come!" When she said this, Paebaengi's mother hurried out, and while standing behind the shaman, she listened to see if her daughter had truly come this time. It was just then that the young charlatan began telling them about the situation as he had heard it in the tavern:

I'm happy, I'm happy, I'm happy. I'm happy to see the mountains and streams of my hometown. I'm happy to see the mountains and streams as well as the plants of my hometown. But when my mum and dad pretend they don't know me like this, then, please, also bring out the copper money that my grandfather gave me when I was growing up, at the age of three, saying I was cute, the 99 yang, 7 ton, 7 pennies, and 5 li, which I had bound together tightly and put in a string-knit wicker basket. Mother, mother, mother. Even though you made a promise, you're still cruel. Even if I'm just an unworthy daughter, you're being cold-hearted. Mother, mother!

When Paebaengi's mother heard these words, she became very sad and burst into tears:

Oh God, it's my daughter, it's my daughter. When my daughter was still alive, she had a sound mind and that's still the case even now she's dead. It's my daughter. My dear, come out quickly! This time our daughter Paebaengi has truly come. Come out quickly, come quickly!

Mother, for what purpose did you raise an unworthy daughter like me? Mum, dad, I died before I could pay back as much as one ten thousandth of my debt. When the sun sets over the mountains in the West, does it go down because it wants to? And, when I leave my old grey-haired parents behind, do I do so because I want to? I died a natural death. You shouldn't be sad at all and be well. Mother, mother, I've seen you now before I leave, but where's my father? Father, father! Let's see your face, father.

"Child, child, your daddy is here! What's all that about your trousseau? Take your mum and your dad, take everything, even the pillars of our house. This is so heartbreaking." When he looked at the two who had come out crying like this, it was obvious that these two old people were Paebaengi's mum and dad. Having identified them like this, the charlatan shaman looked to one side and noticed two young women with babies on their backs who could not stop crying. When the shaman studied them for a bit it occurred to him that the two women crying like that might be Sewŏlle and Newŏlle, as he had been told that Paebaengi had grown up together with a Sewŏlle from the house in front and a Newŏlle from the house in the back. If he were to call them and engage with them, it would be clear evidence that Paebaengi's spirit had come, allowing him to take off with all her money.

Mother, there is one more infuriating and regrettable matter. Sewŏlle from the house in front and Newŏlle from the house in the back, with whom I grew up and who always woke me up to go digging out wild rocamboles on faraway mountains or gather wild herbs in spring and play dangerous games, have come to stand here next to me, but they pretend they don't know me. I want to meet you, Sewŏlle and Newŏlle. Come closer so we can meet. If you just go home without having come to see me today, I will grab those cute children of yours and take them with me when I go back after the ritual.

Oh no, Sewŏlle and Newŏlle, terrified, hearing she would take their children with her, checked for the heads of the babies they were carrying on their backs, but they were just very hot. They had become so hot because they had been carried on their mother's hot backs all day. However, thinking they were hot because the spirit inside the shaman had said that she would get them, the two women rushed forward and quickly sat down on the ritual ground. But, was this Sewŏlle and that Newŏlle? He had to find out their names again.

Sewŏlle and Newŏlle, even though I died and went to the hereafter, I still haven't changed my name, but have you not changed your name since I died?

"Hey, why would I change my name? Even after you died I'm still just Sewŏlle." When she said she was Sewŏlle, the one sitting on the other side had to be Newŏlle.

Sewŏlle and Newŏlle, I'm happy to see you. Just now I was angry and resentful in my desire to see you, but even though you can't give me sisterly love, why would I be angry? Praying for the long life of Dongfang Shuo,[10] *praying for the old age of Jiang Taigong,*[11] *I bless you with longevity of 160 years, the first eighty years and the second eighty years. Stop burning up inside and live good lives. On this last visit I have one more request for you. When we grew up together, and you woke me up from my sleep, we went out to do the washing on the side of a stream and bathe on top of the washing stones and play touching each other; are my wrists bigger, or are yours?*[12] *Let's hold each other's wrists once more.*

"I seriously can't put out my wrists to him, I can't!" Then, an old lady from the village said, "Eh, Sewŏlle and Newŏlle! Paebaengi's spirit has really come now; go on, hold each other's wrists for a bit." "If she really died, then she's dead; I really can't put out my wrists to him!" Embarrassed, Sewŏlle and Newŏlle got up together and put out their wrists to him.

When I look at your wrists, they are still as soft as they were when I was alive. Let me fully enjoy touching once more the wrists of my Sewŏlle and Newŏlle whom I'll never see again.

He kept fumbling them endlessly as if they were bean curd sacks on New Year's Eve. The onlookers watched the shaman in silence, but they found him impudent, this shaman fellow. "Geez, that's odd, let's find out if Paebaengi's spirit has come to that fellow." "Let's test him once more." "What if we collect all the horsehair hats in the neighborhood, pile them up on the ritual ground and put the fairly large hat of Paebaengi's father at the very bottom . . . Oi, you, shaman, has Paebaengi really come to you?" "Yes, she's here." "Then if you truly are her spirit, you must pick out the horse-hair hat of your father. But if you don't, you'll die right here on the spot." This led to much commotion. "Well, I should now be able to find out which horsehair hat is that of Paebaengi's father. Otherwise I'm dead. Well, if I'm to die, so be it." He bawled and tore up one of the hats.

> *When it's offensive, it's offensive. How can you lay the hat of a noble man among those of commoners? I will tear up all of them and only leave my dad's horsehair hat untouched. When I pick up and look at this hat, it's not that of my father.*

When he tore up the hat, a man standing on one side said, "Damn, he's tearing up my hat!" Excellent. Seeing that all the hat owners had now come close, he continued to tear up hats while carefully looking in all directions.

> *When I pick up and look at this hat, it's not that of my father either.*

When he tore it up just like that, a man standing on the other side said, "Damn, he's tearing up my hat!" He now had to tear them up more quickly.

> *When I pick up and look at this hat, it's not that of my father either, and if I look at this one, or this one . . . then they aren't my father's hat either.*

When the owners of the hats watched him for a while, they felt that all hats were going to be torn up with the exception of Paebaengi's father's hat. It would be a tearing-up spectacle. The hat owners then all came forward and after each of them had made off wearing their hats saying, "You wear your hat and I will wear mine," only one fairly large hat remained. When he saw that Paebaengi's father was crying while he examined the horsehair hat, it was obvious that it was his. He picked it up and sang:

> *When I look at this hat, a horsehair hat from T'ongyŏng, onto which a satin band is sown, my skills are proven. This is undoubtedly the hat of my father. Although it is all dusty, nobody's here to dust it. How regrettable.*

He patted off the dust. “Oh my, Paebaengi’s spirit has truly come!” Having conned them into giving him Paebaengi’s money and silk, the charlatan took the money and left, singing,

> *She’s leaving, she’s leaving, Paebaengi’s spirit is leaving. Oh Buddha Amitabha. I conned them well, I conned them well, I conned Paebaengi’s parents well. Oh Buddha Amitabha. The fact that I earned a lot of money with this ritual is because of the old lady of the tavern. Oh Buddha Amitabha. Old lady of the tavern, please accept this money. Although I owe you 1,000 yang, I will give you 10,000 yang. Oh Buddha Amitabha. Half of the money I spent in Pyongyang I have earned back with the ritual.*

NOTES

Introduction

1. Replicas continue to be widely used by museums in Korea. See Veldkamp, "Keeping It Real: The Exhibition of Artifact Replicas in National Museums of Korea."

2. See, for example, Hyung Il Pai, *Constructing "Korean" Origins: A Critical Review of Archeology, Historiography, and Racial Myth in Korean State-Formation Theories; Heritage Management in Korea and Japan: The Politics of Antiquity and Identity.*

3. See Yang, *Cultural Protection Policy in Korea* and "Seoul-shi muhyŏng munhwajae."

4. Keith Howard's work on heritage management comprises two monographs published in 2006, *Creating Korean Music* and *Preserving Korean Music,* and the edited volume *Music as Intangible Cultural Heritage.*

5. Chung Hee Park, *Our Nation's Path,* pp. 242–243.

6. Sang Mi Park, "The Paradox of Postcolonial Korean Nationalism," p. 70. Oskar Elschek notes that "cultural policies have more to do with politics than with culture i.e. they have to do with politically and ideologically targeted goals" ("Traditional Music and Cultural Politics," p. 32). Throughout the 1990s, leading economic magazines continued to tie the promotion of economic activity to that of Korea's cultural heritage. The front cover of the monthly *Korean Business Review,* for example, which regularly included an article under the title "Korean Heritage," always displayed an image related to Korea's cultural past. The monthly *Economic Report* also had a section called "Culture" that usually focused on Korea's tangible heritage.

7. See, for example, Sorensen, "Rural Modernization under the Park Regime in the 1960s," pp. 154–161.

8. Sorensen, "Folk Religion and Political Commitment in South Korea in the 1980s," pp. 343–344; Jung-kwon Chin, "The Dead Dictator's Society," p. 303; Sang Mi Park, "The Paradox," pp. 77, 84.

9. Gi-wook Shin, "Nation, History, and Politics," pp. 152–153.

10. Sang Mi Park, "The Paradox," p. 72.

11. Chatterjee, *The Nation and Its Fragments,* pp. 6, 120–121.

12. Chung Hee Park, *Rebuilding a Nation,* p. 25.

13. Sang Mi Park, "The Paradox," p. 77.

14. Chung Hee Park, *Major Speeches by Korea's Park Chung Hee,* p. 288.

15. For more on postcolonial contra-modernity with which this is associated, see Bhabha, *The Location of Culture,* pp. 6, 245.

16. Sorensen, "Folk Religion and Political Commitment," p. 342.

17. In the 1950 editorial in which he coined the term "cultural cringe," Arthur Phillips deplored the lack of confidence among Australians in the standard of their own art. Comparisons, so he argued, were inevitable, but the preferred British standard ultimately diminished the volume of art that sought to depict the complex idiosyncrasies of Australian life (Phillips, "The Cultural Cringe," p. 299). In early twentieth-century India, however, the Bengal school of art already recognized the importance of a national standard of art independent from that of colonial powers. The school sought to eschew comparison with European standards by being "modern and national, and yet recognizably different from the Western" (Chatterjee, *The Nation and Its Fragments,* p. 8).

18. The left side of each page gives excerpts, the underlined parts of which should be corrected according to the suggestion on the righthand side of the page. One such excerpt from an Indonesian textbook reads as follows: "The Japanese people have always loved to fight. Their history is filled with warfare. In 1375 A.D., there was a princess named Ingo. *She was successful in conquering parts of Korea.*" In this case, the recommendation was simply to delete the underlined sentence (Samsung Co., Ltd., *Misconceptions about Korean History,* p. 86).

19. *Maeil kyŏngje* (Economy daily), February 17, 1994, 25.

20. Roger Janelli, "The Origins of Korean Folklore Scholarship," p. 102; Chungmoo Choi, "The Minjung Culture Movement and Popular Culture," p. 111. E. Taylor Atkins argues that the notion of Japanese colonial policy in Korea having been aimed at eradicating Korean culture remains strong among historians. Atkins, *Primitive Selves,* pp. 3, 201n2.

21. Han'guk munhwa yesul chinhŭngwŏn, *Munye chinhŭngwŏn 20-nyŏnsa,* p. 98.

22. Kwŏn Osŏng, "Kugak chŏngch'aek chedo-ŭi pyŏnch'ŏn-gwa mirae-ŭi chŏnmang," p. 164.

23. Kim Yŏngt'ae, "Munhwa sanŏp chinhŭng kigŭm 500 ŏk chosŏng." A remarkable 70.2 percent of the first five-year plan's budget was spent on renovation and preservation (Hongik Chung, "Cultural Policy and Development in Korea," p. 2).

24. Grayson, *Korea: A Religious History,* pp. 204, 206.

25. Kwang-ok Kim, "Socio-Cultural Implications of the Recent Invention of Tradition in Korea," pp. 12–15; Tangherlini, "Shamans, Students and the State," pp. 139–143.

26. To nurture goodwill, people were sent to villages to organize cultural community events, including campfires, games, and folk dances. An undated guidebook for such event organizers, probably from the early 1970s, emphasizes the importance of good organization and leadership as well the organizer's appearance and use of humor (Min'gan tanch'e saemaŭl undong chungang hyŏbŭihoe, pp. 4–5).

27. Sorensen, "Folk Religion and Political Commitment," p. 344; Steinberg, "Civil Society and Human Rights in Korea," p. 155.

28. Jung-kwon Chin, "The Dead Dictator's Society," p. 304; Sang Mi Park, "The Paradox," pp. 78–79.

29. Brandt, "Rural Development and the New Community Movement in South Korea," pp. 34–35.

30. Robinson, "Enduring Anxieties," p. 184; Hagen Koo, "The State, *Minjung,* and the Working Class in South Korea," pp. 144–145.

31. Sorensen, "Folk Religion and Political Commitment," p. 345.

32. Abelmann, "Minjung Theory and Practice," p. 143.

33. See also Wells, "The Cultural Construction of Korean History," p. 12.

34. Namhee Lee, *The Making of Minjung,* p. 203.

35. Kwang-ok Kim, "Socio-Cultural Implications of the Recent Invention of Tradition in Korea," pp. 22–23.

36. Tangherlini, "Shamans, Students and the State," pp. 131–132.

37. Sang Mi Park, "The Paradox," p. 83.

38. *Wŏlbo kongyŏn yulli* (Public screening monthly), May 15, 1977, p. 8.

39. Sung Suh, *Unbroken Spirits,* pp. 71–81; Maliangkay, "Pop for Progress," pp. 51–52.

40. In 1997, the Ministry of Culture and Tourism began to revise its censoring apparatus (Mun Okpae, *Han'guk kŭmjigog-ŭi sahoe sa,* pp. 20, 159).

41. Chang Chansŭp and Chang Nanju appear to be in denial of this possibility when they say, "the Korean culture is a stockpile of more than 2000 years of heritage. The culture will abandon some of its components and absorb some new elements, but the basic framework of the culture will remain. The Koreans remain Koreans with their unique culture no matter what happens to them" (*The Korean Management System,* pp. 71–72).

42. Howard, "Authenticity and Authority," pp. 12–13.

43. Han'guk pŏpche yŏn'guwŏn, *Pukhan pŏpche punsŏk,* p. 39.

44. Howard, "Authenticity and Authority," p. 158.

45. Howard, "Minyo in Korea," pp. 19–20n1.

46. Howard, *Creating Korean Music,* p. 6, and "Authenticity and Authority," p. 116.

47. Jongsung Yang, *Cultural Protection Policy in Korea,* p. 39.

48. Messenger and Smith, *Cultural Heritage Management,* p. 261; Pigliasco, "Intangible Cultural Property," p. 260; *Economist,* July 14, 2012, pp. 69–70.

49. Miksic, "Introduction," pp. xiii–xiv.

50. Gillman, *The Idea of Cultural Heritage,* p. 196.

51. Hobsbawm, "Introduction," pp. 7–8.

52. Hughes, "The Heart's Home Town," p. 3.

53. Killick, *In Search of Korean Traditional Opera,* p. 212.

54. Delissen, "The Aesthetic Pasts of *Space,*" p. 252.

55. *Tonga ilbo* (Tonga daily), February 4, 1997, p. 45.

56. Interview with Han Ch'anggi, December 24, 1995.

57. Ibid.

58. Jongsung Yang, *Cultural Protection Policy in Korea,* p. 112; Howard, "Authenticity and Authority," p. 133.

59. Kendall, "Introduction," p. 15.

60. Hesselink, *SamulNori,* p. 134; Howard, "Authenticity and Authority." In 1996, the succession of the martial art *t'aekkyŏn* polarized the CPC and the Korean T'aekkyŏn Organization (Taehan t'aekkyŏn hyŏphoe). The latter disagreed with plans to appoint Chŏn Kyŏnghwa, the main student of Shin Hansŭng, as one of the two holders who had passed away in 1987, because Chŏn was said to represent a less authentic version of the martial art than the organization's preferred candidate, Yi Yongbok (Chŏng Namgi, "Muhyŏng munhwajae chijŏng chedo kaesŏn moksori").

61. Kwang-ok Kim, "Socio-Cultural Implications of the Recent Invention of Tradition in Korea," pp. 24–27; Chaehae Im, "Tradition in Korean Society," pp. 13–30; Tae-soo Sohn, "Scholars Debate Definition of Mask Dance."

62. See Hobsbawm, "Introduction," pp. 3–4.

63. Takashi Fujitani, "Inventing, Forgetting, Remembering," p. 77.

64. Eyerman and Jamison, *Music and Social Movements,* p. 30.

65. Tomlinson, *Cultural Imperialism,* p. 91.

66. Young-soo Kim, "Legitimacy and Korean Traditional Culture and Thought," p. 106.
67. Anderson, *Imagined Communities*, pp. 5, 135.
68. Handler, "Creation Myths and Zoning Boards," pp. 63–64.
69. Ibid., p. 67.
70. Staub, "Folklore and Authenticity," p. 171.
71. Office of Cultural Properties, *The Preservation and Transmission System for the Intangible Cultural Properties of the Republic of Korea*, p. 9.
72. Nettl, *The Study of Ethnomusicology*, p. 177. Nettl adds that the preservation systems in some "rapidly westernizing Asian societies" are the exception. In these cases, he finds, the attempts to fully preserve traditional music remove it from its earlier social context.
73. Ibid., p. 177.
74. Ibid., p. 190.
75. Janelli and Dawnhee Yim Janelli, "The Functional Value of Ignorance at a Korean Seance," p. 90.
76. Pilzer, *Hearts of Pine*, p. 45.
77. Nettl, *The Study of Ethnomusicology*, p. 177.
78. Yi Yongshik, "Ch'angga-esŏ minyo-ro"; Maliangkay, "The Revival of Folksongs in South Korea."
79. Im Tonggwŏn, *Han'guk minyo sa*, p. 216; Howard, "Minyo in Korea," p. 15.
80. The Korean Music Research Society, *Korean Folk Songs*, p. 54.
81. *The Korea Herald*, November 28, 2014, 16.
82. Maliangkay, "The Revival of Folksongs in South Korea," p. 228.
83. Atkins, *Primitive Selves, 1910–1945*, p. 157.
84. The Korean Music Research Society, *Korean Folk Songs*, p. 5.
85. In 1993 Ahn Sook-Sun (An Suksŏn), renowned vocalist of *p'ansori* (folk dramatic song), expressed her concern over the iconic power of Japanese traditions: "Their *kabuki* is no match for the richness and maturity of our *p'ansori*. Yet they have made it known to the world through decades of concerted efforts. Today, they have exclusive *kabuki* theaters in downtown Tokyo. We should learn a lesson from the Japanese" (Jung-nam Chi, "Ahn Sook-sun," p. 47).
86. See Maliangkay, "There Is No Amen in Shaman."
87. In the past few years, I have encountered many young female performers of traditional music who had had cosmetic surgery. In doing so, they were following the trend that has seen a growing number of young Korean women, and men, opting for cosmetic surgery in order to increase their chances of success in finding the right partner or job (see Verbeek, "Koreaanse man zweert bij cosmetica").
88. Elschek, "Traditional Music and Cultural Politics," p. 32.
89. See Rosaldo, *Culture & Truth*, pp. 42–43.
90. Hammersley, *Reading Ethnographic Research*, p. 36.
91. Scheper-Hughes, "The Margaret Mead Controversy," p. 450.
92. Rice, "Time, Place, and Metaphor in Musical Experience and Ethnography," pp. 154, 157–158.
93. Ruskin and Rice, "The Individual in Musical Ethnography," pp. 308–309.

Chapter 1 Colonial Foundations of Korean Cultural Policy

1. Bourdieu, *The Field of Cultural Production*, pp. 77, 121.
2. Hobsbawm, "Mass-Producing Traditions," p. 263.
3. Deuchler, *The Confucian Transformation of Korea*, pp. 8, 229.

4. Gellner, *Nations and Nationalism*, p. 12; see also pp. 36, 111, 141; Kwang-ok Kim, "Colonial Body and Indigenous Soul," p. 271.

5. In Japan, on the other hand, the Meiji Restoration of 1868 intended to restore the emperor's position of authority. Upon recognizing the potential use of associating objects with symbolic capital, the authorities began to effectively seek the wide valorization of a range of uniquely Japanese objects in the 1870s, albeit in the first instance for the purpose of boosting overseas trade (Ivy, *Discourses of the Vanishing*, pp. 37–38).

6. See Chin Kim, "Legal Privileges under the Early Yi Dynasty Criminal Codes," p. 19; Yi Sŏngmu et al., *Yŏkchu kyŏngguk taejŏn* (Translation and annotation of the Great Code of Administration), 2: p. 682; Deuchler, *The Confucian Transformation of Korea*, pp. 121–122.

7. These government offices dealt with the general affairs of the palace and the surrounding buildings, respectively (see Yi Sŏngmu et al., *Yŏkchu kyŏngguk taejŏn*, 1, pp. 483–484).

8. Ibid. Translated from modern Korean.

9. Pak Pyŏngho, *Han'gug-ŭi chŏnt'ong sahoe-wa pŏp* (Korea's traditional society and legislation), pp. 295–296.

10. The plan to reconstruct Kyŏngbok Palace, which had been destroyed by fire at the time of the Hideyoshi invasions (1592–1598), came from the father of King Kojong, the prince regent Hŭngsŏn Taewŏn'gun. To fund the expensive restoration and hire the enormous number of workers required, special taxes were raised and new money printed (see Ki-Baik Lee, *A New History of Korea*, pp. 260–263; De Ceuster, "The Changing Nature of National Icons in the Seoul Landscape," pp. 79–80).

11. Lew, "Growth of the Forces of Enlightenment," pp. 224–226; Wilkinson, *The Corean Government*, pp. 46, 52–53, 57–59. On October 12, 1897, the Korean royal house announced that as a reaction to Japanese aggression it had assumed the title of emperor. In the thirteen-point edict, the royal house condemned corruption among officials and emphasized the court's concern for the people. It appears that the court did not rule out the possibility that Japanese pressure was the result of deities being displeased, as point eleven reads as follows: "Let local authorities send to the proper department an estimate of the cost of repairing all dilapidated temples sacred to mountains and streams. Such repairs should be made at once to show reverence to gods" ("The Edict," in *The Korean Repository* 4, pp. 388–390). Although the edict would be aimed at Confucian temples and shrines in general, a statement made by officials on the day of the declaration suggests a primary concern with the safeguard of royal ancestral temples: "When we passed through calamitous times, many dangers only strengthened the country and great anxieties displayed your ["Your Majesty"] powers. Through your exertions disorders have been rectified; and the royal ancestral temples have been kept safe" (*The Korean Repository* 4, p. 387).

12. Moon, *Populist Collaborators*, p. 33.

13. Atkins, *Primitive Selves*, p. 80.

14. Henry, "Respatializing Chosŏn's Royal Capital," p. 22.

15. See Pai, *Heritage Management in Korea and Japan*, p. 116.

16. Munhwa kongbobu (Ministry of Culture and Information), *Munhwa kongbo 30-nyŏn* (Thirty years of culture and public information), p. 311.

17. Edict no. 162, Munhwajae kwalliguk, "Kuhwangshil kwan'gye pŏmnyŏng mit chaesan mongnokchip" (Property inventory and statute regarding the former royal household), pp. 6–7.

18. Chōsen sōtokufu (Government-General of Korea), *Chōsen sōtokufu shisei nenpō—Meiji 41 nenpō* (Yearbook of the Government-General of Korea—1908), pp. 11–13.

19. Ibid., pp. 12–13, Court Order nos. 16 and 17; Chōsen sōtokufu, *Chōsen hōrei shūran* (Compilation of Korean laws), p. 71.

20. Ki-Baik Lee, *A New History of Korea*, p. 331; Maliangkay, "New Symbolism and Retail Therapy," pp. 35–36.

21. Kimura, "Standards of Living in Colonial Korea," pp. 641–642.

22. Bishop, *Korea and Her Neighbours*, p. 21. When around the turn of the century a large number of Confucian schools, *sŏdang*, were modernized, their curriculum came to even include some English (Kwang-ok Kim, "Colonial Body and Indigenous Soul," p. 269). Caprio, *Japanese Assimilation Policies in Colonial Korea, 1910–1945*, pp. 94–99.

23. Ibid., pp. 92–93.

24. Min Kyŏngch'an, "Chosŏn ch'ongdokpu-ŭi ŭmak kyoyuk-kwa ilche kangjŏmgi ttae Pusan-esŏ palgandoen 'Ch'angga kyojae sŏnjib'-e taehayŏ" (On the music education of the Government-General of Korea and the "Anthology of *ch'angga* for educational purposes" published in Pusan during the period of Japanese colonial rule), pp. 72, 82–83.

25. Caprio, *Japanese Assimilation Policies in Colonial Korea*, pp. 99–100.

26. Janelli, "The Origins of Korean Folklore Scholarship," p. 86; Kwang-ok Kim, "Colonial Body and Indigenous Soul," p. 280; Caprio, *Japanese Assimilation Policies in Colonial Korea*, pp. 104–105.

27. Ki-Baik Lee, *A New History of Korea*, p. 334; Mason et al., *The Economic and Social Modernization of the Republic of Korea*, p. 344; Robinson, "Chapter 15: The First Phase of Japanese Rule, 1910–1919," pp. 262–264.

28. Ki-Baik Lee, *A New History of Korea*, p. 331; Maliangkay, "New Symbolism and Retail Therapy," pp. 35–36.

29. Kwang-ok Kim, "Colonial Body and Indigenous Soul," pp. 265, 270.

30. For more on these "fake religions" (*ruiji shūkyō*), see Atkins, *Primitive Selves*, pp. 72–73.

31. Ibid., p. 105.

32. Kwang-ok Kim, "Colonial Body and Indigenous Soul," pp. 273, 289–290.

33. Caprio, *Japanese Assimilation Policies in Colonial Korea*, p. 109; Atkins, *Primitive Selves*, p. 72.

34. Dudden, *Japan's Colonization of Korea: Discourse and Power*, p. 121.

35. Government-General of Chosen, *Annual Report on Reforms and Progress in Chosen (1912–1913)*, pp. 37–38; Chōsen sōtokufu, *Chōsen hōrei shūran* (Compilation of Korean laws), chap. 7, 25, Article 2, *Jisatsurei shikō kisoku* (Temple Act Enforcement Regulations); Sørensen, "The Attitude of the Japanese Colonial Government," pp. 54–55; Grayson, *Korea: A Religious History*, p. 190; Hwansoo Ilmee Kim, *Empire of the Dharma*, pp. 4, 306–308.

36. Robinson, "Chapter 17: Forced Assimilation, Mobilization, and War," p. 315; Sørensen, "The Attitude of the Japanese Colonial Government Towards Religion in Korea (1910–1919)," pp. 61–62.

37. Hwansoo Ilmee Kim, *Empire of the Dharma*, pp. 2–4.

38. Hyung Il Pai, *Constructing "Korean" Origins*, pp. 36–37, 260.

39. Yŏnhap News Agency, *Korea Annual 1991*, p. 298.

40. Munhwajae kwalliguk (Cultural Properties Management Office), *Uri nara-ŭi munhwajae* (Korea's cultural properties), p. 575; Yi Kuyŏl, *Han'guk munhwajae pihwa* (Secret stories of Korean cultural properties), pp. 62–76.

41. Pai, *Heritage Management in Korea and Japan*, pp. 108–109.

42. Yi Kuyŏl, *Han'guk munhwajae pihwa*, p. 87.

43. Mong-Lyong Choi, *A Study of the Yŏngsan River Valley Culture*, p. 13; Janelli, "The Origins of Korean Folklore Scholarship," p. 87; Hyung Il Pai, "The Politics of Korea's Past," p. 29, and *Constructing "Korean" Origins*, p. 279.

44. Pai, "The Politics of Korea's Past," p. 39, and "Resurrecting the Ruins of Japan's Mythical Homelands," pp. 100–103.

45. Pai, "The Politics of Korea's Past," pp. 29–31.

46. Tadashi Sekino, "Ancient Remains and Relics in Korea," p. 4.

47. Pai, "The Politics of Korea's Past," p. 38.

48. Reischauer, "Japanese Archeological Work on the Asiatic Continent in 1937 and 1938," p. 87.

49. Ibid., pp. 90–91, 96.

50. Pai, *Constructing "Korean" Origins*, p. 35.

51. Janelli, "The Origins of Korean Folklore Scholarship," p. 88.

52. Ibid., pp. 90–91.

53. Ibid., pp. 102–103; Brandt, "Objects of Desire,"; Kikuchi, *Japanese Modernisation and* Mingei *Theory*, pp. 2, 129–131.

54. Ivy, *Discourses of the Vanishing*, pp. 71–72, 85–86, 94, 104.

55. Grayson, *Korea*, pp. 221–222; Hwansoo Ilmee Kim, *Empire of the Dharma*, p. 2.

56. Chōsen sōtokufu, *Chōsen hōrei shūran*, chap. 7, 25, Article 7, *Jisatsurei shikō kisoku*; Government-General of Chosen, *Annual Report on Reforms and Progress in Chosen*, p. 108; Pai, "The Politics of Korea's Past," p. 37.

57. See Chōsen sōtokufu, *Chōsen sōtokufu tōkei nenpō* (Statistical yearbook of the Government-General of Korea), vols. 1911–1917, 1920, 1924, 1925 and 1928.

58. Sekino, "Ancient Remains and Relics in Korea," p. 4.

59. Woo-keun Han, *The History of Korea*, p. 471.

60. Chōsen sōtokufu, *Chōsen hōrei shūran*, chap. 7, 24, Articles 5 and 6. The penalty for not abiding by this rule was set at a maximum of fifty yen. A 1923 annual report of the Government-General of Korea stated that the regulations were enacted for the purpose of "removing all restrictions, giving freedom of propagation, guaranteeing temples their properties and raising the status of the priests" (Government-General of Chosen, *Annual Report on Reforms and Progress in Chosen*, p. 108).

61. Kim Chongyŏm, "Oegug-ŭi munhwajae kwalli chedo" (Foreign cultural properties management systems), p. 252; Pai, "The Politics of Korea's Past," p. 37.

62. Chōsen sōtokufu, *Chōsen koseki chōsa hōkoku* (Reports on investigations of ancient sites in Korea). p. 6. This so-called Ancient Shrines and Temples Research Committee (*Koshaji chōsa iinkai*), has incorrectly been named "Kōseki kenkyū iinkai" (Munhwajae kwalliguk, *Uri nara-ŭi munhwajae*, p. 575).

63. Atkins, *Primitive Selves*, p. 49; Pai, "Resurrecting the Ruins of Japan's Mythical Homelands." Article 2 stipulated that if relics were deemed important enough for preservation, the respective owner or manager, the location, the presumed origin, and the recommended method of protection were all to be registered. Articles 3 to 8 constituted precautionary measures with regard to the future discovery of relics, stating that no relics were to be disposed of or changed in any way without prior approval from the colonial government. Included in protected sites were those containing shell mounds or tombs and ancient buildings such as town fortresses, palaces, and barrier gates (Chōsen sōtokufu, *Chōsen koseki chōsa hōkoku*, pp. 3–5). Although the law included items such as old buildings and images of Buddha, all properties belonging to temples would in effect still fall under the *Jisatsurei* (Sekino, "Ancient Remains and Relics in Korea," pp. 18–19; Chōsen sōtokufu, *Chōsen sōtokufu shisei nenpō—Showa 15 nenpō* [1940], p. 638). Links with Japanese legislation abound. In Japan, there was the Antiques and Relics Preservation Law (*Koki kyūbutsu hozonhō*) of 1870. This was followed by the Ancient

Shrines and Temples Preservation Law (*Koshaji hozonhō*) on June 5, 1897, which in turn was succeeded by the Law for the Preservation of Natural Monuments and Places of Scenic Beauty and Historic Interest (*Shiseki meishō tennenkinenbutsu hozonhō*) on April 10, 1919. While the former had only been concerned with buildings and treasures that belonged to temples, the latter also included land, flora, and fauna (see Mo Uchida, "Introduction," pp. iii–v).

64. Chōsen sōtokufu, *Chōsen hōrei shūran*, chap. 8, pp. 26–27.

65. Woo-keun Han, *The History of Korea*, p. 470.

66. Ibid.

67. Chōsen sōtokufu, *Chōsen hōrei shūran*, chap. 8, pp. 26–27, Articles 4, 7.

68. Ibid., chap. 8, p. 26.

69. Chōsen sōtokufu, *Chōsen sōtokufu shisei nenpō*, pp. 639–640. It was very similar to the Law with Regard to the Preservation of Important Artifacts and the Like (*Jūyō bijutsuhinto no hozon ni kansuru hōritsu*) that had been enacted in Japan on April 1, 1933, and it incorporated the 1919 law as well as the National Treasures Preservation Law (*Kokuhō hozonhō*), which had been promulgated on March 28, 1929, as a continuation of the Ancient Shrines and Temples Preservation Law (Ch'oe Tŏkkyŏng, "Munhwajae-ŭi poho-wa taech'aeg-e tae-han koch'al" [A study of the protection and control of cultural properties], p. 311; Kim Chongyŏm, "Oegug-ŭi munhwajae kwalli chedo," pp. 251–252).

70. Although a previously formed Society for the Preservation of Natural Monuments, Places of Scenic Beauty and Historic Interest, and Treasures in Korea (*Chōsen hōmotsu koseki meishō tennenkinenbutsu hozonkai*) was in charge of overseeing the law's execution, the colonial government maintained executive power (Munhwajae kwalliguk, *Uri nara-ŭi munhwajae*, pp. 575–576; Chōsen sōtokufu, *Chōsen sōtokufu shisei nenpō*, pp. 639–640).

71. Pai, *Heritage Management in Korea and Japan*, p. 125.

72. Chōsen sōtokufu, *Chōsen sōtokufu kanpō* (Government-General of Korea gazette), pp. 201–205.

73. Chōsen sōtokufu, *Chōsen sōtokufu shisei nenpō*, pp. 639–640.

74. Ibid., pp. 639–640. According to Sekino, the reconstruction of Pulguk Temple was the most costly of all repair works carried out between 1913 and 1931. It took eleven years and cost 48,456 yen ("Ancient Remains and Relics in Korea," p. 20).

75. Seidel, "Kokuho: Note à Propos du Terme 'Trésor National' en Chine et au Japon," p. 229.

76. Pai, "The Politics of Korea's Past," p. 34.

77. A report by Frederick McCormick shows that in northern China, too, the antiques trade had been the cause of much looting since 1900 (*The North-China Herald and Supreme Court & Consular Gazette*, July 25, 1914, p. 266; see also December 6, 1913, p. 722).

78. Pai, *Heritage Management in Korea and Japan*, p. 54. On one occasion, the Japanese government-general invited a number of Chinese professors from Beijing University to come to Korea to visit an archeological site. Among the inviting party was associate professor Kuroda Kanichi, who is reported to have been a serial collector of old coins (Ma Heng, "Canguan Chaoxian guwu baogao" [Report on a visit to an archeological site in Korea], p. 5).

79. Brandt, "Objects of Desire," p. 742n19.

80. *The North-China Herald and Supreme Court & Consular Gazette*, August 17, 1912, p. 442; December 6, 1913, p. 722. Looting and theft have long threatened the safeguarding of relics in China. In 1934, *The China Press* reported that foreigners nicknamed the Antiques and Jade Bazaar in Shanghai "the thieves market" (*The China Press*, January 30, 1934, p. 9).

81. The number of dealers grew from 1,074 in 1912, to 13,767 in 1927, to 15,650 in 1933, and to 23,031 in 1939 (Chōsen sōtokufu, *Chōsen sōtokufu tōkei nenpō*, 1914, p. 454; 1918,

p. 416; 1929, p. 373; 1931, p. 392; 1935, p. 320; 1938, p. 358; 1941, p. 366). In 1934, the majority of the antiques traders were Korean (86.1 percent). By 1939, the percentage of Korean businesses had further grown to 94 percent (Chōsen sōtokufu, *Chōsen sōtokufu tōkei nenpō,* 1935, p. 320; 1941, p. 366). During the colonial period, foreign businesses became equally involved in the antiques trade, but their numbers never exceeded a few dozen and they dwindled again during the Pacific War (ibid., 1935, p. 320; 1938, p. 358; 1941, p. 366).

82. The annual number of violations of the 1916 law was small and rarely exceeded ten. The violators were usually Korean, although from the late 1920s, sometimes Japanese were among those arrested. Not all cases resulted in penal action, but those that did were usually settled through fines (see ibid., 1928, p. 365; 1930, p. 355, 1930, p. 355; 1932, p. 340; 1934, p. 380). Particular lenience may have been applied in cases involving Westerners. In August 1929, for example, a large number of rare Korean treasures, collected by a Sir MacLeavy Brown, who had worked as a commissioner of customs until the Japanese annexation, were discovered buried under rubbish in the basement of the prison warden's training school in Seoul. Even after their salvage, the treasures were still forwarded to Brown in London (N.C.D.N. [North China Daily News] Special Service, "Important Find of Treasure," *The North-China Herald and Supreme Court & Consular Gazette,* August 31, 1929, p. 329).

83. The law had first been enacted in Japan in 1895 but was promulgated by the Japanese government in Korea in 1916 (*Maeil shinbo* [Daily report], February 9, 1916, p. 2). The total number of reported violations of this law increased from 6 in 1916, to 324 in 1926, to 684 in 1936, and to 1143 in 1939. Again, the majority of these violations were settled through fines (Chōsen sōtokufu, *Chōsen sōtokufu tōkei nenpō,* 1918, p. 594; 1928, p. 370; 1938, p. 358; 1941, p. 356).

84. Pai, "The Politics of Korea's Past," p. 37.

85. Ibid., p. 32.

86. Seidel, "Kokuho." One of the first official uses of the term was on December 19, 1952, by the then minister of education, Kim Pŏmnin, when establishing the Interim Committee for the Preservation of Natural Monuments, Places of Scenic Beauty and Historic Interest, and National Treasures (*Kukpo kojŏk myŏngsŭng ch'ŏnyŏn kinyŏmmul imshi pojon wiwŏnhoe*) for the purpose of carrying out repairs on cultural properties damaged during the Korean War (Chŏng Chaejong, "Munhwajae wiwŏnhoe yaksa," p. 2).

87. Yi Kyŏngnyŏl. "Munhwa-ŭi ŭiŭi," p. 35. One of the first uses of the term *munhwa yusan* was in the North Korean journal of the same name, published since 1957 by the Democratic Republic of Korea's Research Institute for Archaeology and Folklore (*Chosŏn minjujui inmin konghwaguk kwahagwŏn kogohak mit minsokhak yŏn'guso*) in Pyongyang.

88. Atkins, *Primitive Selves,* p. 105.

89. Janelli, "The Origins of Korean Folklore Scholarship," p. 87.

90. Munhwajae kwalliguk, "Kuhwangshil kwan'gye pŏmnyŏng," pp. 20–21.

91. Among those lost were Treasure no. 240, Porim Temple in south Chŏlla province's Changhŭng County; and Treasure no. 276, Ch'oksŏng Pavilion, a former command post located in the southern city of Chinju (Yi Kuyŏl, *Han'guk munhwajae pihwa,* pp. 243–245).

92. Pai, *Constructing "Korean" Origins,* p. 240; *Heritage Management in Korea and Japan,* pp. 176, 181.

93. The Office of the Former Royal Household, which was renamed again on June 8, 1955, this time as Office for the Management of Property of the Former Royal Household (Kuhwangshil chaesan samuch'ongguk), supervised the law's implementation. In June 1955, a total of 132 people were officially employed at the office (Munhwa kongbobu, *Munhwa kongbo 30-nyŏn,* p. 280).

94. Munhwajae kwalliguk, "Kuhwangshil kwan'gye pŏmnyŏng," p. 22. None of the previous ordinances regarding the royal household had been specific about what was to be considered a cultural property. Instead, they focused on the number and type of positions that needed to be created to oversee the management of all associated responsibilities, which included the museums, gardens, and the zoo (Munhwajae kwalliguk, "Kuhwangshil kwan'gye pŏmnyŏng," pp. 5–19).

95. The unit's inauguration coincided with the official decommissioning of the Society for the Preservation of Natural Monuments and Places of Scenic Beauty and Historic Interest (Munhwa kongbobu, *Munhwa kongbo 30-nyŏn*, p. 282).

96. Ibid., pp. 279–283; Munhwajae kwalliguk, *Chosŏn ch'ongdokpu mit mun'gyobu palhaeng munhwajae kwan'gye charyojip* (Collection of materials related to cultural properties as published by the Government-General of Korea and the Ministry of Culture), pp. 163, 415. According to Hyung Il Pai, the reassignment of treasures designated during the colonial era did not take place until December 20, 1962 (*Heritage Management in Korea and Japan*, p. 21).

97. Chŏng Chaejong, "Munhwajae wiwŏnhoe yaksa," p. 4.

98. Uchida, "Introduction," p. iv.

99. David Hughes believes there is a consensus among scholars and the laity that *minzoku bunkazai* are, among other things, usually tied to religion in the broad sense, closely linked to a particular local community, and held at fixed places on fixed occasions (Hughes, "The Heart's Home Town," p. 26; see also Fujie, "A Comparison of Cultural Policies Towards Traditional Music in the United States and Japan," p. 71; Thornbury, "The Cultural Properties Protection Law and Japan's Folk Performing Arts," pp. 214, 222n2).

100. Cang, "Defining Intangible Cultural Heritage and Its Stakeholders," p. 47.

101. Thornbury, "The Cultural Properties Protection Law and Japan's Folk Performing Arts," pp. 211, 225; Pimpaneau, "Living National Treasures in Japan," p. 3; Aikawa-Faure, "Excellence and Authenticity," p. 39.

102. Aikawa-Faure, "Excellence and Authenticity," p. 41.

103. Chungmoo Choi, "Hegemony and Shamanism," p. 23.

104. Howard, *Preserving Korean Music*, pp. 4–6. Ye used the term to refer to master artists and craftsmen (Ye Yonghae, *In'gan munhwajae*). In Japan, the corresponding (and equally unofficial) term is *nin'gen kokuhō* (human national treasures).

105. Munhwa ch'eyukpu (Ministry of Culture and Sports), *Munhwajae kwan'gye pŏmnyŏngjip* (Collection of laws and regulations regarding the management of cultural properties), p. 11. For a description of the amendments, see Han'guk pŏpche yŏn'guwŏn, *Pukhan pŏpche punsŏk*, pp. 13–15.

106. Office of Cultural Properties, *The Preservation and Transmission System*, p. 37, Article 1.

107. Han'guk yŏn'gam p'yŏnch'an wiwŏnhoe (Compilation Committee of the Yearbook of Korea), *Han'guk yŏn'gam 1960* (1960 yearbook of Korea), pp. 501–507. Henrik Sørensen argues that the Law for the Management of Buddhist Property (*Pulgyo chaesan kwallipŏp*), which was enacted in 1961, was intended to control the property of Buddhist temples under the veil of protection ("'Protecting the Nation'," p. 197). Thus this law could be considered a copy of the 1911 Temple Act.

108. The importance of intangible cultural properties had already been recognized as part of the Cultural Properties Preservation Committee Regulations (*Munhwajae pojon wiwŏnhoe kyujŏng*) of November 10, 1960. The committee was replaced by the Cultural Properties Committee (*Munhwajae wiwŏnhoe*) on March 27, 1962 (Chŏng Chaejong, "Munhwajae wiwŏnhoe yaksa," pp. 3–4).

109. Aikawa-Faure, "Excellence and Authenticity, p. 44.

110. Pai, *Heritage Management in Korea and Japan*, p. 180.

111. Apart from the role collectors played in the smuggling of Korean artifacts abroad, scholars have recognized the hand Yanagi played in supporting the system of colonial rule that broke many traditions of folk performing arts. They nevertheless credit him for championing Korean art and crafts, and for successfully opposing the planned demolition of Kwanghwamun, the front gate of Kyŏngbok Palace, in 1922 (Brandt, "Objects of Desire,' pp. 713–714, 726, 737; Kikuchi, *Japanese Modernisation and* Mingei *Theory*, pp. 127–129, 138).

112. Thornbury, "The Cultural Properties Protection Law and Japan's Folk Performing Arts," p. 215.

113. See also Schmid, *Korea Between Empires: 1895–1919*, p. 277.

114. Chŏng Chaejong, "Munhwajae wiwŏnhoe yaksa," p. 5; Office of Cultural Properties, *The Preservation and Transmission System*, p. 39, Article 5.

115. The law also included a provision aimed at improving the control over the illegal trade in cultural relics.

116. See Munhwa ch'eyukpu, *Munhwajae kwan'gye pŏmnyŏngjip*, p. 41, Article 93. See also pp. 59–62, Articles 18, 19, and 26 (regarding the conditions for performance).

117. Munhwajae kwalliguk, *Chosŏn ch'ongdokpu*, p. 161.

118. Munhwa ch'eyukpu, *Munhwajae kwan'gye pŏmnyŏngjip*, p. 13.

119. See Ibid., pp. 69–75.

120. When it moved to Taejŏn, the *Munhwajae yŏn'guso* was given the English title National Research Institute of Cultural Heritage (NRICH).

121. Munhwajae kwalliguk, *Munhwajae kwalli yŏnbo* (Annual report on the management of cultural properties), p. 14.

122. The CPC's directive and structure were laid out before the CPPL in a separate law, the Cultural Properties Committee Regulations (*Munhwajae wiwŏnhoe kyujŏng*) of March 27, 1962 (Chŏng Chaejong, "Munhwajae wiwŏnhoe yaksa," p. 4).

123. Munhwajae kwalliguk, *Munhwajae* (Cultural properties), pp. 1–4.

124. Ibid., pp. 24–27.

125. Pai, "The Politics of Korea's Past," p. 29.

126. Two other former graduates of the Court Music Office of the Yi Royal Household, Kim Kisu and Chang Sahun, would also write many reports as members of the subcommittee (Howard, *Preserving Korean Music*, p. 53).

127. Ibid., p. 50.

128. Sorensen, "Success and Education in South Korea," pp. 22–23, 34.

129. The law dictates that the total number of CPC members must not exceed 120.

130. Munhwa ch'eyukpu, *Munhwajae kwan'gye pŏmnyŏngjip*, p. 30.

131. Kim Okkyŏng, "Muhŏng munhwajae chŏkkŭkchŏk kwanshim-gwa chiwŏn-ŭl" (A positive interest in and support for intangible cultural properties); Munhwajaech'ŏng (Cultural Heritage Administration), "Chŏnsŭng chiwŏn kyehoek annae" (Transmission support planning guide), p. 3; Kim Chuyŏng, "Chorye chejŏng tŭng chŏnsŭng wihan taech'aek maryŏn shigŭp" (Urgent need to prepare measures such as regulations to secure tradition).

132. Kim Kwanghŭi, "Han'guk nongag-ŭi pop'yŏnsŏng-gwa t'ŭksu" (The universality and particularity of Korean folk music), p. 15.

133. Interview with Bang So-Yeon, September 12, 2012. See also So Pyŏnghŭi and Chin Hyeyŏng, "Chungyo muhyŏng munhwajae pojŏn chŏngch'aek kaesŏn pangan yŏn'gu" (A study of ways to improve the policy towards the preservation of important intangible

cultural properties), p. 180. In January each year, the CHA decides which applications it will further examine and what items it should investigate for possible future inclusion in the system (interview with Bang So-Yeon, September 12, 2012).

134. Interview with Bang So-Yeon, September 12, 2012.

135. Howard, "Introduction: East Asian Music as Intangible Cultural Heritage," p. 11.

136. See Im Chunsŏ, "Chŏnt'ong yŏnhŭi 50-nyŏn" (Fifty years of traditional plays), pp. 339–340, 343.

137. Maliangkay, "The Revival of Folksongs in South Korea," pp. 239–240.

138. Interview with Han Ch'anggi, December 24, 1995. In an interview with Keith Howard, Yi Pohyŏng also expressed his concern over the appointment of regional genres putting their local identity at risk (Howard, "Minyo in Korea," p. 16).

139. See Hesselink, *P'ungmul: South Korean Drumming and Dance*, pp. 40–41.

140. Clark Sorensen, pers. comm., April 28, 2016.

141. Munhwajae kwalliguk, *Munhwajae* 11, p. 284.

142. Munhwajae kwalliguk, *Munhwajae* 12, p. 231.

143. Munhwajae kwalliguk, *Chungyo muhyŏng munhwajae hyŏnhwang 1997* (Present state of important intangible cultural properties), p. 33.

144. Munhwa kongbobu, "Yesan kangmok myŏngsesŏ" (Detailed account of all budgetary items), pp. 849–855.

145. Janelli, "The Origins of Korean Folklore Scholarship," pp. 86, 101.

146. Sang Mi Park, "The Paradox," pp. 74–77.

147. Interview with Yi Pohyŏng, August 14, 1995.

148. Interview with Im Tonggwŏn, September 15, 1995.

149. Interview with Kwŏn Osŏng, December 11, 1995; interview with Yi Pohyŏng, August 14, 1995.

150. Interview with Yi Pohyŏng, August 14, 1995.

151. Interview with Kim Sam Dae Ja, October 4, 1995.

152. Interview with Hong Chonguk, November 10, 1995.

153. See http://www.law.go.kr/법령/무형문화재보전및진흥에관한법률. UNESCO's categories of intangible cultural heritage cover a broader range of cultural expressions than those protected under Korea's Cultural Properties Protection Law. In addition to traditional performing arts, practices, rituals, and events, they include "oral traditions and expressions, including language as a vehicle of the intangible cultural heritage" (UNESCO, "Convention for the Safeguarding of the Intangible Cultural Heritage," p. 2).

154. Han'guk pŏpche yŏn'guwŏn, *Pukhan pŏpche punsŏk*, p. 20; Kim Hŭit'ae, "Pŏmnyŏnggwa chedo" (Statute and system), p. 50.

155. The story of Ch'ŏyong, the son of the Dragon King of the Eastern Sea, is included in the compilation of myths, legends, and songs called the *Samguk yusa* (Remnants of the Three Kingdoms), dating from the late thirteenth century.

156. Munhwajae kwalliguk, *Chungyo muhyŏng munhwajae hyŏnhwang 1997*, pp. 11, 44.

157. See Munhwajae kwalliguk, *Munhwajae*, 7, p. 209; 18, pp. 385, 389.

158. Munhwajae kwalliguk, *Chungyo muhyŏng munhwajae hyŏnhwang 1997*, p. 7.

159. Munhwajae kwalliguk, *Munhwajae*, 15, p. 255; 18, p. 413.

160. In the official listing of IICPs, *chŏnsusaeng* were sometimes referred to as *pojoja* (assistants) (see Munhwajae kwalliguk, *Chungyo muhyŏng munhwajae hyŏnhwang 1996*).

161. During the Chosŏn dynasty, people working for the *Changagwŏn* (Music Affairs Bureau) were also called *aksa* (Chang Sahun, *Kugak taesajŏn* [Great dictionary of Korean traditional music], p. 478).

162. Office of Cultural Properties, *The Preservation and Transmission System,* p. 56.

163. Munhwajae kwalliguk, *Chungyo muhyŏng munhwajae hyŏnhwang 1996,* p. 39; *Poyuja ŏmnŭn hubo chogyo yenŭng chosa* (Study of the art of candidate holders and assistant teachers without a holder), p. 27; Sorensen, "Folk Religion and Political Commitment," pp. 325–326.

164. Interview with Bang So-Yeon, September 12, 2012.

165. Interview with Im Tonggwŏn, September 15, 1995.

166. Munhwajae kwalliguk, *Chungyo muhyŏng munhwajae hyŏnhwang 1997.*

167. September 26, 1992, interview transcript courtesy of Howard. For a discussion of rivalry in the tradition of Chindo *Ssikkim kut,* see Howard, *Preserving Korean Music,* p. 144.

168. Interview with Im Tonggwŏn, November 9, 1995.

169. Howard, *Creating Korean Music,* p. 182.

170. Sŏng Kyŏngnin, "Chungyo muhyŏng munhwajae-ŭi pojon chŏnsŭng" (The preservation and transmission of important intangible cultural properties), p. 6; Maliangkay, "Choosing the Right Folk," pp. 97–98.

171. Munhwajae kwalliguk, *Munhwajae kwalli yŏnbo,* p. 14.

172. Maliangkay, "Choosing the Right Folk," p. 100; Munhwajaech'ŏng, "Chŏnsŭng chiwŏn kyehoek annae," p. 3

173. Kang Ŭn'gyŏng, pers. comm. via Jocelyn Clark, December 11, 2016.

174. Eun-mi Byun, "'Human Cultural Asset System' Struck by Corruption, Scandal, Stagnation," p. 30; interview with Yi Ŭnju, October 26, 1997; Yi Hŭijŏng, "In'gan munhwajae chedo kaesŏn-ŭl: puliik, kŭmp'um nobi" (A reform of the system of human cultural properties: Disadvantage and cash and gift lobbying); Howard, *Preserving Korean Music,* pp. 10–11, 33–34.

Chapter 2 Defining Korean Folksongs

1. Bohlman, *The Study of Folk Music in the Modern World,* xviii.

2. Harker, *Fakesong: The Manufacture of British "Folksong,"* p. ix.

3. International Folk Music Council (1955).

4. Howard, "Korean Folk Songs for a Contemporary World," pp. 153–154.

5. Man-young Hahn, "Folksong," p. 313; "Folksongs," pp. 14, 19; Kim Muhŏn, *Han'guk minyo munhak non* (A literary discourse on Korean folksongs), p. 11.

6. In a long scene of the quintessential *Minjung* movie *Sŏp'yŏnje* (dir. Im Kwon-taek), which came out a year earlier, in 1993, the three protagonists sing this song in its entirety.

7. Ko Chŏngok, *Chosŏn minyo yŏn'gu* (A study of Korean folksongs), p. 19; Kim Muhŏn, *Han'guk nodong minyo non (munhak, sahoehakchŏk haesŏk)* (A discourse on Korean working songs: A literary and sociological interpretation), pp. 11–12, 44.

8. Im Tonggwŏn, *Han'guk minyo sa,* pp. 13–15, 17–46; "Folksong," p. 74. The terms used to refer to folksongs have varied considerably over time, but "yo" and "ka" are predominant (Yi Tuhyŏn, Chang Sugŭn, and Yi Kwanggyu, *Han'guk minsokhak kaesŏl* [Introduction to Korean folklore studies], pp. 321–322).

9. Im Tonggwŏn, *Han'guk minyo yŏn'gu* (A study of Korean folksongs), p. 173; Hahn, "Folksongs," p. 14.

10. Williams, *Keywords,* pp. 136–137.

11. Yi Tongsun, *Pŏnji ŏmnŭn chumak* (The tavern without a number), pp. 128, 201–204.

12. Maliangkay, "Their Masters' Voice: Korean Traditional Music SPs (Standard Play Records) under Japanese Colonial Rule," pp. 63–64; Son Minjŏng, *T'ŭrot'ŭ-ŭi chŏngch'ihak* (A study of the politics of trot), pp. 56–57.

13. Pilzer, "The Twentieth-Century 'Disappearance' of the Gisaeng," p. 118; Maliangkay, "Their Masters' Voice," pp. 62–63, 70n18; Atkins, *Primitive Selves*, pp. 150–166.

14. Robinson, "Broadcasting, Cultural Hegemony, and Colonial Modernity in Korea," p. 62.

15. Ibid., pp. 53, 64–65. A fictional representation of the channel's operations can be seen in Ha Kiho's 2008 comic drama *Radio Dayz* (Radŭio teijŭ).

16. Ibid., pp. 53, 66.

17. Atkins, *Primitive Selves*, pp. 79–81.

18. *Tonga ilbo*, July 11, 1935, p. 3.

19. Maliangkay, "Their Masters' Voice," p. 61.

20. Pak Sŏngso, *Han'guk chŏnjaeng-gwa taejung kayo, kirok-kwa chŭngŏn* (The Korean War and popular songs: Records and testimonies), pp. 127, 244.

21. Ch'oe Hyŏnch'ŏl and Han Chinman, *Han'guk radio p'ŭrogŭraem-e taehan yŏksajŏk yŏn'gu: P'yŏnsŏng hŭrŭm-ŭl chungshim-ŭro* (A historical study of radio programming in Korea: Focusing on trends in the organization), pp. 66–67.

22. Koo, "The State," pp. 131–132.

23. Pak Sŏnghŭi, *I saram ihu*, p. 80; Suk-jay Im and Yŏlgyu Kim, "Korean Folk Culture, A Dialogue," p. 137; interview with Ch'oe Sangil, August 26, 1995; Howard, *Bands, Songs, and Shamanistic Rituals*, p. 105; Yang, *Cultural Protection Policy in Korea*, p. 80. As one example, *t'osok* folksongs are considered inferior, and so when talking about these songs informants may omit base language, a common aspect of many other folksongs as well. Ch'oe Ch'ŏl notes that many of the song collections published throughout the colonial period under the direct or indirect supervision of the Japanese likely suffer from self-censorship (*Han'guk minyohak* [Korean folksong studies], p. 57).

24. Maliangkay, "Choosing the Right Folk," p. 98.

25. By omitting transcriptions of dance and music, as well as details on the informants and the data collected, the value of the collection for the study of Korean folklore is limited. The speed with which recordings were made may have prevented singers from elaborating on songs and from improvising during singing. There are cases in which, on a single day, several singers were recorded in two separate regions or more than thirty folktales from different singers were recorded. See Han'guk chŏngshin munhwa yŏn'guwŏn (Academy of Korean Studies), *Han'guk kubi munhak taegye* (A compendium of Korean oral literature), 1: pp. 4, 23; 3: pp. 1, 13; and 7: pp. 14, 12. See also Howard, "Minyo in Korea," pp. 6–7.

26. See Howard, *Creating Korean Music*, pp. 37–38.

27. Man-young Hahn, *Kugak: Studies in Korean Traditional Music*, pp. 185–189; see also Park, *Voices from the Straw Mat*, p. 51; Kim Insuk and Kim Hyeri, *Sŏdo sori* (Folksongs from the Western Provinces), pp. 60–63.

28. Hye-Ku Lee, *Essays on Korean Traditional Music*, p. 178.

29. Howard, *Bands, Songs, and Shamanistic Rituals*, p. 148.

30. Although the techniques and timbres are similar to those of *p'ansori* singers, the latter commonly have a broader timbral palette. For more on the timbres of *p'ansori* singers, see Park, *Voices from the Straw Mat*, pp. 192–197; Killick, *In Search of Korean Traditional Opera*, p. 179.

31. Pilzer, "The Twentieth-Century 'Disappearance,'" p. 45.

32. See, for example, O Pongnyŏ, *Sŏdo sori* (Folksongs from the Western Provinces).

33. Shin Taech'ŏl, *Uri ŭmak, kŭ mat-kwa sorikkal* (Our music: Its flavor and songs), pp. 70–71, 225.

34. Howard, *Bands, Songs, and Shamanistic Rituals*, pp. 168–169.

35. Kyung-hee Kim, "Theory of *Pansori*," pp. 36–37.

36. Im Tonggwŏn, "Folksong," p. 85; Killick, *In Search of Korean Traditional Opera*, p. 182; Howard, *Bands, Songs, and Shamanistic Rituals*, pp. 169–170.

37. Im Tonggwŏn, *Han'guk minyo sa*, p. 6

38. Im Tonggwŏn, "Kanggangsullae," p. 219; Pak Sunho, "'Kanggangsullae' sogo" (Some thoughts on "Kanggangsullae"), p. 18. The term *sŏnch'ang* comes from *sŏn*, which can mean "first" or "standing" (see also chapter 3), and from *ch'ang*, which means "singing." *Tok* in *tokch'ang* means "solo," while *ap* in *apsori* means "first" or "front." The term *hap* in *hapch'ang* means "all" or "combined," while *che* in *chech'ang* means "altogether" or "in chorus."

39. The scene runs from 1:34:40 to 1:37:47.

40. Im Tonggwŏn, "Folksong," p. 91.

41. Ibid., p. 73; Yi Ch'angbae, *Han'guk kach'ang taegye* (A compendium of vocal music in Korea), 1: p. 161; Chang Sahun, *Han'guk chŏnt'ong ŭmag-ŭi ihae* (An understanding of Korean traditional music), p. 102.

42. Im Tonggwŏn, "Folksong," p. 77.

43. Man-young Hahn, "Change and Innovation in Traditional Music and Dance in Folklore Festivals"; Maliangkay, "The Revival of Folksongs in South Korea," pp. 233, 238–239.

44. Ch'oe Ch'ŏl, *Han'guk minyohak*, pp. 197, 212–221.

45. Im Tonggwŏn, *Yŏsŏng-gwa minyo* (Women and folksongs), p. 16.

46. Ibid., p. 116.

47. Im Tonggwŏn, "Folksong," pp. 104, 112.

48. See Mun Sunt'ae, "Han" (Bitterness), p. 852; Pak Kyŏngsu, *Sorikkundŭl, kŭ salm-ŭl ch'ajasŏ* (Singers, looking at their lives); Kim Myŏnggon, *Han, Kim Myŏnggon-ŭi kwangdae kihaeng* (Han: Kim Myŏnggon's kwangdae tour); Shin Kyŏngnim, *Minyo kihaeng* (Folksong tour), pp. 37–41.

49. Shin Kyŏngnim, *Minyo kihaeng*, pp. 37–40.

50. Sasse, "Minjung Theology and Culture," pp. 29–31. Shin Taech'ŏl argues that the sentiment is not unique to Korea: "It is only one out of many characters. It has been given too much emphasis. . . . *Han* is not something only we [Koreans] have. Every country in the world has a history of grief and resentment" (*Uri ŭmak*, pp. 307–308).

51. Frank Tedesco documents several occurrences of Christians targeting the Buddhist faith between 1982 and 1996 ("Questions for Buddhist and Christian Cooperation in Korea," pp. 184–192). Chong-Ho Kim records a violent attack by Christians on a group of shamans in 1993 ("Cultural Politics or Cultural Contradiction?" p. 40).

52. Yi Kyŏngyŏp, "Kidokkyo-ŭi chŏnp'a-wa ŭirye saenghwar-ŭi pyŏnhwa" (The spread of Christianity and changes in rites).

53. Kim Chongch'ŏl writes that some people consider gospel in the Korean traditional music style as "music for evil spirits" (*kwishin ŭmak*; see "Chil nop'ŭn uri ch'ansongga pogŭp shigŭphae" [We must urgently popularize our fantastic hymns], p. 37).

54. Pak Minhŭi, *Kugak ch'anyang* (Traditional Korean songs of praise), CD, Digital Records, March 28, 2012.

55. The English title is *Park Min Hee: Traditional Folk*.

56. Shin Chŏnghŭi, "Myŏngin myŏngjang 28 (Famous people famous artisans 28).

57. Yu Yŏngdae, "Mokhoeja-ro ch'ŏt in'gan munhwajae chijŏng sŏdo sori myŏngch'ang Yi Munju moksa" (Renowned singer of songs from the western provinces, Minister Yi Munju, becomes the first pastor to be appointed a human cultural property).

58. See Maliangkay, "There Is No Amen in Shaman," p. 91.

59. Chŏng Tonghwa, *Han'guk minyo-ŭi sajŏk yŏn'gu* (Historical research on Korean folksongs), p. 8.

60. Yi Ch'angshik, "Han'guk minyohak kwan'gye mongnok" (List of works related to the study of Korean folksongs), p. 187.

61. Hughes, "The Heart's Home Town," pp. 12–13. For parallel events in Japan—the introduction of the term *min'yō* and subsequent attempts at defining various terms relating to folksongs, professionalization, government policy, and the like—see Hughes, "The Heart's Home Town"; "Japanese 'New Folk Songs,' Old and New"; "'Esashi Oiwake' and the Beginnings of Modern Japanese Folk Song."

62. Bohlman, *The Study of Folk Music in the Modern World,* p. ix.

63. Biddle and Gibson, *Masculinity and Western Musical Practice,* p. 136; Anderson, *Imagined Communities,* pp. 67–68, 118–119.

64. Yi Tuhyŏn, Chang Sugŭn, and Yi Kwanggyu, *Han'guk minsokhak kaesŏl,* p. 15.

65. Anderson, *Imagined Communities,* pp. 77–78.

66. Robinson, *Korea's Twentieth-Century Odyssey,* pp. 24, 27–28.

67. Yi Tuhyŏn, Chang Sugŭn, and Yi Kwanggyu, *Han'guk minsokhak kaesŏl,* p. 15.

68. Robinson, *Korea's Twentieth-Century Odyssey,* pp. 28–29; Gi-Wook Shin, *Ethnic Nationalism in Korea,* pp. 56–57.

69. Song Bangsong, "Chosŏn hugi-ŭi ŭmak" (Music in the late Chosŏn period), p. 370; *Han'guk ŭmak t'ongsa* (A comprehensive history of Korean music), p. 470; Chang Sahun, *Chŏngbo han'guk ŭmak sa* (A new history of Korean music), p. 478.

70. Janelli, *Making Capitalism,* p. 136; Keedon Kwon, "Regionalism in South Korea," pp. 547–548.

71. Kwang-ok Kim, "Colonial Body and Indigenous Soul:," p. 265.

72. A precedent for this can be found in Ross King's study of early 1900s "script nationalism," which shows that Christians in the northwestern province of P'yŏngan strongly opposed proposals to standardize the Korean orthography on the basis that it did away with historic continuity and tradition and shunned the region's unique identity (King, "Dialect, Orthography, and Regional Identity," pp. 146–161, 173).

73. Howard, *Bands, Songs, and Shamanistic Rituals,* p. 99.

74. Interview with Im Tonggwŏn, September 15, 1995.

75. Interview with Song Minsŏn, October 4, 1995.

76. Kim Muhŏn, *Han'guk nodong minyo non,* p. 9.

77. Chŏng Tonghwa, *Han'guk minyo-ŭi sajŏk yŏn'gu,* p. 105.

78. *Yŏmbul sori* is probably best described as a Buddhist busking chant.

79. Interview with Hwang Yongju, November 18, 1995.

80. Howard, *Bands, Songs, and Shamanistic Rituals,* p. 103; Chang Sahun, *Kugak taesajŏn,* p. 761.

81. Chŏng Tonghwa, *Han'guk minyo-ŭi sajŏk yŏn'gu,* p. 105.

82. There are many theories regarding the meaning of *Arirang.* For a summary, see Kim Chŏmdo, *Uri minyo taebaekkwa* (Great encyclopedia of Korean folksongs), pp. 305–307.

83. Pilzer, "The Twentieth-Century 'Disappearance,'" p. 42.

84. Chang Sahun, *Kugak taesajŏn,* p. 129; *Han'guk chŏnt'ong ŭmag-ŭi ihae,* p. 92; Wha-Byong Lee, *Studien zur Pansori-Musik in Korea* (Studies of *p'ansori* in Korea), p. 153; Yun Kihong, "Chapka-ŭi sŏngkyŏk-kwa minyo, p'ansori-wa-ŭi kwan'gye" (Folksongs, the character of *chapka,* and their relation to *p'ansori*)," p. 208.

85. Chang Sahun, *Kugak taesajŏn,* p. 633; Song Bangsong, *Han'guk ŭmak t'ongsa,* p. 469.

86. Kim Hŭnggyu, *Han'guk munhag-ŭi ihae* (An understanding of Korean literature), p. 50.

87. Im Tonggwŏn, *Han'guk minyo chip* (Collections of Korean folksongs) 6, p. 8.

88. Clark, *Christianity in Modern Korea*, p. 3; Sørensen, "The Attitude of the Japanese Colonial Government," p. 57.

89. Yi Yusŏn, *Han'guk yangak p'alshimnyŏnsa* (An eighty-year history of Western music in Korea), pp. 89–90; see also Yi Yongshik, "Ch'angga-esŏ minyo-ro" (From ch'angga to folksong), p. 205; Son Minjŏng, *T'ŭrot'ŭ-ŭi chŏngch'ihak*, p. 42. According Pak Sŏngso, the collection was published in 1872 (*Han'guk chŏnjaeng-gwa taejung kayo*, p. 309).

90. Yi Yusŏn, *Han'guk yangak p'alshimnyŏnsa*, p. 162; Song Bangsong, *Han'guk ŭmak t'ongsa*, p. 573.

91. Hwang Munp'yŏng, "Yusŏnggi-wa kayo-ŭi yŏkchŏng" (A history of gramophones and popular songs), pp. 85–95.

92. The present Korean national anthem, composed by An Ikt'ae in 1936, is also called "Aegukka" (Chang Sahun, *Kugak taesajŏn*, p. 489).

93. Yi Yongshik, "Ch'angga-esŏ minyo-ro." In Japan, the *yonanuki* scale was greatly influenced by the introduction of Scottish and Irish music at schools (Yano, *Tears of Longing*, p. 220n9; see also Pilzer, "The Twentieth-Century 'Disappearance,'" p. 161n8).

94. Yi Yusŏn, *Han'guk yangak p'alshimnyŏnsa*, pp. 98–117; Song Bangsong, *Han'guk ŭmak t'ongsa*, pp. 569–571.

95. For more on the history of record companies during Korea's colonial period, and recordings of traditional music in particular, see Maliangkay, "Their Masters' Voice."

96. Yi Kŭnt'ae, "Shin minyo-ŭi t'ansaeng" (The birth of new folksongs). The music of "The Nodŭl Riverside" was composed by Mun Howŏl (Yi Ch'angbae, *Han'guk kach'ang taegye*, 1: p. 784; see also Hwang Munp'yŏng, "Yusŏnggi-wa kayo-ŭi yŏkchŏng," p. 85).

97. Nodŭl is located in Bon-dong, a small area located in Seoul's Tongjak District, just south of the river Han.

98. Yi Ch'angbae, *Han'guk kach'ang taegye*, 1: p. 784.

99. Yi Kŭnt'ae, "Shin minyo-ŭi t'ansaeng"; Chang Yujŏng, *Oppa-nŭn p'unggakchaengi-ya* (My brother is a busker), pp. 68–69. According to Hwang Munp'yŏng, Yi Hwaja lived from 1915 to 1950 ("Yusŏnggi-wa kayo-ŭi yŏkchŏng," p. 74). The birth and death dates of Yi Ŭnp'a are unknown. Kim Muhŏn argues that Yi Hwaja's popularity made her "the queen of *kisaeng* singers" (*kisaeng kasu-ŭi yŏwang*) (*Han'guk minyo munhak non*, p. 139).

100. Chang Yujŏng, *Oppa-nŭn p'unggakchaengi-ya*, p. 83.

101. See Hughes, "Japanese 'New Folk Songs.'"

102. Chang Sahun, *Kugak taesajŏn*, pp. 735, 811; interview with Yi Pohyŏng, September 26, 1995.

103. Yi Pohyŏng, "'Arirang' sori-ŭi kŭnwŏn-gwa kŭ pyŏnch'ŏn-e kwanhan ŭmakchŏk yŏn'gu" (The origin of "Arirang" and a musicological study of its change), p. 114. A simplified version of the song had already been transcribed in February 1896 by Homer Hulbert, who wrote that even at that time it had been popular for fourteen years running ("Korean Vocal Music," pp. 49–51). The origins of "Han obaengnyŏn" and "Ch'ŏngch'un'ga" have as yet not been found to go back farther than the colonial period.

104. Ko Chŏngok, *Chosŏn minyo yŏn'gu*, pp. 47–49, 57.

105. Im Tonggwŏn, *Han'guk minyo yŏn'gu*, pp. 73, 168–169.

106. Hwang Munp'yŏng, "Yusŏnggi-wa kayo-ŭi yŏkchŏng," p. 30.

107. See Han Munp'yŏng, "Yi Hwaja"; Yi Kŭnt'ae, "Shin minyo-ŭi t'ansaeng"; Chang Yujŏng, *Oppa-nŭn p'unggakchaengi-ya*, p. 132; Pak Ch'anho, *Han'guk kayo sa* (A history of Korean popular songs), 1: pp. 258, 265.

108. Hwang Munp'yŏng, "Taejung kayo" (Popular songs), p. 483; Maliangkay, "Their Masters' Voice," p. 67.

109. The former term seems to have been coined following the publication of a collection of songs called *Yuhaeng sogajip* (Collection of short popular songs) in 1913. Since then, other names have also been used, including *yuhaeng chapka, t'ongsok chapka,* and *yuhaeng soga* (Hwang Munp'yŏng, "Yusŏnggi-wa kayo-ŭi yŏkchŏng," p. 482).

110. Yi Yusŏn, *Han'guk yangak paengnyŏnsa* (A one-hundred-year history of Western music in Korea), p. 186; Hwang Munp'yŏng, "Yusŏnggi-wa kayo-ŭi yŏkchŏng," pp. 23, 29.

111. Yi Yusŏn, *Han'guk yangak paengnyŏnsa,* pp. 184–185.

112. Ch'ŏn Yŏngju, "Ilche kangjŏmgi-ŭi ŭmak kyokwasŏ yŏn'gu" (A study of the music schoolbooks from the period of Japanese colonial rule), p. 218; Chang Yujŏng, *Oppa-nŭn p'unggakchaengi-ya,* pp. 82, 378n79; Son Minjŏng, *T'ŭrot'ŭ-ŭi chŏngch'ihak,* p. 21.

113. Yi Yŏngmi, "Ilche shidae-ŭi taejung kayo" (Popular songs from the period of Japanese colonial rule), p. 105; Pilzer, "The Twentieth-Century 'Disappearance'," pp. 79–80.

114. An early radio show dedicated to *kayo,* called *Shinjak taejung kayo palp'yo* (Newly composed pop song show), was broadcast on June 24, 1948 (*Tonga ilbo,* June 24, 1948, 2). During the Korean War, a growing number of radio programs were devoted to the new music genre, but none of them were regular. From the mid 1950s, however, the genre began to pervade the airwaves with the emergence of regular *kayo* programs (see, for example, *Tonga ilbo,* January 7, 1955, 3; January 18, 1955, 4; January 28, 1955, 4). Because idol K-pop is sometimes also referred to as *kayo,* in recent years the genre is increasingly referred to as *chŏnt'ong* (traditional) *kayo* or trot (Son Minjŏng, *T'ŭrot'ŭ-ŭi chŏngch'ihak,* pp. 48, 190).

Chapter 3 Masculinity in Demise

1. Although the term *sŏdo* literally means "western provinces," the provinces are located in the northwestern part of the peninsula that now forms part of North Korea.

2. In an interview on July 8, 2013, *Sŏdo sori* singer Pak Chunyŏng told me that 90 percent of his students were women and he expected that percentage to increase.

3. Yi Pohyŏng, "Sŏnsori sant'aryŏng" (Standing Mountain Songs), p. 166.

4. See also Chang Tŏksun et al., *Kubi munhak kaesŏl* (Introduction to oral literature), p. 75.

5. Hwang Yongju, *Han'guk kyŏng/sŏdo ch'angak taegye* (A compendium of the vocal music from Korea's Kyŏnggi and western provinces), 1: p. 164.

6. Interview with Yi Pohyŏng, October 22, 1997.

7. Yi Pohyŏng, "Sŏnsori sant'aryŏng," p. 163.

8. Chang Sahun, *Kugak taesajŏn,* p. 397; Hahn, *Kugak,* p. 137; Hwang Yongju, *Han'guk kyŏng/sŏdo ch'angak taegye,* 1: p. 155.

9. See pictures in ibid., pp. 141–143. See also Sŏnsori sant'aryŏng pojonhoe (Society for the Preservation of Standing Mountain Songs), "Chungyo muhyŏng munhwajae che-19-ho kihoek kongyŏn" (Planned performances of IICP no. 19), p. 12.

10. For more on the *sogo,* see Hesselink, *P'ungmul,* p. 60.

11. Hahn, *Kugak,* p. 137. See also pictures in Hwang Yongju, *Han'guk kyŏng/sŏdo ch'angak taegye,* 1: pp. 140–143, 145.

12. Chang Sahun, *Kugak taesajŏn,* p. 313.

13. Paek Taeung, "Kyŏnggido sori" (Songs from Kyŏnggi province), pp. 14–15.

14. Quoted in Pak Sŏnghŭi, *I saram ihu* (From this person onwards), p. 50.

15. Hwang Yongju, *Han'guk kyŏng/sŏdo ch'angak taegye,* 1: p. 163.

16. Ibid., p. 164.

17. Hahn, *Kugak,* p. 158; Munhwa kongbobu, *Chungyo muhyŏng munhwajae haesŏl* (Commentary on important intangible cultural properties), p. 103.

18. Man-young Hahn, "Chapka," p. 233.

19. Yi Pohyŏng believes that "Hwach'o sagŏri" may have been composed by the singer Shin Pangch'o ("Sŏnsori sant'aryŏng," p. 168).

20. Hahn, *Kugak,* pp. 155–158, 187.

21. Sŏng Kyŏngnin, *Han'guk ŭmak non'go* (A study of Korean music), p. 138; Han Manyŏng, "Sŏnsori sant'aryŏng" (Standing Mountain Songs), p. 261.

22. Hwang Yongju, *Han'guk kyŏng/sŏdo ch'angak taegye,* 1: p. 183n8.

23. See Han'guk minsok taesajŏn p'yŏnch'an wiwŏnhoe (Compilation Committee of the Great Dictionary of Korean Folklore), *Han'guk minsok taesajŏn* (Great dictionary of Korean folklore), 2: p. 840. The term also appears in the northwestern version of "Twissan t'aryŏng" (Song of the Rear Mountain; see Hwang Yongju, *Han'guk kyŏng/sŏdo ch'angak taegye,* 1: p. 239).

24. Hahn, *Kugak,* p. 145.

25. Paek Taeung, "Kyŏnggido sori," pp. 15–16; Han Manyŏng, "Sŏnsori sant'aryŏng," p. 261.

26. Chang Sahun, *Kugak taesajŏn,* p. 202.

27. Hwang Yongju, *Han'guk kyŏng/sŏdo ch'angak taegye,* 1: pp. 181–182, 227.

28. A translation of the verse can be found in Hahn, *Kugak,* p. 150.

29. Ibid.

30. Hwang Yongju, *Han'guk kyŏng/sŏdo ch'angak taegye,* 1: pp. 187, 233–234.

31. Chang Sahun, *Kugak taesajŏn,* p. 254. The term *kŏri* can also be used to indicate a break in a piece of music (ibid., p. 86).

32. Han Manyŏng, "Sŏnsori sant'aryŏng," p. 261.

33. Hwang Yongju, *Han'guk kyŏng/sŏdo ch'angak taegye,* 1: p. 196.

34. Ibid., p. 239. See also Yi Ch'angbae, *Han'guk kach'ang taegye,* 1: p. 350; Chang Sahun, "Sŏdo sŏnsori" (Standing songs from the western provinces), p. 106.

35. This song must not be mistaken for the *shin minyo* of the same name (Yi Ch'angbae, *Han'guk kach'ang taegye,* 1: p. 783; Chang Sahun, *Kugak taesajŏn,* p. 240).

36. Yi Ch'angbae, *Han'guk kach'ang taegye,* 1: p. 783.

37. Hwang Yongju, *Han'guk kyŏng/sŏdo ch'angak taegye,* 1: p. 211.

38. Ibid., p. 246.

39. Paek Taeung, "Kyŏnggido sori," p. 16; Hahn, *Kugak,* pp. 151–152.

40. The use of the term *kŏri* in this song title could be similar to its use in "Ch'angbu kŏri," part of a shaman ritual, where it signifies "part" or "section."

41. Shin Ch'an'gyun, *Minsog-ŭi kohyang* (The birthplace of folklore), p. 99.

42. Kim was a former graduate of holder Yu Kaedong and not, therefore, as Shin Ch'an'gyun claims, a holder of *Sant'aryŏng* (Yi Pohyŏng, "Sŏnsori sant'aryŏng," p. 169; Shin Ch'an'gyun, *Minsog-ŭi kohyang,* p. 103). Hwang Yongju claims that Yu Kaedong did not have any graduates (*Han'guk kyŏng/sŏdo ch'angak taegye,* 1: p. 160).

43. Shin Ch'an'gyun, *Minsog-ŭi kohyang,* pp. 99–101, 104–108; Yi Pohyŏng, "Sŏnsori sant'aryŏng," p. 170.

44. Chang Sahun, *Kugak taesajŏn,* p. 370; Yi Pohyŏng, "Sŏnsori sant'aryŏng," pp. 163–164; Han Manyŏng, "Sŏnsori sant'aryŏng," p. 260. For a discussion of *kwangdae* and *kŏllipp'ae,* see Hesselink, *SamulNori,* pp. 21–22.

45. According to Sung Soon Kim, the troupes consisted of lay monks who were forced into a life as itinerant entertainers when the dynasty's new philosophy devastated livelihoods reliant on Buddhist faith ("Priests, Entertainers, or Prostitutes," p. 41).

46. Ki-Baik Lee, "Chapter 9: The Creation of a Yangban Society," pp. 130–131.

47. Yi Nŭnghwa, *Chosŏn haeŏhwa sa* (A history of Korean *kisaeng*), p. 283.

48. Son Inae, *Hyangt'o minyo-e suyongdoen sadangp'ae sori* (The songs of *sadangp'ae* among folksongs), p. 10.

49. Chang Sahun, "Kyŏnggido ipch'ang-gwa sŏdo ipch'ang" (Standing songs from Kyŏnggi province and the western provinces), p. 9; Shim Usŏng, *Namsadangp'ae yŏn'gu* (A study of namsadang groups), p. 34; Han'guk minsok taesajŏn p'yŏnch'an wiwŏnhoe, *Han'guk minsok taesajŏn* (Great dictionary of Korean folklore), 2: p. 728. Shim Usŏng argues that *sadangp'ae* were "composed of women," with each *sadang* having several male *kŏsa* assigned to her ("Namsadang," p. 456). For more on the etymology of both terms, see Sung Soon Kim, "Priests, Entertainers, or Prostitutes," pp. 39–43.

50. Yi Pohyŏng, "Sŏnsori sant'aryŏng," p. 164.

51. Interview with Yi Pohyŏng, November 28, 1995.

52. Song Sŏkha, *Han'guk minsok ko* (Studies on Korean folklore), p. 102; "Sadang go" (Scrutinizing sadang), p. 164.

53. Janelli, "The Origins of Korean Folklore Scholarship," p. 93.

54. Interview with Yi Pohyŏng, October 29, 1995.

55. See Yi Nŭnghwa, *Chosŏn haeŏhwa sa*, p. 287. For more examples of *sadanggol*, see Hahn, *Kugak*, p. 142; Shim Usŏng, "Namsadang 'tŏppoegi' yŏn'gu" (A study of namsadang's "Tŏppoegi"), p. 97n2; Sung Soon Kim, "Priests, Entertainers, or Prostitutes," pp. 53–54.

56. Sim Woo-Sung, "Namsadang," p. 456; interview with Shim Usŏng, December 1, 1995.

57. Shim Usŏng refers to the women as part of a couple with the *kŏsa;* Howard translates this as "married" (Shim Usŏng, *Namsadangp'ae yŏn'gu*, p. 34; Howard, *Bands, Songs, and Shamanistic Rituals*, p. 94).

58. Shim Usŏng, *Namsadangp'ae yŏn'gu*, pp. 33–34.

59. Hahn, *Kugak*, p. 142.

60. Interview with Shim Usŏng, December 1, 1995. Pictures (dated April 25, 1938) of one of the last *sadangp'ae* can be found in Song Sŏkha, *Minsok sashil t'ŭkpyŏl chŏndo nok* (A special complete record of the state of folklore), pp. 88–89.

61. Interview with Yi Pohyŏng, October 29, 1995.

62. Sung Soon Kim, "Priests, Entertainers, or Prostitutes," p. 46.

63. Son Inae, *Hyangt'o minyo-e suyongdoen sadangp'ae sori*, pp. 11, 13. An official *namsadangp'ae* still exists today. On August 1, 1988, twenty-four years after the appointment of Pak Kyesun (b. 1934) as holder of one aspect of this group's repertoire, *Kkoktugakshi norŭm* (Puppet Play; IICP no. 3), the group's entire repertoire was officially acknowledged (Munhwajae kwalliguk, *Chungyo muhyŏng munhwajae hyŏnhwang 1997*, p. 14). Whereas the group recognizes both its male and female ancestries, and is keenly nurturing an interest among young practitioners, it is unlikely that *mudong* (dancing boys) will resurface, having disappeared toward the end of the colonial period.

64. While most of the boys had been given to the group by parents unable to provide for them, some of them were orphans or runaways, or had been kidnapped (Shim Usŏng, *Namsadangp'ae yŏn'gu*, p. 41).

65. Chang Sahun, *Kugak taesajŏn*, p. 170; Han'guk minsok taesajŏn p'yŏnch'an wiwŏnhoe, *Han'guk minsok taesajŏn*, 1: p. 536; Sŏmundang, *Sajin-ŭro ponŭn Chosŏn shidae: saenghwalgwa p'ungsok* (Chosŏn dynasty shown through pictures: Daily life and customs), 1: p. 112; interview with Yi Pohyŏng, October 22, 1997.

66. Sŏng Kyŏngnin, *Han'guk ŭmak non'go*, p. 140.

67. Interview with Shim Usŏng, December 1, 1995.

68. Han'guk minsok taesajŏn p'yŏnch'an wiwŏnhoe, *Han'guk minsok taesajŏn*, 2: p. 728.

69. Sŏ Chŏngbŏm, *Sumŏsanŭn oet'olbagi 1* (Single-bur chestnuts living in secret 1), pp. 198–199.

70. The collection of money during the singing was called *tunyang mŏri* (Yi Pohyŏng, "Sŏnsori sant'aryŏng," p. 165; Chang Sahun, "Kyŏnggido ipch'ang-gwa sŏdo ipch'ang," pp. 14, 19; Paek Taeung, "Kyŏnggido sori," p. 14).

71. Yi Ch'angbae, *Han'guk kach'ang taegye,* 1: p. 271; Kwŏn Tohŭi, *Han'guk kŭndae ŭmak sahoesa* (A social history of Korean music from modern times), p. 146.

72. Yi Ch'angbae, *Han'guk kach'ang taegye,* 1: pp. 271, 330; Yi Pohyŏng, "Sŏnsori sant'aryŏng," p. 167. Yi Pohyŏng believes that Shin Nakt'aek was born around 1840 (ibid., 164).

73. Kim Hyeri and Chang Hwiju, *Sŏnsori san'taryŏng* (Standing mountain songs), pp. 52–53. Chang Sahun claims that Shin was married to Wŏlsŏn and that he owed his success to his wife (*Yŏmyŏng-ŭi tongsŏ ŭmak* [Eastern and western music in the new age], pp. 143–146). A *kisaeng* by the same name appears in the songs "P'yŏngyangga" and "Sŏnyuga" that form part of the core repertoire of *Kyŏnggi minyo,* described later in this chapter.

74. Myŏnghŭi Han, "Performance of Bridge-Treading Festival," p. 36.

75. Chang Sahun, *Kugak kaeyo* (An outline of Korean traditional music), p. 220; Im Tonggwŏn, "Folk Plays," p. 98.

76. Ch'oe Sangsu, "Folk Plays," p. 259.

77. Kwŏn Tohŭi, *Han'guk kŭndae ŭmak sahoesa,* p. 148.

78. Pan Chaeshik, *Chaedam ch'ŏnnyŏn sa* (A thousand-year history of comic storytelling), p. 235; see also picture in Kim Hyeri and Chang Hwiju, *Sŏnsori san'taryŏng,* p. 56.

79. Chang Sahun, *Kugak kaeyo,* p. 221; "Kyŏnggido ipch'ang-gwa sŏdo ipch'ang," p. 13; *Yŏmyŏng-ŭi tongsŏ ŭmak,* pp. 145–146; Song Sŏkha, *Minsok sashil t'ŭkpyŏl chŏndo nok,* p. 159; Kim Hyeri and Chang Hwiju, *Sŏnsori san'taryŏng,* pp. 52–53.

80. Chang Sahun, *Yŏmyŏng-ŭi tongsŏ ŭmak,* p. 145; Yi Pohyŏng, "Sŏnsori sant'aryŏng," p. 164; Hahn, *Kugak,* p. 145.

81. Yi Ch'angbae, *Han'guk kach'ang taegye,* 1: pp. 328, 352; Yi Pohyŏng, "Sŏnsori sant'aryŏng," p. 165; Hahn, Kugak, pp. 139–145; Hwang Yongju, *Han'guk kyŏng/sŏdo ch'angak taegye,* 1: pp. 181, 246.

82. Yi Ch'angbae, *Han'guk kach'ang taegye,* 1: p. 319.

83. Cho Yumi, "Yusŏnggi ŭmban-e tamgin sant'aryŏng," p. 102.

84. See Jigu Records Corp., *Han'guk ŭmak sŏnjip che-21-chip: Sŏnsori-wa chapka* (Selections of Korean music, vol. 21, Sŏnsori and chapka), JCD-9311, 1993. The CDs were produced for the National Gugak Center Library and were not commercially released. Remastered Victor recordings of northwestern versions of "Apsan t'aryŏng," "Twissan t'aryŏng," and "Chajin sant'aryŏng" from 1939 are included on the CD *Sŏdo sori sŏnjip* (A Selection of Songs from the Western Provinces), Seoul Records SRCD-1202, 1994.

85. Hahn, *Kugak,* pp. 138–139, 150; Yi Pohyŏng, "Sŏnsori sant'aryŏng," pp. 164, 166–167.

86. Chŏng Chaeho, *Han'guk chapka chŏnjip* (Complete collection of Korean chapka), p. 174; Chang Sahun, "Kyŏnggido ipch'ang-gwa sŏdo ipch'ang," pp. 20–52.

87. Haekyung Um, *Korean Musical Drama,* p. 23.

88. Hwang Yongju, *Han'guk kyŏng/sŏdo ch'angak taegye,* 2: pp. 48, 57n123.

89. Chang Sahun, "Kyŏnggido ipch'ang-gwa sŏdo ipch'ang," p. 20.

90. Hong-key Yoon, *Geomantic Relationships between Culture and Nature in Korea,* pp. 34–38.

91. Chang Sahun, "Kyŏnggido ipch'ang-gwa sŏdo ipch'ang," pp. 31, 50.

92. Hahn, *Kugak,* p. 143; Chŏng Chaeho, *Han'guk chapka chŏnjip,* pp. 296, 491. See also excerpt from the old publication *Shinjŏng chŭngbo shin'gu chapka* (Revised and complemented old and new chapka), transcribed in Kim Insuk and Kim Hyeri, *Sŏdo sori,* pp. 37–38.

93. Hwang Yongju, *Han'guk kyŏng/sŏdo ch'angak taegye,* 1: p. 240.

94. Chang Sahun, "Kyŏnggido ipch'ang-gwa sŏdo ipch'ang," p. 12.

95. Yu Iksŏ, "Chŏng Tŭngman," p. 218.

96. Yi Pohyŏng, "Sŏnsori sant'aryŏng," p. 169; Pak Sŏnghŭi, *I saram ihu,* p. 49.

97. Reports on Chŏng's study with Ch'oe differ. Yi Pohyŏng reports that Chŏng studied *shijo* and *chapka,* but Pak Sŏnghŭi reports that Chŏng was taught *kagok* and *kasa* (Yi Pohyŏng, "Sŏnsori sant'aryŏng," p. 169; Pak Sŏnghŭi, *I saram ihu,* p. 49). The accounts are likely complementary, because Ch'oe and many of his peers, including his well-known student Ch'oe Chŏngshik, mastered all four song types (Yu Iksŏ, "Chŏng Tŭngman," p. 220; Hahn, *Kugak,* pp. 22–23).

98. Yu Iksŏ, "Chŏng Tŭngman," p. 221.

99. Pak Sŏnghŭi, *I saram ihu,* p. 49.

100. Yu Iksŏ, "Chŏng Tŭngman," pp. 221–222.

101. Yi Pohyŏng, "Sŏnsori sant'aryŏng," pp. 168–170.

102. Hahn, *Kugak,* pp. 23–24.

103. Yu Iksŏ, "Chŏng Tŭngman," p. 223; Hahn, *Kugak,* p. 30.

104. Yu Iksŏ, "Chŏng Tŭngman," p. 223; Pak Sŏnghŭi, *I saram ihu,* p. 49. In Yu Iksŏ's elaborate account of the singer's life, there is no mention of Chŏng's work as a gardener for Japanese residents ("Chŏng Tŭngman," pp. 217–225). Chŏng presumably felt reluctant to talk about it, given that anti-Japanese sentiments remained strong at the time of Yu's interview.

105. Quoted in Yu Iksŏ, "Chŏng Tŭngman," p. 222.

106. Chang Sahun, "Kyŏnggido ipch'ang-gwa sŏdo ipch'ang," p. 11. See also Howard, *Bands, Songs, and Shamanistic Rituals,* p. 103; and Hahn, *Kugak,* p. 53.

107. Yi Ch'angbae, *Han'guk kach'ang taegye,* 1: p. 178; Yu Iksŏ, "Chŏng Tŭngman," p. 224. Chŏng was also put forward as a candidate holder of *Kyŏnggi minyo* in 1969 (Hong Hyŏnshik and Pak Hŏnbong, *Chwach'ang Kyŏnggi kin chapka* (Long chapka from Kyŏnggi province sung seated), pp. 377–378).

108. Yi Pohyŏng, "Sŏnsori sant'aryŏng," p. 170.

109. No Chaemyŏng, "1962-nyŏn Han'guk minyo yŏn'guhoe 'minyo Yo-ŭi hyangyŏn' inswaemul charyo haeje" (Bibliographical notes on the Korean Folksong Research Society's 1962 publication "Delights of the folksong show"), p. 400. The society had been managed by Yi Sohyang until An Pich'wi took over the helm, probably around the mid 1960s. See Kim Ŭnjŏng, "An Pich'wi," p. 25; see also figure 3.5.

110. *Maeil kyŏngje,* February 23, 1971, 5; Kim Ŭnjŏng, "An Pich'wi," p. 25.

111. Shin Chŏnghŭi, "An Pich'wi yŏsa 13-se-e immun Kyŏnggi minyo-ro muhyŏng munhwajae" (Madame An Pich'wi from her debut at the age of thirteen to intangible cultural property of *Kyŏnggi minyo*); No Chaemyŏng, "1962-nyŏn Han'guk minyo yŏn'guhoe," p. 400.

112. *Maeil kyŏngje,* August 21, 1982, 9.

113. *Tonga ilbo,* January 15, 1964, 5; Yu Iksŏ, "Chŏng Tŭngman," p. 224; Hahn, *Kugak,* p. 30.

114. Quoted in Pak Sŏnghŭi, *I saram ihu,* p. 48.

115. Interview with Hwang Yongju, November 18, 1995; Paek Taeung, "Kyŏnggido sori," p. 21.

116. Yi Ch'angbae, *Han'guk kach'ang taegye,* 1: p. 326.

117. Interview with Hwang Yongju, November 18, 1995.

118. Ibid.; see also Hwang Yongju, *Han'guk kyŏng/sŏdo ch'angak taegye*, 1: p. 175.

119. Yi Ch'angbae, *Han'guk kach'ang taegye*, 1: p. 326.

120. Yi Pohyŏng, "Sŏnsori sant'aryŏng," p. 170.

121. Hwang Yongju, *Han'guk kyŏng/sŏdo ch'angak taegye*, 1: p. 160; Kim Hyeri and Chang Hwiju, *Sŏnsori san'taryŏng*, pp. 163–165. On November 30, 2009, Pang Yŏnggi replaced then holder-elect Yun Chongp'yŏng (1945–2009), who passed away that year (Bang So-Yeon, pers. comm., July 22, 2013).

122. Interview with Hwang Yongju, September 19, 2012; see also Sŏnsori sant'aryŏng pojonhoe, "Chungyo muhyŏng munhwajae che-19-ho," p. 10.

123. Yi Ch'angbae, *Han'guk kach'ang taegye*, 2: p. 315.

124. Paek Taeung, "Kyŏnggido sori," p. 15; Hwang Yongju, *Han'guk kyŏng/sŏdo ch'angak taegye*, 1: pp. 141–143.

125. A picture in Sŏk Chusŏn shows the singers performing without the silk waistcoats (*Han'guk pokshik sa* [A history of Korean dress and accessories], p. 225).

126. Interview with Yi Pohyŏng, September 26, 1995.

127. Yi Pohyŏng, "Sŏnsori sant'aryŏng," p. 164; Sŏmundang, *Sajin-ŭro ponŭn Chosŏn shidae*, 1: p. 112; Paek Hwarang, "Ŏpsŏjin minsok sadangp'ae" (The lost folklore of *sadangp'ae*), p. 187; Hahn, *Kugak*, p. 142.

128. Hwang Yongju, *Han'guk kyŏng/sŏdo ch'angak taegye*, 1: pp. 141–143. A picture in Sŏk Chusŏn shows the singers performing without hairbands (*Han'guk pokshik sa*, p. 225).

129. Yi Pohyŏng, "Sŏnsori sant'aryŏng," p. 165.

130. Yi Ch'angbae, *Han'guk kach'ang taegye*, 1: p. 315.

131. See Maliangkay, "There Is No Amen in Shaman."

132. See Ch'oe Sangsu, "Folk Plays," p. 257; Paek Taeung, "Kyŏnggido sori," p. 15; Yi Pohyŏng, "Sŏnsori sant'aryŏng," p. 169; Hwang Yongju, *Han'guk kyŏng/sŏdo ch'angak taegye*, 1: pp. 140–143, 145; Kungnip kugagwŏn, "Ipch'ang sant'aryŏng" (Mountain Songs performed standing), p. 6.

133. Howard, "Gender Issues in the Conservation of Korean Music," p. 182; interview with Yi Pohyŏng, August 14, 1995.

134. Interview with Im Tonggwŏn, September 15, 1995.

135. When Hwang Yongju and his senior students were invited to perform at Seoul's Chŏngdong Theater on September 30, 1995, he brought along only male senior students.

136. According to Yi Pohyŏng, *Kyŏnggi minyo* should all be regarded as refined folksongs, *chapka*, because like *Sŏdo sori*, they had been elevated through stage performances and recordings over a long period of time (interview with Yi Pohyŏng, October 29, 1995).

137. Former holder Muk Kyewŏl has commented that although she used to sit throughout her performance, by the 1990s she had become accustomed to occasionally getting up and dancing with an hourglass drum (Muk, cited in Pak Sŏnghŭi, *I saram ihu*, p. 22).

138. Ryu Ŭiho, *Muk Kyewŏl Kyŏnggi sori yŏn'gu* (A study of Muk Kyewŏl's Kyŏnggi folksongs), p. 34.

139. For more on the relation between *kasa* and *chapka*, see Hong Hyŏnshik and Pak Hŏnbong, *Chwach'ang Kyŏnggi kin chapka*, p. 375; Hahn, "Chapka," p. 235; Yi Ch'angbae, *Han'guk kach'ang taegye*, 1: pp. 162–163; Yun Kihong, "Chapka-ŭi sŏngkyŏk-kwa minyo," pp. 209, 212; and Chang Sahun, *Han'guk chŏnt'ong ŭmag-ŭi ihae*, p. 101.

140. According to legend, in China's ancient times King Fu Xi was the first to teach his people how to fish, hunt, and farm livestock (Hwang Yongju, *Han'guk kyŏng/sŏdo ch'angak taegye*, 1: p. 306).

141. Yi Ch'angbae, *Han'guk kach'ang taegye*, 1: pp. 189–190.

142. Kim Yŏngun and Kim Hyeri, *Kyŏnggi minyo* (Folksongs from Kyŏnggi Province), p. 38.

143. Hahn, "Chapka," p. 239; Chang Sahun, *Kugak taesajŏn,* p. 855; Paek Taeung, "Kyŏnggido sori," p. 18.

144. An example can be found on Seoul Records 9407-G526 (1994), *Hŭnggyŏun sorip'anesŏ* (On the joyous folk scene).

145. Hwang Yongju, *Han'guk kyŏng/sŏdo ch'angak taegye,* 1: p. 287; Kim Yŏngun and Kim Hyeri, *Kyŏnggi minyo,* p. 95.

146. Hwang Yongju, *Han'guk kyŏng/sŏdo ch'angak taegye,* 1: p. 287.

147. An example of this style of singing can be found on Oasis ORC-1233 (1991), *Muhyŏng munhwajae che-57-ho* (ICCP no. 57). Typical *Kyŏnggi* folksongs that are not regarded as *t'ongsok minyo,* but are sung in very much the same way, include the *hwimori chapka,* songs such as "Kŭmgangsan t'aryŏng" (Ballad of Mount Kŭmgang) and a number of *shin minyo.* The latter include "P'ungdŭngga," which was composed by Ch'oe Chŏngshik in 1903, and "T'aep'yŏngga" (Song of Peace), composed shortly after the Pacific War (Yi Ch'angbae, *Han'guk kach'ang taegye,* 1: pp. 213, 790).

148. Chŏng Tŭngman, quoted in Pak Sŏnghŭi, *I saram ihu,* p. 51.

149. Interview with Yi Ŭnju, October 26, 1997.

150. See Taedo Records, *Muk Kyewŏl Kyŏnggi chapka wanch'angjip* (Muk Kyewŏl, a complete recital of *Kyŏnggi chapka*), JCDS-0542, 1997; see also Ryu Ŭiho, *Muk Kyewŏl Kyŏnggi sori yŏn'gu,* p. 289.

151. Nipponophone K210-A/B.

152. See Jigu Inc., *Kyŏnggi myŏngch'ang Pak Ch'unjae* (Pak Ch'unjae, the famous singer from Kyŏnggi province), JCDS-0542, 1996.

153. Day, *A Century of Recorded Music,* p. 9; Barfe, *Where Have All the Good Times Gone,* p. 32; Maliangkay, "Their Masters' Voice," p. 64.

154. Yi Ch'angbae, *Han'guk kach'ang taegye,* 1: pp. 162–164; Pan Chaeshik, *Chaedam ch'ŏnnyŏn sa,* pp. 251–253; Kim Yŏngun and Kim Hyeri, *Kyŏnggi minyo,* pp. 26–30; Ryu Ŭiho, *Muk Kyewŏl Kyŏnggi sori yŏn'gu,* p. 29.

155. Hong Hyŏnshik and Pak Hŏnbong, *Chwach'ang Kyŏnggi kin chapka,* p. 371.

156. Shin Ch'an'gyun, *Minsog-ŭi kohyang,* p. 104; Kim Ŭnjŏng, "An Pich'wi," p. 24.

157. Interview with Yi Pohyŏng, October 29, 1995; Ryu Ŭiho, *Muk Kyewŏl Kyŏnggi sori yŏn'gu,* p. 29.

158. Yi Ch'angbae, *Han'guk kach'ang taegye,* 1: pp. 164–165; Shin Ch'an'gyun, *Minsog-ŭi kohyang,* pp. 103–104; Kim Ŭnjŏng, "An Pich'wi," p. 24; Yi Pohyŏng, "Chŏnt'ong sahoe-esŏ minyo-rŭl yŏnhaenghanŭn sahoe chiptan-gwa kŭ munhwa haengwi" (The social groups who sang folksongs in traditional society and their cultural behavior), p. 148.

159. Yi Ch'angbae, *Han'guk kach'ang taegye,* 1: p. 165; interview with Yi Pohyŏng, October 29, 1995.

160. Interview with Yi Pohyŏng, November 18, 1998. See also Howard, *Bands, Songs, and Shamanistic Rituals,* p. 93; Sŏl Hojŏng, "Nŭlgŭn kisaeng Ch'ohyangi" (The old entertainment girl Ch'ohyang), p. 69; Hwang Miyŏn, *Kwŏnbŏn-gwa kisaeng-ŭro pon shingminji kŭndaesŏng,* (Colonial modernity from the viewpoint of *kwŏnbŏn* and *kisaeng*), pp. 50–55.

161. Yi Ch'angbae, *Han'guk kach'ang taegye,* 1: pp. 163–168; Shin Ch'an'gyun, *Minsog-ŭi kohyang,* p. 100; Hahn, *Kugak,* pp. 21–22.

162. Robinson, "Growth of the Forces of Enlightenment," p. 227.

163. Hwang Miyŏn, *Kwŏnbŏn-gwa kisaeng-ŭro,* pp. 66–67.

164. Robinson, *Cultural Nationalism in Colonial Korea, 1920–1925*, p. 63; Young Ik Lew, "Growth of the Forces of Enlightenment," pp. 228–229.

165. Maliangkay, "New Symbolism and Retail Therapy," pp. 30–31.

166. Michael Robinson notes that some listeners complained that the radio was using *kisaeng* ("Broadcasting, Cultural Hegemony," p. 65).

167. See *Tonga ilbo*, September 22, 1921, 3; November 30, 1921, 3; May 13, 1922, 3; November 28, 1923, 3; May 20, 1924, 7; August 17, 1926, 5; December 17, 1930, 5; April 8, 1931, 3; April 24, 1938, 3; and *Chosŏn ilbo* (Korea daily) January 26, 1926, 2; September 6, 1927, 2; August 7, 1931, 7. In several cases, it was reported that the girls had committed suicide because they were unable to be with a man they loved (*Tonga ilbo*, December 20, 1923, 3; December 11, 1925, 3; and *Chosŏn ilbo*, July 17, 1925, 2; October 24, 1929, 7). For more on the various reasons behind young women's suicide and their reportage during the colonial period, see Theodore Jun Yoo, *The Politics of Gender in Colonial Korea*, pp. 2, 59, 162, 175. For more on the use of drugs among *kisaeng*, see Hwang Miyŏn, *Kwŏnbŏn-gwa kisaeng-ŭro*, p. 231.

168. Pilzer, "The Twentieth-Century 'Disappearance'," p. 298.

169. Hwang Miyŏn, *Kwŏnbŏn-gwa kisaeng-ŭro*, p. 44.

170. Kawamura Minato, *Malhanŭn kkot: Kisaeng* (Speaking flowers: Courtesans), pp. 193–199; Atkins, *Primitive Selves*, p. 181; Hwang Miyŏn, *Kwŏnbŏn-gwa kisaeng-ŭro*, pp. 162, 222.

171. Yi Ch'angbae, *Han'guk kach'ang taegye*, 1: pp. 163, 166; Hahn, *Kugak*, p. 22.

172. *Tonga ilbo*, May 2, 1927, 3; Hwang Miyŏn, *Kwŏnbŏn-gwa kisaeng-ŭro*, pp. 70, 76.

173. Han'guk minsok taesajŏn p'yŏnch'an wiwŏnhoe, *Han'guk minsok taesajŏn*, 1: p. 189. According to Sŏl Hojŏng, the *Hansŏng* and *Hannam kwŏnbŏn* mostly attracted students from the area around Pusan, while the *Chosŏn kwŏnbŏn* drew mainly students from Seoul (Sŏl Hojŏng, "Nŭlgŭn kisaeng Ch'ohyangi," p. 73).

174. Yi Ch'angbae, *Han'guk kach'ang taegye*, 1: p. 166; Chosŏn yŏn'guhoe (Research Society of Colonial Korea), *Chosŏn miin pogam* (Handbook of Korean beauties), p. 9; Kim Ŭnjŏng, "An Pich'wi," p. 23; No Tongŭn, *Han'guk kŭndae ŭmak sa* (A modern history of Korean traditional music), p. 559. According to Sŏl Hojŏng, the school was established in 1919. He notes that the *Chosŏn kwŏnbŏn* had initially been known as the *Taejŏng kwŏnbŏn* ("Nŭlgŭn kisaeng Ch'ohyangi," p. 73; see also Chosŏn yŏn'guhoe, *Chosŏn miin pogam*).

175. Yi Ch'angbae, *Han'guk kach'ang taegye*, 1: pp. 163–168; Hahn, *Kugak*, pp. 21–23.

176. Han'guk chŏngshin munhwa yŏn'guwŏn, *Kyŏngsŏng pangsongguk kugak pangsong kok mongnok* (Kyŏngsŏng Broadcast Corporation's playlist of Korean traditional music), pp. 24–27.

177. Hong Hyŏnshik and Pak Hŏnbong, *Chwach'ang Kyŏnggi kin chapka;* interview with Yi Ŭnju, October 26, 1998; Pak Sŏnghŭi, *I saram ihu*, p. 23; Pak Kyŏngsu, *Sorikkundŭl*, pp. 215–219.

178. Quoted in ibid., p. 271.

179. Kim Ŭnjŏng, "An Pich'wi," p. 23.

180. Yi Sŏngbu, "Shin in'gan munhwajae 23" (New human cultural property no. 23), p. 8; Pak Kyŏngsu, *Sorikkundŭl*, p. 221. Yi Chinhong's and Yi Chinbong's profiles are included on respectively page 3 and 21 of the *Taejŏng kwŏnbŏn* section of the *Chosŏn miin pogam* (Handbook of Korean beauties) (Chosŏn yŏn'guhoe, *Chosŏn miin pogam*).

181. Kim Ŭnjŏng, "An Pich'wi," p. 24; Yi Sŏngbu, "Shin in'gan munhwajae 23," p. 8; Pak Kyŏngsu, *Sorikkundŭl*, pp. 270–271.

182. See Sŏng Kyŏngnin, *Han'guk ŭmak non'go*, p. 7; Hwang Yongju, *Han'guk kyŏng/sŏdo ch'angak taegye*, 1: p. 269.

183. Wŏlgan munhwajaesa, *Wŏlgan munhwajae,* p. 10; Yi Ch'angbae, *Han'guk kach'ang taegye,* 1: p. 180.

184. Kim Ŭnjŏng, "An Pich'wi," p. 24; Hahn, *Kugak,* p. 22; Pak Kyŏngsu, *Sorikkundŭl,* p. 271.

185. Quoted in Kim Myŏnggon, *Han, Kim Myŏnggon-ŭi kwangdae kihaeng,* p. 273.

186. Kim Ŭnjŏng, "An Pich'wi," p. 24.

187. An's recollection of her first performance for SBC bears witness to the strong bond between the group members (Kim Myŏnggŏn, *Han, Kim Myŏnggon-ŭi kwangdae kihaeng,* p. 274).

188. Kim Ŭnjŏng, "An Pich'wi," p. 24; Maliangkay, "Koreans Performing for Foreign Troops."

189. Kim Myŏnggon, *Han, Kim Myŏnggon-ŭi kwangdae kihaeng,* p. 275.

190. Kim Ŭnjŏng, "An Pich'wi," p. 25.

191. Quoted in Kim Myŏnggon, *Han, Kim Myŏnggon-ŭi kwangdae kihaeng,* p. 276.

192. Quoted in Kim Myŏnggon, *Han, Kim Myŏnggon-ŭi kwangdae kihaeng,* p. 278.

193. Quoted in Kim Ŭnjŏng, "An Pich'wi," p. 25.

194. Quoted in Ku, "Sŭsŭng-ŭi salm-gwa yesur-ŭi chase-rŭl" (The life of teachers and a detailed account of their art).

195. Kim Myŏnggon, "Muk Kyewŏl," p. 193; Ryu Ŭiho, *Muk Kyewŏl Kyŏnggi sori yŏn'gu,* p. 24.

196. Song Bangsong, "1910-nyŏndae chŏngjae-ŭi chŏnsŭng yangsang" (Looking at the tradition of benefit performances in the 1910s), pp. 153–154, 166.

197. Chang Sahun, *Kugak taesajŏn,* p. 430.

198. Kim Myŏnggon, "Muk Kyewŏl," pp. 193–194; Ryu Ŭiho, *Muk Kyewŏl Kyŏnggi sori yŏn'gu,* pp. 24–26.

199. The fact that Muk's husband had already been married suggests that even popular *kisaeng* were not in the position to be choosy about their husbands-to-be.

200. Ryu Ŭiho, *Muk Kyewŏl Kyŏnggi sori yŏn'gu,* p. 21.

201. Pak Kyŏngsu, *Sorikkundŭl,* p. 200; Ryu Ŭiho, *Muk Kyewŏl Kyŏnggi sori yŏn'gu,* pp. 31–32.

202. Koreans have long celebrated sixtieth birthdays (*hwan'gap*) elaborately because at this age a person has arrived at the start of a second cycle of the Korean sexagenary calendar. Ryu Ŭiho, *Muk Kyewŏl Kyŏnggi sori yŏn'gu,* p. 34.

203. See Hwang Yongju, *Han'guk kyŏng/sŏdo ch'angak taegye,* 1: p. 267.

204. Kim Yŏngun and Kim Hyeri, *Kyŏnggi minyo,* p. 136.

205. Quoted in Kim Myŏnggon, "Muk Kyewŏl," p. 198.

206. Ryu Ŭiho, *Muk Kyewŏl Kyŏnggi sori yŏn'gu,* p. 36.

207. Kim Munsŏng, "Mudae taeshin kaeksŏk chik'in Kim Yŏngim-sshi, che-2-ŭi Kim Okshimin'ga?" (Could Kim Yŏngim who was told to take a seat rather than the stage be the second Kim Okshim?).

208. *Maeil kyŏngje,* April 27, 1968, 3; Hwang Yongju, *Han'guk kyŏng/sŏdo ch'angak taegye,* 1: pp. 273–277.

209. Yi Misuk, "Ŭnt'oe mudae kannŭn *Kyŏnggi minyo* 1-inja Muk Kyewŏl yŏsa" (*Kyŏnggi minyo*'s no. 1 performer Muk Kyewŏl goes into retirement).

210. The government report states that Yi Ŭnju was born in Seoul (Hong Hyŏnshik and Pak Hŏnbong, *Chwach'ang Kyŏnggi kin chapka,* p. 379). Paek Taeung, "Kyŏnggido sori," p. 20; Kim Yŏngun and Kim Hyeri, *Kyŏnggi minyo,* p. 125.

211. Pak Kyŏngsu, *Sorikkundŭl,* p. 217.

212. The government report gives his name as On Kyŏngt'ae (Hong Hyŏnshik and Pak Hŏnbong, *Chwach'ang Kyŏnggi kin chapka,* p. 379).

213. Pak Kyŏngsu, *Sorikkundŭl,* pp. 217–218; interview with Yi Ŭnju, October 26, 1997.

214. Yi Ch'angbae, *Han'guk kach'ang taegye,* 1: p. 790; Chang Sahun, *Kugak taesajŏn,* p. 765.

215. Interview with Yi Ŭnju, July 8, 2013.

216. Interview with Yi Ŭnju, October 26, 1997.

217. Ibid; Kim Yŏngun and Kim Hyeri, *Kyŏnggi minyo,* pp. 125–126.

218. Interview with Yi Ŭnju, October 26, 1997.

219. Interview with Yi Ŭnju, April 23, 2001.

220. Hwang Yongju, *Han'guk kyŏng/sŏdo ch'angak taegye,* 1: pp. 267–268; interview with Yi Ŭnju, April 23, 2001.

221. Interview with Yi Ŭnju, October 26, 1997.

222. Interview with Yi Ŭnju, July 8, 2013.

223. Quoted in Ku, "Mokp'yo nopko tturyŏthan sorikkun" (A distinguished singer aims high), p. 23.

224. Munhwajae kwalliguk, *Munhwajae* 5, pp. 142–143.

225. Kim Yŏngjo, "Chaeya myŏngch'ang 'Kim Okshim'-ŭl ashinayo?" (Have you ever heard of the late renowned singer Kim Okshim?).

226. Hong Hyŏnshik and Pak Hŏnbong, *Chwach'ang Kyŏnggi kin chapka,* pp. 380–381.

227. Yi Ch'angbae, *Han'guk kach'ang taegye,* 1: pp. 179, 181; Song Bangsong, *Han'guk ŭmak t'ongsa,* p. 560.

228. *Maeil kyŏngje,* April 27, 1968, 3.

229. Munhwajae kwalliguk, *Munhwajae,* 10: p. 225.

230. Han'guk munhwa yesul chinhŭngwŏn, *Munye yŏn'gam 1974* (1974 yearbook of culture and arts), p. 128; *Munye yŏn'gam 1978* (1978 yearbook of culture and arts), p. 103; Yesurwŏn, *Han'guk yesulchi* (Record of Korean arts), p. 342.

231. Chŏng Shihaeng, "Sarachyŏ kanŭn uri sori sallyŏ naenŭn poram" (The value of reviving the Korean folksongs that survive today).

232. Interview with Yi Ŭnju, July 8, 2013.

233. Hong Hyŏnshik and Pak Hŏnbong, *Chwach'ang Kyŏnggi kin chapka,* p. 371.

234. Martin Stokes, "Introduction: Ethnicity, Identity and Music," p. 22.

235. Lucy Green, *Music, Gender, Education,* pp. 14–15, 55.

Chapter 4 Embodying Nostalgia

1. Howard, "*Juche* and Culture," pp. 174–176.

2. See Im Tonggwŏn, "Pukhan minyo-ŭi yŏn'gu" (A study of North Korean folksongs), p. 59.

3. Quoted in Pak Sŏnghŭi, *I saram ihu,* pp. 43–44.

4. Interview with Ch'oe Sŏngnyong, May 21, 2012; Pak Chunyŏng, pers. comm., November 23, 2014.

5. Yi Ch'angbae, *Han'guk kach'ang taegye,* I1: pp. 271, 844; Kwŏn Osŏng, "Sŏdo minyo" (Folksongs from the western provinces), p. 703; Hwang Yongju, *Han'guk kyŏng/sŏdo ch'angak taegye,* 2: p. 193. People once had a different impression of the adjacent Hamgyŏng province. Those born there were long believed to have strong characters and to be self-sufficient, diligent, and dedicated (Sŏng Kyŏngnin, *Minyo kihaeng,* p. 172; interview with Im Tonggwŏn, November 9, 1995).

6. Paul S. Crane, *Korean Patterns,* pp. 94, 96.

7. Quoted in Yu Iksŏ, "Kim Chŏngyŏn," p. 179.

8. Im Tonggwŏn and Chŏng Tonghwa argue that the use of Chinese historical stories and Chinese phrasing indicates that the song was influenced by *kasa* (narrative songs) (Im Tonggwŏn, *Han'guk minyo sa*, p. 223; Chŏng Tonghwa, *Han'guk minyo-ŭi sajŏk yŏn'gu*, p. 334n407).

9. Han'guk chŏngshin munhwa yŏn'guwŏn, *Han'guk yusŏnggi ŭmban ch'ongmongnok* (Complete list of Korean gramophone records from the colonial period), pp. 19–20; Kim Insuk and Kim Hyeri, *Sŏdo sori*, p. 74.

10. Yi Yunsŏn, *Han'guk yangak p'alshimnyŏnsa* (An eighty-year history of Western music in Korea).

11. For more on lyrics sheets, see Maliangkay, "Their Masters' Voice," p. 6.

12. Kim Insuk and Kim Hyeri, *Sŏdo sori*, pp. 75–76.

13. Yi Ch'angbae, *Han'guk kach'ang taegye*, 1: pp. 842–843; Paek Taeung, "P'yŏngando sori" (Songs from P'yŏngan province), p. 62; Pak Sŏnghŭi, *I saram ihu*, p. 40; Hwang Yongju, *Han'guk kyŏng/sŏdo ch'angak taegye*, 2: p. 192.

14. Han Kisŏp, *Chŏnt'ong sŏdo sori chŏnjip* (Complete collection of traditional songs from the western provinces), 1: pp. 50–68.

15. This line also appears in the *chapka* "Kwansanyungma" (Hwang Yongju, *Han'guk kyŏng/sŏdo ch'angak taegye*, 1: p. 135).

16. The connotation here is sexual.

17. See Im Tonggwŏn, *Han'guk minyo sa*, p. 223; Chang Sahun, *Yŏmyŏng-ŭi tongsŏ ŭmak*, p. 160; "Sŏdo-ŭi Kwansanyungma-wa Sushimga mit Ch'up'ung kambyŏlgok" (*Kwansanyungma, Sushimga* and *Ch'up'ung kambyŏlgok* from the western provinces), pp. 131, 139; Yi Ch'angbae, *Han'guk kach'ang taegye*, 1: pp. 271, 289, 292, 844, 852; Paek Taeung, "P'yŏngando sori," p. 57; Kwŏn Osŏng, "Minyo-nŭn minjung-ŭi noraeida" (Folksongs are the songs of the people), p. 8; Cho Myŏngju, "Yu Chisuk," p. 92.

18. Paek Taeung, "P'yŏngando sori," p. 58; Hwang Yongju, *Han'guk kyŏng/sŏdo ch'angak taegye*, 2: pp. 115–120, 205–208, 350.

19. Paek Taeung, "Hwanghaedo sori," pp. 29, 31–32.

20. A transcription of the *ŏtchungmori* rhythmic cycle can be found in Kyung-hee Kim, "Theory of *Pansori*," pp. 36–37.

21. Kwŏn Osŏng, "Minyo-nŭn minjung-ŭi noraeida," p. 8; Chang Sahun, *Han'guk chŏnt'ong ŭmag-ŭi ihae*, pp. 221, 225–227.

22. Hahn, *Kugak*, p. 161.

23. Van Zile, *Perspectives on Korean Dance*, p. 5.

24. Kim Insuk and Kim Hyeri, *Sŏdo sori*, p. 63.

25. Paek Taeung, "Hwanghaedo sori," p. 29; Kwŏn Osŏng, "Sŏdo minyo," p. 702. Yi Ch'angbae suggests that "Kwansanyungma" may also have been influenced by *kasa* from the Seoul region (*Han'guk kach'ang taegye*, 1: p. 271). It is believed that the author Shin Kwangsu (1712–1775) composed the song based on a poem by the Chinese poet Du Fu (712–770) (Chang Sahun, "Sŏdo-ŭi Kwansanyungma-wa Sushimga," p. 133; *Han'guk kach'ang taegye*, 1: pp. 398–399).

26. Yi Pohyŏng, *Sŏdo minyo-wa Kyŏnggi minyo-ŭi sŏnyul kujo yŏn'gu* (A study of the melodic structure of Sŏdo minyo and Kyŏnggi minyo), pp. 72–73.

27. Chang Sahun, *Yŏmyŏng-ŭi tongsŏ ŭmak*, p. 115.

28. Yi Ch'angbae used to sing the southwestern "Chŏkpyŏkpu," a *tan'ga* (short poem), in the *Sŏdo* style. Another music piece he converted to the *Sŏdo* style was "Kwandong p'algyŏng" (The eight sights of the Kwandong region), the lyrics of which were written by Pak Hŏnbong

(1907–1977), a former principal of the *Kugak yesul hakkyo* (Korean Traditional Music and Arts School). Yi Ch'angbae, *Han'guk kach'ang taegye*, 1: pp. 162, 169, 271.

29. Yi Pohyŏng argues that no singer ever truly mastered both genres (*Sŏdo minyo-wa Kyŏnggi minyo-ŭi sŏnyul kujo yŏn'gu*, pp. 7–8, 16).

30. The dates given for Pak's life differ considerably. According to Yi Ch'angbae, for example, Pak lived from 1877 to 1947 (*Han'guk kach'ang taegye*, 1: p. 237). For a discussion, see Pan Chaeshik, *Chaedam ch'ŏnnyŏn sa*, pp. 247–249.

31. Yi Ch'angbae, *Han'guk kach'ang taegye*, 1: pp. 237, 272–273; Chang Sahun, *Kugak taesajŏn*, p. 587; Chosŏn yŏn'guhoe, *Chosŏn miin pogam*. Pak Wŏlchŏng (born Pak Kŭmhong) even included folksongs from the southwestern region and *p'ansori* in her repertoire. Chang Sahun, *Han'guk chŏnt'ong ŭmag-ŭi ihae*, p. 159. As I discuss below, later holder of *Sŏdo sori* Yi Ŭn'gwan was renowned for his ability to mimic the singing styles and dialects of several regions.

32. Han'guk chŏngshin munhwa yŏn'guwŏn, *Han'guk yusŏnggi ŭmban ch'ongmongnok*, pp. 23–24.

33. *Chaedam* implies the improvisation (creation) or re-creation of witty dialogues, often by one performer. This is intrinsic to many types of folk performing arts, including *p'ansori* (Pan Chaeshik, *Chaedam ch'ŏnnyŏn sa*, pp. 121–142).

34. Chang Sahun, *Yŏmyŏng-ŭi tongsŏ ŭmak*, p. 116; Yi Ch'angbae, *Han'guk kach'ang taegye*, 1: p. 272; Taehan min'guk yesurwŏn, *Han'guk yesul sajŏn III* (Dictionary of Korean arts III), p. 164.

35. Chang Yŏngch'ŏl, *Chosŏn ŭmak myŏngin chŏn* (Dictionary of famous Korean musicians), pp. 208–209; Yi Pohyŏng, Hong Kiwŏn, and Pae Yŏnhyŏng, *Yusŏnggi ŭmban kasajip* (Collection of song texts from gramophone records), pp. 151–152.

36. Shin Ch'an'gyun, *Minsog-ŭi kohyang*, p. 103; Yi Ch'angbae, *Han'guk kach'ang taegye*, 1: p. 164.

37. Chang Sahun, "Sŏdo-ŭi Kwansanyungma-wa Sushimga," p. 193; Yi Ch'angbae, *Han'guk kach'ang taegye*, 1: p. 273. According to another report, Chang won the contest in 1959, when she was fifty-three years old (Taehan min'guk yesurwŏn, *Han'guk yesul sajŏn III*, p. 330).

38. Yi Ch'angbae, *Han'guk kach'ang taegye*, 1: p. 273.

39. Ibid.; Shin Chŏnghŭi, "Myŏngin myŏngjang 28; Yu Iksŏ, "Kim Chŏngyŏn," pp. 176–181; Kim Insuk and Kim Hyeri, *Sŏdo sori*, pp. 155–156.

40. In 1991, Yi Ch'unmok noted that three former students of Kim Chŏngyŏn had stopped performing (Ku Hŭisŏ, "Sŭsŭng-ŭi salm-i nae chwaumyŏng" [The life of a teacher is my motto], p. 23).

41. Quoted in Pak Sŏnghŭi, *I saram ihu*, p. 42.

42. Yi Chongsŏk, "Sŏdo sori O Pongnyŏ yŏsa" (Madame O Pongnyŏ and songs from the western provinces).

43. Yi Ch'angbae, *Han'guk kach'ang taegye*, 1: p. 166; Yi Chongsŏk, "Sŏdo sori O Pongnyŏ yŏsa," p. 7.

44. O Pongnyŏ, *Sŏdo sori* (Songs from the western provinces).

45. Yi Chongsŏk, "Sŏdo sori O Pongnyŏ yŏsa"; Pak Sŏnghŭi, *I saram ihu*, p. 42.

46. Ibid., p. 43. Yi Chongsŏk claims that O's first return to the stage was at the 1966 *Chŏn'guk minsok yesul kyŏngyŏn taehoe* (National Folk Arts Contest), but *Sŏdo sori* were not performed at the contest that year and would not be performed until 1970 (Yi Chongsŏk, "Sŏdo sori O Pongnyŏ yŏsa"; Im Chunsŏ, "Chŏnt'ong yŏnhŭi 50-nyŏn," pp. 347–349).

47. Paek Taeung, "P'yŏngando sori," pp. 60–61.

48. Pak Sŏnghŭi 1991: 42. Hwang Yongju has mistaken Kim Kwangsuk for being Kim Chŏngyŏn's student (*Han'guk kyŏng/sŏdo ch'angak taegye,* 1: p. 451).

49. Kim Insuk and Kim Hyeri, *Sŏdo sori,* pp. 179–180.

50. Quoted in Pak Sŏnghŭi, *I saram ihu,* p. 41.

51. Yi Chongsŏk, "Sŏdo sori O Pongnyŏ yŏsa."

52. O Pongnyŏ, *Sŏdo sori.*

53. Quoted in Cho Myŏngju, "Yu Chisuk," p. 93.

54. *Maeil kyŏngje,* April 19, 1980, 1.

55. In an interview with Kim Myŏnggŏn, Yi Ŭn'gwan said he won the contest by singing "Ch'angbu t'aryŏng" and a more elaborate version of "Nanbongga," "Sasŏl nanbongga," even though he had said in an earlier interview that he won the contest by singing "Yangsangdo" (Kim Myŏnggŏn, *Han, Kim Myŏnggon-ŭi kwangdae kihaeng,* p. 191; Ppuri kip'ŭn namu, *T'ŏrŏnok'o hanŭn mal 2* (Frank discussions 2), p. 187). In yet another interview, Yi said he competed at the contest at the age of twenty-one (Ch'oe Hongsun, "Sŏdo-ŭi kŭkch'ang *Paebaengi kut*" [*Ritual for Paebaengi,* the operetta from the western provinces], p. 174).

56. Han Manyŏng argues that although the term *rang* literally means "fishermen," it may well be a nonsense syllable and simply chosen for its sound (Hahn, *Kugak,* p. 182).

57. Sŏng Kyŏngnin and Yi Pohyŏng, "Chŏngsŏn 'Arirang' mit *Paebaengi kut* chosa pogosŏ" (Research report on "Arirang" from Chŏngsŏn and *Ritual for Paebaengi*), p. 118; Ppuri kip'ŭn namu, *T'ŏrŏnok'o hanŭn mal 2,* pp. 187–190; Kim Myŏnggon, *Han, Kim Myŏnggon-ŭi kwangdae kihaeng,* pp. 191–192.

58. Sŏng Kyŏngnin and Yi Pohyŏng, "Chŏngsŏn 'Arirang' mit *Paebaengi kut* chosa pogosŏ," p. 118; Kim Myŏnggon, *Han, Kim Myŏnggon-ŭi kwangdae kihaeng,* p. 192.

59. Ppuri kip'ŭn namu, *T'ŏrŏnok'o hanŭn mal 2,* p. 191.

60. Pan Chaeshik also believes that it was Pak Ch'ŏnbok who introduced Yi Ŭn'gwan to Shin Pulch'ul, but in an earlier interview Yi is quoted as saying that he was introduced to Shin by Pak Chin, a veteran of the theater world and a member of the Arts Academy (Yesurwŏn) (Pan Chaeshik, *Chaedam ch'ŏnnyŏn sa,* p. 66; Ppuri kip'ŭn namu, *T'ŏrŏnok'o hanŭn mal 2,* p. 192).

61. Yi Ch'angbae, *Han'guk kach'ang taegye,* 1: p. 275; interview with Yi Ŭn'gwan, October 23, 1997; Pan Chaeshik, *Chaedam ch'ŏnnyŏn sa,* p. 190.

62. Kim Myŏnggon, *Han, Kim Myŏnggon-ŭi kwangdae kihaeng,* p. 194.

63. Quoted in ibid., p. 194.

64. Ppuri kip'ŭn namu, *T'ŏrŏnok'o hanŭn mal 2,* p. 191.

65. Yi Ch'angbae, *Han'guk kach'ang taegye,* 1: p. 174; Hahn, *Kugak,* p. 30.

66. Kim Myŏnggon, *Han, Kim Myŏnggon-ŭi kwangdae kihaeng,* p. 196.

67. Ppuri kip'ŭn namu, *T'ŏrŏnok'o hanŭn mal 2,* p. 193.

68. Interview with Yi Ŭn'gwan, October 26, 1997. The other players included Cho Miryŏng (Paebaengi), Pok Hyesuk, and Pak Hŭngsu (Kim Myŏnggŏn, *Han, Kim Myŏnggon-ŭi kwangdae kihaeng,* p. 196; Taehan min'guk yesurwŏn, *Han'guk yesul sajŏn III* [Dictionary of Korean arts III], p. 213).

69. Ppuri kip'ŭn namu, *T'ŏrŏnok'o hanŭn mal 2,* p. 194.

70. Chang Ch'ŏnho, *"Paebaengi,"* pp. 3–4.

71. No Chaemyŏng, *Paebaengi kut* (*Ritual for Paebaengi*), pp. 131–149.

72. Both Kim Hyŏn'gyu, a former graduate of *Sant'aryŏng,* and former holder Kim Sunt'ae have taught at Yi's Institute (Yi Pohyŏng, "Sŏnsori sant'aryŏng," p. 170; Yi Ch'angbae, *Han'guk kach'ang taegye,* 1: p. 326).

73. Ch'oe Hongsun, "Sŏdo-ŭi kŭkch'ang *Paebaengi kut,*" p. 175.

74. Kim Wansu is also a graduate of *Sant'aryŏng* (Hwang Yongju, *Han'guk kyŏng/sŏdo ch'angak taegye,* 1: p. 29).

75. Ch'oe Hongsun, "Sŏdo-ŭi kŭkch'ang *Paebaengi kut,*" p. 174; Hwang Yongju, *Han'guk kyŏng/sŏdo ch'angak taegye,* 1: p. 451.

76. Interview with Yi Ŭn'gwan, October 23, 1997.

77. Pak Chunyŏng, pers. comm., June 24, 2014.

78. For details on *p'ansori* in performance, see Marshall R. Pihl, *The Korean Singer of Tales,* pp. 4–5.

79. Sŏng Kyŏngnin and Yi Pohyŏng, "*Paebaengi kut,*" p. 592; Hahn, *Kugak,* pp. 188–189.

80. Sŏng Kyŏngnin and Yi Pohyŏng, "*Paebaengi kut,*" pp. 598, 614; Detlef Nolden, "Das Koreanische Volksstück *Paebaengi-kut*" (The Korean folk play *Ritual for Paebaengi*), p. 34.

81. Detlef Nolden writes that some of the songs that Yi introduces by name during the opera are not performed in their "original form" ("Das Koreanische Volksstück *Paebaengi-kut,*" p. 34). Since the notion of a single origin only applies to a form of recorded music, Nolden presumably referred to the songs' common form.

82. Sŏng Kyŏngnin and Yi Pohyŏng, "*Paebaengi kut,*" pp. 592–623; Yi Ch'angbae, *Han'guk kach'ang taegye,* 1: pp. 714–715.

83. See, for example, the Hyundai Records cassette recording *Chŏngt'ong Paebaengi kut* (SSP-1016, 1979; *chŏngt'ong/chŏnt'ong* = traditional). The cassette sleeve does not provide any information other than the title, but there seem to be two or more accompanying musicians on the recording.

84. Oasis 5531–5534, Silver Star M501, and Shinsegi N182/N184/N187/N189.

85. See pictures of shaman fans in Sŏk Chusŏn, *Han'guk pokshik sa,* p. 632. See also Han'guk minsok taesajŏn p'yŏnch'an wiwŏnhoe, *Han'guk minsok taesajŏn,* 2: p. 816.

86. See the picture in Sŏk Chusŏn, *Han'guk pokshik sa,* p. 594. Other pictures of Yi Ŭn'gwan in performance appear in Hwang Yongju, *Han'guk kyŏng/sŏdo ch'angak taegye,* 2: p. 295; and Kim Insuk and Kim Hyeri, *Sŏdo sori,* pp. 74–76.

87. Sŏng Kyŏngnin and Yi Pohyŏng, "Chŏngsŏn 'Arirang' mit *Paebaengi kut* chosa pogosŏ," p. 126.

88. Chang Sahun, *Kugak kaeyo,* pp. 130–131.

89. Pak Chŏnghong, "Paro chabaya hal *Paebaengi kut*" (The *Ritual for Paebaengi* we must get right), p. 39.

90. Kim Tonguk, *Han'guk kayo-ŭi yŏn'gu* (A study of Korean popular ballads), p. 418; Ch'oe Sangsu, "*Paebaengi kut* taesa," part 2, p. 230.

91. Yi Pohyŏng, "*Paebaengi kut*-kwa tari kut" (*Ritual for Paebaengi* and the bridge ritual), p. 11.

92. Interview with Im Tonggwŏn, November 9, 1997.

93. Bo-hyŏng Yi, "P'ansori," p. 295; Yi Ch'angbae, *Han'guk kach'ang taegye,* 1: p. 231.

94. Chang Sahun, *Kugak kaeyo,* p. 131.

95. Sŏng Kyŏngnin and Yi Pohyŏng, "Chŏngsŏn 'Arirang' mit *Paebaengi kut* chosa pogosŏ," p. 129.

96. Han Kisŏp, *Chŏnt'ong sŏdo sori chŏnjip,* 2: p. 376.

97. Ch'oe Sangsu, "*Paebaengi kut* taesa," part 1, p. 183.

98. Nolden surmises that *pang* means "room," *-i* being a vocative suffix ("Das Koreanische Volksstück *Paebaengi-kut,*" p. 91n103). Given that the family loved the servant enough to name their daughter after her, it is unlikely that they would have given the servant such a condescending name.

99. Nolden, "Das Koreanische Volksstück *Paebaengi-kut,*" p. 26.

100. Yi Ch'angbae argues that *sangjwajung,* the Korean term used by Yi Ŭn'gwan for "monk," indicates that the character in the story was a higher monk, eligible to become a teacher (*Han'guk kach'ang taegye,* 1: p. 715).

101. Interview with Pak Chunyŏng, March 11, 2014.

102. Ch'oe Sangsu, "*Paebaengi kut* taesa," part 2, p. 245; Kim Tonguk, *Han'guk kayo-ŭi yŏn'gu,* p. 430.

103. Sŏng Kyŏngnin and Yi Pohyŏng, "Chŏngsŏn 'Arirang' mit *Paebaengi kut* chosa pogosŏ," pp. 126–153.

104. Ch'oe Kilsŏng, "Sejon kut-kwa 'todukchabi'-ŭi kujo punsŏk" (A structural analysis of *Sejon kut* and "catching the thief"), pp. 198–199; Park, *Voices from the Straw Mat.* p. 43.

105. Sŏng Kyŏngnin and Yi Pohyŏng, "*Paebaengi kut,*" p. 583.

106. Boudewijn Walraven, "Muga: The Songs of Korean Shamanism," pp. 40, 87.

107. See Man-young Hahn, "Religious Origins of Korean Music," p. 24; and Lee, *Studien zur Pansori-Musik in Korea,* p. 28.

108. Kim Tonguk, *Han'guk kayo-ŭi yŏn'gu,* p. 320; Sŏng Kyŏngnin and Yi Pohyŏng, "Chŏngsŏn 'Arirang' mit *Paebaengi kut* chosa pogosŏ," p. 123; "*Paebaengi kut,*" p. 581.

109. Interview with Yi Pohyŏng, September 26, 1995. For more details on the social status of *p'ansori* singers, see Pihl, *The Korean Singer of Tales,* pp. 60–61.

110. Interview with Yi Pohyŏng, September 26, 1995.

111. Detlef Nolden finds that the similarities relate only to one particular *p'ansori* piece, "Shimch'ŏngga" (Song of Shimch'ŏng) ("Das Koreanische Volksstück *Paebaengi-kut,*" pp. 37–38).

112. See, for example, the Buddhist chant in both the prologue and epilogue of Yi Ŭn'gwan's version (Ch'oe Sangsu, "*Paebaengi kut* taesa," part 2, pp. 229, 255).

113. Cho Tongil, *P'ansori-ŭi ihae* (An understanding of *p'ansori*), pp. 16–17.

114. Yi Ch'angbae, *Han'guk kach'ang taegye,* 1: p. 275.

115. Pihl, *The Korean Singer of Tales,* pp. 6–7.

116. Kim Tonguk, *Han'guk kayo-ŭi yŏn'gu,* pp. 320–321.

117. Sŏng Kyŏngnin and Yi Pohyŏng, "Chŏngsŏn 'Arirang' mit *Paebaengi kut* chosa pogosŏ," p. 124.

118. Yi Ch'angbae, *Han'guk kach'ang taegye,* 1: p. 272.

119. Han'guk chŏngshin munhwa yŏn'guwŏn, *Han'guk yusŏnggi ŭmban ch'ongmongnok,* pp. 711, 760.

120. Kim Myŏnggŏn, *Han, Kim Myŏnggon-ŭi kwangdae kihaeng,* p. 192.

121. See Sŏng Kyŏngnin and Yi Pohyŏng, "*Paebaengi kut,*" p. 586.

122. The Han'gyŏre reported (May 31, 1991, p. 11) that Yang also studied singing with Kim Chinmyŏng (1913–1997), whom she was able to meet again in 1990 when he visited Seoul as a member of the P'yŏngyang Minjok Ŭmaktan (Pyongyang People's Orchestra).

123. Sŏng Kyŏngnin and Yi Pohyŏng, "*Paebaengi kut,*" pp. 585–586, 594; No Chaemyŏng, *Paebaengi kut,* p. 128; Kim Insuk and Kim Hyeri, *Sŏdo sori,* p. 118.

124. Interview with Yi Ŭn'gwan, October 23, 1997.

125. Yi Ch'angbae, *Han'guk kach'ang taegye,* 1: p. 274; Pak Chŏnghong, "Paro chabaya hal *Paebaengi kut,*" p. 38; Sŏng Kyŏngnin and Yi Pohyŏng, "*Paebaengi kut,*" p. 586.

126. No Chaemyŏng lists a number of additional singers reported in a North Korean directory of folk musicians (*Paebaengi kut,* pp. 106–108).

127. No Chaemyŏng *Paebaengi kut,* pp. 65, 77.

128. Yi Ch'angbae, *Han'guk kach'ang taegye,* 1: p. 272.

129. Kim Yangsam, "K'ol taekshi-ga kaegŭ mudae" (Call taxi serves as comedy stage); No Chaemyŏng *Paebaengi kut,* pp. 130, 155.

130. Sŏng Kyŏngnin and Yi Pohyŏng, "*Paebaengi kut,*" p. 590.

131. Han Kisŏp, *Chŏnt'ong sŏdo sori chŏnjip,* 2: p. 370.

132. Ch'oe Sangsu, "*Paebaengi kut* taesa," part 1, pp. 181–226.

133. Ibid., part 2, pp. 181, 229.

134. Im Tonggwŏn, *Han'guk minyo chip,* 5: pp. 218–222.

135. Ibid., p. 219.

136. Chang Tongun, *Min'gan sŏsashi Paebaengi kut* (The folk epic *Ritual for Paebaengi*), p. 3.

137. Ibid., p. 5.

138. Nolden, "Das Koreanische Volksstück *Paebaengi-kut,*" p. 7.

139. Kim T'aejun, "Kogŭk *Paebaengi kut*" (The old play *Ritual for Paebaengi*).

140. Kim Insuk and Kim Hyeri, *Sŏdo sori,* pp. 178–179.

141. Munhwajaech'ŏng, "2013-nyŏndo munhwajae wiwŏnhoe (The 2013 cultural properties committee), pp. 19–20. Although Pak may eventually also become a holder, he does not currently have a student specializing in *Paebaengi kut.* When I asked Pak about his own successor, he replied, "In the future, I will have to set up a plan, starting with Ms Yuri [Kim; his graduate] . . ." (*ap'ŭro-nŭn chido-rŭl haeyachiyo, Yuri-sshi-but'ŏyo . . .*) (Pak Chunyŏng, pers. comm., December 21, 2014).

142. Pak Chunyŏng, pers. comm., April 26, 2015.

143. Chang Sahun, *Kugak taesajŏn,* p. 619; "Sŏdo-ŭi Kwansanyungma-wa Sushimga," p. 194; interview with Yi Pohyŏng, September 26, 1995.

144. *Tonga ilbo,* May 6, 1976, p. 5.

145. Interview with Yi Pohyŏng, October 22, 1997.

146. Ch'oe Sangsu, "Folk Plays," p. 255.

147. Sŏng Kyŏngnin and Yi Pohyŏng, "Chŏngsŏn 'Arirang' mit *Paebaengi kut* chosa pogosŏ," p. 123; "*Paebaengi kut,*" p. 590.

148. Yi Ŭn'gwan did not wish to give me a name, but he did say that this was a member of the CPC who had transcribed *Paebaengi kut* in a book. Han Manyŏng's transcription of Kim Yonghun's version had only just come out that same year, so I infer that Yi meant the folklorist Kim Tonguk.

149. Interview with Yi Ŭn'gwan, October 23, 1997.

150. Yi Ŭn'gwan, *Kach'ang ch'ongbo* (Full song scores), p. 395. In 1999, musicologist Rowan Pease filmed Yi playing his saxophone during a performance in Yanji, Yanbian. Yi is also shown with the saxophone around his neck on the cover of the CD set *Paebaengi kut* (Hana Records Co., 1353) from 2010.

151. When holders-elect Kim Kyŏngbae and Pak Chunyŏng were asked to carry out a trial performance in October 2012, they were given up to forty minutes to perform the entire piece (Munhwajaech'ŏng, "2013-nyŏndo munhwajae wiwŏnhoe, p. 19).

152. Pak Chŏnghong, "Paro chabaya hal *Paebaengi kut,*" pp. 38–39.

153. Ch'oe Sangsu, "*Paebaengi kut* taesa," part 2, pp. 234–238; Kim Tonguk, *Han'guk kayo-ŭi yŏn'gu,* pp. 422–424.

154. Shinsegi SLN 10607.

155. Seoul Music Sound Co. Ltd. SM-2013.

156. JCDS-0447. Although the record company released a new recording of Yi's *Paebaengi kut* in 2005 (JMCD-0039), it was a reissue of the 1994 recording.

157. The four mountains are located in the four corners of the Korean peninsula. Mount Kŭmgang is located in Kangwŏn province in the eastern part of the peninsula in what is now North Korea, Chiri Mountain stretches from north and south Chŏlla to part of south Kyŏngsang province, Kuwŏl Mountain is located in south Hwanghae province in the west, and Myohyang Mountain is located in what is now North Korea, where it stretches from north and south P'yŏngan to Chagang province.

158. Yi Ŭn'gwan, *Kach'ang ch'ongbo,* p. 297.

159. Pak Chunyŏng, pers. comm., July 9, 2013. See also recording on Synnara, *Pak Chunyŏng-ŭi Paebaengi kut-kwa Sŏdo sori* (Pak Chunyŏng's *Paebaengi kut* and folksongs from the western provinces), NSC-225, 2010.

160. Pak Kyŏngsu, *Sorikkundŭl,* pp. 202–203.

161. Interview with Yi Ŭn'gwan, October 23, 1997.

162. Office of Cultural Properties, *The Preservation and Transmission System,* pp. 9–10.

163. Sŏng Kyŏngnin and Yi Pohyŏng, "Chŏngsŏn 'Arirang' mit *Paebaengi kut* chosa pogosŏ," p. 123; "*Paebaengi kut,*" pp. 581–582.

164. Pak Chunyŏng, pers. comm., September 29, 2009.

165. Shin Chŏnghŭi, "Myŏngin myŏngjang 28."

166. Quoted in Yu Iksŏ, "Kim Chŏngyŏn," p. 181.

167. Cho Myŏngju, "Yu Chisuk," p. 92.

168. Ivy, *Discourses of the Vanishing,* p. 10.

169. Pak Kyŏngsu, *Sorikkundŭl,* p. 202.

Conclusion

1. Cohen, "The Commercialization of Ethnic Crafts," p. 164.

2. See Howard, "Introduction: East Asian Music as Intangible Cultural Heritage," pp. 6–7.

3. Hesketh, "A. A. Phillips and the 'Cultural Cringe'," p. 102.

4. Maliangkay, "Staging Korean Traditional Performing Arts Abroad," p. 52.

5. Michael Robinson notes that *Sŏdo sori* was among the folksong genres favored by the radio station dedicated to Korean listeners in the late 1920s and early 1930s ("Broadcasting, Cultural Hegemony," p. 65).

6. Sŏ Chiyŏng, "Sangshil-gwa pujae-ŭi shigonggan" (The temporal space of loss and absence), p. 173.

7. Howard, "Namdo Tŭl Norae," pp. 204, 215n4; Maliangkay, "Staging Korean Traditional Performing Arts Abroad," pp. 55–58.

8. Yi Ŭn'gwan, *Kach'ang ch'ongbo,* p. 395; Hwang Yongju, *Han'guk kyŏng/sŏdo ch'angak taegye,* 1: p. 485.

9. Ch'oe Chongmin, "Kwangbok 50-nyŏn kugak kyoyug-ŭi hyŏnhwang-gwa munjejŏm" (The present state and problems of the education of Korean traditional music 50 years after liberation), p. 53.

10. See Kungnip kugagwŏn, *Kugak kyoyug-ŭi iron-gwa shilgi* (Theory and training of Korean traditional music education). Ch'oe Chongmin, one of the book's contributors, notes that the transcriptions of a song's music and lyrics constitutes only one version of many; the transcriptions are to be used merely as the basis from which to improvise (p. 3).

11. See also Im Tonggwŏn, *Han'gug-ŭi minyo* (Korea's folksongs), p. 14.

12. Sŏng Kiryŏn, "2007-nyŏn kaejŏng kyoyuk kwajŏng-e ttarŭn minyo kwallyŏn chido naeyong koch'al" (An inquiry into the guidelines for folksong teaching on the basis of the

Revised Curriculum of 2007), pp. 188–189, 192–194, 218. A recent approach to young children's traditional music education proposes simple physical jumping games to familiarize students with the various rhythmic patterns (Kwŏn T'aeryong, Kwŏn Ŭnju and Ko Yŏnghŭi, *Ŏrini kugak kyoyuk* [Korean traditional music education for children], p. 61).

13. Yersu Kim, *Cultural Policy in the Republic of Korea,* p. 52. Sungmun Kim argues that this was mainly due to a lack of finances, as a large number of stations had to rely heavily on advertising (*Die Geschichte, Struktur und Politische Funktion der Koreanische Medien* [The history, structure and political function of the Korean media], p. 57).

14. Interview with Ch'oe Sangil, August 26, 1995.

15. Tu-hyŏn Yi, "Mask Dance-Dramas," pp. 41, 63; Munhwa ch'eyukpu, *Che-36-hoe chŏn'guk minsok yesul kyŏngyŏn taehoe* (36th national folk arts contest), p. 37.

16. Ibid., p. 12.

17. Ko Chŏngok, *Chosŏn minyo yŏn'gu,* pp. 510–511; Im Tonggwŏn, *Han'guk minyo yŏn'gu,* pp. 12–13.

Appendix

1. Sŏng Kyŏngnin and Yi Pohyŏng, "*Paebaengi kut,*" pp. 595–624.

2. In a later version published by Yi himself, the women pray for a son and a daughter (*Kach'ang ch'ongbo,* p. 294).

3. The mountain located on the southern periphery of the old city center of Seoul.

4. Sound of baby crying.

5. Surprisingly, this phrase also appears in the lyrics Yi Ŭn'gwan published in 1999, in which the ministers have in fact prayed for both a boy and a girl (*Kach'ang ch'ongbo,* p. 296).

6. *Kamŭng/Kamang* is the name of a god, whom Laurel Kendall describes as "a spirit of suicides, violent deaths, and deaths far from home" (Kendall, "Caught Between Ancestors and Spirits," p. 17).

7. The association here is phallic.

8. Zhuge Liang (181–234), a Confucian advisor to the king during the Chinese Three Kingdoms period, is famous for his loyalty and wisdom. His pseudonym was Kongmyŏng (Fairness) and his title Wolong (Sleeping Dragon) (West, "Drama," p. 23).

9. Despite their relative complexity, almost exclusively Sino-Korean passages such as these sometimes appear in the repertoire of professional folksong singers. It is, however, unlikely that a lay audience these days would automatically understand all the words and connotations.

10. For more on Dongfang Shuo, see Vos, "Tung-fang Shuo, Buffoon and Immortal, in Japan and Korea."

11. Jiang Taigong (Kor. Kang T'aegong) was a Chinese statesman/sage who lived around the twelfth century BCE (Yi Ch'angbae, *Han'guk kach'ang taegye,* 1: p. 716). According to legend, Kang was eighty years old when he began serving King Wen (Kor. Mun), after which he lived for another eighty years. This particular phrase is commonly used in combination with his name in, for example, *muga* (shaman songs), mask plays, puppet plays, and folksongs (Walraven, "Muga," p. 122).

12. Wrists are a metaphor for breasts here.

GLOSSARY

Aegukka 愛國歌
Aksa 樂士
An Ch'angho 安昌浩
Aniri 아니리
An Pich'wi 安翡翠
An Pokshik (=An Pich'wi) 安福植
Ansan 安山
Apsan t'aryŏng 앞 山打令
Apsori 앞소리
Ari 아리
Arirang 아리랑
Ayam 아얌
Bunkazai hogohō (=Munhwajae pohopŏp)
Chaedam 才談
Chajin/-ŭn 자진/잦은
Chajinmori 자진모리
Chamunbak Troupe 자문밖 牌
Ch'ang 唱
Changagwŏn 掌樂院
Ch'angbu t'aryŏng 倡夫打令
Changdaejang t'aryŏng 張大將打令
Changdan 長短
Ch'angga 唱歌
Changgu/-go 장구/-고
Ch'anggŭk 唱劇
Chang Haksŏn 張鶴仙
Chang Hyŏn'gil (=Chang Haksŏn) 張賢吉
Chang Kŭmhwa 張錦花
Chang Sahun 張師勛
Chang t'aryŏng 場打令
Chang Yangsŏn 張良善
Chapchapka 雜雜歌
Chapka 雜歌
Chebiga (=Yŏnjaga)
Chech'ang 齊唱
Chejŏn 祭奠
Cheju minyo 濟州民謠
Cheshil chaesan chŏngniguk 帝室財產整理局
Chijŏng munhwajae-ioe-ŭi munhwajae 指定文化財以外의 文化財
Chipchangga 執杖歌
Chipch'e ch'angjak 集體創作
Chipch'e yesul 集體藝術
Chirŭm shijo 지름 時調
Cho 調
Cho Cho 曺操
Ch'oe Chŏngshik 崔貞植
Ch'oe Kyŏngshik 崔景植
Ch'oe Sŏngnyong 崔成龍
Ch'oe Sun'gyŏng 崔順慶
Chogyo 助敎
Ch'ohan'ga 楚漢歌
Ch'ohye 草鞋
Cho Kijun 曺基俊
Chŏkpyŏkka 赤壁歌
Chŏkpyŏkpu 赤壁賦
Ch'ŏllima undong 千里馬運動
Ch'omogi 草木이
Cho Moran 趙牧丹
Ch'ŏngch'un'ga 青春歌

Chongdae 鐘大
Ch'ŏnggu kojŏn sŏngak hagwŏn 青丘古典聲樂學院
Chŏng Hakki 鄭學基
Chongmyo cheryeak 宗廟祭禮樂
Chongno kwŏnbŏn 鐘路劵番
Ch'ŏngnyong 青龍
Ch'ŏngsonyŏn kyohwa yŏnhaphoe 青少年教化聯合會
Chŏng sori 情소리
Ch'ŏng Troupe 青牌
Chŏng Tŭngman 鄭得晚
Chŏn'guk kugak kyŏngyŏn taehoe 全國國樂競演大會
Chŏn'guk minsok yesul kyŏngyŏn taehoe 全國民俗藝術競演大會
Ch'ŏngnyong Temple 青龍寺
Chŏnmun wiwŏn 傳門委員
Chŏnsu changhaksaeng 傳受獎學生
Chŏnsu kyoyuk chogyo 傳受教育助教
Chŏnsusaeng 傳受生
Ch'ŏnyŏn kinyŏmmul 天然記念物
Chŏnyŏnsa 典涓司
Ch'oriptong 초립동
Chosan 朝山
Chōsen hōmotsu koseki meishō tennenki-nenbutsu hozonkai 朝鮮寶物古蹟名勝天然記念物保存會
Chōsen hōmotsu koseki meishō tennenki-nenbutsu hozonrei 朝鮮寶物古蹟名勝天然記念物保存令
Chōsen koseki chōsa hōkoku 朝鮮古蹟調查報告
Chōsen koseki kenkyūkai 朝鮮古蹟研究會
Chōsen sōtokufu 朝鮮總督府
Chōsen sōtokufu hakubutsukan 朝鮮總督府博物館
Chosŏn kamu yŏn'guhoe 朝鮮歌舞研究會
Chosŏn kamudan 朝鮮歌舞團
Chosŏn kwŏnbŏn 朝鮮劵番
Chosŏn wangjo shillok 朝鮮王朝實錄
Ch'ŏyongmu 處容舞
Ch'uimsae 추임새
Chujak 朱雀
Ch'u Kyoshin 秋教信
Chul t'agi 줄타기
Ch'ung 忠
Chunggŏri 중거리
Chungjungmori 중중모리
Chungmori 중모리
Chungyo minsok charyo 重要民俗資料
Chungyo muhyŏng munhwajae 重要無形文化財
Ch'unhyangga 春香歌
Ch'up'unggam pyŏlgok 秋風感別曲
Ch'urin'ga 出引歌
Chusan 主山
Chu Subong 朱壽奉
Chwach'ang 坐唱
Dentōteki kenzōbutsugun 傳統的建造物群
Dozoku (=t'osok)
Du Fu 杜甫
Enka 演歌
Fūzoku 風俗
Haegŭm 奚琴
Haktoga 學徒歌
Ha Kyuil 河圭一
Han 恨
Hanbok 韓服
Han'gang Troupe 漢江牌
Han'guk chŏngshin munhwa yŏn'guwŏn 韓國精神文化研究院
Han'guk kach'ang taegye 韓國歌唱大系
Han'guk kubi munhak taegye 韓國口碑文學大系
Han'guk kugak hyŏphoe 韓國國樂協會
Han'guk kyŏng/sŏdo ch'angak taegye 韓國京西道唱樂大系
Han'guk minyo taejŏn 한국민요대전
Han'guk minyo yŏn'guhoe 韓國民謠研究會
Han Kyŏngshim 韓瓊心
Han Int'aek 韓仁澤
Hannam yegi kwŏnbŏn 漢南藝妓劵番
Han obaengnyŏn 恨五百年
Hansŏng kwŏnbŏn 漢城劵番
Hapch'ang 合唱
Ha Sunil 河順一
Hojo Tari Troupe 戶曹다리 牌
Homi kŏri 호미거리
Hong Nanp'a 洪蘭坡
Hŏ Tŏksŏn 許德善
Hŭimangga 希望歌
Hŭngboga 興甫歌
Hŭng t'aryŏng 흥 打令
Hwach'o sagŏri 花草사거리
Hwang Kiun 黃琪運

Hwang Yongju 黃龍周
Hwarot 활옷
Hwimori 휘몰이
Hyangga 鄕歌
Hyo 孝
Hyŏn Ch'ŏl 玄哲
Hyŏngjangga 刑杖歌
Hyŏnhaeng ilsŏn chapka 現行日鮮雜歌
Ilp'ae 一牌
Imjin waeran 壬辰倭亂
Im Tonggwŏn 任東權
In'gan munhwajae 人間文化財
Ip'ae 二牌
Ip'al ch'ŏngch'un'ga 二八青春歌
Ipch'ang 立唱
Isuja 履修者
Isusaeng 履修生
Jiang Taigong 姜太公
Jisatsurei 寺刹令
Jisatsurei shikō kisoku 寺刹令施行規則
Jūyō bijutsuhintō no hozon ni kansuru hōritsu 重要美術品等ノ保存ニ關スル法律
Jūyō mukei minzoku bunkazai 重要無形民俗文化財
Jūyō yūkei minzoku bunkazai 重要有形民俗文化財
Kabo kyŏngjang 甲午更張
Kaeguri t'aryŏng 개구리 打令
Kagok 歌曲
Kamŭng/Kamang 가믕/가망
Kanggangsullae 강강술래
Kangnŭng tanoje 江陵端午祭
Kasa 歌辭
Kashiryŏmnikka 가시렵니까
Kat 갓
Kayo 歌謠
Kayo chipsŏng 歌謠集成
Kibu 妓夫
Kidungsŏbang 기둥서방
Kiji-shi chul tarigi 機池市줄다리기
Kim Ch'ilsŏng 金七星
Kim Chongjo 金宗朝
Kim Chŏngyŏn 金正淵
Kim Ch'ŏnhŭng 金千興
Kim Chuho 金周鎬
Kim Chuksa 金竹史 (=Kim Suyŏng)
Kim Ch'unhong 金春紅
Kim Hyŏn'gyu 金鉉圭
Kim Inshik 金仁湜
Kim Kwanjun 金寬俊
Kim Kyech'un 金桂春
Kimmaegi sori 김매기소리
Kim Milhwaju 金蜜花珠
Kim Okshim 金玉心
Kim Pyŏnggyu 金炳奎
Kim Sŏngmin 金成敏
Kim Sunt'ae 金順泰
Kim Suyŏng 金守英
Kim T'aebong 金泰鳳
Kim Tuch'il 金斗七
Kim Ŭngnyŏl 金應烈
Kim Yonghun 金龍勳
Kin 긴
Kinyŏmmul 記念物
Kip'ŭn sarang 깊은 사랑
Kisaeng 妓生
Kkoktugakshi norŭm 꼭두각시놀음
Kkwaenggwari 꽹과리
Kobutsushō torishimarihō 古物商取締法
Koki kyūbutsu hozonhō 古器舊物保存方
Kokuhō 国宝
Kokuhō hozonhō 国宝保存法
Kŏllipp'ae 乞粒牌
Kombo t'aryŏng 곰보 打令
Komul 古物
Kŏmun'go sanjo 거문고 散調
Kongboch'ŏ 公報處
Kongch'ŏga 恐妻家
Kongch'ŏng 公廳
Kongmyŏngga 孔明歌
Kongnosang 功勞賞
Kŏsa 居士
Koseki oyobi ibutsu hozon kisoku 古蹟及遺物保存規則
Koshaji chōsa iinkai 古社寺調查委員會
Koshaji hozonhō 古社寺保存法
Kosŏng nongyo 固城農謠
Kugag-ŭi hyanggi 國樂의 香氣
Kugak ch'anyang kasu hyŏphoe 國樂讚揚歌手協會
Kugak yŏnyesa 國樂演藝社
Kuhwangshil chaesanpŏp 舊皇室財產法
Kuhwangshil chaesan samuch'ongguk 舊皇室財產事務總局
Kukpo 國寶

Kukpo kojŏk myŏngsŭng ch'ŏnyŏn kinyŏmmul imshi pojon wiwŏnhoe 國寶古蹟名勝天然記念物臨時保存委員會
Kŭkpon paebaengi kut 劇本배뱅이굿
Kukp'ung 國風
Kŭmch'ŏn taejwa 金千代座
Kŭmgangsan t'aryŏng 金剛山打令
Kungnaebu kamubyŏlgam 宮內府歌舞別監
Kungnip kugagwŏn 國立國樂院
Kut 굿
Kutkŏri 굿거리
Kuwanggung 舊王宮
Kuwanggung chaesan ch'ŏbunpŏp 舊王宮財處分法
Kwach'ŏn Panga Tari Troupe 果川방아다라牌
Kwana 官衙
Kwandong p'algyŏng 關東八景
Kwangdae 광대
Kwanggyo kwŏnbŏn 廣橋券番
Kwansanyungma 關山戎馬
Kwan U 關羽
Kwanuhŭi 觀優戲
Kwŏnbŏn 券番
Kyobangch'ŏng 敎坊廳
Kyodokwa 敎導科
Kyōkō zaisan kanri kitei 鄕校財產管理規定
Kyŏngballim 경발림
Kyŏngbokkung t'aryŏng 景福宮打令
Kyŏnggi minyo 京畿民謠
Kyŏngguk taejŏn 經國大典
Kyŏnghwa kwŏnbŏn 京華券番
Kyŏngjo 京調
Kyŏngnodang 敬老堂
Kyŏng sagŏri 경사거리
Maengho ch'ullim 猛虎出林
Maettol sori 맷돌소리
Maizō 埋藏
Mandam 漫談
Manggŏn 網巾
Menarijo 메나리 調
Miryang arirang 密陽아리랑
Mingei 民芸
Minjok 民族
Minjung 民衆
Minsok charyo 民俗資料
Minyo 民謠
Minzoku 民俗
Minzoku bunkazai 民俗文化財
Minzoku geinō 民俗芸能
Miryang paekchung nori 密陽百中놀이
Modaeyŏk 謀大逆
Mogap 某甲
Monggŭmp'o t'aryŏng 夢金浦打令
Mudang 巫堂
Mudang kwahak kŭpche 巫堂과학급제
Mudang satto 巫堂삿도
Mudong 舞童
Muga 巫歌
Muhyŏng munhwajae 無形文化財
Muhyŏng munhwajae chosa pogosŏ 無形文化財調查報告書
Muhyŏng munhwajae pojŏn mit chinhŭng-e kwanhan pŏmnyul 무형문화재 보전 및 진흥에 관한 법률
Mukei 無形
Mukei bunkazai (=Muhyŏng munhwajae)
Muk Kyewŏl 墨桂月
Mun Ch'anggyu 文昌圭
Mun Howŏl 文湖月
Munhwajae charyo 文化財資料
Munhwajaech'ŏng 文化財廳
Munhwajae kwalliguk 文化財管理局
Munhwajae kwalli t'ŭkpyŏl hoegyepŏp 文化財管理特別會計法
Munhwajae pohopŏp 文化財保護法
Munhwajae pohopŏp shihaengnyŏng 文化財保護法施行令
Munhwajae pojon wiwŏnhoe kyujŏng 文化財保存委員會規定
Munhwajae wiwŏnhoe 文化財委員會
Munhwajae wiwŏnhoe kyujŏng 文化財委員會規定
Munhwajae yŏn'guso 文化財研究所
Munhwa pojonkwa 文化保存科
Munhwa sanŏp chinhŭng kibonpŏp 文化產業振興基本法
Munhwa yesul chinhŭngpŏp 文化藝術振興法
Munhwa yusan 文化遺產
Mun Segŭn 文세근
Myŏngsŭng 名勝
Nakhwa yusu 落花流水
Nalt'ang Troupe 날탕 牌
Namdo 南道
Namdo tŭl norae 南道들노래

Namsadang 男寺黨/-社堂/-寺堂
Nanbongga 難逢歌
Nin'gen kokuhō 人間国宝
Nodŭl kangbyŏn 노들 江邊
Nollyang/-lyŏng 놀량/-령
Nongak 農樂
Nongch'on chinhŭng undong 農村振興運動
Norae 노래
Nori 놀이
Nunmul chŏjŭn Tuman'gang
 눈물젖은 豆滿江
O Pongnyŏ 吳福女
O T'aesŏk 吳太石
Obongsan t'aryŏng 五峯山打令
Odolttogi 오돌또기
Ŏkkae ch'um 어깨춤
Ŏnmori 엇모리
Ŏrang t'aryŏng 어랑 打令
Ŏtchungmori 엇중몰이
Ŏu yadam 於于野談
P'ae 牌
Paebaengi kut 배뱅이굿
Paekho 白虎
Paekkot t'aryŏng 배꽃 打令
Paek Shinhaeng 白信行
Paennorae 뱃노래
Paeogae Majŏn Tari Troupe
 배오개마전다리 牌
Pak Chŏnghŭi 朴正熙
Pak Ch'un'gyŏng 朴春景
Pak Ch'unjae 朴春載
Pak Insŏp 朴仁燮
Pak Kŭmhong 朴錦紅
Pak Nokchu 朴綠珠
Pak Puyong 朴芙蓉
Pak Samsoe 朴三釗
Pallim ch'um 발림춤
Palt'al 발탈
P'alto myŏngch'ang taehoe 八道名唱大會
Pangan sori 방안소리
Panga t'aryŏng 방아 打令
Pangmulga 房物歌
P'ansori 판소리
P'an yŏmbul 판 念佛
Para 바라
Park Chung Hee (=Pak Chŏnghŭi)
Pawi t'aryŏng 바위타령
P'iri 피리
Pomul 寶物
Pongsan t'alch'um 鳳山탈춤
Poryŏm 보렴
Poyuja 保有者
Poyuja hubo 保有者候補
Ppongtchak 뽕짝
Ppuri kip'ŭn namu 뿌리깊은 나무
Pudongsan 不動産
Pujŏk 符籍
Puk 북
Pulgyo chaesan kwallipŏp 佛教財産管理法
P'ungdŭngga 豊登歌
P'ungmul 風物
P'ungnyu 風流
P'yŏng shijo 平時調
Pyŏngshin nanbongga 病身難逢歌
P'yŏngyangga 平壤歌
P'yŏngyang kyŏnggaega 平壤景概歌
P'yŏngyang mudang sori 平壤巫堂소리
Riōke hakubutsukan 李王家博物館
Sabalga 沙鉢歌
Sach'ŏlga 四節歌
Sadang 寺黨/社堂/寺堂
Sadanggol 사당골
Saemaŭl chŏngshin 새마을 精神
Saemaŭm undong 새마음 運動
Saengmae chaba 생매잡아
Sae t'aryŏng 새타령
Sagŏri 사거리
Sagyech'uk 四契軸
Sajang 社長 (=sadang)
Sajŏk 史蹟
Samgukchi yŏnŭi 三國志演義
Samhwa kwŏnbŏn 三和券番
Samp'ae 三牌
Sangjwajung 上佐중
Sangsapyŏng 相思病
Sangyŏ sori 喪輿소리
San yŏmbul 山念佛
Sasŏl shijo 辭說時調
Sejon-kut 世尊굿
Semach'i 세마치
Shibak 十惡
Shibi 十二
Shich'ang 詩唱
Shi-do chijŏng munhwajae 市道指定文化財
Shijo 時調
Shimch'ŏngga 沈淸歌

Shinawi 시나위
Shin Kwangsu 申光洙
Shin minyo 新民謠
Shin Nakt'aek 申洛澤
Shin Pangch'o 申芳草
Shin Pulch'ul 申不出
Shin seikatsu undō 新生活運動
Shipchangga 十杖歌
Shiseki meishō tennenkinenbutsu hozonhō 史蹟名勝天然記念物保存法
Soebunggu Troupe 西氷庫牌
So Ch'unhyangga 小春香歌
Sŏdo sori 西道소리
Sŏdo sori hagwŏn 西道소리 學院
Sŏdo sori pojonhoe 西道소리 保存會
Sogo 小鼓
Sogyo 俗謠
Sŏkchŏn kyŏngu 石田耕牛
Sŏnch'ang 先唱
Sŏngbuk-tong Troupe 城北東牌
Sŏng Kyŏngnin 成慶麟
Song Man'gap 宋萬甲
Songsŏ 誦書
Song Sŏkha 宋錫夏
Sŏnsori sant'aryŏng 선소리 山打令
Sŏnsori sant'aryŏng yŏn'gu pojonhoe 선소리 山打令研究保存會
Sŏnyuga 船遊歌
Sori 소리
Sorikkun 소릿군/소리꾼
So Wanjun 蘇完俊
Sshirŭm 씨름
Sŭngmu 僧舞
Sŭri sŭri pom param 스리스리 봄바람
Sushimga 愁心歌
Ta-dong chohap 茶洞組合
Taedong kwŏnbŏn 大同券番
Taegŭm 대금
Taehan kugagwŏn 大韓國樂院
Taehan min'guk ibuk 5-do-e kwanhan t'ŭkpyŏl choch'ipŏp 대한민국 이북5도에 관한 특별조치법
Taehan minsok yesul hagwŏn 大韓民俗藝術學院
Taejŏng kwŏnbŏn 大正券番
T'aekkyŏn 택견
Tae myŏngnyul chikhae 大明律直解
T'aep'yŏngga 太平歌
T'aep'yŏngso 太平簫
Talbi 달비
Talkŏri 달거리
Tan'ga 短歌
Tanggŭm aegi 당금애기
Tapkyo 踏橋
Tari 다리
T'aryŏng 打令
T'aryŏngkkun 타령꾼
Tchanji Troupe 짠지 牌
Todŭri 도드리
Tohwa t'aryŏng 桃花打令
Tokch'ang 獨唱
Tondollari 돈돌라리
Tongi kimil 동이기밀
Tongmak Troupe 東幕牌
Tongsan 動産
T'ongsok 通俗
Tongyun 洞允
Toraji t'aryŏng 도라지 打令
T'ori 토리
T'osok 土俗
Trot 트로트
Ttuksŏm Troupe 뚝섬 牌
Tugyŏnsae unŭn maŭl 두견새 우는 마을
Tungdung t'aryŏng 둥둥 打令
Twissan t'aryŏng 뒷 山打令
Twit sori 뒷소리
Ŭijŏngbu 議政府
Ŭit'aek 義澤
Umjip 움집
Unsan paebaengi kut 雲山배뱅이굿
Wangshimni Troupe 往十里牌
Wang Subok 王壽福
Wimun 慰問
Wŏlsŏn 月仙
Wŏnhyŏng 原形
Wŏn Kyŏngt'ae 元慶兌
Yangban 兩班
Yanggŭm 洋琴
Yangsando 陽山道
Yangsan hakch'um 梁山鶴춤
Yang Soun 楊蘇云
Yech'ŏn t'ongmyŏng nongyo 醴泉通明農謠
Yesurwŏn 藝術院

Yi Ch'angbae 李昌培
Yi Chŏngnyŏl 李貞烈
Yi Ch'unhŭi 李春羲
Yi Ch'unmok 李春木
Yi Hwaja 李花子
Yi Hwajungsŏn 李花仲仙
Yi Insu 李仁洙
Yi Kyewŏl 李桂月
Yi Kyŏngok (=Muk Kyewŏl) 李瓊玉
Yi Mansŏk 李萬石
Yi Myŏnggil 李命吉
Yi Nŭnghwa 李能和
Yi Pandohwa 李半島花
Yi Pohyŏng 李輔亨
Yi Sangsu 李祥洙
Yi Sohyang 李少香
Yi Sŏnggye 李成桂
Yi Sora 李素羅
Yi Sŭngch'ang 李承昌
Yi T'oegye 李退溪
Yi Tongshik 李東植
Yi Tongun 李東運
Yi Toryŏng 李道令
Yi Ŭn'gwan 李殷官
Yi Ŭnju 李銀珠
Yiwangjik 李王職
Yi Yullan (=Yi Ŭnju) 李潤蘭
Yi Yusaek 李柳色
Yŏkkŭm 엮음
Yŏmbul 念佛
Yonanuki ヨナ抜き
Yŏngbyŏn'ga 寧邊歌
Yongsan Samgae Troupe 龍山삼개 牌
Yŏngsŏn 營繕
Yŏnjaga 燕子歌
Yŏsadang 女寺黨
Yuhaeng chapka 流行雜歌
Yuhaengga 流行歌
Yuhaeng soga 流行小歌
Yuhyŏng munhwajae 有形文化財
Yu Inman 柳寅晩
Yu Kaedong 柳開東
Yukchabaegi 六字배기
Yukch'irwŏl hŭrin nal 六七月 흐린 날
Yūkei 有形
Yukkuhamdo 六衢咸道
Yu Mongin 柳夢寅
Yusan'ga 遊山歌
Zhuge Liang 諸葛亮

BIBLIOGRAPHY

Abelmann, Nancy. "Minjung Theory and Practice." In *Cultural Nationalism in East Asia: Representation and Identity,* edited by Harumi Befu, 139–165. Berkeley: Institute of East Asian Studies, University of California, 1993.

Aikawa-Faure, Noriko. "Excellence and Authenticity: 'Living National (Human) Treasures' in Japan and Korea." *International Journal of Intangible Heritage* 9 (2014): 37–51.

Anderson, Benedict. *Imagined Communities: Reflections on the Origin and Spread of Nationalism.* London: Verso, 2006.

Atkins, E. Taylor. *Primitive Selves: Koreana in the Japanese Colonial Gaze, 1910–1945.* Berkeley: University of California Press, 2010.

Barfe, Louis. *Where Have All the Good Times Gone: The Rise and Fall of the Record Industry.* London: Atlantic Books, 2005.

Bhabha, Homi K. *The Location of Culture.* London and New York: Routledge, 1994.

Biddle, Ian, and Kirsten Gibson, eds. *Masculinity and Western Musical Practice.* Farnham, UK: Ashgate, 2009.

Bishop, Isabella Bird. *Korea and Her Neighbours.* New York: Fleming H. Revell Co., 1898.

Bohlman, Philip V. *The Study of Folk Music in the Modern World.* Bloomington: Indiana University Press, 1988.

Bourdieu, Pierre. *The Field of Cultural Production.* New York: Colombia University Press, 1993.

Brandt, Kim. "Objects of Desire: Japanese Collectors and Colonial Korea." *Positions* 8, no. 3 (2000): 711–746.

Brandt, Vincent. "Rural Development and the New Community Movement in South Korea." *Korean Studies Forum* 1 (Autumn-Winter 1976–1977): 32–39.

Byun, Eun-mi. "'Human Cultural Asset System' Struck by Corruption, Scandal, Stagnation." *Newsreview* 5 (March 1994): 30–31.

Cang, Voltaire Garces. "Defining Intangible Cultural Heritage and Its Stakeholders: The Case of Japan." *International Journal of Intangible Heritage* 2 (2007): 45–55.

Caprio, Mark E. *Japanese Assimilation Policies in Colonial Korea, 1910–1945.* Seattle: University of Washington Press, 2009.

Chang, Chansŭp, and Nanju Chang. *The Korean Management System: Cultural, Political, Economic Foundations.* Westport, CT: Quorum Books, 1994.

Chang Ch'ŏnho. "*Paebaengi.*" Unpublished film script, commissioned by Haptong yŏnghwa chushik hoesa (United Cinema Co. Ltd.). Korean Film Archives, Seoul, 1973.

Chang Sahun. *Chŏngbo han'guk ŭmak sa* (A new history of Korean music). Seoul: Segwang ŭmak ch'ulp'ansa, 1993.

———. *Han'guk chŏnt'ong ŭmag-ŭi ihae* (An understanding of Korean traditional music). Seoul: Seoul University Press, 1994.

———. *Kugak kaeyo* (An outline of Korean traditional music). Seoul: Chŏngyŏnsa, 1961.

———. *Kugak taesajŏn* (Great dictionary of Korean traditional music). Seoul: Segwang ŭmak ch'ulp'ansa, 1984.

———. "Kyŏnggido ipch'ang-gwa sŏdo ipch'ang" (Standing songs from Kyŏnggi province and the western provinces). *Muhyŏng munhwajae chosa pogosŏ: Sŏnsori sant'aryŏng* (Research report regarding the appointment of intangible cultural properties: Standing mountain songs) 30 (1966): 2–58.

———. "Sŏdo sŏnsori" (Standing songs from the western provinces). *Muhyŏng munhwajae chosa pogosŏ* 51 (1968): 83–123.

———. "Sŏdo-ŭi Kwansanyungma-wa Sushimga mit Ch'up'ung kambyŏlgok" (*Kwansanyungma, Sushimga* and *Ch'up'ung kambyŏlgok* from the western provinces). *Muhyŏng munhwajae chosa pogosŏ* 52 (1968): 127–194.

———. *Yŏmyŏng-ŭi tongsŏ ŭmak* (Eastern and western music in the new age). Seoul: Pojinjae, 1974.

Chang Tŏksun, Cho Tongil, Sŏ Taesŏk, and Cho Hŭiung. *Kubi munhak kaesŏl* (Introduction to oral literature). Seoul: Ilchogak, 1971.

Chang Tongun. *Min'gan sŏsashi Paebaengi kut* (The folk epic *Ritual for Paebaengi*). Shenyang: Liaoning renmin chubanshe, 1982.

Chang Yŏngch'ŏl. *Chosŏn ŭmak myŏngin chŏn* (Dictionary of famous Korean musicians). Vol. 1. P'yŏngyang: P'yŏngyang insoe kongjang, 1998.

Chang Yujŏng. *Oppa-nŭn p'unggakchaengi-ya: taejung kayo-ro pon kŭndae-ŭi p'unggyŏng* (My brother is a busker: Looking at modernity through popular songs). Seoul: Minŭm, 2006.

Chatterjee, Partha. *The Nation and Its Fragments: Colonial and Postcolonial Histories.* Princeton, NJ: Princeton University Press, 1993.

Chi, Jung-nam. "Ahn Sook-sun." *Koreana* 7, no. 4 (1993): 44–47.

Chin, Jung-kwon. "The Dead Dictator's Society." In *Developmental Dictatorship and the Park Chung-hee Era: The Shaping of Modernity in the Republic of Korea,* edited by Lee Byeong-cheon, 294–311. Paramus, NJ: Homa & Sekey Books, 2003.

Ch'oe Ch'ŏl. *Han'guk minyohak* (Korean folksong studies). Seoul: Yonsei University Press, 1992.

Ch'oe Chongmin. "Kwangbok 50-nyŏn kugak kyoyug-ŭi hyŏnhwang-gwa munjejŏm" (The present state and problems of the education of Korean traditional music fifty years after liberation). Paper presented at a National Gugak Center forum celebrating fifty years of independence, Seoul, September 27–28, 1995, pp. 43–62 in the unedited pre-forum collection of papers.

Ch'oe Hongsun. "Sŏdo-ŭi kŭkch'ang *Paebaengi kut*" (*Ritual for Paebaengi*, the operetta from the western provinces). *Pukhan-ŭi minsok kihaeng* (Travelogs of North Korean folk) 3 (1985): 167–175.

Ch'oe Hyŏnch'ŏl and Han Chinman. *Han'guk radio p'ŭrogŭraem-e taehan yŏksajŏk yŏn'gu: P'yŏnsŏng hŭrŭm-ŭl chungshim-ŭro* (A historical study of radio programming in Korea: Focusing on trends in the organization). Seoul: P'aju: Hanul ak'ademi, 2004.

Ch'oe Kilsŏng. "Sejon kut-kwa 'toduk chabi'-ŭi kujo punsŏk" (A structural analysis of *Sejon kut* and "catching the thief"). *Han'guk minsokhak* (Korean folklore studies) 12 (1980): 193–205.

Ch'oe Sangsu. "Folk Plays." In *Survey of Korean Arts: Folk Arts*, edited by the National Academy of Arts, 240–269. Seoul: National Academy of Arts, 1974.

———. "*Paebaengi kut* taesa" (The words of *Ritual for Paebaengi*). Part 1. *Minsok hakpo* (Folk studies gazette) 1 (1956): 179–188; and 2 (1957): 200–226; Part 2. *Minsok hakpo* 2 (1957): 227–255.

Ch'oe Tŏkkyŏng. "Munhwajae-ŭi poho-wa taech'aeg-e taehan koch'al" (A study of the protection and control of cultural properties). *Munhwajae* 26 (1993): 302–315.

Choi, Chungmoo. "Hegemony and Shamanism: The State, the Elite, and Shamans in Contemporary Korea." In *Religion and Society in Contemporary Korea*, edited by Lewis R. Lancaster and Richard K. Payne, 19–48. Berkeley, CA: Institute of East Asian Studies, 1997.

———. "The Minjung Culture Movement and Popular Culture." In *South Korea's Minjung Movement*, edited by Kenneth Wells, 105–18. Honolulu: University of Hawai'i Press, 1995.

Choi, Mong-Lyong. *A Study of the Yŏngsan River Valley Culture: The Rise of Chiefdom Society and State in Ancient Korea*. Seoul: Tongsŏngsa, 1984.

Cho Myŏngju. "Yu Chisuk." *Wŏl'gan ŭmak* (Music monthly) 286 (1995): 90–93.

Chŏng Chaeho, ed. *Han'guk chapka chŏnjip* (Complete collection of Korean chapka). Seoul: Kyemyŏng munhwasa, 1984.

Chŏng Chaejong. "Munhwajae wiwŏnhoe yaksa" (A short history of the Cultural Properties Committee). *Munhwajae* 18 (1985): 1–18.

Chŏng Namgi. "Muhyŏng munhwajae chijŏng chedo kaesŏn moksori" (Calls for a reform of the system of appointing intangible cultural properties). *Han'gyŏre* (July 16, 1996): 16.

Chŏng Shihaeng. "Sarachyŏ kanŭn uri sori sallyŏ naenŭn poram" (The value of reviving the Korean folksongs that survive today). *Chosŏn ilbo* (Korea daily) (July 9, 2004): A30.

Chŏng Tonghwa. *Han'guk minyo-ŭi sajŏk yŏn'gu* (Historical research on Korean folksongs). Seoul: Ilchogak, 1981.

Ch'ŏn Yŏngju. "Ilche kangjŏmgi-ŭi ŭmak kyokwasŏ yŏn'gu" (A study of the music schoolbooks from the period of Japanese colonial rule). Ŭmak-kwa minjok (Music and people) 13 (1997): 212–229.

———. *Chōsen koseki chōsa hōkoku* (Reports on investigations of ancient sites in Korea). Seoul: Chōsen sōtokufu, 1916.

———. *Chōsen sōtokufu kanpō* (Government-General of Korea gazette) #2290 (August 27, 1934): 201–212.

———. *Chōsen sōtokufu shisei nenpō—Meiji 41 nenpō* (Yearbook of the Government-General of Korea—1908). Tokyo: Kuresu shuppan, 1992 (1909).

———. *Chōsen sōtokufu shisei nenpō—Shōwa 15 nenpō* (1940). Tokyo: Kuresu shuppan, 1992 (1941).

———. *Chōsen sōtokufu tōkei nenpō* (Statistical yearbook of the Government-General of Korea). Vols. 1912, 1916, 1920, 1926, 1927, 1928, 1930, 1932, 1933, 1934, 1936, 1939. Seoul: Chōsen sōtokufu, 1914–1941.

Chosŏn yŏn'guhoe (Research Society of Colonial Korea). *Chosŏn miin pogam* (Handbook of Korean beauties). Seoul: Minsokwŏn, 1984 (1918).

Cho Tongil. *P'ansori-ŭi ihae* (An understanding of *p'ansori*). Seoul: Ch'angjak-kwa pip'yŏngsa, 1978.

Cho Yumi. "Yusŏnggi ŭmban-e tamgin sant'aryŏng" (Mountain ballads preserved on chronograph records). *Han'guk ŭmbanhak* (Studies of Korean records) 6 (1996): 101–114.

Chōsen sōtokufu (Government-General of Korea). *Chōsen hōrei shūran* (Compilation of Korean laws). Vol. 1. Seoul: Chōsen sōtokufu, 1932.

Chung, Hongik. "Cultural Policy and Development in Korea." *Korean Journal of Policy Studies* 7 (1992): 1–7.

Clark, Donald N. *Christianity in Modern Korea.* Lanham, MD: University Press of America, 1986.

Cohen, Erik. "The Commercialization of Ethnic Crafts." *Design History* 2, no. 2/3 (1989): 161–168.

Crane, Paul S. *Korean Patterns.* Seoul: Royal Asiatic Society, 1967.

Day, Timothy. *A Century of Recorded Music: Listening to Musical History.* New Haven, CT: Yale University Press, 2000.

De Ceuster, Koen. "The Changing Nature of National Icons in the Seoul Landscape." *Review of Korean Studies* 3, no. 2 (2000): 73–103.

Delissen, Alain. "The Aesthetic Pasts of *Space* (1960–1990)." *Korean Studies* 25, no. 2 (2001): 243–260.

Deuchler, Martina. *The Confucian Transformation of Korea: A Study of Society and Ideology.* Cambridge, MA: Harvard University Press, 1992.

Dudden, Alexis. *Japan's Colonization of Korea: Discourse and Power.* Honolulu: University of Hawai'i Press, 2005.

Elschek, Oskar. "Traditional Music and Cultural Politics." In *Music in the Dialogue of Cultures, Traditional Music and Cultural Policy,* edited by Max P. Baumann, 32–55. Wilhelmshaven, Germany: Florian Noetzel Verlag, 1991.

Eyerman, Ron, and Andrew Jamison. *Music and Social Movements: Mobilizing Traditions in the Twentieth Century.* Cambridge: Cambridge University Press, 1998.

Fujie, Linda. "A Comparison of Cultural Policies Towards Traditional Music in the United States and Japan." In *Music in the Dialogue of Cultures, Traditional Music and Cultural Policy,* edited by Max P. Baumann, 68–76. Wilhelmshaven, Germany: Florian Noetzel Verlag, 1991.

Fujitani, Takashi. "Inventing, Forgetting, Remembering: Toward a Historical Ethnography of the Nation-State." In *Cultural Nationalism in East Asia: Re-presentation and Identity,* edited by Harumi Befu, 77–106. Berkeley: Institute of East Asian Studies, University of California, 1993.

Gellner, Ernest. *Nations and Nationalism.* Oxford: Blackwell, 1983.

Gillman, Derek. *The Idea of Cultural Heritage.* Cambridge, UK: Cambridge University Press, 2010.

Government-General of Chosen. *Annual Report on Reforms and Progress in Chosen (1912–1913).* Seoul: Chōsen sōtokufu, 1914.

———. *Annual Report on Reforms and Progress in Chosen (1921–1922).* Seoul: Chōsen sōtokufu, 1923.

Grayson, James Huntley. *Korea: A Religious History.* Oxford: Clarendon Press, 1989.

Green, Lucy. *Music, Gender, Education.* Cambridge, UK: Cambridge University Press, 1997.

Hahn, Man-young (Han Manyŏng). "Change and Innovation in Traditional Music and Dance in Folklore Festivals." *Seoul Journal of Korean Studies* 2 (1989): 92–105.

———. "Chapka." In *Survey of Korean Arts: Traditional Music,* edited by the National Academy of Arts, 229–241. Seoul: National Academy of Arts, 1974.

———. "Folksong." In *Survey of Korean Arts: Folk Arts,* edited by the National Academy of Arts, 306–315. Seoul: National Academy of Arts, 1974.

———. "Folksongs." In *Traditional Performing Arts of Korea,* edited by the Korean National Commission for UNESCO, 15–26. Seoul: UNESCO, 1983.

———. *Kugak: Studies in Korean Traditional Music.* Seoul: Tamgudang, 1990.

———. "Religious Origins of Korean Music." In *Traditional Korean Music,* edited by the Korean National Commission for UNESCO, 23–34. Seoul: Si-sa-yong-o-sa Publishers, Inc., 1983.

Hammersley, Martin. *Reading Ethnographic Research: A Critical Guide.* London: Longman, 1998.

Handler, Richard. "Creation Myths and Zoning Boards: Local Uses of Historic Preservation." In *The Politics of Culture,* edited by Brett Williams, 63–74. Washington, DC: Smithsonian Institution Press, 1993.

Han'guk chŏngshin munhwa yŏn'guwŏn (Academy of Korean Studies). *Han'guk kubi munhak taegye* (A compendium of Korean oral literature). Vols. 1–10. Seoul: Ŏmun yŏn'gushil, 1979–1990.

———. *Han'guk yusŏnggi ŭmban ch'ongmongnok* (Complete list of Korean gramophone records from the colonial period). Seoul: Minsokwŏn, 1998.

———. *Kyŏngsŏng pangsongguk kugak pangsong kok mongnok* (Kyŏngsŏng Broadcast Corporation's playlist of Korean traditional music). Seoul: Minsokwŏn, 2000.

Han'guk minsok taesajŏn p'yŏnch'an wiwŏnhoe (Compilation Committee of the Great Dictionary of Korean Folklore). *Han'guk minsok taesajŏn* (Great Dictionary of Korean Folklore). 2 vols. Seoul: Minjok munhwasa, 1991.

Han'guk munhwa yesul chinhŭngwŏn (Korean Culture and Arts Foundation). *Munye chinhŭngwŏn 20-nyŏnsa* (Twenty years of the Korean Culture and Arts Foundation). Seoul: Paeksang Printing Co., 1993.

———. *Munye yŏn'gam 1974* (1974 yearbook of culture and arts). Seoul: Kwangdŏk sangsa, 1975.

———. *Munye yŏn'gam 1978* (1978 yearbook of culture and arts). Seoul: Kwangdŏk sangsa, 1979.

Han'guk pŏpche yŏn'guwŏn (Korean Legislative Research Institute). *Pukhan pŏpche punsŏk* (Analyses of North Korean legislation) 95, no. 1, 1995. Seoul: Han'guk pŏpche yŏn'guwŏn.

Han'guk yŏn'gam p'yŏnch'an wiwŏnhoe (Compilation Committee of the Yearbook of Korea). *Han'guk yŏn'gam 1960* (1960 yearbook of Korea). Seoul: Han'guk yŏn'gam p'yŏnch'an wiwŏnhoe, 1961.

Han Kisŏp. *Chŏnt'ong sŏdo sori chŏnjip* (Complete collection of traditional songs from the western provinces). 2 vols. Seoul: Eunha Publishing Co., 1997.

Han Manyŏng. "Sŏnsori sant'aryŏng" (Standing Mountain Songs). In *Han'guk minjok munhwa taebaekkwa sajŏn*, vol. 12, edited by the Han'guk chŏngshin munhwa yŏn'guwŏn (Academy of Korean Studies), 260–261. Seoul: Samhwa Printing Co., 1992.

Han Munp'yŏng. "Yi Hwaja." In *Han'guk minjok munhwa taebaekkwa sajŏn*, vol. 18, edited by the Academy of Korean Studies, 374. Seoul: Samhwa Printing Co., 1992.

Han, Myŏnghŭi. "Performance of Bridge-Treading Festival." *Korea Journal* 9, no. 4 (1969): 36–38.

Han, Woo-keun. *The History of Korea*. Seoul: Eul-Yoo Publishing Co., 1970.

Harker, Dave. *Fakesong: The Manufacture of British 'Folksong' 1700 to the Present Day*. Milton Keynes: Open University Press, 1985.

Henry, Todd A. "Respatializing Chosŏn's Royal Capital: The Politics of Japanese Urban Reforms in Early Colonial Seoul, 1905–1919." In *Sitings: Critical Approaches to Korean Geography*, edited by Timothy R. Tangherlini and Sallie Yea, 15–38. Honolulu: University of Hawai'i Press, 2008.

Hesketh, Rollo. "A. A. Phillips and the 'Cultural Cringe': Creating an 'Australian Tradition'." *Meanjin* 72, no. 3 (2013): 92–103.

Hesselink, Nathan. *P'ungmul: South Korean Drumming and Dance*. Chicago: University of Chicago Press, 2006.

———. *SamulNori: Contemporary Korean Drumming and the Rebirth of Itinerant Performance Culture*. Chicago: University of Chicago Press, 2012.

Hobsbawm, Eric. "Introduction: Inventing Traditions." In *The Invention of Tradition*, edited by E. Hobsbawm and T. Ranger, 1–14. Cambridge, UK: Cambridge University Press, 1983.

———. "Mass-Producing Traditions: Europe, 1870–1914." In *The Invention of Tradition*, edited by E. Hobsbawm and T. Ranger, 263–307. Cambridge, UK: Cambridge University Press, 1983.

Hong Hyŏnshik and Pak Hŏnbong. *Chwach'ang Kyŏnggi kin chapka* (Long chapka from Kyŏnggi province sung seated). *Muhyŏng munhwajae chosa pogosŏ* 57 (1969): 355–409.

Howard, Keith. "Authenticity and Authority: Conflicting Agendas in the Preservation of Music and Dance at Korea's State Sacrificial Rituals." In *Music as Intangible Cultural Heritage: Policy, Ideology, and Practice in the Preservation of East Asian Traditions*, edited by Keith Howard, 113–139. Aldershot, UK: Ashgate, 2012.

———. *Bands, Songs, and Shamanistic Rituals: Folk Music in Korean Society*. Seoul: Royal Asiatic Society, 1989.

———. *Creating Korean Music: Tradition, Innovation and the Discourse of Identity*. Aldershot, UK: Ashgate, 2006.

———. "Gender Issues in the Conservation of Korean Music: Presumptive Observations." In *Lux Oriente: Begegnungen der Kulturen in der Musikforschung* (A light on the Orient: Encounters of cultures in musicology), edited by Klaus Wolfgang

Niemöller, Uwe Pätzold, and Chung Kyo-chul, 181–195. Cologne, Germany: Gustav Bosse Verlag, 1996.

———. "*Juche* and Culture: What's New?" In *North Korea in the New World Order*, edited by Hazel Smith, Chris Rhodes, Diana Pritchard, and Kevin Magill, 169–195. London: Macmillan, 1996.

———. "Korean Folk Songs for a Contemporary World." In *Contemporary Directions: Korean Folk Music Engaging the Twentieth Century and Beyond*, edited by Nathan Hesselink, 149–172. Berkeley: Institute of East Asian Studies, University of California, 2001.

———. "Minyo in Korea: Songs of the People and Songs for the People." *Asian Music* 30, no. 2 (1999): 1–37.

———. "Namdo Tŭl Norae: Ritual and the Korean Intangible Cultural Asset System." *Journal of Ritual Studies* 3, no. 2 (1989): 203–216.

———. *Preserving Korean Music: Intangible Cultural Properties as Icons of Identity*. Aldershot, UK: Ashgate, 2006.

Howard, Keith, ed. *Music as Intangible Cultural Heritage: Policy, Ideology, and Practice in the Preservation of East Asian Traditions*. "Introduction," 1–21. Aldershot, UK: Ashgate, 2012.

Hughes, David Weirick. "The Heart's Home Town: Traditional Folksong in Modern Japan." PhD dissertation, University of Michigan, 1985.

———. "Japanese 'New Folk Songs,' Old and New." *Asian Music* 22, no. 1 (1991): 1–49.

———. "'Esashi Oiwake' and the Beginnings of Modern Japanese Folk Song." *World of Music* 34, no. 1 (1992): 35–56.

Hulbert, Homer B. "Korean Vocal Music." In *The Korean Repository*, vol. 3, 45–53. New York: Paragon Book Reprint Corp., 1964 (1896).

Hwang Miyŏn. *Kwŏnbŏn-gwa kisaeng-ŭro pon shingminji kŭndaesŏng: Ilche kangjŏmgi Chŏlla pukto-rŭl chungshim-ŭro* (Colonial modernity from the viewpoint of *kwŏnbŏn* and *kisaeng*: Focusing on the period of Japanese colonial rule in north Chŏlla province). Seoul: Minsokwŏn, 2013.

Hwang Munp'yŏng. "Taejung kayo" (Popular songs). In *Han'guk minjok munhwa taebaekkwa sajŏn*, vol. 6, edited by the Academy of Korean Studies, 482–484. Seoul: Samhwa Printing Co., 1992.

———. "Yusŏnggi-wa kayo-ŭi yŏkchŏng" (A history of gramophones and popular songs). In CD booklet, Shin Nara Records, SYNCD-001524, *Yusŏnggi-ro tŭttŏn kayosa, 1925–1945* (A history of ballads through the gramophone, 1925–1945), 1992: 20–46. Article is followed by biographies of main singers, writers, and composers, 47–108.

Hwang Yongju. *Han'guk kyŏng/sŏdo ch'angak taegye* (A compendium of the vocal music from Korea's Kyŏnggi and western provinces). 2 vols. Seoul: Tosŏ ch'ulp'an orŭn'gil, 1993.

Im, Chaehae. "Tradition in Korean Society: Continuity and Change." *Korea Journal* 31, no. 3 (1991): 13–30.

Im Chunsŏ. "Chŏnt'ong yŏnhŭi 50-nyŏn" (Fifty years of traditional plays). Paper presented at a National Gugak Center forum celebrating fifty years of independence, Seoul, September 27–28, 1995, pp. 329–365 in the unedited pre-forum collection of papers.

Im, Suk-jay, and Yŏlgyu Kim. "Korean Folk Culture, A Dialogue." In *Folk Culture in Korea* (Korean Culture Series 4), edited by Chŏn Shinyong, 131–138. Seoul: Kukche munhwajaedan ch'ulp'anbu, 1974.

Im Tonggwŏn. "Folk Plays." In *Traditional Performing Arts of Korea,* edited by the Korean National Commission for UNESCO, 81–99. Seoul: UNESCO, 1983.

———. "Folksong." In *Survey of Korean Arts: Folk Arts,* edited by the National Academy of Arts, 73–114. Seoul: National Academy of Arts, 1974.

———. *Han'guk minyo chip* (Collections of Korean folksongs). Vols. 1–7. Seoul: Chimmundang, 1961–1995.

———. *Han'guk minyo sa* (A history of Korean folksongs). Seoul: Chimmundang, 1964.

———. "Kanggangsullae." *Muhyŏng munhwajae chosa pogosŏ* 7 (1965): 137–241.

———. *Han'guk minyo yŏn'gu* (A study of Korean folksongs). Seoul: Sŏnmyŏng munhwasa, 1974.

———. *Han'gug-ŭi minyo* (Korea's folksongs). Seoul: Ilchisa, 1989.

———. "Pukhan minyo-ŭi yŏn'gu" (A study of North Korean folksongs). *Han'guk minyohak* (Korean folksong studies) 1 (1991): 38–77.

———. *Yŏsŏng-gwa minyo* (Women and folksongs). Seoul: Chimmundang, 1989.

International Folk Music Council. *Journal of the International Folk Music Council* 7 (1955): 23.

Ivy, Marilyn. *Discourses of the Vanishing: Modernity, Phantasm, Japan.* Chicago: University of Chicago Press, 1995.

Janelli, Roger L. "The Origins of Korean Folklore Scholarship." *Pikyo minsokhak* (Comparative folk studies) 2 (1986): 81–112.

Janelli, Roger L., and Dawnhee Yim Janelli. "The Functional Value of Ignorance at a Korean Seance." *Asian Folklore* 38, no. 1 (1979): 81–90.

Janelli, Roger L., with Dawnhee Yim Janelli. *Making Capitalism: The Social and Cultural Construction of a South Korean Conglomerate.* Stanford, CA: Stanford University Press, 1993.

Jeon Yeo-ok (Chŏn Yŏok). *Ilbon-ŭn ŏpta* (There is no Japan). Seoul: Chishik kongjakso, 1993.

Kawamura Minato. *Malhanŭn kkot: Kisaeng* (Speaking flowers: Courtesans). Translated by Yu Chaesun. Seoul: Sodam, 2002.

Kendall, Laurel. "Caught Between Ancestors and Spirits: Field Report of a Korean Mansin's Healing Kut." *Korea Journal* 17, no. 8 (1977): 8–23.

———. "Introduction: Material Modernity, Consumable Tradition." In *Consuming Korean Tradition in Early and Late Modernity: Commodification, Tourism, and Performance,* edited by Laurel Kendall, 1–17. Honolulu: University of Hawai'i Press, 2011.

Kikuchi, Yuko. *Japanese Modernisation and* Mingei *Theory: Cultural Nationalism and Oriental Orientalism.* London: RoutledgeCurzon, 2004.

Killick, Andrew. *In Search of Korean Traditional Opera: Discourses of Ch'anggŭk.* Honolulu: University of Hawai'i Press, 2010.

Kim, Chin. "Legal Privileges under the Early Yi Dynasty Criminal Codes." *Korea Journal* 15, no. 4 (1975): 34–44; and 15, no. 5 (1975): 19–28.

Kim Chŏmdo. *Uri minyo taebaekkwa* (Great encyclopedia of Korean folksongs). Seoul: Se-Kwang Music Publishing Co., 1990.

Kim Chongch'ŏl. "Chil nop'ŭn uri ch'ansongga pogŭp shigŭphae" (We must urgently popularize our fantastic hymns). *Sae kajŏng* (New family) 405 (August 1990): 37.

Kim, Chong-Ho. "Cultural Politics or Cultural Contradiction? Prejudice against Shamanism in Korean Society." In *Proceedings of the Second Biennial Conference of the Korean Studies Association of Australasia*, edited by Young-A Cho, 38–50. Melbourne: Monash University, 2001.

Kim Chongyŏm. "Oegug-ŭi munhwajae kwalli chedo" (Foreign cultural properties management systems). *Munhwajae* (Cultural properties) 17 (1984): 248–260.

Kim Chuyŏng. "Chorye chejŏng tŭng chŏnsŭng wihan taech'aek maryŏn shigŭp" (Urgent need to prepare measures such as regulations to secure tradition). *Ulsan shinmun* (Ulsan newspaper), September 24, 2012, 10.

Kim Hŭit'ae. "Pŏmnyŏng-gwa chedo" (Statute and system). In *Munhwajaehak: Iron-gwa shilche* (Studying cultural properties: Theory and practice), edited by Kim Hŭit'ae, Cho Ung, and Kim Kyŏngch'il, 28–72. Seoul: Hyangjisa, 1998.

Kim Hŭnggyu. *Han'guk munhag-ŭi ihae* (An understanding of Korean literature). Seoul: Minŭm, 1992.

Kim, Hwansoo Ilmee. *Empire of the Dharma: Korean and Japanese Buddhism, 1877–1912.* Cambridge, MA: Harvard University Press, 2012.

Kim Hyeri and Chang Hwiju. *Sŏnsori sant'aryŏng* (Standing Mountain Songs). Seoul: Minsokwŏn, 2008.

Kim Insuk and Kim Hyeri. *Sŏdo sori* (Folksongs from the Western Provinces). Seoul: Minsokwŏn, 2009.

Kim Kwanghŭi. "Han'guk nongag-ŭi pop'yŏnsŏng-gwa t'ŭksusŏng" (The universality and particularity of Korean folk music). *Wŏlgan munhwajae* (Cultural heritage monthly) 11, no. 362 (2014): 13–15.

Kim, Kwang-ok. "Colonial Body and Indigenous Soul: Religion as a Contested Terrain of Culture." In *Colonial Rule and Social Change in Korea, 1910–1945*, edited by Hong Yung Lee, Yong Chool Ha, and Clark W. Sorensen, 264–313. Seattle: University of Washington Press, 2013.

———. "Socio-Cultural Implications of the Recent Invention of Tradition in Korea: An Overview." *Papers of the British Association for Korean Studies* 1 (1991): 7–28.

Kim, Kyung-hee. "Theory of *Pansori*." In *Korean Musicology Series 2: Pansori*, edited by the National Gugak Center, 31–69. Seoul: Kungnip kugagwŏn, 2008.

Kim Muhŏn. *Han'guk minyo munhak non* (A literary discourse on Korean folksongs). Seoul: Chimmundang, 1991.

———. *Han'guk nodong minyo non (munhak, sahoehakchŏk haesŏk)* (A discourse on Korean working songs: A literary and sociological interpretation). Seoul: Chimmundang, 1986.

Kim Munsŏng. "Mudae taeshin kaeksŏk chik'in Kim Yŏngim-sshi, che-2-ŭi Kim Okshimin'ga?" (Could Kim Yŏngim who was told to take a seat rather than the stage be the second Kim Okshim?). *OhmyNews*, July 14, 2006. www.ohmynews.com.

Kim Myŏnggon. *Han, Kim Myŏnggon-ŭi kwangdae kihaeng* (Han: Kim Myŏnggon's kwangdae tour). Seoul: Tosŏ ch'ulp'ansa, 1994.

———. "Muk Kyewŏl." In *Myŏngin myŏngch'ang* (Famous people, famous singers), edited by Yu Iksŏ et al., 191–198. Seoul: Dong-a Ilbo, 1987.

Kim Okkyŏng. "Muhŏng munhwajae chŏkkŭkchŏk kwanshim-gwa chiwŏn-ŭl" (A positive interest in and support for intangible cultural properties). *Mudŭng ilbo* (Peerless daily), March 24, 2010, 16.

Kim, Sungmun. *Die Geschichte, Struktur und Politische Funktion der Koreanische Medien* (The history, structure and political function of the Korean media). Frankfurt: Peter Lang, 1993.

Kim, Sung Soon. "Priests, Entertainers, or Prostitutes: The Three Roles of the Female Performers (*Sadang*) in Chosŏn Korea." *Seoul Journal of Korean Studies* 27, no. 1 (2014): 37–58.

Kim T'aejun. "Kogŭk *Paebaengi kut*" (The old play *Ritual for Paebaengi*), *Wŏlgan yadam* (Historical tales monthly) 46 (1938): 64–69.

Kim Tonguk. *Han'guk kayo-ŭi yŏn'gu* (A study of Korean popular ballads). Seoul: Ŭlyu munhwasa, 1961.

Kim Ŭnjŏng. "An Pich'wi." *Chŏnt'ong munhwa* (Traditional culture) 5 (1986): 22–25.

Kimura, Mitsuhiko. "Standards of Living in Colonial Korea: Did the Masses Become Worse Off or Better Off under Japanese Rule?" *Journal of Economic History* 53, no. 3 (1993): 629–652.

Kim Yangsam. "K'ol taekshi-ga kaegŭ mudae" (Call taxi serves as comedy stage). *Kyŏnghyang shinmun* (Capital and country news), August 2, 1986, 7.

Kim, Yersu. *Cultural Policy in the Republic of Korea*. Paris: UNESCO, 1976.

Kim Yŏngjo. "Chaeya myŏngch'ang 'Kim Okshim'-ŭl ashinayo?" (Have you ever heard of the late noted singer Kim Okshim?). *OhmyNews*, July 26, 2004. www.ohmynews.com.

Kim Yŏngt'ae. "Munhwa sanŏp chinhŭng kigŭm 500 ŏk chosŏng" (Creation of a fifty billion fund for the promotion of the culture industry). *Maeil kyŏngje* (Economy daily), May 12, 1999, 3.

Kim Yŏngun and Kim Hyeri. *Kyŏnggi minyo* (Folksongs from Kyŏnggi Province). Seoul: Minsokwŏn, 2008.

Kim, Young-soo. "Legitimacy and Korean Traditional Culture and Thought." In *The Identity of the Korean People: A History of Legitimacy on the Korean Peninsula*, edited by the Research Centre for Peace and Unification, 106–170. Seoul: Samhwa Printing Co., 1983.

King, Ross. "Dialect, Orthography, and Regional Identity: P'yŏngan Christians, Korean Spelling Reform, and Orthographic Fundamentalism." In *The Northern Region of Korea: History, Identity, and Culture*, edited by Sun Joo Kim, 139–180. Seattle: University of Washington Press, 2010.

Ko Chŏngok. *Chosŏn minyo yŏn'gu* (A study of Korean folksongs). Seoul: Susŏnsa, 1947.

Koo, Hagen. "The State, *Minjung*, and the Working Class in South Korea." In *State and Society in Contemporary Korea*, edited by Hagen Koo, 131–162. Ithaca, NY: Cornell University Press, 1993.

The Korean Music Research Society. *Korean Folk Songs*. Seoul: National Music Research Society of Korea, 1954.

The Korean Repository. Vols. 3–5. New York: Paragon Book Reprint Corp., 1964 (1896, 1897, 1899).

Ku Hŭisŏ. "Mokp'yo nopko tturyŏthan sorikkun" (A distinguished singer aims high). *Ilgan sŭp'och'ŭ*, January 19, 1991, 23.

———. "Sŭsŭng-ŭi salm-gwa yesur-ŭi chase-rŭl" (The life of teachers and a detailed account of their art). *Ilgan sŭp'och'ŭ* (Sports daily), October 27, 1990, 23.

———. "Sŭsŭng-ŭi salm-i nae chwaumyŏng" (The life of a teacher is my motto). *Ilgan sŭp'och'ŭ,* March 2, 1991, 23.

Kungnip kugagwŏn (National Gugak Center). "Ipch'ang sant'aryŏng" (Mountain songs performed standing). *Kugangnuri* (Folk play) 84 (April 2007): 6–7.

———. *Kugak kyoyug-ŭi iron-gwa shilgi* (Theory and training of Korean traditional music education). Seoul: Kungnip kugagwŏn, 1997.

Kwon, Keedon. "Regionalism in South Korea: Its Origins and Role in Her Democratization." *Politics & Society* 32, no. 4 (2004): 545–574.

Kwŏn Osŏng. "Kugak chŏngch'aek chedo-ŭi pyŏnch'ŏn-gwa mirae-ŭi chŏnmang" (Transition and future outlook of the policy for Korean traditional music). Paper presented at a National Gugak Center forum celebrating fifty years of independence, Seoul, September 27–28, 1995, pp. 161–181 in the unedited pre-forum collection of papers.

———. "Minyo-nŭn minjung-ŭi noraeida" (Folksongs are the songs of the people). *Ppuri kip'ŭn namu p'alto sori* (The deep-rooted tree collection of Korean folksongs). Vol. 1. Seoul: Ppuri kip'ŭn namu, 1984.

———. "Sŏdo minyo" (Folksongs from the western provinces). In *Han'guk minjok munhwa taebaekkwa sajŏn,* vol. 11, edited by the Han'guk chŏngshin munhwa yŏn'guwŏn, 702–703. Seoul: Samhwa Printing Co., 1992.

Kwŏn T'aeryong, Kwŏn Ŭnju, and Ko Yŏnghŭi. *Ŏrini kugak kyoyuk* (Korean traditional music education for children). Seoul: Tongmunsa, 2010.

Kwŏn Tohŭi. *Han'guk kŭndae ŭmak sahoesa* (A social history of Korean music from modern times). Seoul: Minsokwŏn, 2012.

Lee, Hye-Ku. *Essays on Korean Traditional Music.* Translated by Robert C. Provine. Seoul: Royal Asiatic Society, 1981.

Lee, Ki-Baik. "The Creation of a Yangban Society." In *Korea Old and New, A History,* edited by Carter J. Eckert et al., pp. 107–131. Seoul: Ilchogak, 1991.

———. *A New History of Korea.* Translated by Edward W. Wagner and Edward J. Schultz. Seoul: Ilchogak, 1984.

Lee, Namhee. *The Making of Minjung: Democracy and the Politics of Representation in South Korea.* Ithaca, NY: Cornell University Press, 2007.

Lee, Wha-Byong. *Studien zur Pansori-Musik in Korea* (Studies of *p'ansori* in Korea). Frankfurt: Peter Lang, 1991.

Lew, Young Ik. "Growth of the Forces of Enlightenment." In *Korea Old and New: A History,* edited by Carter J. Eckert et al., 199–230. Seoul: Ilchogak, 1991.

Maeil kyŏngje (Economy daily), February 17, 1994, 25.

Ma Heng. "Canguan Chaoxian guwu baogao" (Report on a visit to an archeological site in Korea). *Beijing daxue yanjiusuo guoxue yuekan* (Beijing University's Chinese Studies Institute Monthly) 4 (1925): 1–5.

Maliangkay, Roald. "Choosing the Right Folk: The Appointment of 'Human Cultural Properties' in Korea." In *Folksong: Tradition, Revival, and Re-Creation,* edited by Ian Russell and David Atkinson, 95–107. Aberdeen, UK: Elphinstone Institute, University of Aberdeen, 2004.

———. "Koreans Performing for Foreign Troops: The Occidentalism of the C.M.C. and K.P.K." *East Asian History* 37 (2011): 59–72.

———. "New Symbolism and Retail Therapy: Advertising Novelties in Korea's Colonial Period." *East Asian History* 36 (2008): 29–54.

———. "Pop for Progress: South Korea's Propaganda Songs." In *Korean Pop Music: Riding the Korean Wave,* edited by Keith Howard, 48–61. Folkestone, Kent, UK: Global Oriental, 2006.

———. "The Revival of Folksongs in South Korea: The Case of Tondollari." *Asian Folklore Studies* 61 (April 2002): 223–245.

———. "Staging Korean Traditional Performing Arts Abroad: Important Intangible Intercultural Performance Issues." *Sungkyun Journal of East Asian Studies* 7, no. 2 (2008): 49–68.

———. "Their Masters' Voice: Korean Traditional Music SPs (Standard Play Records) under Japanese Colonial Rule." In "Music and Politics on the Korean Peninsula," special issue, *The World of Music* 49, no. 3 (2007): 53–74.

———. "There Is No Amen in Shaman: Music Preservation and Christianity in South Korea." *Asian Music* 45, no. 1 (2014): 77–97.

Mason, Edward S., Mahn Je Kim, Dwight H. Perkins, Kwang Suk Kim, and David C. Cole. *The Economic and Social Modernization of the Republic of Korea: Studies in the Modernization of the Republic of Korea, 1945–1975.* Cambridge, MA: Council on East Asian Studies, Harvard University Press, 1980.

Messenger, Phyllis Mauch, and George S. Smith. *Cultural Heritage Management: A Global Perspective.* Tampa: University Press of Florida, 2010.

Miksic, John N. "Introduction." In *Rethinking Cultural Resource Management in Southeast Asia: Preservation, Development, and Neglect,* edited by John N. Miksic, Geok Yian Goh, and Sue O'Connor, xiii–xxi. London: Anthem Press, 2011.

Min'gan tanch'e saemaŭl undong chungang hyŏbŭihoe (Central Council for Civil Groups' New Village Movement). *Saemaŭl rek'ŭreisyŏn kyobon* (Manual for New Village Recreation). Internal publication, n.d. N.p.

Min Kyŏngch'an. "Chosŏn ch'ongdokpu-ŭi ŭmak kyoyuk-kwa ilche kangjŏmgi ttae Pusan-esŏ palgandoen 'Ch'angga kyojae sŏnjib'-e taehayŏ (On the music education of the Government-General of Korea and the "Anthology of *ch'angga* for educational purposes" published in Pusan during the period of Japanese colonial rule), *Ŭmakhak* (Musicology) 8 (2001): 67–83.

Moon, Yumi. *Populist Collaborators: The Ilchinhoe and the Japanese Colonization of Korea, 1896–1910.* Ithaca, NY: Cornell University Press, 2013.

Munhwa ch'eyukpu (Ministry of Culture and Sports). *Munhwajae kwan'gye pŏmnyŏngjip* (Collection of laws and regulations regarding the management of cultural properties). Seoul: The Korea Herald, 1983.

———.*Che-36-hoe chŏn'guk minsok yesul kyŏngyŏn taehoe* (36th national folk arts contest). Contest program. Seoul: Ministry of Culture and Sports, 1995.

Munhwajaech'ŏng (Cultural Heritage Administration). "Chŏnsŭng chiwŏn kyehoek annae" (Transmission support planning guide). Internal publication, 2012. N.p.

———. "2013-nyŏndo munhwajae wiwŏnhoe: che-2-ch'a muhyŏng munhwajae punkwa wiwŏnhoe hoeŭirok (The 2013 cultural properties committee: Second proceedings of the committee of the intangible cultural properties division). Internal publication, 1–53, 2013.

Munhwajae kwalliguk (Cultural Properties Management Office). *Chosŏn ch'ongdokpu mit mun'gyobu palhaeng munhwajae kwan'gye charyojip* (Collection of materials related to cultural properties as published by the Government-General of Korea and the Ministry of Culture). Seoul: Munhwajae kwalliguk, 1992.

———. *Chungyo muhyŏng munhwajae hyŏnhwang* (Present state of important intangible cultural properties) *1996*. Seoul: Munhwajae kwalliguk, 1996.

———. *Chungyo muhyŏng munhwajae hyŏnhwang 1997.* Seoul: Munhwajae kwalliguk, 1997.

———. "Kuhwangshil kwan'gye pŏmnyŏng mit chaesan mongnokchip" (Property inventory and statute regarding the former royal household). Internal publication, 1992. N.p.

———. *Munhwajae* (Cultural properties). Vols. 1, 5, 7, 10, 11, 12, 15, 18. Seoul: Munhwajae kwalliguk, 1965–1985.

———. *Munhwajae kwalli yŏnbo* (Annual report on the management of cultural properties). Seoul: Munhwajae kwalliguk, 1994.

———. *Poyuja ŏmnŭn hubo chogyo yenŭng chosa* (Study of the art of candidate holders and assistant teachers without a holder). Seoul: Munhwajae kwalliguk, 1996.

———. *Uri nara-ŭi munhwajae* (Korea's cultural properties). Seoul: Munhwajae kwalliguk, 1970.

Munhwa kongbobu (Ministry of Culture and Information). *Chungyo muhyŏng munhwajae haesŏl: ŭmak* (Commentary on important intangible cultural properties: Music). Seoul: Munhwajae kwalliguk, 1985.

———. *Munhwa kongbo 30-nyŏn* (Thirty years of culture and public information). Seoul: Ministry of Culture and Information, 1979.

———. "Yesan kangmok myŏngsesŏ" (Detailed account of all budgetary items). Unpublished, Munhwajae yŏn'guso, Taejŏn, 1988.

Mun Okpae. *Han'guk kŭmjigog-ŭi sahoe sa* (A social history of banned Korean music). Seoul: Yesol, 2004.

Mun Sunt'ae. "Han" (Bitterness). In *Han'guk minjok munhwa taebaekkwa sajŏn*, vol. 23, edited by the Han'guk chŏngshin munhwa yŏn'guwŏn, 852–857. Seoul: Samhwa Printing Co., 1992.

Nettl, Bruno. *The Study of Ethnomusicology: Twenty-Nine Issues and Concepts.* Urbana: University of Illinois Press, 1983.

No Chaemyŏng. *Paebaengi kut* (*Ritual for Paebaengi*). Seoul: Arŭm ch'ulp'ansa, 2002.

———. "1962-nyŏn Han'guk minyo yŏn'guhoe 'minyo Yo-ŭi hyangyŏn' inswaemul charyo haeje" (Bibliographical notes on the Korean Folksong Research Society's 1962 publication, "Delights of the folksong show"). *Han'guk ŭmak sa hakpo* (Bulletin of Korean music history) 48 (2012): 395–407.

Nolden, Detlef. "Das Koreanische Volksstück *Paebaengi-kut*" (The Korean folk play *Ritual for Paebaengi*). Master's thesis, University of Bochum, 1985.

No Tongŭn. *Han'guk kŭndae ŭmak sa* (A modern history of Korean traditional music). Seoul: Tosŏ ch'ulp'an han'gilsa, 1996.

Office of Cultural Properties. *The Preservation and Transmission System for the Intangible Cultural Properties of the Republic of Korea.* Internal publication. Seoul: Munhwajae kwalliguk, 1994.

O Pongnyŏ. *Sŏdo sori* (Folksongs from the Western Provinces). Seoul: Kwangjin munhwasa, 1978.

Paek Hwarang. "Ŏpsŏjin minsok sadangp'ae" (The lost folklore of *sadangp'ae*). In *Yŏmyŏng-ŭi kugakkye* (The Korean traditional music scene in the new age), edited by Chang Sahun, 186–197. Seoul: Se-Kwang Music Publishing Co., 1989.

Paek Taeung. "Hwanghaedo sori" (Songs from Hwanghae province). *Ppuri kip'ŭn namu p'aldo sori* (The deeply rooted tree collection of Korean folksongs), vol. 1, edited by Ppuri kip'ŭn namu, 29–41. Seoul: Ppuri kip'ŭn namu, 1984.

———. "Kyŏnggido sori" (Songs from Kyŏnggi province). *Ppuri kip'ŭn namu p'aldo sori,* vol. 2, edited by Ppuri kip'ŭn namu, 9–35. Seoul: Ppuri kip'ŭn namu, 1984.

———. "P'yŏngando sori" (Songs from P'yŏngan province). *Ppuri kip'ŭn namu p'aldo sori,* vol. 1, edited by Ppuri kip'ŭn namu, 57–66. Seoul: Ppuri kip'ŭn namu, 1984.

Pai, Hyung Il. *Constructing "Korean" Origins: A Critical Review of Archeology, Historiography, and Racial Myth in Korean State-Formation Theories.* Cambridge, MA: Harvard University Press, 2000.

———. *Heritage Management in Korea and Japan: The Politics of Antiquity and Identity.* Seattle: Washington University Press, 2014.

———. "The Politics of Korea's Past: The Legacy of Japanese Colonial Archaeology in the Korean Peninsula." *East Asian History* 7 (1994): 25–48.

———. "Resurrecting the Ruins of Japan's Mythical Homelands: Colonial Archaeological Surveys in the Korean Peninsula and Heritage Tourism." In *The Handbook of Post-colonialism and Archaeology,* edited by Jane Lydon and Uzma Rizvi, 93–112. Walnut Creek, CA: Left Coast Press, 2010.

Pak Ch'anho. *Han'guk kayo sa* (A history of Korean popular songs) 1. Seoul: Mizi Books, 2009.

Pak Chŏnghong. "Paro chabaya hal *Paebaengi kut*" (The *Ritual for Paebaengi* we must get right). *Wŏlgan munhwajae* 6/7 (1973): 38–40.

Pak Kyŏngsu. *Sorikkundŭl, kŭ salm-ŭl ch'ajasŏ: han, sori, sorikkun* (Singers, looking at their life: Bitterness, songs and singers). Seoul: Irwŏl sŏgak, 1993.

Pak Pyŏngho. *Han'gug-ŭi chŏnt'ong sahoe-wa pŏp* (Korea's traditional society and legislation). Seoul: Seoul taehak ch'ulp'anbu, 1988.

Pak Sŏnghŭi. *I saram ihu* (From this person onwards). Seoul: World Book Publishers, 1991.

Pak Sŏngso. *Han'guk chŏnjaeng-gwa taejung kayo, kirok-kwa chŭngŏn* (The Korean War and popular songs: Records and testimonies). Seoul: Ch'aeg-i innŭn p'unggyŏng, 2010.

Pak Sunho. "'Kanggangsullae' sogo" (Some thoughts on "Kanggangsullae"). In *Han'guk minyohak* 1, edited by the Han'guk minyo hakhoe, 1–19. Seoul: Kyomunsa, 1991.

Pan Chaeshik. *Chaedam ch'ŏnnyŏn sa* (A thousand-year history of comic storytelling). Seoul: Paekchungdang, 2000.

Park, Chan E. *Voices from the Straw Mat: Towards an Ethnography of Korean Story Singing.* Honolulu: University of Hawai'i Press, 2003.

Park, Chung Hee (Pak Chŏnghŭi). *Major Speeches by Korea's Park Chung Hee.* Seoul: Hollym Corporation Publishers, 1970.

———. *Our Nation's Path.* Seoul: Dong-a Publishing Company, 1962.

———. *Rebuilding a Nation.* Seoul: n.p.

Park, Sang Mi. "The Paradox of Postcolonial Korean Nationalism: State-Sponsored Cultural Policy in South Korea, 1965–Present." *Journal of Korean Studies* 15, no. 1 (2010): 67–93.

Phillips, Arthur. "The Cultural Cringe." *Meanjin* 9, no. 4 (Summer 1950): 299–302.

Pigliasco, Guido Carlo. "Intangible Cultural Property, Tangible Databases, Visible Debates: The Sawau Project." *International Journal of Cultural Property* 16 (2009): 255–272.

Pihl, Marshall R. *The Korean Singer of Tales.* Cambridge, MA: Harvard University Press, 1994.

Pilzer, Joshua D. *Hearts of Pine: Songs in the Lives of Three Korean Survivors of the Japanese "Comfort Women."* New York: Oxford University Press, 2012.

———. "The Twentieth-Century 'Disappearance' of the Gisaeng during the Rise of Korea's Modern Sex-and-Entertainment Industry." In *The Courtesan's Arts: Cross-Cultural Perspectives,* edited by Martha Feldman and Bonnie Gordon, 295–311. New York: Oxford University Press, 2006.

Pimpaneau, Sara. "Living National Treasures in Japan." Master's thesis, University of London, 1995.

Ppuri kip'ŭn namu (The deep-rooted tree). *T'ŏrŏnok'o hanŭn mal 2: Han'guk hyŏndae yŏksa-ŭi chuch'ŭttoldŭrin sŭmulhan sŏn'guja-ga ta t'ŏrŏnohŭn chŏngshin-ŭi mohŏmdam* (Frank discussions 2: The truthful adventures of 21 important figures in modern Korean history). Seoul: Ppuri kip'ŭn namu, 1980.

Reischauer, Edwin O. "Japanese Archeological Work on the Asiatic Continent in 1937 and 1938." *Harvard Journal of Asiatic Studies* 4 (1939): 87–100.

Robinson, Michael E. "Broadcasting, Cultural Hegemony, and Colonial Modernity in Korea, 1924–1945." In *Colonial Modernity in Korea,* edited by Gi-Wook Shin and Michael Robinson, 52–69. Cambridge, MA: Harvard University Press, 1999.

———. "Chapter 13: Growth of the Forces of Enlightenment." In *Korea Old and New: A History,* edited by Carter J. Eckert et al., 199–230. Seoul: Ilchogak, 1991.

———. "Chapter 15: The First Phase of Japanese Rule, 1910–1919." In *Korea Old and New: A History,* edited by Carter J. Eckert et al., 254–275. Seoul: Ilchogak, 1991.

———. "Chapter 17: Forced Assimilation, Mobilization, and War." In *Korea Old and New, A History,* edited by Carter J. Eckert et al., 305–346. Seoul: Ilchogak, 1991.

———. *Cultural Nationalism in Colonial Korea, 1920–1925.* Seattle: University of Washington Press, 1988.

———. "Enduring Anxieties: Cultural Nationalism and Modern East Asia." In *Cultural Nationalism in East Asia,* edited by Harumi Befu, 167–186. Berkeley: Institute of East Asian Studies, University of California, 1993.

———. *Korea's Twentieth-century Odyssey: A Short History.* Honolulu: University of Hawai'i Press, 2007.

Rosaldo, Renato. *Culture & Truth: The Remaking of Social Analysis.* Boston, MA: Beacon Press, 1993.

Rice, Timothy. "Time, Place, and Metaphor in Musical Experience and Ethnography." *Ethnomusicology* 47, no. 2 (2003): 151–179.

Ruskin, Jesse D., and Timothy Rice. "The Individual in Musical Ethnography." *Ethnomusicology* 56, no. 2 (2012): 299–327.

Ryu Ŭiho. *Muk Kyewŏl Kyŏnggi sori yŏn'gu* (A study of Muk Kyewŏl's Kyŏnggi folksongs). Seoul: Kip'ŭn saem, 2003.

Samsung Co., Ltd. *Misconceptions about Korean History.* Samsung Co., Ltd., 1991.

Sasse, Werner. "Minjung Theology and Culture." *Papers of the British Academy of Korean Studies* 1 (1991): 29–43.

Scheper-Hughes, Nancy. "The Margaret Mead Controversy: Culture, Biology and Anthropological Inquiry." In *Perspectives in Cultural Anthropology,* edited by Herbert Applebaum, 443–454. Albany: State University of New York Press, 1987.

Schmid, Andre. *Korea Between Empires: 1895–1919.* New York: Columbia University Press, 2002.

Seidel, Anna. "Kokuho: Note à Propos du Terme 'Trésor National' en Chine et au Japon" (National treasures: A note regarding the term 'national treasure' in China and Japan). *Bulletin de l'École Française d'Extrême-Orient* (Journal of the French School of East Asia) 69 (1981): 229–261.

Sekino, Tadashi. "Ancient Remains and Relics in Korea: Efforts toward Research and Preservation." Paper presented at a conference of the Institute of Pacific Relations, Hangzhou, China, October 21–November 4, 1931.

Shin Ch'an'gyun. *Minsog-ŭi kohyang* (The birthplace of folklore). Seoul: Chinmun ch'ulp'ansa, 1978.

Shin Chŏnghŭi. "An Pich'wi yŏsa 13-se-e immun Kyŏnggi minyo-ro muhyŏng munhwajae" (Madame An Pich'wi from her debut at the age of thirteen to intangible cultural property of *Kyŏnggi minyo*). *Maeil kyŏngje,* June 9, 1984, 9.

———. "Myŏngin myŏngjang 28: Sŏdo sori Kim Chŏngyŏn yŏsa" (Famous people famous artisans 28: *Sŏdo sori*'s Madame Kim Chŏngyŏn). *Maeil kyŏngje,* July 17, 1982, 9.

Shin, Gi-wook. *Ethnic Nationalism in Korea: Genealogy, Politics, and Legacy.* Stanford, CA: Stanford University Press, 2006.

———. "Nation, History, and Politics." In *Nationalism and the Construction of Korean Identity,* edited by Hyung Il Pai and Timothy R. Tangherlini, 148–165. Berkeley: Institute of East Asian Studies, University of California, 1998.

Shin Kyŏngnim. *Minyo kihaeng* (Folksong tour). Seoul: Han'gilsa, 1994.

Shin Taech'ŏl. *Uri ŭmak, kŭ mat-kwa sorikkal* (Our music: Its flavor and songs). Seoul: Kyobo mun'go, 1993.

Sim, Woo-Sung (Shim Usŏng). "Namsadang." In *Survey of Korean Arts: Folk Arts,* edited by the National Academy of Arts, 455–471. Seoul: National Academy of Arts, 1974.

Shim Usŏng. *Namsadangp'ae yŏn'gu* (A study of namsadang groups). Seoul: Tonghwa ch'ulp'an kongsa, 1974.

———. "Namsadang 'tŏppoegi' yŏn'gu" (A study of namsadang's "Tŏppoegi"). *Sŏnangdang* (Shrine of a patron god) 2 (1972): 91–123.

Sŏ Chiyŏng. "Sangshil-gwa pujae-ŭi shigonggan: 1930-nyŏndae yorijŏm-gwa kisaeng" (The temporal space of loss and absence: Restaurants and kisaeng in the 1930s). *Chŏngshin munhwa yŏn'gu* (Studies of spiritual culture) 32, no. 3 (2009): 167–194.

Sŏ Chŏngbŏm. *Sumŏsanŭn oet'olbagi 1: Chŏnt'ong sahoe-ŭi hwanghon-e sŏn saramdŭl* (Single-bur chestnuts living in secret 1: People in the twilight of traditional society). Seoul: Ppuri kip'ŭn namu, 1977.

Sohn, Tae-soo. "Scholars Debate Definition of Mask Dance." *The Korea Herald*. August 31, 1994, 7.

Sŏk Chusŏn. *Han'guk pokshik sa* (A history of Korean dress and accessories). Seoul: Pojinjae, 1971.

Sŏl Hojŏng. "Nŭlgŭn kisaeng Ch'ohyangi" (The old entertainment girl Ch'ohyang). In *Sumŏ sanŭn oet'olbagi* (Single-nut chestnut burs living in secret), vol. 1, edited by Ppuri kip'ŭn namu, 68–81. Seoul: Ppuri kip'ŭn namu, 1977.

Sŏmundang. *Sajin-ŭro ponŭn Chosŏn shidae: saenghwal-gwa p'ungsok* (Chosŏn dynasty shown through pictures: Daily life and customs). 2 vols. Seoul: Sŏmundang, 1988.

Song Bangsong (Song Pangsong). "Chosŏn hugi-ŭi ŭmak" (Music in the late Chosŏn period). In *Han'guk yesul saŏpsŏ III: Han'guk ŭmak sa* (An account of Korean art activities III: A history of Korean music), edited by the Taehan min'guk yesurwŏn, 279–408. Seoul: P'yŏnghwadang Printing Co., 1985.

———. *Han'guk ŭmak t'ongsa* (A comprehensive history of Korean music). Seoul: Ilchogak, 1988.

———. "1910-nyŏndae chŏngjae-ŭi chŏnsŭng yangsang: kisaeng chohab-ŭi chŏngjae kongyŏn-ŭl chungshim-ŭro" (Looking at the tradition of benefit performances in the 1910s: Focusing on kisaeng organisations' benefit shows). *Kugagwŏn nonmunjip* (Journal of the National Gugak Center) 17 (June 2008): 147–185.

Sŏng Kiryŏn. "2007-nyŏn kaejŏng kyoyuk kwajŏng-e ttarŭn minyo kwallyŏn chido naeyong koch'al" (An inquiry into the guidelines for folksong teaching on the basis of the Revised Curriculum of 2007). *Han'guk minyohak* 25 (2007): 187–224.

Sŏng Kyŏngnin. "Chungyo muhyŏng munhwajae-ŭi pojon chŏnsŭng" (The preservation and transmission of important intangible cultural properties). *Munhwajae* 15 (1982): 1–6.

———. *Han'guk ŭmak non'go* (A study of Korean music). Seoul: Tonghwa ch'ulp'an kongsa, 1976.

———. *Minyo kihaeng* (Folksong tour). Seoul: Han'gilsa, 1994.

———. "Sŏul sŏnsori: Kyŏnggi ipch'ang" (Standing songs from Seoul: Songs from Kyŏnggi province performed standing). *Sŏnsori sant'aryŏng, Muhyŏng munhwajae chosa pogosŏ* 30 (1966): 60–81.

Sŏng Kyŏngnin and Yi Pohyŏng. "Chŏngsŏn 'Arirang' mit *Paebaengi kut* chosa pogosŏ" (Research report on "Arirang" from Chŏngsŏn and *Ritual for Paebaengi*). *Muhyŏng munhwajae chosa pogosŏ* 135 (1980): 121–155.

———. "*Paebaengi kut*" (*Ritual for Paebaengi*). *Muhyŏng munhwajae chosa pogosŏ* 156 (1984): 577–624.

Song Sŏkha. *Han'guk minsok ko* (Studies on Korean folklore). Seoul: Ilshinsa, 1960.

———. *Minsok sashil t'ŭkpyŏl chŏndo nok* (A special complete record of the state of folklore). Seoul: Han'guk minsok pangmulgwan, 1975.

———. "Sadang go" (Scrutinizing sadang). In *Chosŏn minsok* (Korean folklore), 163–202. Seoul: Minsokwŏn, 1998 (1940).

Son Inae. *Hyangt'o minyo-e suyongdoen sadangp'ae sori* (The songs of *sadangp'ae* among folksongs). Seoul: Minsokwŏn, 2007.

Son Minjŏng. *T'ŭrot'ŭ-ŭi chŏngch'ihak* (A study of the politics of trot). P'aju: Ŭmak segye, 2009.

Sŏnsori sant'aryŏng pojonhoe (Society for the Preservation of Standing Mountain Songs). "Chungyo muhyŏng munhwajae che-19-ho kihoek kongyŏn: Sŏnsori sant'aryŏng palp'yo kongyŏn" (Planned performances of IICP no. 19: Public performance of Standing Mountain Songs). Internal publication, 2012. N.p.

So Pyŏnghŭi and Chin Hyeyŏng. "Chungyo muhyŏng munhwajae pojŏn chŏngch'aek kaesŏn pangan yŏn'gu" (A study of ways to improve the policy towards the preservation of important intangible cultural properties). *Munhwa chŏngch'aek nonch'ong* (Cultural policy journal) 26, no. 1 (2012): 175–199.

Sorensen, Clark W. "Folk Religion and Political Commitment in South Korea in the 1980s." In *Render Unto Caesar: The Religious Sphere in World Politics,* edited by Sabrina Petra Ramet and Donald W. Treadgold, 325–353. Washington, DC: The American University Press, 1995.

———. "Rural Modernization under the Park Regime in the 1960s." In *Reassessing the Park Chung Hee Era, 1961–1979: Development, Political Thought, Democracy, and Cultural Influence,* edited by Clark W. Sorensen and Hyung-A Kim, 145–165. Seattle: University of Washington Press, 2011.

———. "Success and Education in South Korea." *Comparative Education Review* 38, no. 1 (1994): 10–35.

Sørensen, Henrik H. "The Attitude of the Japanese Colonial Government Towards Religion in Korea (1910–1919)." *Copenhagen Papers in East and Southeast Asian Studies* 8 (1993): 49–69.

———. "'Protecting the Nation': Korean Buddhism under the Rule of Park Chung Hee, 1961–1979." In *Korea: The Past and the Present,* 2 vols., edited by Susan Pares and J. E. Hoare, 191–204. Folkestone, Kent, UK: Global Oriental, 2008.

Staub, Shalom. "Folklore and Authenticity: A Myopic Marriage in Public Sector Programs." In *The Conservation of Culture: Folklorists and the Public Sector,* edited by Burt Feintuch, 166–179. Lexington: University Press of Kentucky, 1988.

Steinberg, David I. "Civil Society and Human Rights in Korea: On Contemporary and Classical Orthodoxy and Ideology." *Korea Journal* 37, no. 3 (1997): 145–165.

Stokes, Martin. "Introduction: Ethnicity, Identity and Music." In *Ethnicity, Identity and Music: The Musical Construction of Place,* edited by Martin Stokes, 1–27. Oxford: Berg, 1994.

Suh, Sung. *Unbroken Spirits: Nineteen Years in South Korea's Gulag.* Lanham, MD: Rowman and Littlefield, 2001.

Taehan min'guk yesurwŏn (Korean Academy of Arts). *Han'guk yesul sajŏn III: Han'guk yŏn'gŭk, muyong, yŏnghwa sajŏn* (Dictionary of Korean arts III: Dictionary of Korean plays, dance and films). Seoul: P'yŏnghwadang Printing Co., 1985.

———. *Han'guk yesul sajŏn III: Han'guk ŭmak sajŏn* (Dictionary of Korean arts III: Dictionary of Korean music). Seoul: P'yŏnghwadang Printing Co., 1985.

Tangherlini, Timothy R. "Shamans, Students and the State: Politics and the Enactment of Culture in South Korea, 1987–1988." In *Nationalism and the Construction of Korean Identity,* edited by Hyung-Il Pai and Timothy R. Tangherlini, 126–147. Berkeley: Institute of East Asian Studies, University of California, 1999.

Tedesco, Frank. "Questions for Buddhist and Christian Cooperation in Korea." *Buddhist-Christian Studies* 17 (1997): 179–195.

Thornbury, Barbara E. "The Cultural Properties Protection Law and Japan's Folk Performing Arts." *Asian Folklore Studies* 53 (1994): 211–225.

Tomlinson, John. *Cultural Imperialism: A Critical Introduction*. London: Pinter Publishers, 1991.

Uchida, Mo. "Introduction." In *Bunkazai hogo jitsumu hikkei* (Handbook of the administration of cultural properties protection), edited by the Bunkachō bunkazai hogo kenkyūkai, iii–v. Tokyo: Daiichi hoki shuppan kabushiki kaisha, 1978.

Um, Haekyung. *Korean Musical Drama:* P'ansori *and the Making of Tradition in Modernity*. Farnham, Surrey, UK: Ashgate, 2013.

UNESCO. "Convention for the Safeguarding of the Intangible Cultural Heritage." Paris: UNESCO, 2003.

Van Zile, Judy. *Perspectives on Korean Dance*. Middletown, CT: Wesleyan University Press.

Veldkamp, Elmer. "Keeping It Real: The Exhibition of Artifact Replicas in National Museums of Korea." *Acta Koreana* 17, no. 2 (2014): 557–581.

Verbeek, Bas. "Koreaanse man zweert bij cosmetica" (Korean men swear by cosmetics). *Trouw*, January 5, 2013, 12.

Vos, Frits. "Tung-fang Shuo, Buffoon and Immortal, in Japan and Korea." *Oriens Extremus* 26, no. 1/2 (1979): 189–204.

Walraven, Boudewijn. "Muga: The Songs of Korean Shamanism." PhD dissertation, Leiden University, 1985.

Wells, Kenneth M. "The Cultural Construction of Korean History." In *South Korea's Minjung Movement: The Culture and Politics of Dissidence*, edited by Kenneth M. Wells, 11–29. Honolulu: University of Hawai'i Press, 1995.

West, Stephen H. "Drama." In *The Indiana Companion to Traditional Chinese Literature*, vol. 1, edited by William H. Nienhauser, Jr., 13–30. Bloomington: Indiana University Press, 1986.

Wilkinson, W. H. *The Corean Government: Constitutional Changes, July 1894 to October 1895*. Shanghai: Kelly & Walsh, 1897.

Williams, Raymond. *Keywords: A Vocabulary of Culture and Society*. London: Croom-Helm, 1976.

Wŏlgan munhwajaesa. *Wŏlgan munhwajae* (Cultural properties monthly) 8–9, 1972.

Yang, Jongsung (Yang Chongsŭng). *Cultural Protection Policy in Korea: Intangible Cultural Properties and Living National Treasures*. Seoul: Jimoondang International, 2003.

———. "Seoul-shi muhyŏng munhwajae, musok ŭirye yŏn'gu (Investigative research towards the designation of shamanic village rituals as 'intangible cultural properties' of the Seoul Metropolitan government)." *International Journal of Intangible Heritage* 4 (2009): 75–86.

Yano, Christine R. *Tears of Longing: Nostalgia and the Nation in Japanese Popular Song*. Cambridge, MA: Harvard University Press, 2002.

Yesurwŏn (Art Academy). *Han'guk yesulchi* (Record of Korean arts). Seoul: Yesurwŏn, 1980.

Ye Yonghae. *In'gan munhwajae* (Human cultural properties). Seoul: Ŏmun'gak, 1963.

Yi, Bo-hyŏng (Yi Pohyŏng). "P'ansori." In *Survey of Korean Arts: Folk Arts*, edited by the National Academy of Arts, 295–305. Seoul: National Academy of Arts, 1974.

Yi Ch'angbae. *Han'guk kach'ang taegye* (A compendium of vocal music in Korea). 2 vols. Seoul: Hongin munhwasa, 1976.

Yi Ch'angshik. "Han'guk minyohak kwan'gye mongnok" (List of works related to the study of Korean folksongs). *Han'guk minyohak* (Korean folksong studies), vol. 1, edited by the Han'guk minyo hakhoe, 185–227. Seoul: Kyomunsa, 1991.

Yi Chongsŏk. "Sŏdo sori O Pongnyŏ yŏsa" (Madame O Pongnyŏ and songs from the western provinces). *Chungang ilbo,* November 15, 1988, 7.

Yi Hŭijŏng. "In'gan munhwajae chedo kaesŏn-ŭl: puliik, kŭmp'um nobi" (A reform of the system of human cultural properties: Disadvantage and cash and gift lobbying). *Han'guk ilbo* (Korea daily), July 25, 2002, 25.

Yi Inmuk. "'No Chŏnggwŏn ttae immyŏng ibuk 5 do chisa 3 myŏng kyoch'e hara' posu tanch'e hoewŏndŭl t'oejin undong" (A move to resign by members of the conservation organization demanding the replacement of 3 members of the branch for the 5 provinces north of Korea who were appointed during No's administration). *Chosŏn ilbo,* May 12, 2009, 12.

Yi Kŭnt'ae. "Shin minyo-ŭi t'ansaeng" (The birth of new folksongs). In CD booklet, Seoul Records Inc., 9501-G17, *30-nyŏndae shin minyo* (New folksongs from the 1930s), 1995.

Yi Kuyŏl. *Han'guk munhwajae pihwa* (Secret stories of Korean cultural properties). Seoul: Han'guk misul ch'ulp'ansa, 1973.

Yi Kyŏngnyŏl. "Munhwa-ŭi ŭiŭi" (The significance of culture). *Tonggwang* (Dawn) 1 (January 1927): 32–39.

Yi Kyŏngyŏp. "Kidokkyo-ŭi chŏnp'a-wa ŭirye saenghwar-ŭi pyŏnhwa: Shinan-gun Chŭngdo-rŭl chungshim-ŭro" (The spread of Christianity and changes in rites: Centering on Jeungdo, Shinan County). *Tosŏ munhwa* (Island culture) 28 (2006): 177–221.

Yi Misuk. "Ŭnt'oe mudae kannŭn *Kyŏnggi minyo* 1-inja Muk Kyewŏl yŏsa" (*Kyŏnggi minyo*'s no. 1 performer Muk Kyewŏl goes into retirement). *Munhwa ilbo,* September 11, 1995, 22.

Yi Nŭnghwa. *Chosŏn haeŏhwa sa* (A history of Korean *kisaeng*). Seoul: Shinhan sŏrim, 1968 (1927).

Yi Pohyŏng. "'Arirang' sori-ŭi kŭnwŏn-gwa kŭ pyŏnch'ŏn-e kwanhan ŭmakchŏk yŏn'gu" (The origin of "Arirang" and a musicological study of its change). *Han'guk minyohak* 5 (1997): 81–120.

———. "Chŏnt'ong sahoe-esŏ minyo-rŭl yŏnhaenghanŭn sahoe chiptan-gwa kŭ munhwa haengwi" (The social groups who sang folksongs in traditional society and their cultural behavior). In *Minyo-wa minjung-ŭi salm* (Folksongs and people's lives), edited by the Han'guk yŏksa minsok hakhoe, 142–160. Seoul: Usŏk, 1994.

———. "*Paebaengi kut*-kwa tari kut" (*Ritual for Paebaengi* and the bridge ritual). In CD booklet, Seoul Records 9303-G123, *Paebaengi kut,* 1993: 1–17.

———. *Sŏdo minyo-wa Kyŏnggi minyo-ŭi sŏnyul kujo yŏn'gu* (A study of the melodic structure of folksongs from the western and Kyŏnggi provinces). Seoul: Munhwajae yŏn'guso, 1992.

———. "Sŏnsori sant'aryŏng" (Standing Mountain Songs). *Munhwa yesul* 100 (1985): 163–171.

Yi Pohyŏng, Hong Kiwŏn, and Pae Yŏnhyŏng. *Yusŏnggi ŭmban kasajip* (Collection of song texts from gramophone records). Vol. 4. Seoul: Minsokwŏn, 1999.

Yi Sŏngbu. "Shin in'gan munhwajae 23" (New human cultural property no. 23). *Ilgan sŭp'och'ŭ*, July 28, 1986, 8.

Yi Sŏngmu, Han Ugŭn, Min Hyŏn'gu, Yi T'aejin, and Kwŏn Oyŏng. *Yŏkchu kyŏngguk taejŏn* (Translation and annotation of the Great Code of Administration). 2 vols. Seoul: Han'guk chŏngshin munhwa yŏn'guwŏn, 1986.

Yi Tongsun. *Pŏnji ŏmnŭn chumak* (The tavern without a number). Seoul: Sŏn, 2007.

Yi, Tu-hyŏn (Yi Tuhyŏn). "Mask Dance-Dramas." In *Traditional Performing Arts of Korea*, edited by the Korean National Commission for UNESCO, 35–80. Seoul: UNESCO, 1983.

Yi Tuhyŏn, Chang Sugŭn and Yi Kwanggyu. *Han'guk minsokhak kaesŏl* (Introduction to Korean folklore studies). Seoul: Ilchogak, 1991.

Yi Ŭn'gwan. *Kach'ang ch'ongbo* (Full song scores). Seoul: Cheil akposa, 1999.

Yi Yongshik. "Ch'angga-esŏ minyo-ro: Hamgyŏngdo Pukch'ŏng minyo "Tondollari"-ŭi hyŏngsŏng-e kwanhan yŏn'gu" (From ch'angga to folksong: A study of the formation of the folksong "Tondollari" from Hamgyŏng province). *Han'guk minyohak* 7 (1999): 199–224.

Yi Yŏngmi. "Ilche shidae-ŭi taejung kayo" (Popular songs from the period of Japanese colonial rule). In *Norae* (Songs). Vol. 1, edited by Kim Ch'angnam, Yi Yŏngmi, Pak Yunu and Kim Haeshik. Seoul: Shilch'ŏn munhaksa, 1980.

Yi Yunsŏn. "'Sushimga' sasŏr-ŭi maech'ebyŏl pyŏni yangsang-gwa ŭimi" (Variations in the lyrics of "Sushimga" and their meaning). *Han'guk minyo hak* 26 (2009): 159–195.

Yi Yusŏn. *Han'guk yangak paengnyŏnsa* (A one-hundred-year history of Western music in Korea). Seoul: Ŭmak ch'unch'usa, 1985.

———. *Han'guk yangak p'alshimnyŏnsa* (An eighty-year history of Western music in Korea). Seoul: Chungang taehakkyo ch'ulp'ansa, 1968.

Yŏnhap News Agency. *Korea Annual 1991*. Seoul: Yŏnhap News Agency, 1991.

Yoo, Theodore Jun. *The Politics of Gender in Colonial Korea: Education, Labor, and Health, 1910–1945*. Berkeley: University of California Press, 2008.

Yoon, Hong-key. *Geomantic Relationships between Culture and Nature in Korea*. Taipei: Orient Culture Service, 1976.

Yu Iksŏ. "Chŏng Tŭngman." In *Myŏngin myŏngch'ang*, edited by Yu Iksŏ et al., 217–225. Seoul: Dong-a Ilbo, 1987.

———. "Kim Chŏngyŏn." In *Myŏngin myŏngch'ang* (Famous people, famous singers), edited by Yu Iksŏ et al., 174–181. Seoul: Dong-a Ilbo, 1987.

Yun Kihong. "Chapka-ŭi sŏngkyŏk-kwa minyo, p'ansori-wa-ŭi kwan'gye" (Folksongs, the character of *chapka*, and their relation to *p'ansori*). In *Han'guk minyo non* (A study of Korean folksongs), edited by Ch'oe Ch'ŏl, 206–239. Seoul: Chimmundang, 1992.

Yu Yŏngdae. "Mokhoeja-ro ch'ŏt in'gan munhwajae chijŏng sŏdo sori myŏngch'ang Yi Munju moksa" (Noted singer of songs from the western provinces, Minister Yi Munju, becomes the first pastor to be appointed a human cultural property). *Kungmin ilbo* (People's daily), September 3, 2009, 27.

INDEX

ABOUT THE AUTHOR

Roald Maliangkay is associate professor of Korean Studies and director of the Korea Institute at the Australian National University. He has published widely on broad developments in Korean folk and popular entertainment and is coeditor of *K-pop: The International Rise of the Korean Music Industry* (Routledge, 2015).